Schooling Jim Crow

CARTER G. WOODSON INSTITUTE SERIES
Deborah E. McDowell, Editor

SCHOOLING
Jim Crow

The Fight for Atlanta's
Booker T. Washington High School
and the Roots of Black Protest
Politics

JAY WINSTON DRISKELL JR.

University of Virginia Press
CHARLOTTESVILLE AND LONDON

University of Virginia Press
© 2014 by the Rector and Visitors of the University of Virginia
All rights reserved
Printed in the United States of America on acid-free paper

First published 2014
First paperback edition published 2019

ISBN 978-0-8139-3614-7 (cloth)
ISBN 978-0-8139-4258-2 (paper)
ISBN 978-0-8139-3615-4 (ebook)

1 3 5 7 9 8 6 4 2

Library of Congress Cataloging-in-Publication Data
Driskell, Jay Winston, 1973–
Schooling Jim Crow : the fight for Atlanta's Booker T. Washington High School
and the roots of Black protest politics / Jay Winston Driskell Jr.
pages   cm — (Carter G. Woodson Institute series)
Includes bibliographical references and index.
ISBN 978-0-8139-3614-7 (cloth : alkaline paper) — ISBN 978-0-8139-3615-4 (e-book)
1. African Americans—Education—Georgia—Atlanta—History—20th century. 2. Booker T.
Washington High School (Atlanta, Ga.)—History—20th century. 3. African American schools—
Georgia—Atlanta—History—20th century. 4. Segregation in education—Georgia—Atlanta—
History—20th century. 5. African Americans—Segregation—Georgia—Atlanta—History—20th
century. 6. African Americans—Civil rights—Georgia—Atlanta—History—20th century. 7. National
Association for the Advancement of Colored People—History—20th century. 8. African Americans—
Georgia—Atlanta—Politics and government—20th century. 9. Protest movements—Georgia—
Atlanta—History—20th century. 10. Atlanta (Ga.)—Race relations—History—20th century. I. Title.
LC2803.A85D75 2014
371.829'960758231—dc23
2014009609

For Lauren

Contents

Acknowledgments   ix

Introduction   1

1   "Manhood Rights": Progress and the Politics
of Respectability, 1899–1906   24

2   "To Humiliate the Progressive Negro": The Atlanta
Race Riot of 1906   61

3   "Respectable Militants": The Neighborhood Union and the
Transformation of the Politics of Respectability, 1908–1913   106

4   "Close Ranks": World War I as a Crucible for Black
Solidarity, 1913–1919   148

5   "A Satisfied Part of Our Composite Citizenship": The Fight for
Booker T. Washington High School, 1918–1924   196

Epilogue: "Self-Determination at the Ballot Box"   235

Notes   243

Bibliography   281

Index   291

Acknowledgments

I'd like to begin by thanking my parents for telling me to be the best at what I did and for showing me the value of hard work. My ability to wake day after day and take my licks came from your example. I only wish, Dad, that you had lived to see this moment. A special thank-you goes to my uncle Stan, who convinced me to go to college—if only to learn enough to win at least one of our epic four-hour arguments. In all seriousness, I've learned as much from him as I have from any of my colleagues.

When I was seventeen years old and homeless, there was one teacher who looked out for me, took me into his home now and then, and encouraged me to develop my writing. At Whitney Young High School, Jim English taught me poetry and introduced me to Jorge Luis Borges, Gabriel García Márquez, and William Carlos Williams. He continually fed me with new books and ideas that enticed me to stick it out and finish high school. Jim really was "the first English teacher to ever give me an A." Many thanks to you, Jim.

My mentors at the University of Wisconsin at Madison have also been decisive influences on my—admittedly intermittent—intellectual development while at Wisconsin. Thanks to Stephen Kantrowitz for recognizing me as a scholar despite my absences. Thanks to Florencia Mallon for your demonstration of what politically committed scholarship could look like. And very special thanks to Tim Tyson, who convinced me to do this for a living. If there were one person besides myself responsible for me becoming a historian, it would be him. Having read and critiqued hundreds of pages of writing I did under his supervision, I also owe Tim a great debt for encouraging me to find and refine my writing voice.

At Yale, I was fortunate to have the guidance of several great mentors.

Glenda Gilmore's comments on a very early version of this project contributed significantly to its present shape. Matt Jacobson's encouragement helped me to think big about this project, stretching my understanding of African American history, while the insightful and critical readings by Michael Denning and Jonathan Holloway forced me to sharpen my argument and bring it back down to earth. While all the mistakes in this book are assuredly mine, a good deal of its coherence can be attributed to the contributions made by my advisers.

Additionally, I'd like to thank Emilie Amt, Eric Arnesen, Dennis Burke, Susan Carle, Stan Driskell, David Fort Godshalk, Cindy Hahamovitch, Donna Haverty-Stacke, Sophia Lee, Danielle McGuire, Barry Muchnick, Paul Ortiz, James Palmer, Theresa Runstedtler, Anita Seth, Melissa Stuckey, and Andrew Zimmerman for their helpful comments on various drafts of this book. A special shout-out goes to Cindy Hahamovitch and Jennifer Luff for assembling the DC-Area Working-Class Studies Seminar, which has become a continual source of intellectual nourishment. At Hood College, I've found a stimulating and supportive intellectual community that has also challenged me to approach history in new ways. Thanks go to my new colleagues Emilie Amt, Trevor Dodman, Amy Gottfried, Karen Hoffman, Lisa Algazi Marcus, Heather Mitchell-Buck, Jennifer Ross, Tamelyn Tucker-Worgs, and Hoda Zaki.

Along the way, I've also had the support of an incredibly large number of people who provided both friendship and moral support. At Duke, I'd like to thank Ian Lekus, Lisa Hazirjian, James Palmer, Alejandro Velasco, and Ivonne Wallace-Fuentes for making my brief sojourn in North Carolina both pleasant and productive. I'd especially like to thank Lawrence Goodwyn for sharing with me his vast knowledge of the intricacies of southern politics. At Yale, I was lucky to find a community of scholars committed not just to the study of history but also to the making of it. My fellow union brothers and sisters in the Graduate Employees and Students Organization (GESO) helped me realize that it is not enough to change the world; one must be a part of it as well. In addition to broadening my political imagination, these and others at Yale challenged me intellectually, profoundly influencing my ideas on history and social change. As an organizer for GESO, I engaged in hundreds, if not thousands, of conversations about the meaning of both our work and what it meant to build real solidarity with other campus workers, our union brothers and sisters in UNITE HERE Locals 34 and 35. The process of organizing my colleagues and comrades to take a stand for the things they believed in helped me think about the struggles of the past in completely different terms. This book is as much a product of my formal education as it is of my organizing experience. So, special thanks to my intellectual comrades in arms: Carlos Aramayo, Ben Begleiter, Jeffrey Boyd, Alison Bruey, Antony Dugdale, Adam Franklin-Lyons, Sarah Haley, Kate Reed Hauenstein, Naomi Shar-Yin Huang, David Huyssen, Lucas Klein, Sophia Lee, Manuella Meyer, Bethany Moreton, Barry Muchnick, Michael Mullins, Lisabeth Pimentel, Shana Redmond, Peter Reed, Mary Reynolds, Justin Ruben, Jake Ruddiman, Theresa Runstedtler, Andrew Sackett, David Sanders, Anita Seth, Ashley Riley Sousa, Kristie Starr, Melissa Stuckey, Rachel Sulkes, Kate Unterman, Sam Vong, Louise Walker, Brendan Walsh, Wendi Walsh, Philip Ziesche, and Maris Zivarts.

Of this illustrious roll call, a few deserve special mention: Melissa Stuckey, for being a true friend and ally across the years—you have been an inspiration to me and an emotional anchor, and your contribution to my success as a scholar remains inestimable; David Sanders, for believing in me and helping me realize that I did not have to forfeit who I was in order to succeed at Yale; Kristie Starr, for being there when my father passed away; Jeffrey Boyd, Carlos Aramayo, and Anita Seth, for pushing me to take myself seriously; and, finally, Barry Muchnick, for helping me to not take myself too seriously and dragging me away from my work to take walks through the woods.

I'd like to thank the staff of the Atlanta History Center, the Schomburg Center for the Study of Black Culture, Emory University's Manuscripts and Rare Books Library, the Beinecke Rare Books Library, the microfilm room at Yale's Sterling Library, the newspaper reading room at the Library of Congress, and the Beneficial-Hodson Library at Hood College for the assistance they provided in helping me complete my research. *Schooling Jim Crow* was also made possible in part due to several generous grants and fellowships. A Beinecke Library Fellowship freed a productive summer for writing and research. A generous grant from Gilder Lehrman Institute of American History allowed me to spend a summer working at the Schomburg Center. My research in Atlanta was underwritten by a MARBL Research Fellowship provided by Emory University as well as the Albert J. Beveridge Grant for Research in the History of the Western Hemisphere provided by the American Historical Association. And special thanks goes to my copyeditor, Robert Burchfield, whose exacting attention to detail rescued me from my grammatical shortcomings.

Finally, my deepest debt of gratitude goes to Lauren Burke. She has remained (mostly) patient and always loving through the roller coaster of submission deadlines, job interviews, revisions, and writer's block, and has forgiven me time and again for vanishing into the depths of my own head. Lauren has also been a model for me of a soldier for justice, fierce and compassionate. I aspire always to be as committed as she. Lauren has contributed to this work in ways for which I'll never be able to fully account. She has been a patient listener, a generous critic, and, above all else, an unfailing source of support, encouragement, and love.

Schooling Jim Crow

Introduction

A white man once had a colored man in a buggy beside him driving. He was skillful with the whip. He could take his whip and pick a fly off a rose. As he drove along whenever he saw a fly on a rose or a bush, he would take his whip and just pick him off. Finally, he came to a hornets' nest. The white man said, "Jim, there is a chance to show your skill, why not pick that fellow off the hornets' nest?" Jim said, "No sir, boss, they's organized." That is what the black man has got to do—organize to protect himself and his family.

—CAPTAIN JACKSON MCHENRY, ATLANTA (1919)

On Saturday mornings just after World War I, subscribers to the city's leading black newspaper, the *Atlanta Independent,* read Captain Jackson McHenry's weekly column, comprising equal parts gossip, political news, and opinion. Here, they would regularly encounter bits of homespun wisdom such as the one above. On the surface, the meaning of this parable seems quite obvious. An organized black community will not be whipped, and stands a better chance at defending its individual members than a disorganized one. This was more than an inspiring fable about organized resistance to oppression, however. McHenry offered his readers a lesson in solidarity.

McHenry placed the whip in the hand of Jim, a black man who works for a white man rich enough to have both a buggy and a driver. When ordered to, he can whip a lone fly off a rose. Taking the lone fly on the rose as a metaphor, McHenry's fable seems to suggest a class-based critique of older forms of black leadership. Just as there was no rosebush beautiful enough to protect a lone, hapless fly from the coachman's whip, there was no escape

1

from the arbitrary violence of Jim Crow for any African American no matter how well situated. But when confronted with the hornet's nest, Jim balks. An attack on the hornet's nest carried with it the threat of retaliation by the entire hive, enough to dissuade the white man's black servant from wielding his whip. The most significant decision made in this parable was not the implied threat of retribution by the hive. Rather, it was Jim's refusal to obey.

In April 1919, McHenry's parable of solidarity and organized black political action had particular resonance for the black citizens of Atlanta. At the dawn of the twentieth century, nearly 90,000 people called Atlanta home. By 1920, that number had swelled to more than 200,000 residents.[1] In order to keep up with its burgeoning population, the city had laid sidewalks and paved roads, installed streetlights and running water, planted public parks, and dug swimming pools. However, decades of racially stratified urban development had built a city in which black citizens were taxed for the construction of an electrical grid that did not illuminate their homes, running water that did not wash their bodies, and public schools from which their children were barred. As Atlanta became a thoroughly twentieth-century city, its black residents were increasingly relegated to nineteenth-century ghettos. In response, two days before McHenry's fable of the hornets' nest appeared in the pages of the *Atlanta Independent,* black voters had gone to the polls to defeat millions of dollars in municipal bond referenda.

Organized by the National Association for the Advancement of Colored People (NAACP) and an organization of progressive black women called the Neighborhood Union, this vote was the latest attempt to compel the city to invest in black Atlanta. It had been the third such vote in less than ten months. Three times the city's urban boosters had appealed to Atlanta's black voters, seeking their support for these bond referenda, and three times they were defeated by a unified black electorate. Despite the imposition in 1908 of numerous legal mechanisms that had disfranchised and decimated the size of the black electorate, African American voters could not legally be barred from voting in municipal referenda. So, the NAACP and the Union organized more than 3,000 African Americans to pay their poll taxes and register to vote in a bloc against the bonds until the city agreed to build a publicly funded high school for the city's black students. Ultimately, these efforts were successful—in 1924 Booker T. Washington Public High School opened its doors. For the first time, the black citizens of Atlanta could at last send their children to one of the high schools that their taxes had been supporting since Reconstruction.

This book tells the story of how Atlanta's black community gradually came to abandon an older strategy of pursuing incremental progress through building alliances between the black middle class and paternalistic white elites. This strategy had developed alongside the advance of Jim Crow and was deeply informed by a *politics of respectability* that publicly accepted the principles of disfranchisement and segregation but sought to redraw the racial exclusions of the new Jim Crow order along the lines of class and gender instead. Based on a shared embrace of respectability with their white counterparts, black elites attempted to transform paternalism into a politics capable of uniting an interracial elite behind a mission to civilize the masses of both races and fit them for citizenship. Basing claims to power upon the reputation of the race in the eyes of influential white elites was a shaky foundation upon which to build a politics. White elites were under no obligation to treat their erstwhile black allies as equals; should political necessity demand the abandonment of black Americans, white leaders could simply discard relationships that African Americans had spent years cultivating. Despite these limitations, the cultivation of these elite interracial relationships was responsible for what few gains were possible in the Jim Crow South.

By contrast, the display of political unity in the 1919 bond fight would have been remarkable in any era, but in the context of Jim Crow Atlanta it was astonishing. Not only did it signify the decline of respectability as the basis of negotiations across the color line, it helped establish a new basis for urban black politics. By holding the entire city budget hostage and preventing desperately needed improvements to the fire department and waterworks, the Atlanta NAACP compelled the city fathers to invest an unprecedented $1.5 million in black public schools. Engaging in such bare-knuckled power politics required tremendous courage. This showdown over the city's future development occurred less than thirteen years after the bloody Atlanta race riot of 1906, and just weeks ahead of the wave of lynchings and the mad, antiblack rampage that swept the nation in the Red Summer of 1919. The fear of this violence had long fed a despairing politics of accommodation to white supremacy, driving the city's black population into political quietude. The power to overcome this deference was based upon a transformation of the understandings of gender and class in response to the upheavals of urban development, the imposition of Jim Crow, and U.S. entry into World War I. The chapters that follow show how black Atlantans used these new understandings to sustain the solidarity that finally allowed them to contend—and not merely negotiate—for their rights. As clubwomen and settlement house workers, patriotic Americans, and municipal taxpayers, these new

3

civic identities gave the black men and women of Atlanta new ways to assert equality with their white fellow citizens outside of the constraints of respectability. Through these identities, they were able to make rights claims not mediated by their relationships with influential white elites. It was atop these new cultural terms of black solidarity that the struggle for black public education by the fighting grassroots of the early NAACP gave birth to a new black protest politics.

"So Vast a Prejudice": Fighting Jim Crow

Between 1890 and 1920, Atlanta had more than tripled in size, growth spurred by the city's location as the hub for ten major railroads and a development strategy that emphasized low taxes and minimal regulation in order to attract investment.[2] Atlanta's rapid development created a broad array of public goods and city services, access to which African Americans began to assert as a fundamental right of citizenship. This also created a whole new range of *civic rights,* benefits attached to urban citizenship such as libraries, parks, and schools, even sidewalks—all of which arise alongside the modern city. These civic rights stood in contrast to the earlier array of formal civil rights—such as the right to vote or the right to trial by jury—for which African Americans had long contended. Asserting equal access to these new urban amenities increasingly became a new vehicle for asserting racial equality. In reaction, even former white allies increasingly sought to restrict the prerogatives of modern urban life to whites only. Or, as the famed black intellectual W. E. B. Du Bois described this process, the modernization of southern cities at the end of the nineteenth century left black Americans "a poor race in a land of dollars . . . the very bottom of hardships."[3] Thus, urbanization created new ways of both asserting equality and reinforcing racial hierarchy. In Atlanta, the tensions generated by this racial tug-of-war over urban development culminated in the passage of laws imposing racial segregation upon the city's new public spaces, the victory of a disfranchisement movement that severely restricted African Americans' voting rights, and a three-day racial pogrom in the summer of 1906 that killed dozens of African Americans—particularly those from the respectable middle class who felt entitled to full access to the fruits of urban citizenship. Bourgeois respectability had done little to guarantee their status as first-class citizens; it also failed to protect them from indiscriminate violence, disfranchisement, and segregation. In McHenry's parable: no rose, regardless of its beauty, would offer protection against the arbitrary violence of the coachman's whip-hand.

Du Bois described the segregation of African Americans from the fruits of economic development as a prejudice "so vast . . . [it] could not but bring the inevitable self-questioning, self-disparagement and lowering of ideals which ever accompany repression."[4] When confronted with the enormity of the oppression African Americans faced at the turn of the twentieth century, it can be difficult to understand how black people fought and, at times, defeated Jim Crow. Traditionally, the term "Jim Crow" has been used to describe the entire series of changes in southern politics and culture that sought to relegate African Americans to an inferior caste, encompassing everything from lynching to disfranchisement and segregation. Without dismissing the role that each of these played in the lived experience of African Americans during the period, this book emphasizes the role played by urban development and reform. A history of Jim Crow that is keyed closely to the racial exclusions built into the Progressive Era expansion of city services makes it possible to more accurately trace the mechanisms through which African Americans were denied access to their civic rights. It also permits the construction of a detailed timeline of local black resistance to segregated development in cities like Atlanta, revealing the oft-hidden contours of organized black resistance to Jim Crow.

Many discussions of Jim Crow focus on the exclusion of African Americans from the benefits of citizenship without linking that exclusion to the Progressive Era expansion of the prerogatives of citizenship or the proliferation of new forms of public space resulting from the rapid economic development following the Civil War.[5] Not only does this tend to homogenize the history of the black South between disfranchisement in the 1890s and the emergence of the civil rights movement in the later 1950s, it also robs organized African Americans of their agency as historical actors. Without a clear chronology of the history of black exclusion from the benefits of progress, it is hard to fathom how African Americans both fought and accommodated themselves to Jim Crow.[6] It was this particular historical juxtaposition of Jim Crow alongside Progressive Era reform and economic development that forced a dilemma upon the black progressives in the NAACP and the Neighborhood Union. At the same time they sought to enlist the state as an ally in reform, that state was inscribing into its laws a second-class status for black Americans. The narrative arc of this book and its argument rests heavily on an exploration of the ways in which black progressives in Atlanta confronted and attempted to solve this dilemma. Their accumulated responses to the chronic crises caused by the expansion of Jim Crow profoundly impacted the future development of black politics in the city, the state, and the nation. The tension between black and white citizens over access to Progressive Era urban amenities created both the impetus for segregation and disfranchisement as well as its antithesis, the movement to democratize access to the pleasures and prerogatives of urban life under the banner of "first-class citizenship."

Complicating this fight for "first-class citizenship" was the fact that the early leaders of the Atlanta NAACP did not campaign for desegregated public schools. Rather, they fought instead for their share of the public wealth. In some cases, this meant a protracted struggle to desegregate streetcars.[7] In others, such as the battle for black public education, this meant the establishment of several segregated schools—victories that did not fit comfortably into the later narratives of the civil rights movement. The fight for Booker T. Washington High School is mentioned in several histories, but never as a pivotal moment in African American political development.[8] After World War II, as the NAACP started on the road to *Brown,* the story of the fight for Atlanta's black public schools dropped from the official memory of the organization.[9] Nonetheless, in its early years, when the NAACP was still small, the magnitude of the victory in Atlanta guaranteed it would become an important model for future organizing—a legacy with profound consequences for African American political development.

The parable that McHenry related in the pages of the *Atlanta Independent* following the third bond election was not his own invention. This story was likely repeated on doorsteps and in barbershops, churches, and lodge halls throughout each of the three bond elections, and may well be an adaptation of an earlier organizing tale that predates the 1919 campaign in Atlanta by several decades. Not only was it a good story for encouraging people to register and vote against the bonds, it helped clarify the impact that the April balloting had on the idea of solidarity in Atlanta's black community. It was upon this cultural foundation that the local NAACP was able to unite black Atlantans across class lines and build a voting bloc powerful enough to prevent the passage of every single municipal bond referendum until the city agreed to build public schools for black students.

The two overarching arguments that run through this book attempt to describe the historical context for the emergence of the sort of autonomous black politics seen in Atlanta in 1919. The first argument is that this new politics was not created out of whole cloth. The story of Atlanta's fight for school equality complicates the much-celebrated transition from Booker T. Washington's politics of accommodation to the protest politics of W. E. B. Du Bois. Washington had famously advised black Americans to accommodate themselves to Jim Crow and suspend their agitation for first-class citizenship, including the right to vote. Given the apparent futility of the fight, he reasoned that the best way for black Americans to advance was to accumulate wealth and thus prove their capacity for self-government and virtue. Over time, through the embrace of respectability, white Americans would finally be able to see black Americans as equals, and it would be upon this foundation of shared virtue that black people could finally assert racial equality. Traditionally, this approach to politics has been understood in opposition to the protest politics championed by Du Bois, who in 1903 publicly rejected the accommodationist strategy. Arguing that a voteless people were a powerless people, he urged black Americans not to abandon their claims on political power and equality and instead fight the spread of disfranchisement and segregation.[10] However, as the Atlanta story demonstrates, the difference between these two approaches was in practice not as great as has often been portrayed. The evolution of accommodation into protest was no sudden rupture. The same late nineteenth-century notions of respectability and virtue that had deeply informed Washington's politics would continue to shape the emergence of black protest politics well into the twentieth century.

The second argument is that the emergence of this autonomous black politics was by no means automatic. Rather, it depended heavily on decades of work by hundreds of organizers, whose efforts in the fight to secure black access to the fruits of Progressive Era reform and development helped create a new form of black politics. Rather than emerging from an arid intellectual debate over the best way for the race to advance, black protest politics emerged from the interaction between the social and economic upheavals of the Progressive Era and organized black attempts to respond to those upheavals. In Atlanta, the turmoil caused by rapid economic development and reform profoundly transformed the ideas of class and gender that informed the discourse of respectability upon which accommodationist politics had rested. The ways in which men and women constructed their gender and class identities, publicly and privately, deeply impacted the ways in which they understood politics itself. The political options open to black Atlantans between 1890 and 1920 were significantly determined by the gender roles available to them. As these gender roles changed in response to urbanization, violence, and war, so, too, could their politics. Most important, the experience of the city presented considerable dangers that black men and women would have to face, but it also offered them new ways of being men and women.[11] This new repertoire of gender roles reshaped the cultural terms of both racial solidarity and interracial politics and formed the foundation necessary for the emergence of a genuinely autonomous black politics—one that would free black Atlantans from the constraints imposed by the politics of respectability and enable black progressives to compel their supposed white allies to act justly toward their black fellow citizens.

The Politics of Respectability

Leading a respectable life entailed emotional and physical self-restraint (especially in public), modest dress, proper speech, the pursuit of self-improvement through education, industriousness, refraining from drinking and gambling, keeping a clean body and a thrifty home, and—perhaps most important—refraining from licentious sexual behavior and, for women, adopting an ethic of sexual purity. Taken together, these informed the discourse of respectability, which reserved social power for those best able to adhere to contemporary bourgeois gender roles.

Respectability formed the basis of interracial politics in the era of Jim Crow. As the historian Evelyn Brooks Higginbotham describes it, respectability comprised a "bridge" discourse that mediated relations between black and white elites.[12] This politics of respectability depended upon an alliance with sympathetic white elites who, together with black elites, would establish the basis for a joint civilizing mission to uplift the masses of both races and fit them for citizenship. Faced with the exclusion of all African Americans from southern "civilization," black elites sought to use their class status to argue for their inclusion as respectable members of the middle class in the full benefits of citizenship. By basing the qualifications for first-class citizenship on the adoption of cultural practices deemed respectable rather than just having the right skin color, those who embraced the politics of respectability sought to replace the stratification of citizenship by race with exclusions based on gender and class.[13]

This was a tenuous strategy at best, based as it was upon reputation rather than the ability to muster political power at the polls. Should it become necessary for white elites to sacrifice the needs of black Americans, interracial relationships that had been painstakingly cultivated for years were simply discarded. This was a common occurrence given the economic chaos that accompanied Progressive Era urban development throughout the South.

Frequently, white city leaders faced the choice between expanding public services such as schools, sewers, and police protection to white citizens only or not at all. In these cases, black citizens were frequently excluded. Despite these limitations, the cultivation of these elite interracial relationships was responsible for what few gains were possible in Jim Crow cities of the South.

For African Americans, the embrace of respectability also served as a cultural form of self-defense against white assaults motivated by racist stereotypes that suggested black men and women were lazy or criminal. Apologists for lynching marshaled stereotypes that black men were unable to control their sexual urges to justify the murder of thousands of African Americans. Even though an NAACP study published in 1919 revealed that fewer than 30 percent of the 2,522 black people lynched nationwide in the preceding three decades had been accused of assaults on white women, and only 19 percent had been specifically accused of rape, it was nevertheless in hopes of deflecting or avoiding such attacks that many black elites sought to enforce a strict adherence to a rigid moral code among all black men and women.[14]

Finally, in the face of such assaults on African American character, the politics of respectability was also a means to defend the very tenuous position of the black middle class. The years since the Civil War had seen the rise of a small yet vibrant black bourgeoisie that did not fit white expectations of how black people should have fared without the discipline of slavery. An elite white southerner, the mistress of a large plantation, who had been a child during Reconstruction, described the "educated negro" as "an artificial production, which does not fit in with our natural order, and for this reason no distance is so wide as that between the people of my class and aspiring, wronged, intelligent, vindictive negroes."[15] Most, if not all, black leaders were acutely aware of this attitude and the accompanying danger posed by the threat of white backlash. As black Americans climbed up into the ranks of the "aspiring, intelligent" middle class, they sought to suppress any suspicion that they might become "vindictive." As one contributor to Du Bois's Atlanta University study on the "College-Bred Negro" put it: "The Negro's ignorance, superstition, vice and poverty do not disturb and unnerve his enemies so much as his rapid strides upward and onward."[16] The dangers of rising too high or too fast could be considerable. In 1906, the city of Atlanta erupted in a three-day race riot that took the lives of dozens of African Americans. Although the riot began in the wake of a rape scare fabricated in the midst of a superheated gubernatorial race by the city's major white dailies, the targets of this riot were almost exclusively members of the city's small black middle class. In the eyes of one prescient observer forced into exile after the riot, the violence was meant "to humiliate the progressive Negro."[17] Embracing respectability as a way of establishing some sort of common ground with white elites was one means—even if undependable— of defending black communities and their middle-class leaders against this sort of bloodshed.

As it shaped understandings of black solidarity, the politics of respectability had three effects that are important for understanding the central argument of this book. First, in setting up the terms for negotiation between black and white elites across the color line, it implicitly—and sometimes explicitly— reaffirmed segregation. However, it would be a mistake to judge the black politicians of respectability too harshly for not committing their full energies to fighting the imposition of Jim Crow laws. While there were significant protests against the imposition of segregation on Atlanta's streetcars in 1892 and 1900, it was much more common for African Americans in Atlanta and other southern cities to confront a choice between *no* access to city services and urban amenities and *segregated* access.[18] Given limited power to wage a frontal assault on segregation, the politics of respectability was part of a broader strategy to ensure that separate facilities were equal, too.[19] This strategy was vital in another way as well. The politics of respectability sought to establish some basis of equality between black and white elites that did not unleash a violent white backlash prompted by fears of social equality. According to the historian Hannah Rosen, the term "social equality" referred "broadly to forms of association between white and black people that did not convey a hierarchal meaning of race and that did not serve to mark racial difference." When used by southern white supremacists in defense of segregation and disfranchisement, the phrase evoked black men's access to the "private spaces" of white society, which extended to the parlors of white men's homes and the bedrooms of their wives and daughters.[20]

White men feared that black men empowered by the vote with the backing of the federal government would undermine the private sources of white men's public power—namely, their mastery over their household and the women and children sheltered therein. In a society where white male claims on citizenship were rooted in the ability to provide for and protect their dependents, the politicians of respectability had to steer clear of seeming to threaten these private sources of white male public power. Or, as Booker T. Washington pithily phrased it in his speech before the white delegates to the 1895 Atlanta Cotton States and International Exposition: "In all things that are purely social we can be as separate as the fingers, yet one as the hand in all things essential to mutual progress."[21] So long as black Americans were outgunned, outnumbered, and relatively powerless in the face of white mob violence, black progress had to occur within the constraints of segregation in order to avoid a potentially deadly backlash.

The second impact of the politics of respectability was to divide the black community—especially as black elites attempted to configure the racial exclusions of Jim Crow along the lines of class and gender instead. For example, in 1906 G. G. McTeir wrote in to the *Savannah Tribune* about the recent moves to segregate Telfair, the local playhouse. He was heartened by news that Telfair was not planning on barring all African Americans, but rather "only the undesirable class . . . showing that there are some respectable Negroes." He then called on these "respectable Negroes to begin to draw a strong line of distinction in [our] own race and until we do so we will be like a big drove of black birds all alike."[22] This was not the same thing as "acting white," nor was it simply mimicking white people—members of the black bourgeoisie like McTeir sincerely embraced leading respectable lives as a positive goal for themselves and those whom they sought to uplift.[23] That the contours of this respectability were profoundly shaped by white cultural practices and racist opinions of what black people were capable of is without question. But black elites embraced Victorian standards of morality as might any materially successful person of their day. Not only did McTeir want to demonstrate that there *were* class distinctions within Savannah's black community and that some African Americans had progressed, he himself did not want to be excluded from one of the leading cultural institutions of his city. This is why respectability—while still serving as a means of cultural self-defense and informing the rituals of interracial negotiation across the color line—was far more than a simple "mask." It is also why the discourse of respectability had such a pervasive influence on Atlanta's black politics in the Progressive Era.

This tactical embrace of respectability—no matter how necessary—held serious consequences for the future of black politics, significantly limiting the political vision of black elites for decades.[24] Higginbotham asserts that "the politics of respectability constituted a deliberate, highly self-conscious concession to hegemonic values." Though she is careful to note that respectability is not reducible to a "front," lacking "substance or content," this ability to make a concession to hegemonic values presumes that there is a space free from hegemonic determination.[25] By this reading, the politics of respectability is still a mask that can be donned or removed with ease in order to conceal a subversive black agenda. However, the need to don such a mask placed severe limits upon the extent to which this masquerade could resist white supremacy. This is because the mask, the face behind the mask, and the audience for whom the mask is donned all participate in a shared universe of meanings even as those meanings are contested. This makes a non-ideological, nonhegemonic space incredibly difficult to maintain. In other words, once the mask is put on, it is very hard to remove. Dissemblance is, of course, still possible, but it only works if there is at least some shared understanding between the deceiver and the deceived of what the "mask" should look like. The politicians of respectability shared too many cultural assumptions about gender, class, and sometimes even race with the advocates of white supremacy to stake out a genuinely oppositional position. This is not to say that the historic proponents of a black politics of respectability were themselves white supremacists. The economic, political, and martial balance of power between black Americans and southern white supremacists militated against any organized aggressive political action African Americans may have chosen. This tactical embrace of respectability was commonly the only strategy open to those African Americans who resisted Jim Crow. Relatively powerless in the face of white supremacy, black elites were compelled to seek an alliance—though unequal—with those white elites with whom it was possible to establish some sort of common ground.

Finally, because respectability was not always premised on the possession of wealth or power, it always held the potential of uniting African Americans across class lines. In her insightful study of community formation among nineteenth-century black Atlantans, Allison Dorsey argues that social stratification within the Gate City is better understood in terms of status rather than class. Measured in terms of their relationship to the world of wage labor and the accumulation of property, the vast majority of black Atlantans would qualify as working class, while the number of African Americans in the city who could stake a claim to middle-class status based on wealth alone was tiny.[26] According to Dorsey, it was possible to gain the social status associated with the middle class by simply behaving respectably. To the extent that it is true, the politics of respectability could in some instances work against the division of the black community by class and gender. In other words, just as respectability could serve as a "bridge discourse" between black and white elites, it also had the capacity to serve as a bridge discourse *within* the black community, uniting black people across the divides of power and wealth. In 1918 and 1919, when Atlanta's black voters united to force the city to build Booker T. Washington High School, they could do so because they shared a common understanding of respectability that was linked to the ability to send their children to public schools. Thus, respectability always had this dual potential to both unite and divide the community. The extent to which it unified or divided black Atlantans depended upon a historically specific definition of respectability.

However, the politics of respectability had long hindered the development of the racial consciousness necessary to give the black vote in Atlanta in 1919 its coherence as *the black vote,* and it was the transformation of the meaning of respectability during the Progressive Era that created a much sounder basis for black political solidarity. The widespread embrace of the politics of respectability as a strategy by the black elite at the end of the nineteenth century guaranteed that it would be one of the key terms that defined black solidarity. It is precisely this aspect of respectability that makes it vital to comprehend the ways in which the Victorian understandings of gender and class that comprised the discourse of respectability changed over time. The challenges posed by Progressive Era urban development, disfranchisement, and indiscriminate antiblack violence repeatedly threw this politics of respectability into turmoil, and as World War I approached, these forces would undermine the cultural foundation of respectability that had shaped political negotiations across the color line. After the war, Atlanta's black elite were able to reinterpret the language and the politics of respectability. Rather than serving as an unstable foundation for *class solidarity across racial lines,* the politics of respectability became instead a means for black Atlantans to establish *racial solidarity across class lines.* Though this new cultural foundation of respectability was still unstable, black Atlantans used it once again to publicly embrace an idea of universal suffrage and full access to the prerogatives of modern urban citizenship that had been difficult for black political leaders to demand since the collapse of Reconstruction. During the 1919 bond fight, the solidarity built atop this new cultural foundation would prove potent enough to sustain the unity of a powerful black voting bloc that could at least partially dictate the terms of its relationship to the power of reform-minded white elites.

Gender, Reform, and the City

Of all the cultural variables that comprised the discourse of respectability, the most significant was gender. Recall from the opening epigraph that Captain Jackson McHenry concluded his 1919 parable by urging "the black man . . . [to] organize to protect himself and his family."[27] As he did so, he equated the participation of Atlanta's black men in the 1919 bond election with the patriarchal defense of the black household. On the most basic level, this speaks to a commonly held expectation that all men have the responsibility to defend their dependents. On a deeper level, by insisting that black men organize to protect themselves and their families, McHenry's patriarchal appeal is a way of asserting the equality of black men and white men, based in a shared understanding of manhood. McHenry's call to arms boldly proclaimed that black men had proven themselves just as capable as white men of defending the interests of their families—in this case, their children's right to attend public school. However, taken as a simple assertion of male equality, McHenry's fable obscures the profound transformations that black Atlantans had undergone in the prior three decades, which had radically reshaped the public roles of black men and women as well as their relationships to one another. The social chaos caused by rapid urban development challenged the gender roles that formed the very foundation of the politics of respectability. Indeed, black middle-class leaders used the language of respectability to describe racial solidarity as well as negotiations across the color line. Necessarily drawing its meaning from the dominant discourses of race, class, and gender, this language both empowered African Americans and constrained the options open to them. However, these underlying discourses changed over time—most significantly in response to the changing role of women in the public sphere. Between the collapse of Reconstruction and the 1910s, black migration into Atlanta allowed women to become more prominent as wageworkers, as heads of household, and as reformers.[28] As they did so, their actions would impact the languages available to describe racial and interracial solidarity.

As Atlanta grew larger and more complex, women increasingly became symbols of social order, morality, and purity. It fell to women, as mothers and moral guardians of the home, to defend the family against the corruptions of urban life. For female reformers, this presented the opportunity to put the stamp of women's superior morality on the new era. Such immense responsibility placed on black women to safeguard the future of the race ensured that they would become one of the predominant symbols for racial progress in Atlanta. As the city's black elite confronted Jim Crow, the public perception of black women's morality became as important, if not more so, than what these women did to uplift the race, and this often reduced them to the dual status of "ornament or outcast in public life."[29] Though women did actively participate in creating this bifurcated symbolism of black womanhood, those voices that most loudly praised black women as mothers, wives, and daughters (and condemned their failings) often belonged to men. As Mary P. Ryan puts it, the gender symbols of the late nineteenth century provided "ample images with which to drape the multifarious interests that competed with one another in the male-dominated political domain."[30] Women frequently became the symbols through which men contested with one another for power, representing all that they as men desired to defend from the aggressions, real or imagined, of other men. Additionally, given the immense influence of a still vibrant ideology of republican motherhood that had first emerged following the American Revolution, women's domestic roles became crucial to the defense of the nation's virtue. As mothers especially, women stood as a wall between the moral home and the corruptions of the public sphere. Grounded in an increasingly strict division between a male public sphere and a female private sphere, women assumed the awesome responsibility of educating their sons and daughters to be virtuous citizens. The willingness of individuals to sacrifice personal advantage for the public good depended upon the private virtue of those individuals, and it fell to women to nurture those virtues in the children that they raised. This responsibility also gave women a large measure of cultural authority over the home, which they were to sustain as a refuge in which children could grow up healthy and morally upright and to which men could return to restore themselves following their daily engagements with other men in the dog-eat-dog world of politics and the marketplace.[31]

Should women fail in their duties to defend the virtue of the home, the result would be both racial and national decline. This also meant that Atlanta's women were also easily associated with anything that might undermine virtue.[32] In placing so much weight on the collective moral responsibilities of the city's mothers, daughters, and wives, women became symbols of potential social disorder and immorality as well. As the Atlanta historian Georgina Hickey aptly framed it, against the background of rapid urban development, women—especially working-class women—became symbols of both hope and danger. For black politicians of respectability, this meant that the image of black working-class women was one of the central terms in their negotiations across the color line. To defend black rights, they embraced a conception of patriarchal manhood, while women's domesticity (or lack thereof) served as a symbol that marked the progress of the race.

However, for black women living in the era of Jim Crow, this idealized vision of domesticity was very difficult to realize. To begin with, their moral capacities—especially in their roles as mothers—were continually under attack by racist white ideologues. In 1889, Philip Bruce devoted two full chapters to black womanhood in his influential history of Reconstruction. Without the discipline of slavery, black mothers became, he said, "morally obtuse and indifferent, and at times even openly or unreservedly licentious." Bruce argued that African American mothers did not instill in their daughters "those moral lessons that they particularly need as members of the female sex." Unable and unwilling to raise their daughters to value chastity and sexual purity, bulwarks of the family, black women instead became the "floodgates of the corrupting sexual influences that are doing so much to sap and destroy it."[33] Additionally, very few black women could lead purely domestic lives at the turn of the twentieth century. Throughout the rural South, 95 percent of black women employed in 1910 were in domestic service or agriculture.[34] Those working as domestic servants in white households faced the constant threat of sexual assault at the hands of the white men who employed them. These women bore the double burden of responsibility for defending the purity of their homes while simultaneously navigating the hazards of the public sphere, where they were often compelled to defend their own purity as well.

Not only was black women's special moral mission to defend the home complicated by their participation in the workforce, Atlanta's rapid development made the defense of that home ever more challenging. As the city grew, it became increasingly segregated by race, with black Atlantans crowded onto land that white people would not live on—near factories, railroads, and low-lying flood zones, all of which exacerbated the incidence of tuberculosis and other urban diseases of poverty.[35] Ever resistant to raising taxes to pay for the expansion of city services, what little public infrastructure the city had was limited to the downtown business district, the city's tonier white neighborhoods, and some white working-class districts. By contrast, *no* black neighborhood enjoyed access to city services; well into the twentieth century, life for most black Atlantans was characterized by unpaved streets, inadequate sanitation, a lack of clean water, insufficient fire and police protection, and the absence of the sorts of parks and swimming pools to which white Atlantans had access in white neighborhoods. Even worse, not only were black Atlantans excluded from the benefits of urban development, but the environmental costs of that development were often displaced onto black communities. According to the urban historian Ron Bayor, sewer lines commonly ended where black property lines began and dumped their contaminated effluvia into black Atlantans' drinking water.[36] The city not only threatened the health of its black citizens but also endangered their morals. Despite periodic crackdowns on prostitution, the police did not close brothels in the city's African American neighborhoods. For Atlanta's powerful leisure industry, the availability of black prostitutes was too big a draw for tourists and conventioneers.[37]

Charged with the responsibility of defending the morality of the household, black women were also compelled to address the consequences of Atlanta's racially stratified urban development. Like female reformers and settlement house workers throughout this period, the urban crisis encouraged some black women in Atlanta to expand the scope of their domestic mission beyond the four walls of their own households and into the surrounding community. As aptly put in 1910 by Marion Talbot, the dean of women at the University of Chicago, "The home does not stop at the street door. It is as wide as the world into which the individual steps forth. The determination of the character of that world and the preservation of those interests which she has safeguarded in the home, constitute the real duty resting upon women."[38] By embracing this sort of public "activist womanhood," black women were able to carve out a space in the public sphere where they were to become more than symbols of racial advance or decline.[39] Expansively interpreting their mandate to defend the home, they became agents of racial uplift and began to assert a greater measure of control over the meaning of black womanhood—particularly the role it played in the politics of respectability. As black men were driven by violence and disfranchisement from the public sphere, especially after the 1906 race riot, this activist womanhood gave women a vehicle to assume the vanguard of race leadership.[40] And, as they did so, they began to reshape black politics.

In Atlanta, the driving force behind this new politics was famed community organizer Lugenia Burns Hope, one of the founders of the Neighborhood Union. Having grown up in Chicago, she got her start in reform work through her involvement with Jane Addams's Hull House. Married in 1897, she followed her husband, John Hope, to Atlanta, where he would eventually become president first of Morehouse College and then, later, of Atlanta University. As she looked forward to starting a family with her husband, she grew increasingly alarmed about the conditions of the city in which she found herself. Her first step was to reach out to the other mothers in the neighborhood, who worked full time and lacked access to day care and playgrounds for their own children. By 1905, Hope and her neighbors had helped organize the Gate City Kindergarten Association, which established five kindergartens for black children across Atlanta. Three years later, in 1908, this same group of women became the core group of leaders that established the Neighborhood Union. Understanding that kindergartens alone were insufficient to defend the health and morals of their children, the Union pressured the city's white progressive leaders to extend the boundaries of the modern city to include the city's black residents. However, lacking the power to demand equal access to public goods such as running water or streetlights as a matter of simple justice—or even a fair return on the taxes they had paid—these women used respectability as a basis for the extension of these city services into black neighborhoods. Skilled practitioners of the politics of respectability, the women of the Union argued that white elites needed to ally themselves with black elites, invest in the city's black neighborhoods, and uplift the race in order to prevent black criminality.[41]

As the women who founded the Neighborhood Union extended their concern for the health and morality of their own children outward into the neighborhoods surrounding their homes, they also moved beyond being mere ciphers for racial progress and decline to being active agents of race uplift. Atlanta's black women were far from passive symbols of domesticity before the founding of the Gate City Kindergarten Association and the Neighborhood Union, but these twin institutions gave them considerably more power over the representations of black women in the public sphere. This power allowed them to use respectability to unify Atlanta's black citizens behind a campaign of active engagement with the city's development.

The Collapse of the Politics of Respectability and the Rise of Modern Black Politics

The social and political order of Jim Crow rested upon an unstable cultural foundation, a gender ideology that demanded men and women, black and white, play their respective roles. White men, of course, were the heroes, whose nobility was able to master their innate capacity for violence, which was unleashed only in the defense of endangered, virtuous white women. The bêtes noires—literally—in this narrative were beastly black men, intent on raping white women, and the sexually depraved and immoral black women who raised beastly sons and depraved daughters.[42] As an ideology, it bore little resemblance to the real world, but the white protagonists were willing to use it to justify all manner of violence and racist oppression during Jim Crow. The politics of respectability challenged this narrative by attempting to deracialize it, recasting the roles of hero and villain in such a way that not all black men were beasts and not all black women were depraved. In this new version of the same narrative, it was elite and respectable men who defended endangered, virtuous women against beastly men from the unrespectable classes and the depraved women who raised them. As a way of asserting equality between black and white elites, this made a certain amount of cultural sense, even though it still accepted the same divisions and exclusions of the Jim Crow gender system. The trick was for it to draw these distinctions based on class and respectability rather than race.

However, this politics of respectability itself was unstable and met considerable resistance from within the black community, primarily from the "unrespectable" black masses who rejected the uplift efforts of their betters and insisted on dancing, drinking, and carousing the night away. There were also families whose lives could not conform to the parameters of respectability due to the racial and gendered structure of the Atlanta job market, which reserved steady, if low-paid, work for black women and relegated most black men to seasonal and migratory work. Finally, those brave and isolated individuals who pierced the gender ideology of Jim Crow also came to question the politics of respectability. When black newspaper editor Alexander Manly suggested in 1898, for example, that white women sometimes preferred the company of black men, it helped spark the Wilmington race riot in North Carolina and forced Manly into exile.[43] Ida B. Wells's 1892 suggestion that "many white women in the South would marry colored men if such an act would not place them at once beyond the pale of society" made it impossible for her to return to Memphis without risking her life.[44] And when Jesse Max Barber, the editor of the *Voice of the Negro*, suggested during the 1906 Atlanta race riot that white men in blackface attacked white women, the city's most powerful white men compelled him to abandon his press and flee to Chicago. By attempting to deracialize the gender system of Jim Crow, the politicians of respectability implicitly suggested that *some* white men may be beastly and *some* white women may be depraved—or worse, some of these white women may reject the protection of white men. However, each of these black commentators, all members of the respectable middle class, had explicitly revealed truths that had to remain unspoken for the politics of respectability to function as a "bridge discourse" between black and white elites. These individual dissidents openly spoke truth to power, but in the face of both white reaction and the response of black leaders anxious to maintain the tenuous foundations of interracial politics, these acts of resistance were unable to change the underlying cultural foundations that undergirded white supremacy.

A politics of respectability that placed heroic black men at its heart also depended upon virtuous, endangered black women to make it work. However, not all black women were content to remain symbols of potential racial decline or endangerment. Some, like Lugenia Burns Hope and the other women who founded Atlanta's Neighborhood Union, came to see themselves as the protagonists in this narrative. Though they began their work accepting the same basic gender system that underlay both the politics of respectability and Jim Crow, they ultimately came to challenge both class-bound and patriarchal visions of respectability. Their engagement with urban development that left black neighborhoods without access to the city services enjoyed by white neighborhoods transformed their uplift work among the working-class women of the city into an effort to forge solidarity among all of the city's black women regardless of class or status. Castigated as "depraved" by the city's white supremacist elite, Atlanta's black women had long tried to keep hearth and home together on a domestic worker's income. And they did so without access to urban amenities like running water and electricity that made it easier for white women to play the role of virtuous mother (amenities that also included command over the low-wage labor of black women). Through their organizing work, the women of the Neighborhood Union came to see the difference between respectable and unrespectable not solely as a moral distinction but also the result of being denied access to city services and decent employment. This realization changed the language of respectability from one that ranked and judged the black community on a scale of worth to a right to which all families should have access.

U.S. entry into World War I presented a further challenge to the politics of respectability as black Americans appropriated Woodrow Wilson's call to "make the world safe for democracy" to make America democratic for black people too. Though asked to risk their lives to defend a Jim Crow nation, millions of African American men and women heeded W. E. B. Du Bois's exhortation published in the NAACP's *Crisis* magazine that they ought to "forget . . . special grievances and close our ranks shoulder to shoulder with our white fellow citizens and the allied nations that are fighting for democracy."[45] At the beginning of the war, the entire size of the U.S. military was only 220,000 men.[46] By war's end, four million men were in uniform—of this number, 367,000 were African American, out of 2.3 million black men who registered for the draft.[47] Even though they were not required to register for the draft, approximately 2,000 black women volunteered for service as Red Cross nurses.[48] Others worked with the Young Women's Christian Association (YWCA) to provide cultural and social services for the millions of young men crowded into the hastily erected cantonments that dotted the nation.[49] In 1918, Neighborhood Union founder Lugenia Burns Hope ran a YWCA hostess house for black soldiers at Camp Upton in New York.[50] Such professions of black loyalty established a new "bridge discourse" through which African Americans could assert equality with white Americans through military valor and patriotic service even as white supremacists violently contested these assertions of racial equality. Fearful that African Americans would bring the fight for democracy home, white supremacist vigilantes used violence to shore up the Jim Crow social order through terror and intimidation, lynching ten black soldiers in their uniforms in the weeks following the Armistice. Northern cities, which had become the destination of thousands of black migrants seeking economic opportunities opened by wartime labor shortages, erupted in a series of antiblack riots that left hundreds of African Americans dead.[51] Despite this widespread white resistance, wartime nationalism had changed the terms of black solidarity and the bounds of interracial politics, making both considerably more expansive. Black claims on racial equality rooted in patriotism were able to occur outside the limits imposed by the politics of respectability—allowing formerly "nonrespectable" types to establish common ground with both white Americans and respectable black elites. Additionally, the language of patriotic sacrifice gave Atlanta's black community a way to assert equality with the city's white taxpayers and—as loyal, taxpaying citizens—insist on equal access to public education and other civic rights.

As the cultural and social upheavals of World War I weakened the hold of the politics of respectability on the imagination of the city's black leadership, it permitted the emergence of an identifiably modern black politics. Whereas before the war interracial politics in Atlanta was rooted in strategic alliances with nominally sympathetic white elites, after the war contending racial voting blocs periodically vied with one another for political power and influence, as seen in the 1919 bond fight. Black journalist Timothy Thomas Fortune articulated just this vision for black politics as early as 1882. In a speech that year before the Colored Press Association, he declared that "in the politics of the country the colored vote must be made as uncertain a quantity as the German and Irish vote. The color of their skin must cease to be an index of their political creed. They must think less of 'the party' and more of themselves."[52] This refrain was repeated every time the Republican Party betrayed its legacy as the party of Lincoln, emancipation, and Reconstruction. In 1883, when the U.S. Supreme Court eviscerated the 1875 Civil Rights Act, black leaders denounced the decision and warned that the Republican Party would pay dearly in the 1884 elections.[53] On the day following the 1906 midterm elections, President Theodore Roosevelt dismissed without honor all 167 black members of the Twenty-Fifth Infantry stationed in Brownsville, Texas, following the unsolved murder of a local bartender. Black leaders across the nation again vowed that they would punish the Republican Party at the polls in 1908.[54] John Mitchell of the *Richmond Planet* condemned the decision and declared an earlier announcement would have changed the outcome of the recent election in several key states and predicted that Brownsville should "figure in many elections to come," especially given the "independent attitude of the Republican voters of the North."[55] Richard W. Thompson of the *Indianapolis Freeman* suggested that not since the *Civil Rights Cases* of 1883 had the black electorate been so aroused and that had the announcement been before the midterms, "there would have been a disastrous slump in the colored Republican vote for Congressmen in the States where the Negroes hold the balance of power."[56] Even staunch party loyalist Ben Davis of the *Atlanta Independent* agreed with Mitchell and said that "no self-respecting Negro man would have voted the [R]epublican ticket last Tuesday in the face of this flagrant violation of our constitutional rights."[57]

The most strident voice calling for black political autonomy in 1906 belonged to T. Thomas Fortune of the *New York Age*. Using a model of ethnic and racial solidarity that was common in urban politics of the North throughout the second half of the nineteenth century, Fortune urged African Americans to reconsider their loyalties to the GOP. He insisted that "the Afro-American people" ought to become "as narrow and self-centered as the white native and foreign Americans are in all matters that concern them." The *Age* criticized black Americans for their "trust in white men," which had "in the past brought upon them most of the troubles that now vex them." Fortunately, the trials of Brownsville and the recent Atlanta race riot were "bringing them into closer sympathy and union." Since "the white man [had] deceived and robbed the Afro-Americans of their faith and their substance . . . it [was] high time for them to . . . look out for themselves and their interests."[58] Black Americans would not be able to follow Fortune's advice until there was a real political alternative to support with their votes. This would not happen until enough black voters had migrated to the cities of the North, where they encountered urban Democratic machines. Nationally, a real political alternative would not emerge until 1936, when millions of black voters "turned Lincoln's picture to the wall" to support the party of the New Deal.[59] However, the 1919 bond fight in Atlanta required African Americans neither to abandon their long-standing loyalties to the GOP nor to support the party of southern white supremacy. As they fought for

Booker T. Washington High School, black Atlantans laid the foundation for a new black politics.

The collapse of the politics of respectability in the face of rapid urbanization, white supremacist violence, and wartime mobilization forced black Atlantans to make their own power, rather than borrowing it from their relationship with capricious white elites. This power enabled the Atlanta branch of the NAACP and the Neighborhood Union to declare themselves ready to stop negotiating for inclusion into a Jim Crow social order and instead start demanding *first-class citizenship* for all black Americans.

1

"Manhood Rights"

Progress and the Politics
of Respectability, 1899–1906

The most telling indicator of the political position that the state's black leadership found itself in was the cartoon on the front page of the *Atlanta Journal* on the day following the defeat of the Hardwick bill in 1899 (see figure 1). This bill, authored by state representative Thomas W. Hardwick, was modeled after similar disfranchisement bills passed earlier in Mississippi and asked the electorate to change the state constitution to include a grandfather clause and literacy test in order to disfranchise Georgia's African American voters.[1] The *Journal* cartoon depicted a former slave, ballot in hand, standing before an arch inscribed with the words "Wisdom, Justice and Moderation," listening to a former slave-owner tell him, "Though I have the power I will not take from you the ballot. Trust the southern white man as your friend. Work to build up Georgia and all your rights, personal and political, will be safe."[2] Although the cartoonist's depiction rendered invisible the efforts of Georgia's black leadership to defeat the bill, he nonetheless captured the limitations within which this resistance was confined. The battle to preserve the right to vote could only be waged using the language of mutual regard within a framework of white paternalism, avoiding any contention over the fundamental rights of citizenship. While the state's black leadership had certainly earned the right to applaud themselves for defeating disfranchisement in 1899, a cautious observer would not clap too loudly.

In the last decade of the nineteenth century, African Americans confronted an increasingly aggressive effort on the part of white southerners to legally exclude them from the full prerogatives of citizenship. State after state enacted laws that both disfranchised black citizens and sought to drive them from public space. These developments strengthened the commitments of black emigrationists like Bishop Henry McNeal Turner to lead black people

FIGURE 1. "Former slave owner to ex-slave: 'Though I have the power I will not take from you the ballot. Trust the southern white man as your friend. Work to build up Georgia and all your rights, personal and political, will be safe,'" *Atlanta Journal,* 29 November 1899.

out of the metaphorical Egypt to a black Israel in Africa. At the same time, black political leaders retreated ever deeper into the Republican Party as the guarantor of their liberties. And even when the party's commitments faltered, loyal Republicans could count on a handful of patronage jobs for themselves and at least some people in their community. Resting somewhat uneasily alongside both of these strategies was a third that accepted the limitations placed on citizenship by Jim Crow even as it rejected the notion that access to the full benefits of citizenship was to be permanently or semipermanently demarcated by race. Rather, those exclusions would depend upon the class and gender discourses that comprised the notion of respectability. By embracing an idea of the citizen that was bounded by the correct performance of bourgeois gender roles, it became possible to use the politics of respectability to assert a formal equality with other respectable *white* citizens. These black politicians of respectability hoped to deracialize citizenship by embracing instead its stratification by gender and class, an embrace that would form some basis for interracial negotiations across the color line.

This politics of respectability posed significant limits to the sorts of demands black leaders could make as well as how they could articulate those demands. Most obviously, white elites were frequently unwilling to see even the most respectable black people as equals—especially if the price for doing so seemed too high. Second, this strategy frequently made its adherents complicit in the project of segregation and disfranchisement. Although the politicians of respectability did reject segregation and disfranchisement based on race, they were still prepared to exclude from the ballot those deemed unworthy, regardless of race. Finally, self-consciously placing the gender and class practices of respectability at the heart of black politics in this era made political discourse within the black community as much a contest over the terms of manhood and womanhood as it was a fight for access to power and resources. This was perhaps the most limiting aspect of the politics of respectability, since it seriously undermined the effort to create a broader black solidarity. Nevertheless, this politics of respectability was crucial in carving out a space for political action for both black men and women during the "nadir" of black history, when the terrors faced by African Americans who dared assert themselves forced black politics to function within narrow limits.

Not only did black people who dared assert their rights risk death, antiblack violence was commonly sanctioned by the highest political authorities in the state. In 1899, the same year that the Hardwick bill went down to defeat, a black farmworker in Coweta County named Sam Hose got into an argument with his employer, Alfred Cranford, demanding the wages due him. During the course of the argument Cranford drew his pistol, and, in self-defense, a frightened Hose killed his employer with an ax. Within two days, newspapers had completely changed the story, arguing that Hose had snuck up behind Cranford and killed him while he was eating dinner. He then dragged Mrs. Cranford into the kitchen, threw her onto the floor, and raped her repeatedly as she lay beside her husband's corpse. When the mob caught Hose in the town of Newnan, they waited to kill him until a special excursion train carrying spectators could make the forty-mile trip from Atlanta.

Their arrival swelled the crowd to more than 2,000 men and women eager to watch the lynching. They chained Hose to a tree, piled high with firewood and doused with oil and kerosene. Before burning him alive, members of the crowd sliced off his ears, fingers, and genitals and removed the skin from his face. At one point in the midst of the ordeal, Hose managed to writhe free of the ropes that bound him to the tree. His killers then extinguished the flames, tied their still-living victim more firmly to the charred trunk of the tree, and set fire to him once again. Once Hose had finally perished, the crowd took out their knives and dismembered the corpse, hoping to take home a souvenir. Rumor had it that the crowd even sent a delegate to the state capital to present a slice of Sam Hose's heart as a gift to Governor Allen D. Candler.[3]

It remains unknown whether the governor ever received his gory tribute; however, he did comment publicly on the lynching of Sam Hose. Instead of condemning the torture and extralegal murder, Governor Candler condemned the assault allegedly committed by Hose as "among the most diabolical committed in the annals of crime." He followed this with a denunciation of Georgia's black community, whose protests against the lynching became evidence of black "race prejudice," blinding them to the true facts of the case—namely, that Hose's heinous crime justified his brutal death. For having failed to assist in the capture of Sam Hose, he criticized the black citizens of Newnan for having "lost the best opportunity they will ever have to elevate themselves in the eyes of their neighbors."[4] Upon hearing of the lynching from the relative safety of Atlanta, W. E. B. Du Bois decided to pen a "careful and reasoned response" in order to correct the governor's commentary. On his way to the office of the *Atlanta Constitution,* he passed a store window on Mitchell Street, where he saw on display the charred knuckles of Sam Hose. In horror, Du Bois returned to his rooms at Atlanta University. His response was never published.[5] This culture of violent impunity, in which white mobs could put black people to death without trial or due process of law, enjoyed the sanction and tolerance of nearly all white people in the state—from the office of the governor to the shopkeeper's storefront. In the age of Jim Crow, black southerners lived their lives under a racial sword of Damocles—every decision was made with this threat hanging above their heads, especially those that involved navigating the color line. This placed hard limits on black political ambitions, and it was within these limits that the black leadership of Georgia employed the politics of respectability to defeat the Hardwick bill.

"Wisdom, Justice, Moderation"

Because the size of the black electorate in Georgia had already been severely curtailed both by the introduction of a cumulative poll tax in 1877 and the white primary at the county level, it would have been difficult at best to rally the state's black voters in opposition to the Hardwick bill.[6] Instead, Georgia's black leaders traded on their reputations with white politicians to defeat this latest attempt to further reduce the black vote in the state legislature, rather than at the polls. Some of these efforts relied on long-standing personal friendships between black and white leaders. John H. Deveaux, the black collector of customs for the port of Savannah, called upon his long-standing relationship with Georgia state representative J. J. McDonough of Chatham to reprint and distribute to every member of the legislature a petition signed by the city's black citizens opposing the Hardwick bill.[7] However, given the recent level of violence directed at black Georgians, most black leaders were initially afraid to speak out against the bill. In the final decade of the nineteenth century, lynch mobs in Georgia assembled eighty-eight times to claim the lives of 106 victims—an average of one killing every five weeks. The violence only intensified with time; of those eighty-eight lynchings, eighteen of them had occurred in 1899, claiming the lives of twenty-five black victims— an average of one killing every two weeks.[8] Though these attacks did not directly target the state's black leadership, they had a profoundly chilling effect on those who attempted to stop the spread of disfranchisement. As novelist Richard Wright later wrote about growing up in the Jim Crow South, "The things that influenced my conduct as a Negro did not have to happen to me directly; I needed but to hear of them to feel their full effects in the deepest layers of my consciousness. Indeed, the white brutality that I had not seen was a more effective control of my behavior than what which I knew."[9]

The climate of fear is perhaps why even a leader as safe and conservative as Booker T. Washington had a difficult time rallying the state's black leadership to oppose the bill. On 7 November 1899, as the bill was making its way through the state legislature, Washington wrote to his friend T. Thomas Fortune about his frustration with the lack of local resistance to the Hardwick measure. "I have been corresponding with the leading people in the state but cannot stir up a single colored man to take the lead in trying to head off this movement. . . . They will not even answer my letters."[10] Deciding to take matters into his own hands, Washington boarded a train for Atlanta to direct this fight himself. After spending a day meeting with the state's black leaders, he gave an interview to the *Atlanta Constitution* regarding his opinions on the Hardwick bill. His conservative reputation and his relationships with Atlanta's prominent white elites allowed Washington to use the interview to both establish the limits of safe discourse in opposition to the proposed disfranchising law and determine the shape that opposition would ultimately take.

Washington had solidified this reputation four years earlier in Atlanta at the 1895 Cotton States and International Exposition. His "Atlanta Compromise" advised African Americans to steer clear of political agitation and abandon the fight for equal voting rights and work instead to build a foundation for black economic self-sufficiency. By working hard and accumulating wealth, Washington believed that in the long run black people would be able to build a firm and defensible foundation upon which to exercise future political power. However, in his imagining, that would be generations in the future. Whatever present progress was possible had to occur within the deadly limits imposed by Jim Crow and the unwillingness of the federal government to take any steps toward protecting black rights in the South; so, he focused instead on what he called the "art of the possible." In addition to steering ambitious young black people away from politics, the Atlanta Compromise defined a racially bifurcated social world, one that reassured white southerners that "in all things that are purely social we can be as separate as the fingers, yet one as the hand in all things essential to mutual progress." By thus capitulating to segregation and disfranchisement, Washington was hoping to avert the complete exclusion of African Americans from American civilization altogether. In other words, a second-class citizenship was better than none.[11] It was this sensibility that framed Booker T. Washington's uncharacteristically public defense of black voting rights in Georgia.

After carefully establishing that "the question of the rights and elevation of the negro" ought to be a decision left to the South, Washington outlined his case against the proposed educational qualification in the Hardwick bill. The most significant of Washington's arguments began by affirming for his audience that Georgia's black electorate posed absolutely no threat to white control over the state. Georgia's cumulative poll tax had reduced the size of the black electorate by so much that, in the most recent statewide election for governor, only 15 percent of eligible black voters had cast a ballot.[12] Washington reasoned that since "the white man controls practically every state and every county and township in the south," the proposed bill would serve no purpose but to purge the rolls of black voters, who could pose no real threat to white supremacy. All disfranchisement would do is encourage interracial strife and "widen the breach between the two races."[13]

Washington was able to make this argument—that black votes would not threaten white rule in the South—by divorcing the franchise from politics altogether. Rather than a means through which black people could collectively voice their dissent with white supremacy, Washington's ballot stands as a signifier describing the man who possesses it as qualified to be a part of white civilization. As one after another of the southern states passed measures to disfranchise black voters, Washington charged the entire South with a great responsibility "to take the negro by the hand and . . . lift him up to the point where he will be prepared for citizenship." In this telling, the ballot was not a means to exercise black political power, but rather the reward given to those "conservative and intelligent negroes" who have proven their fitness for citizenship and cast their lot "more closely with the southern white man and cease[d their] continued senseless opposition to his interests." At the end of his interview, Washington even went so far as to advise African Americans to steer clear of politics, warning them against becoming "mere politicians." Nevertheless, he still claimed to be speaking to "the very fundamental principles of citizenship," a claim that only made sense within the hard limits imposed on black political assertion at the end of the nineteenth century.[14] The only safe way to defend the ballot was for someone as accommodating to the system of Jim Crow as Booker T. Washington to publicly depoliticize black suffrage, even as this defense reduced the vote to a mere ritual undertaken to prove black Americans' capacity for virtuous self-government.

According to Washington, the real danger that the Hardwick bill posed was that it would deprive the process of qualifying for the vote of its power to serve as a vehicle for racial uplift. Even though the poll tax had been introduced as a means of eliminating black voters, he instead reframed the poll tax as a means of demonstrating one's fitness for citizenship. This allowed Washington to criticize the new disfranchisement measures as unfair to those who have prepared themselves for citizenship "by acquiring intelligence . . . education and property." At the same time, it also allowed him to defend the overall principle of suffrage restriction as a positive good. Saving up for the annual poll tax gave black Georgians a reason to work hard, accumulate property, and get ahead. Washington argued that a law that would prevent these worthy voters from exercising a right to vote that they had already earned would only serve to discourage other black Georgians from striving to make themselves respectable members of society. Even worse, he warned should the law "take from the negro all incentive to make himself and his children useful, property-holding citizens . . . can any one blame him for becoming a beast capable of committing any crime?"[15] The effort required to pay the poll tax and qualify to vote transformed black access to the ballot into a way to learn the habits of thrift, industriousness, and self-restraint necessary to become civilized. Foolishly closing down that path put white civilization at risk.

With Washington's support, twenty-four of the state's most prominent black leaders signed a memorial to the state legislature incorporating the points Washington had made in his *Atlanta Constitution* interview. Purporting to speak "in behalf of the Negroes of Georgia," the signatories represented a broad cross section of Georgia's black elite, including influential educators like W. E. B. Du Bois and John Hope alongside important black Republicans William Pledger, Henry L. Johnson, and Henry Rucker. Despite Washington's uncharacteristic leadership in the fight against disfranchisement in Georgia, his separation of the franchise from the exercise of political power severely limited the sorts of political claims these twenty-four men could make on the legislature.[16] By yoking the ballot to the project of race uplift, the Hardwick memorial became yet another invocation of the politics of respectability and a means for asserting equality among elite black and white men rather than a vehicle for demanding fundamental rights.

Reporting on the suffrage fight in Georgia for the *New York Independent,* Du Bois described the bill as going "beyond anything yet proposed in the South," the culmination of a long history of efforts to suppress the black vote from the fraud and violence that brought down Reconstruction to understanding and grandfather clauses recently voted into law in other states.[17] The bill was clearly designed to eliminate the black vote, and the authors of the memorial did not hold back in condemning the provisions of the Hardwick bill as designed to proscribe "color" rather than "ignorance, bribery and vote-selling." Joining the call "of the civilized world in demanding a pure, intelligent ballot," they challenged the state legislature to pass a bill that applied to black and white voters alike. Should the bill "restrict the right of suffrage to all who, irrespective of race or color, are intelligent enough to vote properly," the twenty-four signatories of the memorial would "heartily indorse it."[18]

It is possible to read this "hearty indorsement" of color-blind suffrage restriction as a way of forcing the defenders of the bill into an untenable position where they would have to sanction the disfranchisement of their own white constituents. This echoed the solution that Washington proposed toward the end of his interview with the *Constitution.* Suggesting that the proposed bill would be in violation of the equal protection clause of the Fourteenth Amendment, he proposed that it be amended to disfranchise unqualified black and white voters equally.[19] However, the memorial went a step further than necessary, asserting that racial discrimination in politics was "defensible" when it was "grounded on a real difference in civilization and intelligence. . . . In such case, it is not really discrimination against color, but against ignorance, poverty and vice." In other words, while it was inappropriate to discriminate on the basis of skin color, it was legitimate and even desirable to deny the vote to African Americans due to their inferior development and "civilization."[20]

The authors of the memorial attempted to resolve this contradiction by establishing common ground with the state's white elites, attempting to enlist them as equal partners on a civilizing mission to lift both the black and white working class out of the illiteracy, poverty, and crime that prevented them from being intelligent and responsible voters. Linking the progress of black Georgians to the progress of civilization itself, the authors of the petition argued that "the prosperity of Georgia was bound up with the prosperity of the Georgia negro; that no nation or State can advance faster than its laboring classes, and that whatever hinders, degrades or discourages the negroes weakens and injures the State."[21] At the turn of the century, this discourse of civilization was pervasive and was frequently used by white men to legitimize their claims on domination. By positing an evolutionary development of the races, these white paragons of humanity could place themselves at the top. However, as the authors of the memorial invoked this discourse of civilization, they partially subverted the claims of white men on absolute social power and contested the notion that racial differences between black and white people were biologically determined. They maintained that black men and women were just as capable of attaining the pinnacle of civilization as their white counterparts, and insisted that the survival of the nation itself depended upon interracial elite efforts to uplift the semicivilized masses of both races.[22] Subversive or not, by appropriating this discourse, they validated and became bound by its terms, seriously hindering the longer term development of a genuinely oppositional discourse that could sustain future claims for equal protection under the laws and, in the short term, implicating the authors of the memorial in justifying the project of disfranchisement.

In order to launch this civilizing mission, the signatories of the memorial enrolled the assistance of one of the key institutions of the Progressive Era state-building project: the public school.[23] Establishing that "the governed must be intelligent enough to recognize and choose their own best good," the memorial asserted that "in free government based on universal manhood suffrage, it is fair and right to impose on voters an educational qualification, so long as the State furnishes free school facilities to all children."[24] With this statement, the black leaders of Georgia were in a single breath willing to trade away a large portion of what remained of black political power in the state in exchange for access to universal free public education. Unable in 1899 to use the ballot to compel Georgia to provide adequate school facilities for all of the state's school-age children, they instead chose to exchange one means of race uplift (the ballot) for another (the public school). Acknowledging that these measures would disfranchise a huge number of African Americans who were "in large degree, poor and ignorant" due to the legacy of slavery, the signatories reminded the lawmakers that this was no "light sacrifice."[25] Their choice of the word "sacrifice" in this context suggests that despite all the language they employed to distinguish themselves as leaders of the race from the "ignorant" masses, they fully understood the value of what they were giving up; nonetheless, they thought the price, though steep, was a fair one to pay. Their use of the word "sacrifice" also indicated that they had no choice in the matter. They were subject to a power far greater than their own. In 1899, the leading black men of Georgia were willing to negotiate inclusion into a Jim Crow social order, so long as some of the expanding benefits of the Progressive state would go to the black community—particularly if those benefits gave them at least some access to the means necessary to uplift the black masses.

This sort of sacrifice placed rather severe limitations on the claims black citizens could make on the expanding powers of the Progressive Era state. Arguing that African Americans "have not been sparing in [their] efforts to improve," the memorial pointed out that "the strenuous efforts of the Negroes have reduced their illiteracy from ninety-two to not much over fifty percent in a single generation."[26] While emphasizing the astoundingly successful expansion of literacy among African Americans a generation out of slavery, the authors nonetheless "gladly acknowledge[d]" their "indebtedness to the Public School System of Georgia, supported by the tax-payers of the State. These educational facilities, no less thankfully received than generously tendered, are largely responsible for the measure of good will still remaining between the black and white residents of Georgia."[27] While fitting into the narrative establishing a joint civilizing mission between black and white elites, this story overlooked the glaring inequalities between black and white schools in the state. For example, in 1905 white Georgia schoolteachers earned an average of $42.85 per month as compared to $19.88 for

33

black teachers. In addition, black communities relied upon "second-taxing" in order to pay for the construction of their own school buildings rather than wait for the state to do so.[28] Understanding black access to primary and secondary education as a "thankfully received" act of white "generosity" rather than a right of citizenship did not just erase this history of black self-reliance; it undermined the ability of black Americans to make claims on the state as citizens. Ready to exchange the civil rights of the majority of black Georgians for access to the civic rights of public education, the authors of the Hardwick memorial were willing to accept both inclusion into a racially segregated Progressive state and the classification of the black electorate into those more and less worthy of full citizenship. The embrace of such divisions would make it much more difficult for black Americans to forge the political solidarity necessary for a genuinely autonomous black politics to emerge.

Ultimately, the disfranchisement bill failed in the House, garnering only two votes in favor besides Hardwick's.[29] According to the historian Clarence Bacote, the 1899 defeat of disfranchisement in Georgia was due more to white interests and indifference than black protest. Many legislators realized that the poll tax and white primary had already decimated the black vote, and any action to further disfranchise black Georgians would only incite racial conflict. In addition, some legislators realized the utility of a small and tractable black vote, which could be useful should the Populists reemerge as a political force in the state as they had at the beginning of the decade.[30] Still others from less affluent districts feared the disfranchisement bill would strip their poor white constituents of the right to vote.[31] Historically, the most important thing that the debate over the Hardwick bill demonstrated was not the effectiveness of black protest strategies against disfranchisement, but rather the ways in which both the racial exclusions and terror that lay at the heart of the Progressive Era state-building project shaped black understandings of racial solidarity and expectations of citizenship.

Thomas Hardwick was by no means finished with his campaign to drive African Americans from the polls. The arch in the *Atlanta Journal* cartoon described at the beginning of this chapter symbolized the power of the state of Georgia, before which the best black men of the state made their "sacrifice." As long as their citizenship claims did not conflict with the interests of the so-called best white men of the state, the terms of this sacrifice would be honored and the black citizens of Georgia would retain a qualified suffrage. However, the Progressive Era, with its comparatively vast expansion of the powers of the state, was about to bring into power a new set of architects who would topple the arch of "Wisdom, Justice and Moderation" in order to build a new one christened "Progressivism—for whites only."[32] As African Americans in Georgia confronted this new threat, the ideas of class and gender that sustained the politics of respectability prevented them from articulating a coherent opposition to the project of black disfranchisement. Soon, these older strategies would no longer be able to hold disfranchisement at bay.

The Progressive's Curse

Before the signatories of the Hardwick memorial sought an alliance with the state's conservative white elite, there had been the possibility of an interracial political alliance that was not completely confined within the politics of respectability. Emerging from the Farmers' Alliance in 1891, the People's Party (or the Populist Party as it came to be known) advanced an ambitious platform that included calls for overhauling the nation's monetary and banking systems, a progressive income tax, and public ownership of the railroads. During the height of the Populists' influence between 1891 and 1902, they elected seven governors and forty-five members of Congress (including six senators), sent hundreds of representatives into state legislatures, and carried four states in the 1892 presidential election.[33] The Populists' ambition was to unite Americans across the lines of class, region, and sometimes even race to stand against the rapacity of late nineteenth-century capitalism. As one Populist leader told his supporters in the winter of 1892, "You stand for the yearning, upward tendency of the middle and lower classes. . . . You stand as sworn foes of monopoly—not monopoly in the narrow sense of the word—but monopoly of power, of place, of privilege, of wealth, of progress."[34]

Those words were penned by the irascible Tom Watson, one of the party's earliest and most powerful leaders, then a first-term Democratic representative from Georgia's Tenth Congressional District.[35] Even before finishing his first term, Watson quit the party of his forefathers to take up the Populist banner. What made Watson unique among southern politicians was the extent to which he appeared willing to reach out to black voters even as he tried to convince southern white men to sever their ties of loyalty to the Democrats, a party that not only claimed them politically but also emotionally, historically, and even racially. Careful to distance himself from charges of advocating "social equality," Watson nonetheless proclaimed the need for "political equality" between black and white Georgians. Over the course of his 1892 campaign for Congress, he told his supporters that "the accident of color can make no difference in the interests of farmers, croppers and laborers.... You are kept apart that you may be separately fleeced of your earnings.... You are deceived and blinded that you may not see how this race antagonism perpetuates a monetary system which beggars both."[36] While Watson's language here remains remarkable, his outreach to black voters was not all that unique in the early 1890s. As the historian Charles Crowe points out, in two decades between the collapse of Reconstruction and the imposition of disfranchisement, conservative white Democrats frequently forged alliances of convenience with their black constituencies.[37] And black political leaders often sought to take advantage of splits between white leaders in order to leverage real power for themselves and their communities.[38] If that meant supporting conservative Democrats, they would do so. When black leaders heard Watson's message that the People's Party gave black Georgians a means "to escape the dilemma of selling [their] vote to the Democrats or pledging it blindly to the Republican bosses," some of them also decided to cast their lot with the firebrand Populist.[39]

The 1892 campaign was particularly violent. Before the polls closed, white Democrats had killed at least fifteen black Populists in addition to an indeterminate, though smaller, number of their white allies.[40] The threat of violence, however, forced some extraordinary acts of solidarity. In the weeks before the election, Rev. H. S. Doyle, a black Populist who had given more than sixty speeches in support of Watson, fled the threat of a lynching following a campaign stop in rural Georgia. After having taken refuge on Watson's farm in the town of Thomson, the white Populist leader sent out a call for men to defend Rev. Doyle. Within twenty-four hours, some 2,000 armed men flooded into town from the surrounding countryside in order to defend both Watson and his black allies.[41] All the same, Rev. Doyle did not take refuge in Watson's home. To avoid charges of "social equality," Doyle instead was given a bed in one of the "Negro house[s]" on Watson's property.[42] Even though Watson's 1892 campaign gave black and white Georgians a common struggle during which some racial distinctions could be set aside, there were decided limits to Watson's willingness to see a staunch black ally as his true equal.

Despite these remarkable displays of interracial solidarity, through force and fraud the Democrats still defeated Watson in 1892. Two years later, when Populist power in the state reached its apex, Watson was beaten yet again through "ballot-box stuffing and burning, intimidation, bloodshed and bribery." In both of these campaigns, powerful white planters took advantage of their control of black laborers to compel them to vote against the Populist Party.[43] As Watson failed repeatedly to revive the declining fortunes of the Populist Party, he faced a unified white Democratic Party that, despite its reliance on easily intimidated black voters to maintain power, used the threatening image of "Negro domination" to scare potential white Populists back into line. Even though the voting strength of black Georgians had long ago been decimated by the poll tax and the white primary, the Democrats insisted that any division of white men would allow the few remaining black voters to constitute a "balance of power," which would allow black voters to exploit a divided electorate and pave the way for their return to political power. When he began his career as a Populist, Watson dismissed these racist scare tactics, retorting that "the argument against independent political movement in the South may be boiled down to one word—nigger." However, after more than a decade of defeat, what was once put forth as a critical rejection of the race-baiting of his Democratic opponents would eventually develop into Watson's diagnosis for what had killed his Populist Party. The real turning point in Watson's evolving position on black suffrage was his nomination in 1904 for president of the United States by the remnants of the national Populist Party. On the campaign trail, Watson told his supporters that "in Georgia, [the Democrats] do not dare disfranchise [the Negro], because the men who control the [D]emocratic machine in Georgia . . . need the negro to beat us with."[44] White men could not divide politically without giving black voters an opening to take power. For any independent politics in the South to have a future, the black vote would have to be eliminated.

Following a disastrous showing in the 1904 canvass, Watson was desperate to demonstrate the continuing relevance of the Populists and sustain his political career. In the aftermath of the campaign, Watson publicly offered to throw his weight behind any Democratic candidate who would run on a platform including a pledge to "a change in our Constitution which will perpetuate white supremacy in Georgia."[45] Twenty-three thousand Georgians had voted for Watson in 1904, and he hoped to swing these voters to the Democratic candidate who would meet his demands. If successful, he could position himself as a kingmaker in state politics. Watson, however, was not interested in being merely a kingmaker; he wanted to see the return of his Populist Party as a political force to be reckoned with. His hope was that the complete removal of African Americans from politics would disarm the race-baiters of the Democratic Party and allow white voters to unite behind the banner of the Populist Party.[46]

Watson's sentiments on disfranchisement were similar to those held by the aforementioned Thomas W. Hardwick, who in 1903 had won election to Watson's former seat in the House. Like Watson, Hardwick's primary goal was to secure the further disfranchisement of black voters in Georgia, and throughout his first term in the House, he even repeatedly pressed for the repeal of the Fifteenth Amendment. In late June 1905, Hardwick wrote to Watson to enlist his support in behalf of the gubernatorial race of his friend and ally Hoke Smith. In his missive, he wrote that "until the South is finally rid of the negro even as a *political potentiality* she will never again have either freedom of thought or independence of action. Every Georgian who loves Ga. and who sees this question as you and I do ought to sink all personal feeling, run all political risks, and help rid the state of this *curse; Then,* we can very easily settle everything."[47] It is worth dwelling on the language in Hardwick's letter for a moment. Hardwick is not emphasizing Georgia's past, but rather its future. He is not talking about how the black vote has operated in the past, but as a *"potentiality,"* or how it might be used in the future. Even the way in which he invokes the black vote as a *"curse"* indicates someone who is not seeking to restore an older form of racial domination, but rather is seeking to escape it. In Hardwick's and Watson's narrative, the destiny of the heroic white reformer is cursed by the specter of black political power. This sort of fatalism looks to the future as much as to the past; the prospects of reform will be continually doomed unless the magic spell of disfranchisement can break the curse. To escape destiny, Hardwick argued that white men must unite at all costs—"to sink all personal feeling, run all political risks"—so that "we," the white voters of Georgia, "can very easily settle everything." In other words, once the curse is lifted, a new destiny falls into place. Unburdened, white reformers could remake the state along more humane, progressive lines.

The charge of "Negro domination" had long been used by conservatives to attack interracial movements and political alliances—most infamously, perhaps, during the white supremacy campaign in Wilmington, North Carolina, in 1898.[48] In addition, Populists and progressives had frequently accused the leaders of the Democratic Party machines in the South of manipulating a corruptible and purchasable black vote in order to defeat time and again any reform initiative. These claims were not just electorally convenient bogeymen. The political vilification of Reconstruction between the late 1860s and the dawn of the Progressive Era in the 1880s had caused many white southerners to become suspicious of using government as a means of reform, since the expansion of state power had become linked indissolubly in their minds with Reconstruction. To cite just one example, an 1889 debate over

expanding Georgia's investment in the state's common schools was complicated by the fact that black schools also drew on the common school fund.
Ultimately, this move to expand public education failed in the face of white
resistance.[49] Only after the state could be purged of the influence of black
voters could most white voters embrace the state as a vehicle for reform.
In other words, southern progressivism was utterly inconceivable to most
whites prior to the disfranchisement and segregation of African Americans
beginning in the 1890s. Hoke Smith's stunning victory over *Atlanta Constitution* editor Clark Howell in the 1906 gubernatorial race would cement this
relationship between reform and disfranchisement. In his speech before the
Democratic state convention celebrating Smith's triumph, Thomas Hardwick proclaimed that the white people of Georgia had shown their determination to have "protection against the black cloud of ignorant and purchasable negroes with which they are surrounded . . . that the negro shall not be
left around the corner, awaiting the awakening hand of the corruptionist
whenever division shall again break the white ranks." The victory of Hoke
Smith was a victory for both white supremacy and progressivism, ensuring
that "future economic and political divisions in Georgia shall be fought out
on a strictly white basis."[50]

Only a recent convert to progressivism, Smith was an unlikely standard-
bearer for reform. His support for the 1892 election of Grover Cleveland and
consequent reward with a cabinet-level post at the head of the patronage-
rich Department of the Interior marked him as a prominent national leader
of the conservative wing of the Democratic Party. Unfortunately for Smith,
the ascendancy of William Jennings Bryan within the ranks of the party
in 1896 forced him to retire from politics and return to Atlanta, where he
resumed his legal practice and his position at the reins of the *Atlanta Journal.* Although he remained staunchly opposed to the "socialist" reforms of
Bryan, the power corporations had over the lives of his fellow Atlantans had
encouraged Smith to embrace the state as a means of reform and regulation.[51] Though he remained a Cleveland Democrat in national politics, his
confrontation with corporate power at the local level transformed Smith
into a progressive champion. In 1899, with the assistance of the editorial
pages of the *Journal,* he launched a campaign against the unregulated distribution of city contracts for municipal services. Two years later, the mayor
appointed him as the city's representative in negotiations with the city's electric and streetcar companies over a proposal to consolidate the two into one
company. Over the course of his investigation, Smith discovered that both
companies had managed to avoid paying taxes on almost 80 percent of the

value of their holdings. Arguing against the merger before the city council, Smith also urged the city to use its power to control the depredations of these public utilities. That same year, he lent his strong support to the national campaign against child labor, upon which the state's textile mills had long depended.[52] This agitation not only resulted in the passage of Georgia's child labor law, it also helped launch Smith's career as one of Georgia's most successful Progressive Era reformers.[53]

Despite this momentum, a reform victory in 1906 seemed remote at best. Facing incumbents who had been entrenched in office for a full decade, Smith was willing to do what it took to win Watson and his 23,000 Populist votes. Using Hardwick as a broker, Watson agreed to support Smith in exchange for reassurances that Smith would come out for disfranchisement during the election. With the Populist leader behind him, Smith opened his campaign assailing his opponent as the candidate of big business. He emphasized proposals to reform the state railroad commission and check the power of the railroads and promised to fight for laws that would combat corruption, rein in the power of lobbyists, provide for the popular election of U.S. senators, and modernize the state's antiquated system of public instruction.[54] Most important, however, he made good on his promise to Watson. From the very first speech in his campaign, Smith's argument in favor of disfranchisement highlighted the ways in which black voting strength impeded reform efforts, accusing the corrupt Democratic county "rings" of relying on the purchasable black vote.[55] Every day in the weeks prior to the election, the editorial page of the *Atlanta Journal* reprinted in bold letters the promise embedded in Smith's campaign platform: "THE ELIMINATION OF THE NEGRO FROM POLITICS . . . BY LEGAL AND CONSTITUTIONAL METHODS . . . WITHOUT DISFRANCHISING A SINGLE WHITE MAN."[56] On the hustings and in the media, disfranchisement increasingly played a central role in Smith's campaign for the governor's mansion.

This embrace of disfranchisement was more than mere political calculation. As a reform-minded politician committed to maintaining white supremacy, Smith faced a genuine dilemma. By calling on the state to act on behalf of workers, consumers, and everyday citizens, progressive reformers also expanded the capacity of the state to act on behalf of the rights of African Americans. Thus, the exclusion of African Americans from Progressive Era developments such as public schools and other newly built city amenities was more than a pragmatic measure necessary to marshal these reforms through various legislative bodies. The removal of black citizens from the electorate, from public space, and even from the protections of due process was more than a prerequisite for a progressive development agenda; segregation and disfranchisement soon became crucial reforms in their own right. It was during these years that Atlanta saw its first segregated streetcar laws "to avoid racial clashes" and preserve public order. The improvement of the electorate by removing the influence of corruptible black voters was as much a reform as improving government by removing the influence of lobbyists. Temperance reformers contended that prohibition was necessary "to keep whiskey from the Negro" lest whites become the victims of black crime, and called for black disfranchisement since their votes served only to undermine the democratic process and protect the saloon.[57] This is why Hoke Smith, whose campaign promises included the expansion of the public schools, sought at the same to limit funding for black education.[58] White progress demanded the legal subordination of black Georgians, lest the expansion of the power of the state pave the way for the return of "the hell that is called Reconstruction."[59]

However, according to Smith's opponents in the Howell campaign, there was no risk of "Negro domination." They countered that disfranchisement was a red herring since the state's current voter registration laws had so completely marginalized black Georgians they no longer posed a threat to white rule. Fundamentally, Howell was correct. The requirement that the cumulative $1 annual poll tax be paid in full for every year a prospective voter had been eligible to vote since 1877 had driven all but the wealthiest or most persistent voters, black and white, from the polls.[60] The editor of the *Savannah Morning News,* J. H. Estill, in his campaign for governor that same year, concurred with Howell. Citing the state's comptroller general, the Estill campaign stated that of the 273,000 registered voters eligible to participate in the 1904 election, less than 68,000 were African American, giving white voters a three-to-one advantage over black voters. The comptroller general further stated that in most counties, most eligible black voters were anywhere from ten to twenty-five years behind in paying their poll taxes.[61] Given that the average monthly wage for a farm laborer in Georgia was around $15 in 1906, even paying ten years in back poll taxes would represent a considerable sacrifice for the average black citizen.[62] For those farming on shares and in debt to the landlord or furnishing merchant, it was rare to have even a dollar left over after accounts had been settled at the end of the year. In addition to these obstacles, the rigid exclusion of black voters from the white Democratic Party primary had proven to be even more effective in curtailing black political power. Regardless of how many black voters were able to keep up on their poll taxes, they could not participate in the only election that mattered in a one-party state.

Unlike Smith, Howell was not advocating a dramatic increase in the scope of state power. He ridiculed Smith's call for further disfranchisement since—as long as the power of the state remained minimal—the previously existing mechanisms for disfranchisement would remain sufficient to keep black Georgians politically quiescent. By contrast, progressives like Smith promised to extend state power into a series of relationships that had formerly been deemed outside of the public sphere, such as the workplace or the family. They also promised to expand the role of government to include the development of public parks, schools, and municipal utilities. The dilemma faced by Smith and other reformers committed to white supremacy was how to use the power of the state to level the playing field between the state's farmers and working class and the ruling elite without at the same time leveling the field between black and white Georgians. To that end, in addition to advocating disfranchisement, he also proposed reforms that racially segregated the benefits of the Progressive state. For example, during the campaign, he recalled the attempt to expand public education in 1889 that was defeated because black Georgians would also be able to draw on the common school fund. Deeming it "folly to spend the money of white men to give negroes a book education," he proposed racially segregating the state's school funding so that the money of white taxpayers supported only white schools, while black taxpayers were responsible for their own schools.[63] Additionally, Smith not only proposed limiting the power of black voters in general elections, he also specifically sought to limit their influence during bond referenda, a common tool used to fund Progressive Era municipal development.[64] The Progressive state made white Democracy vulnerable. Both Smith and his supporters knew that African Americans would use these extensions of the state to leverage power for themselves as they had during Reconstruction. As the campaign of 1906 made clear, white progressivism in the South made disfranchisement imperative.

The "Colored Yeomanry" and the
1906 Georgia Equal Rights Convention

In response to the renewed assault on black voting rights, Rev. William Jefferson White issued a call in December 1905 "to the colored men & women of Georgia to meet and confer with one another as to the future."[65] Alongside African Methodist Episcopal (AME) bishop Henry McNeal Turner,

Rev. White, editor of the influential *Georgia Baptist,* attempted to unite black Georgians in defense of their right to vote. Working closely with the young W. E. B. Du Bois, who was seeking to build support for his Niagara movement in the South, Turner and White gathered several hundred black leaders from across the state to attend the Georgia Equal Rights Convention (GERC) in Macon on 13 and 14 February 1906. Both Turner and White, born free prior to the Civil War, were giants in the history of black politics in Georgia. Turner was an influential bishop in the AME Church and the editor of the important Methodist paper *Voice of Missions.* Despite his unorthodox politics as a black Democrat and his advocacy of African emigration, Turner nonetheless commanded the respect of a wide swath of black Georgia. White was known as the "Father of Negro Education" in Georgia. As early as 1853, he operated clandestine schools for enslaved African Americans throughout Georgia, and in 1880 he was instrumental in opening Ware Colored High School in Augusta, the first publicly funded high school in Georgia.[66] Du Bois, the first African American to earn a Ph.D. from Harvard, was a professor of economics and history at Atlanta University. He had recently broken with his former ally Booker T. Washington, rejecting the latter's conservative response to segregation and disfranchisement, and envisioned the GERC as a vehicle that would resist more aggressively the assault on black civil rights.[67] These three men, with their extensive contacts throughout the state, had the potential to politically unite black Georgians.

Given Du Bois's involvement, it would be easy to locate the GERC at one end of the protest versus accommodation continuum; however, this historiographical convention obscures more than it reveals. The magnitude of the crisis facing black Georgians made it clear to Rev. White as he issued the call for the meeting that it was necessary to unite the state's black political community regardless of partisan divisions and public splits between the allies of Washington and Du Bois. In order to get as many people behind the GERC as possible, White made extensive efforts to include Henry A. Rucker in the planning for the meeting. Rucker, as the collector of internal revenue for the state of Georgia, was the most powerful black Republican in the state as well as a loyal supporter of Washington. The week prior to issuing the call, White wrote Rucker asking him for suggestions of local leaders who ought to be invited to the meeting. He added, "I want you to be with me in this movement. It will do you no harm if it does you no good," signaling to the collector that the meeting was not meant as a challenge either to Rucker's political position or the state's black Republican leadership.[68]

The extreme fragmentation of the state GOP meant that reaching out to prominent black Republicans could be tricky. It is unclear from the historical record whether White extended an invitation to *Atlanta Independent* editor Ben Davis, another prominent Republican leader in the state. It is probable that White decided against inviting him, given his public hostility toward Du Bois. This rancor stemmed from Du Bois's recent endorsement of Henry Rucker for another term as collector in the face of President Theodore Roosevelt's threat to remove him.[69] Davis and Rucker had long fought one another for control of the state GOP, and years of infighting had made each the other's nemesis. Despite these efforts, most of the state's Republican leadership declined White's invitation. This failure to engage either the GOP or Washington's forces in the state compelled the GERC to organize outside and to a certain extent in conflict with the state Republican Party. Indeed, instead of offering support, Washington sent a spy, asking Rev. C. T. Walker of Augusta to monitor the meeting. Walker only stayed for the first day of the convention, but managed to get himself elected as a vice president of the GERC and to place "a number of men on guard to watch affairs."[70]

In any case, White, Turner, and Du Bois could not simply call for all black Republicans to unite in opposition to disfranchisement without making the GERC yet another arena for black Republicans to jockey for power. To frame black political solidarity in terms exclusive of the internecine conflicts that had long divided black Republicans, the organizers of the GERC attempted to construct this political unity upon a shared understanding of manhood. White called on the black men of Georgia to "speak for themselves. If they are content with present conditions, let them say so; and if they are not content let them as men, in a manly way, say so. Let us speak as men for ourselves and thus maintain our manhood whether we secure the enjoyment of manhood rights or not."[71] In attempting to avoid importing intrapartisan conflicts of the Republican Party into the GERC, White's appeal to men as men instead imported the conflicted discourse of black Victorian manhood. Rooted in the class and gender suppositions of the politics of respectability, "manhood rights" traditionally signified that the right to vote was rooted in one's possession of manhood, and White's syntax in his call clearly follows this tradition. However, in the face of disfranchisement, black men were not only denied access to the right to vote but also to manhood itself. Not only did this reopen the terms of their relationship, it reversed the equation of manhood and suffrage. It seemed that *manhood,* more than the rights that manhood conferred, was at stake here. As the GERC elaborated its opposition to disfranchisement, it would become evident that manhood conferred the ballot as much as possession of the ballot conferred manhood.

The month prior to the meeting, Rev. White wrote Du Bois about plans for the upcoming convention, "anxious to send forth a statement that will tell among the whites of Georgia and the balance of mankind."[72] Fundamental to this statement were calls for equitable distribution of school taxes, access to jury privileges, the abolition of peonage and the convict-lease system, unfettered access to employment, and an end to both the white primary and the recent moves to disfranchise black Georgians.[73] As important as the demands of the GERC was the way in which they would be delivered. White's letter continued: "We do not want bitter expressions but good strong, manly expressions." He further characterized the statement he wanted to make as a "plea," adding, "I use the word *plea* thoughtfully."[74] In modern usage, the word "plea" is closely associated with "pleading" or "begging," both terms associated with submission to a higher authority. However, at the beginning of the twentieth century, the word more commonly denoted "a suit or an action at law." Drawing on the legal meanings of the term, White was almost certainly insisting that in the eyes of the law, black and white men ought to have equal standing. However, "plea" also represents another form of "appeal." In this sense, the "manly expressions" comprising his "plea" were intended as an appeal to the manhood of the white race. As he phrased it in the closing paragraphs of his call: "The children of a common state with a common destiny should cultivate among themselves a deep and abiding friendship. This cannot be done by unjust laws and practices. . . . Let the colored yeomanry of Georgia get together, and decide what is best for them as a race to do and then as true men stand together." White sought to unify this "colored yeomanry" behind an appeal to the "fair-minded and [C]hristian" white people of Georgia. The GERC would "present our case to them from our standpoint in a straight forward, manly way, with assurance of our readiness to cooperate with them for the highest good and best development of this grand old commonwealth."[75] That is, the leading men of the state, both black and white, together have the power to address the grievances that White listed in his call.

Who exactly was this "colored yeomanry"? Among the most prominent signatories were Du Bois, Turner, and White as well as Atlanta University president John Hope, Rev. Henry Hugh Proctor of the elite First Congregational Church, and editor Jesse Max Barber.[76] The rest of the 265 men and women who signed the call included seventy-six clergy, twenty-five educators, seven doctors, four businessmen, four social workers, three lawyers, three farmers (one of these listed his occupation as "planter"), three newspaper editors, two mechanics, and one former state militia captain.[77]

Given that in 1900, there were only forty-three black doctors and fourteen black lawyers in the entire state, it is evident that the supporters of the GERC in the state represented a significant cross section of the state's black professional elite.[78] In addition, there were only three identifiable Republican officeholders in the entire list.[79] That the convention drew most of its leadership from outside the state Republican machine suggested that this yeomanry had a different outlook on the prospects for the race. Those active in the GOP represented a political class that advanced through means of patronage and looked to the party as the vehicle for progress. By contrast, the men and women who founded the GERC comprised an independent black professional class whose advancement was distinct from party politics. Progress for these professional black elites was rooted in a combination of material success and moral probity.

This black yeomanry was also relatively well-to-do, representing some of the most economically successful African Americans in the state. However, there was an ideology to the concept of the yeomanry that transcended its material base. White's independent black yeomen were not only there to speak "for themselves" as individuals, but sought to represent "themselves" collectively as race leaders. Indeed, a "yeoman" was a man who held a small landed estate, a freeholder or a commoner of respectable standing who could be called upon to defend the community from assault. To call these black leaders members of the "middle class" does not quite capture the ways in which these men and women understood themselves in relationship to other black people. They were more than an economically successful group of African Americans; they also viewed themselves as *morally* successful and hence models for other black people to emulate. In so doing, they sought to define the aims of and membership in the black political community of Georgia.

Another reason the state GOP kept its distance from the GERC may have been the top billing given to AME bishop Henry McNeal Turner at the meeting in Macon. Not only was Turner a prominent black Democrat, since the early 1890s Turner and his Republican opponents had clashed over whether African Americans should stay and fight Jim Crow or whether they should abandon the United States altogether and establish their own independent nation. As this debate progressed, the question of whether black people had a future in America narrowed down to whether black *men* had a future in the United States. So as long as possession of the ballot signified manliness, it would remain very difficult to establish a basis for black political power that was not at the same time a contest over the meaning of black manhood.

"Common Children of a Common State":
First-Class Citizenship and Progressive Georgia

In his speech opening the meeting in Macon, Rev. White appealed to the state's "best" citizens, black and white alike, as "the children of a common state with a common destiny" who should "cultivate among themselves a deep and abiding friendship."[80] Through this familial metaphor, he asserted an interracial equality rooted in a common identity as citizens of Georgia and contested the ideologically charged symbol of family in maintaining the boundaries and privileges of whiteness. White attempted to undermine the utility of the gender and racial discourses inscribed within the idea of family in asserting racial inequality. His identification of membership in the nation with membership in a family was an attempt to deracialize citizenship by drawing the circle of family around all of Georgia's citizens, black and white.

This project was complicated by the fact that the fruits of Progressive Era development had not simply been restricted to "whites only." It depended upon a subject, voteless population to serve as a tax base to sustain the development of public education and to provide African American convict laborers for the construction of roads and other labor-intensive infrastructural improvements. As the assembled delegates tackled the systematic exclusion of African Americans from newly available civic rights such as electricity, plumbing, sanitation, and public education, which were dramatically improving the lives of white families, they could not avoid addressing this contradiction. The GERC charged the state of Georgia with robbing its black citizens to reward and enrich its white ones, observing that the "accumulated wealth of this great state has been built upon our bowed backs . . . [and that] no portion of the community is giving more of its labor and money to support the public burdens" than Georgia's black workers and taxpayers.[81] As might be expected from a movement begun by the "Father of Negro Education," one of the most significant campaigns initiated by the GERC was for the equitable distribution of school taxes. One participant wrote that "the state of Georgia has stolen millions from our people to educate the white children." Research done by Du Bois determined that even though there was a roughly equal number of black and white children enrolled in the state's public schools, only twenty cents out of every dollar spent by the state of Georgia went toward the education of black children.[82] A year later, it emerged that black taxpayers were not only paying to educate their own children, they were disproportionately paying for white children as well.[83] This critique was a far cry from the language used in the memorial against the 1899 Hardwick bill. By asserting an entitlement as tax-paying citizens to the benefits of the state, it was no longer possible to view public education as a gift "generously tendered." Importantly, this also gave rise to a new language with which to criticize the terms on which this "gift" had been "given."

Much of Georgia's development had been driven by the exploitation of black convict labor controlled precisely by those white elites with whom White urged an alliance. This contradiction is embedded in the irony that the railroad on which the GERC delegates traveled to Macon was itself built by unfree African American convict laborers. The convict-lease system got its start in Georgia in May 1868, shortly after the end of the Civil War, when the state signed a lease under which the Georgia and Alabama Railroad acquired 100 black convicts for a sum of $2,500. That same year the state sold 134 prisoners to the Selma, Rome, and Dalton Railroad and sent 109 others to work on the rail line being built between Macon and Brunswick.[84] This labor was indispensable to the railroad development that both integrated Georgia into the postwar economy and made Atlanta the unofficial capital of the New South. By 1880, Georgia's convict laborers had added 1,000 miles of track to the state's rail system, making it the second largest in the South (after Texas). The operation of this labor system was lethal to the workers it exploited, more than 400 of whom had died in the first twelve years of Georgia's convict-lease system.[85] Between 1868 and 1908, when the convict-lease system was finally abolished, more than 1,600 convicts would perish—a rate of more than one per week.[86] One of the reasons behind such a high fatality rate was reflected in one delegate's comments at the 1883 meeting of the National Prison Association: "Before the war, we owned the negroes. . . . If a man had a good negro, he could afford to keep him. . . . But these convicts, we don't own 'em. One dies, get another."[87]

Not only was convict labor vital to rebuilding Georgia after the war, it also built the fortunes of the wealthiest and most powerful white men in Georgia. Both former governor Joseph E. Brown and James W. English, president of Atlanta's Fourth National Bank, had made their millions using the forced labor of black convicts. At one point these two men controlled the labor of nearly half of the state's convicts.[88] Brown had employed hundreds of convicts in his north Georgia coal mines and employed hundreds more to rebuild his iron furnaces, which had been destroyed by Union troops during the Civil War.[89] English, using the connections he had established while serving as mayor of Atlanta, won the contract to supply the bricks to pave the streets and sidewalks for the city's first major suburb, Grant Park. With guaranteed profits, English's Chattahoochee Brick Company sold them in lots of one million bricks each to the Atlanta City Council. By the end of the century, English's company was turning out 300,000 bricks per day— all of which were made by unfree black labor.[90] Modern Atlanta—from its foundations to its skyline—was built atop a mountain of black suffering and misery.

When held up alongside the glittering progress of Atlanta, the convict-lease system highlighted the emergence of a two-tiered state in which black citizens were to be relegated to second-class status. It also highlighted the hypocrisy of well-to-do whites who benefited from this labor—notably men like James W. English. This hypocrisy made the politics of respectability difficult to sustain, based as it was on the myth of white benevolence. When the GERC asked that black education be funded equally alongside white education, they were intimately aware that the bricks with which those schools were built would be made by black workers taken by force from their own communities. Thus, even though the delegates to the GERC sought to extend the benefits of economic development to black communities, they had to insist it be done without depending upon this subject class of unfree black laborers. They charged that the convict-lease system had indiscriminately imprisoned black Georgians, who were then sold as "slaves of the state . . . to private capitalists for the sake of gain."[91] As Rev. White put it, "the fortunes of many a prominent white Georgia family [are] red with the blood and sweat of black men justly and unjustly held to labor in Georgia prison camps." Not only did private employers benefit from the convict-lease system, so did the state. According to the GERC, the state of Georgia, "boasting of her ability to make crime pay," made $225,000 annually from leasing its prisoners.[92] In addition, the city of Atlanta took in $100,000 annually in fines levied against black men charged with vagrancy. This sum represented a significant portion of the city budget, which in 1905 was slightly less than $1.9 million.[93] Between July 1905 and June 1906, the state netted $333,000 from the convict-lease system and $128,000 from leasing these prisoners to counties to build the road system.[94] These revenues ultimately helped fund the expansion of a Progressive Era state that excluded African Americans from its protections. It was precisely this exclusion from the expansion of the early welfare state that created a notion of "second-class citizenship" to which black southerners were being relegated and which made "first-class citizenship" a rallying cry of the twentieth-century civil rights movement.

Fully aware that they lacked the power to compel their erstwhile white allies to reciprocate their offer of "deep and abiding friendship," the delegates to the GERC turned once again to the politics of respectability as they faced the prospect of disfranchisement. Just like the signatories of the 1899 Hard-wick memorial, these politicians of respectability were willing to accept a limited franchise: first-class citizenship for those capable of adhering to the tenets of respectability and a second-class, voteless citizenship for everyone else—regardless of race or color. Despite their sharp critique of who paid the price of Georgia's development, their embrace of respectability disallowed them from staking out a genuinely oppositional position against suffrage restriction. And making respectability the qualification for the right to vote also transformed the struggle against disfranchisement into a divisive fight over the terms of black manhood.

"Manhood Rights"

Jim Crow worked not only to undermine the claims of black men on the benefits of citizenship but also the claims of black men to manliness itself. The GERC's defense of "first-class citizenship" was not just a defense of the right to vote or to have access to the city services that were supported by black tax dollars. It was also a defense of the responsibilities and preroga-tives of black fathers and husbands. In this regard, Georgia's convict-lease and vagrancy laws came under particular fire for creating disorder within black families, which in turn presented a grave threat to black morals. Not only did these laws stunt the development of "honesty, sobriety, industry and chastity," their unjust application left black women in "a defenceless condition."[95] When black women were arrested for vagrancy, they wound up in jail alongside other supposed "vagrants" as well as genuine criminals. In Georgia, these women were sometimes sent to James English's Chatta-hoochee brick yard and other convict labor camps, where they would face the threat of rape and sexual assault at the hands of both male guards and their fellow prisoners.[96] The children born of these assaults would remain with their mothers—and according to one report, there were at one time as many as twenty-five such children living in Georgia's convict labor camps.[97] As the GERC stated, to supply the labor needs of the agricultural sector, "colored men are punished . . . without intelligent discrimination; old and young, thug and mischief-maker, and often men and women are herded together after unfair trials before juries who would rather convict ten in-nocent Negroes rather than let one guilty one escape."[98] The convict-lease system profoundly disorganized black communities—arbitrarily mixing the criminal and virtuous—regardless of the responsibility of black patriarchs to defend and protect their wives and children.

Further, the GERC delegates charged that as long as the "open traffic in Negro crime" encouraged by these laws taught white men open "disrespect for black womanhood, so long will his degradation be the damnation of some black man's daughter."[99] This disregard for the integrity of the black household left defenseless those black women whose male protectors had been put on the chain gang. The loss of a man's wages could drive wives and daughters into the formal economy, where they would encounter the most dangerous place for black women to be in Jim Crow Georgia: the homes of their white employers, where they faced the constant threat of sexual harassment and assault. While Atlanta was unique among southern cities in offering employment opportunities for working-class women, few of these jobs were open to African Americans. As white women entered the wage-labor force as textile workers, secretaries, and shopgirls, black domestic workers absorbed the household duties that white women could not or would not perform due to their participation in the workforce.[100] By the end of the nineteenth century, this dynamic helped draw some 50 to 70 percent of adult black females living in the major cities of the South into employment outside the home for at least part of the year.[101] While a small minority of these women chose to work as live-in servants, the majority sought to maintain their own households, even if it meant lower wages. Not only did the life of a live-in servant keep black women from caring for their own families, it also most closely resembled the lack of autonomy that had characterized work under slavery. One live-in domestic worker described her "sunrise to sunrise" toil as reducing her to "the slave, body and soul," of the family for whom she worked.[102]

Most important, black women rejected live-in domestic service to avoid the sorts of sexual exploitation that had also been common under slavery and from which the GERC sought to protect them. In 1912, a black nurse in Georgia who had worked in white households for thirty years recalled in the pages of the *Independent* her experiences with sexual assault in the workplace. Though newly married, she was fired from a job early in her career after refusing to let her white employer kiss her. Once again demonstrating that black communities could not rely on the law to protect them, after this woman's husband went to the police to file a complaint, he was arrested and fined $25 for contradicting the word of a white man.[103] She soon came to the realization that there was no protection for "a colored woman's virtue. . . . Nearly all white men take undue liberties with their colored female servants—not only the fathers, but in many cases the sons also."[104] Another woman, writing to the *Independent* in 1904, described the efforts of her father to support his family through his wages alone, so that his wife and daughters could avoid being "thrown into contact with Southern white men in their homes." When she married and had children of her own, she vowed that she would make every sacrifice to keep her daughters out of domestic service, "where they would be thrown constantly in contact with . . . white men, [who] consider the colored girl their special prey."[105]

The law was utterly useless in defending black women from rape and sexual assault at the hands of white men. Throughout the entire century following emancipation, few white men were ever convicted in the South for the rape or attempted rape of a black woman.[106] Without the effective protection of the law, the GERC called instead for unity in defense of black morals rooted in the patriarchal family, and charged the men assembled to "look to the care and protection of our wives and daughters." In defining these threats to black manhood, the GERC also defined an ideal to which black men ought to aspire. It was as important to defend black women's honor "with our lives" as it was to be able to "keep them at home and support them there."[107] In other words, the idea of manhood with which the GERC sought to unite black Georgians in defense of their right to vote was defined as much by courage as it was by an economic independence that would allow black men to keep their wives and daughters away from the economic and sexual exploitation that domestic service entailed. Equal protection under the laws and access to the ballot would allow black men to defend their households.

As a strategy, this spoke to the lived experience of the economically successful black men and women who headed up the GERC. Georgia's small, but vocal, black middle class owed its existence to male heads of household who managed through considerable effort and no small amount of luck to maintain their positions as skilled craftsmen, professionals, and entrepreneurs within a hostile Jim Crow environment.[108] As black men, they had managed to succeed as doctors, lawyers, newspaper editors, and educators in the harsh environment of Jim Crow America. Although success for these men was hard won and by no means guaranteed, the struggle itself helped them verify their own manliness, which they used to judge the manhood of those whom they could charge with abandoning their duties as fathers and husbands.[109] Additionally, these middle-class black men employed the discourse of patriarchy to counter the white supremacist image of themselves as uncivilized criminals inclined to rape white women and terrorize white communities. By instead defining white men as savage sexual predators, they displaced this racist characterization and created a narrative in

which endangered black women could rely upon a virile black male pro-
tector. Through this process, black men linked their claims on manhood to
the right to vote. As the historian Elsa Barkley Brown argues, "black men's
political rights were essential so that they could do as men should—protect
their communities, homes, families, women."[110]

While the dangers faced by black women were very real, the solution
proposed by the GERC relied upon an idealized patriarchal household that
was impossible to sustain and projected an image of domesticity that did
not accord with the lived experience of most black women. Both black and
white women's participation in Atlanta's labor force was significantly higher
than in the rest of the country. Between 1890 and 1920, the percentage of
women holding jobs in the formal economy climbed from 25 percent to over
40 percent—a participation rate the nation as a whole would not reach until
the 1970s.[111] Black women's participation in the paid workforce far exceeded
their proportion in the population. At the turn of the century, when African Americans represented almost 43 percent of the city's population, black
women comprised roughly three-quarters of the city's paid female workforce.[112] Ten years later, 67 percent of Atlanta's black households contained
working women, and nearly half of all black households (46 percent) were
headed by women, the vast majority of whom were employed as domestic workers.[113] Through this extensive participation in the workforce, many
married black women rivaled or superseded their husbands as the primary
breadwinner for the family. While the bulk of women's work comprised
various forms of domestic service, black working women in the South performed all sorts of work for pay. Capturing just part of the full range of
women's employment in his 1908 study on African American families, Du
Bois noted one woman who "sells vegetables, chickens and eggs, milk and
butter, to neighbors, washes, irons and sometimes cooks." In addition, black
women would also take in boarders, temporarily migrate from the city to
participate in the cotton harvest, and peddle baked goods and hot lunches
on the street.[114] The diversity of black women's employment demonstrates
that, whatever they may have felt about going into service, it is not at all clear
that these women would have wanted to give up the power they enjoyed due
to control over their own wages, however meager.[115]

Moreover, the patriarchal and protective role that the GERC wanted
black men to assume depended on the sorts of steady employment that was
simply not available. Most black men—especially in the urban South—were
relegated to employment in low-paying, unskilled jobs that were commonly

seasonal or temporary. Working as draymen, laborers, and construction workers, most black men brought home less than $30 per month. An 1897 Atlanta University study surveyed 1,100 urban black families. Of that number, less than a quarter were able to rely exclusively on a male breadwinner's wages.[116] The only way for these families to make their monthly budgets was to rely on the wages of wives and children. Not only were there few jobs available to sustain the patriarchal family, the survival of that family commonly depended upon the wages of black women. Even for the elite men who attended the GERC, few of their wives could remain out of the wage market. The finances of black middle-class households were too precarious to dispense with a wife's earnings, and many women were eager to put to use the formal education they had received, working most commonly as schoolteachers but also as dressmakers and milliners, both of which were considered respectable professions for middle-class black women.[117] As the GERC put forward the image of the imperiled black woman as the symbol around which black men rallied to the defense of the right to vote, the battle against disfranchisement became a fight to defend the prerogatives of black male power.

This choice carried with it significant limitations. Based as it was on a shared understanding of Victorian middle-class black manhood, those who violated the terms of behavior demanded of such men were not only excluded from this call, they became scapegoats for the problems facing all African Americans as well. In his speech opening the convention, Rev. White observed that "as individuals, we may have very different views, but since the conditions are racial, it is the duty of the race to decide what to do." The threat of disfranchisement faced by all black Georgians made it imperative to submerge their differences for the sake of racial unity in defense of "manhood rights." Given the vast differences within the black community, however, calling for political unity on these grounds was fraught with difficulty. To defend the right to vote of all black men meant asserting that the criminal, intemperate, and immoral were as fit for self-government as were the assembled bishops, doctors, and lawyers present at the meeting. Unable to define the less respectable out of the race, White aimed his call for unity at the "true-hea[r]ted men and women who have made or are making something of themselves" and commanded the audience to do whatever they could "to redeem the shiftless, worthless class of the race" and not "allow them to drag us down." To White, the choice was between "lift[ing] them up to travel with us . . . or leav[ing] them behind in the great procession."[118] Given this choice, the convention concerned itself extensively with the material condition of Georgia's black working class as well as its moral character.

Du Bois, Turner, and White were all concerned that the disabilities under which the state's black working class labored undermined their ability to lead manfully independent and moral lives. Given the widespread white anxieties over black retrogression to barbarism outside the discipline of slavery, the GERC feared that the progress of the entire race would be judged by the moral and material conditions of its working class.[119] These hazardous conditions were compounded by the disfranchising measures proposed during the governor's race, which threatened to "establish and perpetuate the political outlawry of the colored citizen." Deprived of equal access to education and trapped within a low-wage or, more accurately, *no-wage* agricultural workforce through peonage, vagrancy laws, and the convict-lease system, "the ignorant laborer is held in a net work of debt and petty crime, compelled to work like a slave, unable to leave his master or to demand decent wages." These conditions did not make black Georgians "quick, intelligent and eager as we might be . . . if we did not bend under deadening caste restrictions." Without claiming "any . . . special righteousness" and apologizing for "those among us whose wicked ways shame us bitterly," the convention's address castigated the convict-lease system and the vagrancy laws. "As long as public and private wealth in Georgia fattens on the sale of black criminals, so long will crime be encouraged and the outcry against it will ring with hypocrisy." Disfranchisement threatened to cast black Georgians not only outside the protections of the law as citizens but also outside the bounds of respectable society. Being cast outside of the law, they feared, would make outlaws of black citizens. All of these concerns were embodied in an address "to the world" approved at the close of the convention by 200 of the delegates in attendance and later reprinted in Jesse Max Barber's Atlanta-based *Voice of the Negro.* The document concluded that this state of affairs emerged from the failure of the former slaveholder to honor the agreement embodied in the Civil War amendments to bring "the late slave into equal citizenship with himself." The GERC viewed with alarm the recent movements "to reduce the late bondmen . . . to a condition of helpless dependence that would, in some respects, be worse than . . . slavery." Speaking to the looming threat of disfranchisement, the statement declared that "voteless workingmen are slaves . . . naked to our enemies, helpless victims of jealousy and hate, subjected to and humiliated by an unreasoning caste spirit."[120] This "helpless dependence" upon the tenuous goodwill and honor of their white employers, landlords, and creditors undermined the ability of black working-class men to provide for and defend their families. The ballot was the guarantor of economic independence, the integrity of the black family, and the defense of black morals.

Although they linked the defense of the votes of black "workingmen" to the defense of the morals and integrity of the black family, the GERC delegates had difficulty comprehending the black working class as real allies. Among the greatest fears of the GERC was that powerlessness had already made black working-class men unfit to vote even as the vote was deemed necessary in order to defend the morality of themselves and their families. Just as white opponents of black suffrage feared the black vote as corruptible, black elites viewed the political judgment of the black working class as morally suspect. As seen earlier in the language of the Hardwick memorial of 1899, this caused the black middle class to embrace suffrage restriction as a means of "improving" the black electorate. So long as the goal of black political power was to enable black people to lead respectable lives and climb the rungs of the ladder of civilization, the GERC's call to defend the votes of black working-class men would remain rooted in a concurrent defense of respectable black manhood. This politics of respectability would make it difficult for the delegates to the GERC to bridge the divide between themselves and the black working class.

This linkage between the ballot, the defense of respectable manhood, and the practice of Victorian middle-class virtues obscured the extent to which the state's poll tax laws had already compromised black "manhood rights."[121] Despite the "unmistakable" determination of the "ruling element of the white people of Georgia . . . to eliminate the colored man from the high prerogatives of manhood citizenship," the delegates to the GERC did not describe the previously passed poll tax requirement as a mechanism for disfranchising African American voters. Rather, by embracing the poll tax as a means of excluding the "worthless, shiftless element" from politics, the ability to pay one's poll tax became a test and demonstration of individual manhood. In his speech to the convention, White gave his audience a choice: "Shall we as helpless children sit down and cry over what we regard as wrongs . . . or shall we as men, in a manly way, protest?" To "stand as men among other men" required every black Georgian to "qualify . . . to use the ballot." He insisted, and the black leaders assembled in Macon agreed, that the poll tax was a burden that every citizen should be compelled to bear and believed that "no man should be allowed to avoid paying his tax as his price of disfranchisement."[122] Throughout the surviving documentation of the GERC, White never raises the question of how the black laborer living on less than $30 a month or the sharecropper perpetually in debt to the local furnishing merchant—however hardworking, honest, and respectable he may be—would ever find the money to pay his annual $1 poll tax that had accumulated every year since he turned twenty-one.

White and the GERC did not even necessarily view their primary allies to be Georgia's black electorate. Rather, they sought to share the elective franchise alongside responsible white men in order to establish a common ground on "the highest type of American manhood and citizen sovereignty."[123] The leaders of the GERC thought of their political community as embracing the "best men," black and white, of Georgia.[124] In 1906, the GERC's political strategy was to establish a shared sense of bourgeois manliness with the white middle class, which would then establish grounds for asserting racial equality within this Victorian-era framework of class and gender. However, this strategy also made it difficult to imagine a broader foundation for black political unity, a necessary basis for a genuinely independent black politics. Within the confines of the politics of respectability (in which reputation, and specifically *racial reputation*," was key), the black working class was seen more often as a liability rather than as an ally. In order to understand the black working class as a source of power—and importantly, as a source of the votes needed for modern black politics to emerge—African American leaders would have to reimagine their relationship to the black working class. The most important obstacle facing the development of black political strategy at the dawn of the twentieth century was precisely this inability to understand politics without invoking the language of respectability. Until this understanding emerged, any effective strategy that involved marshaling black political power in defense of "first-class citizenship" would be nearly impossible to conceive, let alone execute.[125]

"The Political Equation of the State"

While Booker T. Washington assured the white South that "in all things that are purely social we can be as separate as the fingers, yet one as the hand in all things essential to social progress," the statement issued by the GERC concluded its published "address to the world" by urging Georgia's black leaders to "organize these million brothers of ours into one great fist which shall never cease to pound at the gates of opportunity until they fly open."[126] This inversion of Washington's famous metaphor may have been unintentional, but the challenge the GERC posed to the Tuskegee machine and its local allies among the black Republican Party leadership was not. Jesse Max

Barber editorialized in his *Voice of the Negro* that those who opposed the convention "say that . . . the demands made [are] so radically different from the concessions that the white people are willing to make as to render our case hopeless."[127] However, the GERC's call for the inclusion of black citizens into the state was neither utopian nor unrealistic. The GERC simply insisted that the inclusion of African Americans in the benefits of Progressive Era development and reform must be based not on the "relationship of master to slave" but on that of "man and man, equal in the sight of God and the eye of the law."[128] Setting aside for the moment the narrow bounds placed on the GERC's notion of manliness, this was truly radical. No longer would it suffice for black Georgians to publicly accept access to public education and other publicly supported services as gifts "generously tendered." These sharp words were pointed as much at the state's white supremacists as they were at the convention's black critics, those men still willing to stand hat in hand before the arch labeled "Wisdom, Justice and Moderation" and negotiate inclusion into a white supremacist political order. Barber's editorial declared that one of the most "gratifying" elements of the convention for those "who believe unalterably in the manhood rights of the Negro" was "the absence of a sickening, ultra-conservatism on the floor." By contrast, Barber praised those who attended the convention as "fearless men . . . who find no pleasure in forever kissing the chastening rod of oppression."[129] The "manly independence" of black Georgians was threatened as much by Jim Crow and disfranchisement as it was by the failings of the established black leadership, which was centered in the Republican Party and grounded in Washington's policy of accommodation.

This drew an angry reaction from Ben Davis in the pages of the *Independent*. The irascible editor criticized the leaders of the convention for irresponsibly raising their protest at a time when "the whites, though split, only differ as to the most effectual means of accomplishing . . . our disfranchisement. . . . Wisdom would suggest that we [not] . . . give the demagogues who are now roving about the State additional pretext to steal our rights as men."[130] As a pragmatist who acknowledged that "both factions of our white neighbors" sought the elimination of black voters from "the political equation of the State," he advised his readers to forgo this "indignation meeting" for the sake of the political future of the race. Accordingly, he warned those who chose to attend the conference "to weigh well your words before you utter them . . . [and] take into consideration the inflamed condition of the white man's mind."[131] Any significant political advance on the part of African Americans would spark a white backlash that would make any of these gains temporary at best. The political realism of men like Davis had given them the skills they needed to survive the age of Jim Crow with their leadership intact, however circumscribed by white supremacy. It was a pragmatism that, based on the bitter experiences of the fall of Reconstruction, was skeptical of the role of the state as an ally in the struggle. While in the short run this caution was wise, in the long run it crippled their ability to imagine a future in which politically assertive African Americans were not hemmed in by the threat of an inevitable white backlash.

Davis's opposition to the convention was more than tactical, however. Just as the GERC's response to disfranchisement was essentially a defense of the prerogatives of black manhood, so also was Davis's response to the GERC. He charged the delegates to the convention with shirking their civic duties, and asking for rights they did not earn. Belittling the GERC's efforts as immature, he commanded his readers, "don't sit down in convention and fret and do the baby act because the white man won't stay at home . . . and send you to represent him without regard to your fitness or qualifications. . . . If you want to go to the legislature, pay tax, register and vote." In a telling phrase, he stated that "civil and political rights do not come to a race or nation collectively." Instead, Davis answered the GERC's demand for "first-class citizenship" by insisting that access to the ballot is earned only by "the individual as he rises in the estimation of his neighbors and becomes useful and helpful in the community where he lives" regardless of the number of conferences he holds.[132] Even as the GERC's understanding of first-class citizenship still presumed a "second-class" to which many, if not most, African Americans would be relegated, this articulation nevertheless changed the terms of asserting equality from a formal equality as masters of households rooted in a gendered and "classed" politics of respectability to equality as citizens entitled to the full range of civic rights. Even though both Davis and the GERC insisted that black men pay their poll tax, it was this implicit challenge to traditional notions of manhood that prompted Davis's characterization of the convention as a "baby act." Real men earned the right to vote—mere babies demanded it.

Despite their differences, the only major thing that distinguished the GERC from Davis and the GOP were the different claims they made on the state. The social and cultural impact of urbanization, economic development, and disfranchisement challenged the patriarchal black family, which was interpreted by black men like Davis and Rev. White as a crisis in manhood. The solutions that both black Republicans and the GERC articulated to this crisis employed the same gender conventions inherent in the politics of respectability and prevented a truly oppositional critique from emerging. White asserted that "voteless workingmen were slaves" and found the moral degradation of the black working class caused by their political subjugation, and Davis attributed this subjugation to the immorality, immaturity, and irresponsibility of the "shiftless and untrustworthy" black masses.[133] Both men sought to challenge the economic and political underpinnings of white supremacy, but they did so in terms limited by the tactical options open to them. Their understandings of respectable manhood limited their ability to imagine a different way of ordering society, and even encouraged them to share the same sorts of ideas about the black working class that their white counterparts did. In any case, without the ability to muster real political power, it would remain difficult to change "the political equation of the State," which demanded the sort of prudence that Davis advocated and commended respectability as a potentially achievable goal for the black freedom struggle. In 1906, it remained impossible to even conceive of autonomous black political power, since the language of respectability continued to confound the establishment of true cross-class solidarity within black communities.

2

"To Humiliate the Progressive Negro"

The Atlanta Race Riot of 1906

When the polls opened at 7 A.M., it was still cool outside, though the mercury would hit a steamy 92 degrees by midafternoon.[1] Despite the heated rhetoric voiced by supporters of both Hoke Smith and Clark Howell, the day passed without incident. Throughout the day, partisans from every campaign sweated and swarmed around the polling stations with placards, signs, slogans, and, where necessary, hard cash in order to cajole the Democrats who showed up to vote that day. Since the state Republican Party had not run a statewide slate for over two decades, the outcome of this Democratic primary on 22 August 1906 would determine the next governor of Georgia. At Five Points in downtown Atlanta, the *Atlanta Georgian* had rigged a set of magic lanterns through which the election results could be projected on the wall above Goodrum's Tobacco Company. As election results were telegraphed in from across the state, the thousands of people who had gathered downtown could cheer for their candidates. Every hour, the city's newspapers issued extras with the latest election returns. As the day faded into evening, it became more and more clear that Hoke Smith was going to win by a landslide. Chattooga County, one of the first to be called for Smith, supported him by a two-to-one margin. In Bartow County, Smith won by 650 votes; he won Polk County by 300 votes.[2] Once the votes were tallied, Smith had garnered 104,796 votes, while 70,471 votes were cast for Howell. To Smith's 118 counties, Howell managed to win only 6.[3]

The result was a stunning victory that decisively affirmed Smith's white supremacist progressive vision for the state. In the months that followed, members of the legislature, emboldened by this mandate, introduced several bills aimed at limiting black access to public space as well as the influence of black institutions. Among these bills was one requiring traveling circuses to segregate their performances in Georgia. In an attack on the state's black colleges, another would have barred white teachers from teaching black students. A third bill, whose sponsor painted fraternal and benevolent orders such as the Negro Knights of Pythias, the Odd Fellows, and the state's black Elks lodges as hotbeds of black agitation, would have required all fraternal orders and "secret societies" in the state to post a bond of up to $20,000.[4] Though none of these bills passed, they were an early indication that the most powerful white citizens of Georgia were not only going to move against the perceived criminality of the black working class but would also act aggressively to undermine the influence of the state's black elite. Within Atlanta itself, Smith's victory signaled that the gentleman's agreement among the city's leading black and white citizens that had long kept the city relatively peaceful had been fatally destabilized. Just after the election, Booker T. Washington wrote a friend about a recent visit to Atlanta. "When I got there," he said, "I found the feeling between the races intensely strong, almost to the breaking point."[5] Washington found this remarkable because he had long considered race relations in the city an exception to the general antiblack feeling that had come to dominate the South since his famous Atlanta Compromise speech in 1895. Even more alarming was the fact that, during the election, calls for disfranchisement had arisen from the ranks of the white middle-class leaders of Atlanta rather than those representing Georgia's poor white rural districts.

Black leaders who had painstakingly cultivated relationships with the two leading candidates were stunned as both men took turns savaging the reputation of African Americans. Both Howell and Smith had formerly been seen as "friends of the Negro," but as both men sought the support of white Georgians in the gubernatorial race, this friendship was cast out the window, and years of arduous alliance building were undone in the heat of political combat. The election demonstrated that the white partners in this alliance would arbitrarily alter the terms of this relationship should it suit them. As this happened, the leaders of the black community were forced to shift their position in order to retain the hard-won common ground they only tenuously shared with their white allies. This not only endangered the interracial alliance between elite black and white men, it also called into question the effectiveness of the shared understandings of respectable manhood upon which this alliance had been based. Though this politics of respectability had long protected the city's black population from the most brutal excesses of white supremacy, the rhetoric of the candidates in the primary clarified the real limitations of this strategy. The bloody events of the next few months would bear this out.

Disfranchisement and the Language of Hypocrisy: Black Responses to Smith's Victory

Smith's victory caused particular difficulties for men like Ben Davis and Jesse Max Barber. Previously, the state's black leadership had counted on an alliance with white elites to preserve a limited franchise for African Americans. Drawing on this relationship, it had been possible to defeat the Hardwick bill in 1899. However, this time around many of the same white men who had voted to defeat the bill—including Smith himself—were clamoring for disfranchisement. The gubernatorial campaign undermined the (unequally) shared ground of responsible manhood upon which black and white elites negotiated their alliances. Despite their differences, the state's black leadership shared with Smith a common language of manhood and citizenship, which made it difficult to articulate an effective response to disfranchisement. When faced with charges that black votes were only worth the money they could fetch on Election Day, they did not attempt to refute these claims or even shift the terms of debate. The editor of the *Colored American Magazine,* commenting in May 1906 on the upcoming gubernatorial race, wrote that out of 223,000 potential black voters in Georgia, 125,000 were "densely ignorant and unable to read or write." Echoing Tom Watson, this ignorance encouraged corrupt politicians to defend black voting rights so that they could keep a reserve of "purchasable" black votes with which to beat back honest reform efforts. Rather than question the accuracy of these charges, the editors of the *Colored American* instead endorsed an educational qualification for suffrage, hoping to improve the black electorate by driving ignorant black voters from the polls.[6] In a similar vein, Ben Davis wrote that Smith's "insanity and greed for office" made him "just about fit to be trusted with the ballot as the average negro." Nonetheless, Davis considered the ballot "a sacred instrument," which should be "surrounded with such safeguards and protection as will insure its purity" against "both the vicious negro and the vicious white man," and supported the educational qualification as long as it was applied to "all men alike."[7] Because they shared the same cultural assumptions of who should have political standing, it was difficult not to use the same language as the supporters of disfranchisement, even as they opposed it.

Though Barber and Davis would soon become political foes, the arcs of their lives were quite similar and seemed to demonstrate that perseverance and hard work would be rewarded with success. These men's lives made it easy for them to believe that the only thing stopping most black people from qualifying to vote was their unwillingness to try. Benjamin Davis Sr. was born in poverty to former slaves in rural Georgia around 1870. After attending Atlanta University, he was a teacher in Terrell County before moving to Dawson in the southwest part of the state, where he learned the newspaper trade working in a white publishing house. In 1904, at the age of thirty-four, he moved to Atlanta to launch his paper, the *Atlanta Independent*, which soon became one of the most prominent black papers throughout Georgia. In his ambition to rise, Davis became a political infighter with no equal, and his weekly paper soon became infamous for the ferocity of its editorials attacking and criticizing other black leaders, especially Davis's opponents in the Republican Party. Nevertheless, his paper was one of the few places where black Georgians could read news about African Americans' travails and triumphs. Davis's son, who went on to become a leading figure within the Communist Party, recalled that his father was the "idol of the backwoods poor Negro farmers . . . for the fearlessness of [the paper's] editorial policy" as well as the fearlessness of its editor. In 1919, he recalled heading out with his father to Covington, Georgia, to personally hand out free copies of the paper after the postmaster had returned a bundle to the *Independent*'s offices with a warning never to return. Despite the editor's brash courage, the paper was one of the few black periodicals successful enough to turn a profit. It was so successful that Davis became one of the first men in Atlanta to own an automobile. Parlaying this success into political power, Davis rose to positions of leadership in the Georgia state Republican Party and the Atlanta branch of the Grand United Order of Odd Fellows, whose Auburn Street building became one of the anchors for what would emerge as the "Sweet Auburn" black business district in the 1910s.[8]

Like Davis, Jesse Max Barber was also the child of former slaves and was born in poverty in rural South Carolina in 1878. The seeming epitome of Booker T. Washington's "bootstraps" ideology, Barber had put himself through high school and ultimately graduated at the head of his class at Virginia Union University in Richmond. After a brief stint working at an industrial school in Charleston, South Carolina, he moved to Atlanta at the age of twenty-six and began publishing the *Voice of the Negro* in January 1904. Though the magazine never turned a profit, it became one of the most influential black periodicals of its day. With a peak readership of 15,000, the *Voice* published work by black leaders and luminaries such as John E. Bruce, T. Thomas Fortune, W. E. B. Du Bois, Kelly Miller, and Mary Church Terrell. One of the twenty-nine men willing to sign on to Du Bois's Niagara movement in 1905, Barber attracted the ire of Booker T. Washington, who had been an early supporter of the *Voice*. Nevertheless, his dissent—though frequently intemperate—was still contained within the cultural framework of respectability.[9] In early 1906, Barber was still seeking some sort of common ground with "the greatest leaders of the white race" to whom he had appealed in the inaugural issue of the *Voice*.[10]

Even as he grew critical of Washington's policy of accommodation, the editor of the dissident *Voice of the Negro* ultimately could not see beyond the class and gender discourses that grounded his political identity. In March 1906, Barber dismissed Smith's call for "a pure and educated ballot" as a hypocritical concoction designed "to rob the Negro of his right to vote." However, without a real political solution to the crisis faced by black Georgians, the only advice Barber could give was to state that the race had "nothing to gain by the election of either one of these gentlemen" and advised his readers to stay out of the contest between Smith and Howell.[11] A few months later, it emerged that during a white primary in Chatham County, roughly 800 white votes had been openly bought for prices ranging between $10 and $40.[12] Barber took this opportunity to remind his readers that "one of the reasons generally given for why the Negro should not be allowed to vote is that his vote is purchasable"; however, he continued, "The only difference between the Negro vote-seller and the white vote-seller is . . . price. The history of Democratic politics in Georgia . . . a very orgy of corruption . . . ought to make such men as . . . Hoke Smith forever hush their rant about 'the purchasable Negro vote.'" Barber charged that "this election should make these egotistical 'superior' hypocrites ashamed, if indeed they are susceptible to such a healthy moral influence."[13]

In criticizing Smith as a hypocrite, Barber pointed out one of the key contradictions in the disfranchiser's argument—the belief that white people were more moral as a race than black people. Thus, after laying the charge of hypocrisy, Barber asserted that "the Negro is no better nor worse than the white man."[14] This is different than simply pointing out these contradictions between the professed beliefs and the actual behavior of white politicians. Were it simply accepted that politicians invariably behaved in this manner, the charge would cease to be hypocrisy and would be cynicism plain and simple. However, Barber's outrage stemmed from a violation of a common standard of correct behavior—articles of faith—that he shared with the pious white supremacists he was attacking. In asserting that Smith and the rest of the disfranchisers *should* act in a moral way, he was implicitly expressing a belief that they *could* act this way. If Barber believed that Smith could not, the charge of hypocrisy would make little sense. Instead, he could have dismissed the lot of them as corrupted by power and irredeemably racist to the core. For the charge of hypocrisy to be conceivable, Barber had to think that he shared with Smith the same cultural universe of moral beliefs that proscribed the appropriate behavior for race leaders, whether white or black.[15] Without this shared universe of meanings, Barber's charges would not have been legible as hypocrisy to his audience. While this made it easier to point out the contradictions in Smith's defense of disfranchisement, it nonetheless deprived Barber of the vision necessary to see beyond those contradictions.

This is why, despite his political differences with more conservative black leaders like Davis, Barber wound up offering essentially the same response to disfranchisement as these other men did. Because he shared the same notion of political manhood, rooted in economic independence, self-control, and respectability, Barber ultimately accepted the imposition of an educational qualification for voting—so long as it was administered with "even-handed justice to both whites and blacks" by registrars from both races. Opposing the implication of "the Southern stump orator that white ignorance is superior to black ignorance," Barber insisted that "all ignorance is dangerous and a black ignoramus no more deserves to be excluded from the ballot than a white thick head."[16] Barber closed with an appeal to white manhood that at the same time affirmed black manhood through a metaphor of manly competition. Echoing President Theodore Roosevelt, he asked only for a "square deal" and a fair fight as he addressed his opponents: "We say to our superior white friends, put yourselves on a level with us; enter the race with us, and if you prove to be swifter of feet and stronger of head and purer of heart than we are, we will take our medicine. Will you do the same should we leave you in the race?"[17] *Independent* editor Ben Davis concurred, asserting that "the Negro will not object to an educational qualification affecting all men alike. We believe ballot reform is necessary but feel that the law ought not inflict unnecessary burdens upon Negro intelligence and place a premium upon white ignorance."[18] Thus Barber and Davis, each alongside his political rivals, were both willing to accept fair racial competition only so long as white men were willing to submit themselves to the same rules as black men.

"The Greatest Social Problem of the American Negro": Gender and Black Migration to Atlanta

Given these metaphors of manly, Darwinian competition, the place of poor and working-class African Americans in American civilization preoccupied of a good deal of elite thought. After all, the bulk of the competitors in the great race Barber described were rural black migrants to Atlanta, whose arrival created the city's black working class for whom this question had a keener edge. Tripling in size between 1890 and 1920, Atlanta became home to thousands of emigrants from smaller towns and rural districts across the South. Just like those from foreign shores who arrived in the towering cities of the North during the great wave of European immigration that peaked at the turn of the century, those who arrived in Atlanta used their new homes to create new lives.

Many, if not most, of Atlanta's black immigrants had left behind them an existence of dismal toil as sharecroppers, growing cotton on someone else's land. Across the Black Belt, where Georgia's African American population was concentrated, nine out of ten black farm families at the turn of the twentieth century were sharecroppers or tenant farmers.[19] They were perpetually in debt to their landlord or the local general store, and had little or no access to the cash needed to adequately feed and clothe themselves and their children, let alone purchase the increasing array of goods available in the burgeoning consumer society of the New South. Locked into a cash-crop economy based on a repressive labor system, sharecropping families led a contradictory existence. Though they labored on farms skillfully coaxing life from the soil, they could not use those skills to sustain their own lives. Forbidden by their landlords to grow anything but cotton, thousands of black farm families suffered from malnutrition. And though they grew nothing but cotton, black women rarely enjoyed the pleasure of a cotton dress on Sundays.[20] The existence of a sharecropping family was so precarious that a single traumatic event—the arrival of the boll weevil, a drought, a flood, a spike in the price of fertilizer, an unexpected injury—could tip a family from survival to starvation. The combination of all of these factors led to real concerns that there would be no future for black people in America, not because they would be defined out of the magic circle of civilization by the state's white supremacist elite, but rather because they would be starved out of existence. Between 1880 and 1910, the fertility of black women declined by one-third due to disease, overwork, and malnutrition. Due to the high rate of infant mortality, the average life expectancy of black men and women in the rural South was only thirty-three years.[21] A black woman who survived to the age of twenty could expect to see one out of three children die before his or her tenth birthday, and she herself would die in her mid-fifties, well before her youngest children left home.[22]

Sharecropping emerged in the aftermath of the Civil War as a compromise between labor-hungry southern planters and black workers anxious to establish a household independent of white authority. However, this compromise left African Americans enmeshed in a coercive system of labor control that undermined the autonomy of black families. Initially, sharecropping appealed to black patriarchs since it allowed them control over which members of the family were sent to work in the fields. In the immediate aftermath of the Civil War, so many black women and children withdrew from the labor force that overall southern agricultural production fell by about a third.[23] But this was not to last. By 1870, 40 percent of black married women worked in the fields or as servants in the homes of white families.[24] And by the end of the century, the attempts by black fathers to assert some control over the labor of their dependents could be overridden by the authority of the landlord to get the cotton crop to market during harvest time. The largest cotton planters, for example, employed armed overseers who patrolled their tenants' holdings. With the knowledge of how large each black family was, these overseers had the authority and power to order all hands into the field at any time.[25] In a 1906 interview with one of these planters, muckraking journalist Ray Stannard Baker asked how he dealt with tenants who resisted this authority. The planter obliged by showing him a hickory wagon spoke about three feet long that he kept on a shelf above his back door. "When there's trouble," he said, "I just go down with that and lay one or two of 'em out. That ends the trouble. We've got to do it; they're like children and once in awhile they have to be punished."[26]

White landlords not only controlled the labor of every member of a sharecropping family, they also controlled that family's access to food and consumer goods. The amount typically cleared at the end of the season was rarely enough to carry a sharecropping family through the year. The only way they could survive was by taking out a loan against the value of their future crops. With no access to a bank, those tenants who came up short were forced to turn to their landlord or the proprietor of the local general store (who were often the same person). The effective interest rate charged on these loans ranged between 40 and 70 percent annually, a rate that—by design—would bury the most hardworking farm family under a burden of inescapable debt.[27] Most landlords never really expected their tenants to be able to pay them back in full; rather, the reason they charged such usurious rates was to bind the tenants to their shares and secure a steady supply of labor. With few other choices, thousands of sharecropping families, both black and white, sustained themselves year after year by going ever deeper into debt.

With their power over access to credit, white landlords exerted extensive control over what black sharecroppers could purchase. Some would forbid their tenants from growing food or raising livestock on their land, so that they would have to buy vegetables and meat from them.[28] More often, these landlords would only extend credit to their tenants to buy certain goods, and, working closely with merchants, they ensured that the color line was drawn between the lowest grade of goods and higher quality merchandise available to white customers. Those fortunate enough to turn a cash profit after selling their crop still had little choice but to spend their money at the local general store, where they faced the same restrictions on consumer spending. Even with cash in hand, storekeepers would still humiliate their black patrons, forcing them to wait until all white customers were served and then charging inflated prices to black customers, selling them only clothing "good enough for a darky to wear." Before the advent of rural free delivery (RFD) mail in 1898, those lucky enough to be able to pick freely what they wanted from a Sears mail-order catalog would still have to send and receive those orders through the local storekeeper, who was often also the local postmaster. Even after the advent of RFD, in order to protect their monopoly on the local trade, the postmaster could refuse to sell money orders and stamps to black customers who still owed money on their accounts.[29]

Despite living such a sharply circumscribed existence, rural black Americans were able to draw on considerable family, social, and community resources while they struggled to survive as sharecroppers. Basing her analysis on a sample of federal census data, the historian Jacqueline Jones has determined that the typical black rural household contained both a husband and a wife (87.8 percent in 1900), and women headed no more than 11 percent of all rural black households between 1880 and 1900. Of those women who headed rural households, not all of them were widows or single mothers. It was not uncommon for sharecropping fathers and husbands to travel for seasonal employment, leaving their wives and children to run the farm. Thus, the typical family remained nuclear, though by 1900 about a quarter of all households contained extended family members and about a third of all families lived near some or all of their relatives. These networks of kin and community helped black families weather the uncertainties of sharecropping. However, these resources allowed them to do little else, especially black farm women. Not only would these women have to help out in the fields when necessary, they also bore the double burden of maintaining the home, under what were effectively primitive conditions. The typical share-cropper's dwelling was little more than a one-room shack, about fifteen to twenty square feet in size, and cobbled together by the white landowner years previously. Without glass windows or even window screens, it was im-possible to keep out bugs and flies, let alone dirt. There was of course no running water, electricity, or sanitary facilities, and all of the business of day-to-day life happened in the same room—cooking, cleaning, mending, sleeping, even acts of love and physical intimacy stolen at the end of a long workday.[30] For black men and women who aspired to something more, the move to the city promised the possibility of a more civilized existence. Just as black elites like Ben Davis Sr. worried about whether black Americans would be able to stake a claim on civilization, so also did black sharecrop-pers who left the countryside to make a new life.

If they arrived in Atlanta in 1880, they would have entered a growing metropolis that was not yet completely segregated. Though the white elite monopolized the homes clustered around the central business district, there were black residents scattered throughout the city. The persistent shortage of housing stock, a legacy of the destruction wrought by Sherman's assault on Atlanta, meant that new settlers had to set up households where they could.[31] The physical conditions of their new urban lives were not that much different from the rural existence they had left behind. Few streets were paved, and there was no citywide gas or electrical grid, nor did the water system extend much past the downtown district. As late as 1910, eighty-two miles of streets were without water mains or sewers, and 50,000 Atlantans had to use surface toilets (that is, outhouses).[32] They also faced housing dis-crimination. While white working-class families were able to rent relatively commodious houses of three to six rooms, the best most black families could hope for was two to three rooms in a house that had been subdivided into two apartments. Nevertheless, these homes were a significant improvement over the one-room plantation shacks in which many new migrants had once lived. For a weekly rent ranging from $1 to $2, they could live in a home with a front porch and well water available through a pump in the yard shared by several tenants.[33] For the first time, it was possible to live an existence that could be deemed respectable.

Those living in Atlanta between 1880 and 1920 witnessed the elaboration of a racially segregated urban geography that pushed African Americans (along with poor whites) to row houses and shanty towns at the outskirts of town and well beyond the reach of the city's newly installed gas, water, streetcar, and sewer lines.[34] Not only did this deprive the majority of Atlanta's black residents access to an expanding range of civic rights available to the city's white residents, black neighborhoods also bore the brunt of the environmental costs of development. Because black neighborhoods largely rested at the bottom of the city's valleys, the waste of the city's white neighborhoods flowed downhill to pollute the water that black Atlantans used to cook, clean, and drink. The inadequacy of the sewer system meant that seasonal flooding caused by summer storms would flush the waste of out of literally hundreds of these surface toilets to fill the streets and yards of homes built on low-lying or poorly graded land and contaminate the drinking water.[35] They lived on marginal land alongside factories and rail lines, where the fumes of the city's tanneries and coal furnaces would fill the air with a miasmic stench.[36] Compounding the impact of industrial pollution, a series of laws passed in the 1870s and 1880s authorized municipal garbage collection within the city's downtown business district, which was then dumped on undeveloped land in the city's black neighborhoods.[37] These environmental factors contributed to persistently high levels of infant mortality among the black population. A study undertaken in 1896 revealed that of the 907 black Atlantans who died in 1890, 230 (25.4 percent) were still-born or perished from cholera infantum and other diseases of childhood, and the infant mortality rate for black Atlantans was almost three times that of white Atlantans.[38] In the five years between 1904 and 1908, 6,047 black Atlantans died. Of that number, 1,115 (18.4 percent) were less than one year old.[39]

These patterns of uneven development pushed an increasing number of black migrants to settle in the mostly black enclaves of Summer Hill, Mechanicsville, and Pittsburg on the south side; Shermantown on the east side; and Jenningstown to the west.[40] By the 1910s, these enclaves would be reshaped as Atlanta's white population moved to the city's north side, while black neighborhoods began to grow around key black community institutions. To the east, Shermantown expanded along Auburn Avenue; growth to the west was anchored by the growth of Atlanta University; and to the south, a small black middle-class neighborhood was established around Clark University and Gammon Theological Seminary. Despite this development, Atlanta's black neighborhoods still remained largely outside the limits of the modern city. As Ben Davis's *Independent* commented in 1908, "Atlanta streets, in which whites and the rich live, are cleaned daily and the pavement is taken up and re-laid every half dozen years, while the Negroes and poor whites . . . live in communities seldom cleaned and never paved."[41]

Despite the disappointing continuities between life in Atlanta and the countryside, the opportunity to work for cash wages in the city offered these migrants the possibility of a better future, if not for themselves, then for their children. Among the best-paying jobs available to black men was employment as bricklayers or plasterers, both of which were fields dominated by skilled African American craftsmen and which paid weekly wages of approximately $23 to $25. As first-coat varnishers in the furniture industry, a black worker could make a little over $9 each week, and as a furnaceman in the city's fertilizer plants, he could make up to $13 per week.[42] Still others worked as self-employed teamsters, hackmen, or draymen moving goods and people from one end of the city to the other.[43] However, outside of a tiny handful of skilled trades, the vast bulk of African American men worked as unskilled day laborers, hired for the duration of a job. When they could string together a week's worth of employment, they could expect to take home anywhere between fifty cents and a dollar.[44] To supplement meager family incomes, black women living in the city also worked for wages. Doing laundry before there was reliable access to indoor plumbing, gas heat, and modern electric washing machines ranked this chore as among the most onerous women had to perform. Combined with the fact that the average income for white working-class families was high enough to at least employ a washerwoman, this created a huge market for the labor of black women. By 1880, at least 98 percent of black wage-earning women were employed in domestic service, the bulk of whom were employed as washerwomen. The hours were long and the pay short. For a month's labor—sunup to sundown, six or seven days per week—these women would earn between $4 and $8, a rate that remained steady for decades, regardless of the type of service performed, whether it be cooking, cleaning, or laundry.[45] Such low wages meant that even the poorest white families could employ black help at least part of the time.

The participation of black families in this urban labor market sparked a profound transformation in the structure of the black household.[46] Because the labor demands of urban employers were not as severe, the move to the city held the potential to draw a distinction between a public sphere in which a black male breadwinner could provide for his dependents and a private sphere where black women could safeguard the family's health and virtue. Paradoxically, however, the structure of urban employment both denied black men's claims to the sorts of authority over the household that a bread-winner would assert and drew women out of the home and into the world of permanent wage labor in unprecedented numbers.[47] The power of segregated urban craft unions and employers wary of angering their white workforce by hiring black men relegated these recent migrants to the margins of the urban economy.[48] And unlike labor-starved rural planters, Atlanta's employers only hired black men as temporary laborers. The sporadic nature of urban employment for black men relegated them to long stretches of idleness or weeks on the road working as seasonal labor in the state's cotton, turpentine, or timber industries. By contrast, black female migrants to the city found steady employment as domestic workers or laundry workers.[49]

Women's wages sustained most black urban households. Edward Bacon, a black brickmason interviewed in the 1930s, recalled the role his wives' wages played in sustaining their household. While his first wife was alive, times were good, and he made enough money so that his wife "never worked out for no family. . . . The only work she did was her own housework." After he remarried, Bacon fell on hard times. and his wife, Susie, had to take in washing: "that dollar a week she gets . . . comes in mighty handy when I'm out of work. A dollar's worth of flour or meal will keep you from going hungry . . . when you're out hunting for a job."[50] This experience was relatively common for black men and women in Atlanta. By 1900, 71.1 percent of all employed black Atlantans worked in domestic and personal service, a field dominated by women like Susie Bacon.[51] In that same year, 67 percent of black households in Atlanta contained working women, and nearly half of all black households (46 percent) were headed by women.[52] Though the move to the city allowed black migrants to lead a moderately more secure existence, urban patterns of black male unemployment and the presence of black women working as servants in white homes presented a threat to black middle-class claims on respectability and civilization. African American elites who observed groups of black men congregating on street corners did not see people hoping to pick up some day labor; they saw idlers and loafers who willing to permit their wives and daughters to support them by working as domestics in white people's homes. When the 1906 Georgia Equal Rights Convention (GERC) exhorted black men to defend black women's honor with their lives and "keep them at home and support them there," it was not only responding to the threat that their wives and daughters faced at the hands of the white men who employed them.[53] The convention was also speaking to what it perceived as a crisis in black manhood that had disordered the black family and put the entire community at risk.

Working-class black Atlantans also displayed little regard for the norms of middle-class respectability as they fought to improve the conditions of their employment. In 1881, 3,000 washerwomen of Atlanta organized themselves into a union they called the Washing Society and struck for higher wages. Despite the union's high-toned name, these women evinced little concern for the conventions of middle-class respectability. Within the first ten days of the strike, six of the strike's leaders were arrested for disorderly conduct, one of whom was sentenced to forty days on the chain gang. On at least two occasions over the course of the strike, police arrested groups of women charged with physically intimidating those washerwomen who insisted on working despite the strike. And after the city council threatened to impose an annual license fee of $25 in order to pressure the strikers into giving up, the women held an outrage meeting openly denouncing and defying the city council. Soon, talk of organizing began to spread among the city's cooks, maids, and nurses, and on the eve of the 1881 Cotton States and International Exposition due to be held in the city in October, the Washing Society threatened a general strike of all domestic workers.[54] Rather than reach across the color line to build alliances with influential white leaders based on a shared embrace of respectability, these strikers instead demanded respect.

With one of the highest per capita arrest records in the nation, the police continuously harassed residents of Atlanta's black neighborhoods, targeting black men and women and subjecting them to public humiliation, bodily searches, arbitrary violence, and arrest. In response, black communities would fight the police in order to resist the arrest of one their own on flimsy or unjust charges. The historian Tera Hunter recounts the story of the arrest of John Burke, who was grabbed by the police for allegedly pushing a white woman off the sidewalk as he climbed the steps to the Opera House. When Burke attempted to escape, a group of policemen began to club him into submission. A crowd of black witnesses to the violence, outnumbering the police by 500 to 6, attempted to liberate the prisoner. In the melee that followed, police from nearby patrols joined the fighting, as did dozens of additional black men and women. In the midst of the chaos, John Burke's mother seized a rifle, aimed it in the face of one of the arresting officers, and pulled the trigger. Fortunately for him, it was not loaded. With reinforcements, the police managed to make several arrests, but were followed all the way to the police station by an enraged mob of 200 people, threatening further violence and retaliation. Throughout the 1880s and 1890s, police entering black neighborhoods to make an arrest faced the possibility of being taunted, harassed, or attacked by a community that did not see them as agents of law and order, but rather as the coercive arm of a racist social and political system. Police were also used to enforce court orders demanding the seizure of personal property on behalf of loan sharks, who charged the city's black population usurious rates ranging from 250 to 3,500 percent on small cash loans. These police officers would also be met by mobs of neighbors armed with clubs and bricks, hoping to chase off the moneylenders' agents.[55] Incidents like these distressed black elites as much as the city's white population—both groups feared that any one of these confrontations could lead to a deadly riot.

The perception that urban disorder presented a grave threat to black morals and white security was exacerbated by the encounter between recent black migrants and the vast world of consumer goods newly available to them. A study conducted by W. E. B. Du Bois revealed that in 1898, 80 percent of black families in Georgia's urban centers earned annual incomes of less than $500, and half of those earned less than $300.[56] Though this was not a great deal of money, it was still far more than they could ever have earned farming on shares. Black shoppers' ability to spend their cash wages to fulfill their desires sparked a cultural backlash that laid the groundwork for legal segregation. With little access to cash in the countryside, it was a relatively simple matter for white southerners to ensure that African Americans did not, for example, purchase clothing that allowed them to dress above their station. However, with cash in pocket and a public street lined with merchants, all competing for the same dollars, both black and white, it became possible for a black shopper to dress as well as or better than a white person. The encounter between poor whites and economically successful African Americans unsettled the cultural signifiers that assured white people that they were superior to their new black neighbors, so the city of Atlanta responded with laws that attempted to segregate consumption and restrict black access to fruits of economic and urban development.[57] For example, in 1913 Atlanta passed a housing ordinance that sought to keep upwardly mobile African Americans from buying homes in the newly built northside subdivisions of Inman Park, Druid Hills, and Ansley Park. When these laws failed—as they did in 1917 when *Buchanan v. Warley* invalidated Atlanta's segregation ordinance—white homeowners would resort to restrictive covenants and extralegal violence to ensure their neighborhoods remained lily-white.[58]

Though Atlanta's housing ordinances targeted the threat to white supremacy posed by black middle-class strivers, working-class entertainments proved more difficult to segregate. These presented different dangers to the racial order that Atlanta sought to establish as it moved into the twentieth century. In 1913, the *Atlanta Journal*'s weekend magazine described the city's infamous entertainment district on Decatur Street as "the melting pot of Dixie. . . . Here bearded mountaineers from Rabun County brush shoulders with laborers fresh from the Old Country. Jewish shopkeepers pass the time o' day with the clerk of the Greek ice cream parlor. . . . The Yankee spieler cries his wares and the Confederate veteran buys 'em, and through it all negroes, yellow black and brown, thread their laughing, shiftless way."[59] Decatur Street was lined with every manner of urban entertainment conceivable— saloons, brothels, poolrooms operated side by side with more respectable dry goods stores, barbershops, and thrift stores—and these attracted shoppers, strollers, and gawkers of all sorts. With money to be made and fun to be had, the conventions of Jim Crow could sometimes be laid aside. In Atlanta, as the historian John Dittmer put it, "vice was integrated."[60]

Decatur Street was also a place where bootleg liquor and the general rowdiness of early twentieth-century working-class culture sometimes contributed to other destructive forms of urban disorder, such as knife fights or all-out barroom brawls.[61] As black blues pioneer Perry Bradford remarked, "It was a tame Saturday night [on] Decatur Street . . . if there were only six razor operations performed."[62] The street's notoriety even sparked a debate in the Atlanta City Council about changing the name of Decatur Street—"an eyesore, an unclean and leprous spot upon the face of our fair city." Only after vigorous debate was the proposal voted down.[63] As a street that flaunted the racial order of Jim Crow, it was also a place where black working-class men and women could flaunt the conventions of respectability. Atlanta's saloons and dance halls were permissive spaces for public sexual expression. After a hard day's labor, female laundry workers and black hackmen alike would dress in the finest clothes they could muster, head down to a Decatur Street saloon for a glass of whiskey and a little blues music, and dance erotically charged dances called the Grind, the Fanny Bump, Ballin' the Jack, and the Funky Butt.[64] In 1915, the leaders of the city's black Odd Fellows lodge condemned these sorts of dance halls as places where the "lower classes of people" engaged in "all kinds of vulgar motions . . . for the purpose of arousing that which is animal in man." Ten years previously, Rev. Henry Hugh Proctor of the First Congregational Church, where many of the city's black elite went to worship, decried the corrupting influences of the public dance halls on Decatur Street as a "stumbling block to the weak and immature of both sexes . . . a center of evil influences and . . . a vestibule to the house of shame."[65] While this sort of language criticized the leisure activities of the black working class as destructive to the habits of self-discipline and control, this sort of consumption evinced a level of control over their lives that these men and women—many of whom had recently migrated to the city—could never have enjoyed as sharecroppers. They could spend their cash wages as easily at the opera as they could at a Decatur Street juke joint, and more than anything, they reveled in the simple fact of having this power.

As Atlanta's black working class enthusiastically embraced all that the city's nightlife had to offer, Rev. Proctor and other middle-class black leaders raised the alarm about the threat Decatur Street posed to black morality. Just as the protection of women from sexual violence at the hands of white employers had become the rallying cry for groups like the GERC, equally strident was the call to defend the morality of those women from the corrupting influences of the city. In both cases, the status of black women—whether protected or endangered, virtuous or fallen—came to symbolize the status of the entire black community.[66] These concerns prompted the Fifth Atlanta University Conference for the Study of Negro Problems to conclude in 1900 that "without doubt the greatest social problem of the American Negro at present is sexual purity."[67] The conference argued that, while slavery had at least forced some regularity on the sexual practices of black Americans, emancipation and the "independent Negro home" run by black women of "poor training" and "field-hands" who "never had the responsibility of family life" had caused a crisis in the black family, resulting from the sexual improprieties of black women.[68] The same conference eight years later concluded that women's sexual immorality was "the greatest single plague spot" on the reputation of the race.[69] To make such claims when black Americans were being driven from politics by disfranchisement, relegated to second-class citizenship, and killed wholesale by lynch mobs highlights the profound anxiety over Jim Crow's impact on constructions of black manhood and womanhood.

These anxieties were profoundly linked to the question of whether black people had a place in American "civilization." In a 1902 pamphlet entitled *Negro Womanhood—Its Present,* Adeline Davis Proctor, the wife of Rev. Henry Hugh Proctor, described "three classes of Negro women, lower, middle and upper." Her major concern was with this lower, less "developed" class of women, which "Southern newspapers hold up as typical. . . . It is from this class that the inmates of the prison and evil resorts [that is, houses of prostitution] come. With their upliftment the redemption of the race is involved."[70] Proctor's invocation of the language of development implicitly links racial development with urban development, and both are informed by the discourse of civilization. As Atlanta, styling itself the capital of the New South, moved into the twentieth century, the city's white elite sought to exclude the "uncivilized"—to figuratively expel the barbarians. Proctor's anxiety—along with that of Du Bois and the other participants in the Atlanta University conferences—was that the perceived sexual immorality and criminality of the "lower class" black men and women would eject African Americans from the magic circle of civilization. At minimum, this would justify their disfranchisement. At worst, it would permit, even demand, their extermination as savage brutes. Facing a mounting threat of violence as the election of 1906 drew to a close, black elites clung to the politics of respectability and attempted to enlist white elites in a joint civilizing mission for the "upliftment and redemption" of the race. This decision would profoundly constrain their ability to respond to the bloodshed and its aftermath.

"A Red Hot Campaign of Death…to Every Brute": Social Equality, Rape, and Politics

In the weeks prior to the 1906 Georgia Democratic primary, Atlanta's newspapers were filled with horror stories of black rapists assaulting defenseless white women. Many of these stories were published by James Gray, the editor of the *Atlanta Journal* as well as Smith's campaign manager.[71] Riding the momentum of a "rape scare" he himself helped generate, Gray repeatedly linked black suffrage to the rape of white women. Southern white men, who had long grounded their claims on social and political authority in their ability to defend a mythic southern white womanhood, feared that black challenges to their authority in the political sphere would unsettle their authority over the domestic sphere. When black men threatened the privileges of white men by exercising political power, they would be emboldened to threaten the prerogatives these men held over white women. On 1 August 1906, less than three weeks before the primary election, the *Atlanta Journal* editorialized that with "political equality being preached to the Negro in the papers and on the stump, what wonder he makes no distinction between political and social equality."[72] By "social equality," editor Gray did not merely mean that black men ought to be held in the same regard as white men when it came to questions of access to public space or decent employment. He was referring in particular to the possibility that a black man and a white woman could meet on a social basis, have sex, raise children, and start a household. On the face of it, this was an absurd claim, and can be characterized as simple fearmongering attributable to the manipulations of cynical politicians seeking to maintain their power. However, this claim would not have been so effective at so many points in southern history had it not been believable to many, many white men. The experience of urbanization, in particular, had confronted them with the specter of social equality as the city's ever-changing geographies obscured the line that demarcated a hierarchical relationship between the races. Or, as Gray pointed out in his editorial, the black man daily "grows more bumptious on the street [and] more impudent in his dealings with white men."[73]

These new urban anxieties dovetailed with an earlier concern over black political power rooted in gendered understandings of citizenship and political solidarity. In the nineteenth and early twentieth centuries, the equation of black suffrage with the rape of white women was one way in which white men in the South called for and enforced white political solidarity within the Democratic Party. White men who appealed to the "corrupt and purchasable" black vote did not just undermine democratic government; they encouraged black men to take their liberties with white women. This was effective because southern white men rooted their claims to independence and citizenship in their control over a household and its dependents. Before the Civil War, this mastery over a household allowed yeoman farmers to assert a formal equality with the masters of large plantations and to separate themselves from those without the economic independence to be politically independent—namely women, recent immigrants, enslaved African Americans, and wage laborers.[74] Following the war, the collapse of the planter class would reorder these latter categories somewhat, but the essential claim that mastery over a household formed the necessary basis for political independence endured. According to the historian Stephen Kantrowitz, this meant that the social and political power of white men could not be "neatly separated into spheres of 'government' and 'household.'" Thus, the efforts of black men to enter politics could be seen as the first step into the bedrooms of white men's households, where their daughters and wives slept.[75] Additionally, mastery over a household as the basis for voting rights found an echo in the somewhat more modern notion of mastery over oneself. Not only was economic independence necessary for the responsible exercise of the vote, so was self-control over the masculine urges that led to crimes like rape and murder. As *Atlanta Journal* editor Gray explained, when the black man became frustrated in his attempts to achieve "social equality, [then] . . . with the instinct of a barbarian to destroy what he cannot attain to, he lies in wait . . . and assaults the fair young girlhood of the South."[76] Without the strength to control these bestial urges, the sexuality of enfranchised and empowered black men represented a grave threat when not under the firm control of responsible white men. It was against this background of racialized sexual anxiety that Hoke Smith was able to urge his followers to support disfranchisement. "Shall it be," he asked them, "ballots now or bullets later?"[77] Such rhetoric utterly contradicted Booker T. Washington's argument against the 1899 Hardwick bill—that qualifying for the ballot could serve as a vehicle for race uplift and would keep black men from "becoming a beast capable of committing any crime."[78] Rather than the responsible use of political power being a way to civilize black men, political power only propelled them further into barbarity.

Similarly, black men also found the sources of their social and political authority in their mastery over a household. The protection of black womanhood against white depredation was a frequent rallying cry in Georgia during these crisis years. While black women, especially those working as domestic servants in white homes, faced very real threats of sexual violence at the hands of their employers, both black and white women became symbols in this contest between men over political power. It was precisely this language of gender, mastery, and citizenship that the GERC invoked when it concluded its address to the world with an exhortation to the black men of Georgia to "look to the care and protection of our wives and daughters." In order to "keep them at home and support them there, and defend their honor with our lives," it was as necessary to "earn a decent living . . . , work hard, [and] buy land and homes," as it was to agitate and protest.[79] In late nineteenth-century Georgia, claims on political power and mastery over a household were inextricably intertwined for black and white men alike.

This call to defend the black family was sharply limited by realities of life under Jim Crow. The white ruling class that stood behind Hoke Smith and Clark Howell did not just wield considerable economic and political clout, but they also had their hand on the lever that could open the floodgates of antiblack violence. While this ever-present threat of violence constituted the most powerful constraint on the political choices of black elites, their choices were even further limited by the affinities they shared with white elites. Occupying the same discursive terrain made the fight to preserve the franchise a fight over the terms of manly independence as much as it was a fight over its political cognate, citizenship. These shared ideas of manhood shaped black men's response to charges they sought the ballot so they could use their political power to compel white women to do their sexual bidding. Instead of simply denouncing the charge as absurd, they frequently joined in the call to punish black rapists and criminals.

This is precisely what Ben Davis did in the pages of the *Independent* in the wake of the media-driven "rape scare" that propelled Smith to victory. Davis was anxious to prevent even "the least racial friction, [which] at this time will precipitate conditions in which the Negro . . . inevitabl[y] must lose out." Rather than publicly question the truth of these allegations of black criminality, he accepted them at face value and called on black and white community leaders to stand together to put an end to the "reign of rapine and terror precipitated in our midst by the black beasts who have been assaulting white women." Although he singled out the editors of the state's major white newspapers for "incendiary editorials . . . appealing to the prejudice and the mob spirit of our white neighbors [and their] indict[ments of] the whole race as rapists," he also criticized "the Negro editors and preachers [for] denouncing lynch law in scathing terms [while] doing nothing to put out of existence the brutes who assault white women." To save the "reputation of the race," he called on black men to unite with white men and "put to death or expel every fiend. . . . Let us get together and map out a red hot campaign of death and damnation to every brute in the community."[80] Davis invoked this image of an interracial lynch mob in a desperate attempt to reestablish common ground lost during the gubernatorial race.[81] Upon this bloody ground, black elites would be able to forge unity with the elite white men of Georgia through the joint policing of black criminality.[82] It might be possible to write off Davis's stridency as a quirk of his truculent personality; however, his was not the only black voice offering this response to the threat of lynching. In early September, the Baptist Ministers Union of Atlanta, while asserting the innocence of "negro preachers, teachers, and editors," attributed Atlanta's crime wave to the "vicious, 'rounders,' loafers and [the] grossly ignorant, . . . [who] frequent the barrooms, pool rooms, gambling dens, dives, and restaurants attached to these bars." Although Davis's rhetoric may have been extreme, the ministers echoed Davis's call for violent retribution, offering their own services as a lynch mob: "if given an opportunity to compose the entire jury, as the evidence warranted, even if circumstantial, we would instantly bring a verdict of death."[83]

If black leaders did not immediately agree with Davis, they certainly did so following the riot that shook Atlanta the month after the election. In measured tones, the *Savannah Tribune* tried to establish an interracial front against crime, writing that "the good colored people and the good white people must join hands and put down lawlessness in every community. The criminals of each race must be apprehended and punished."[84] With considerably less restraint, J. W. E. Bowen, the head of Atlanta's Gammon Theological Seminary, wrote in to the *New York World* that the black race is "afflicted with a small brood of lustful, besotted, worthless and dangerous black harpies who fear neither God nor man and are the worst enemies of society. . . . They do attack white women, and, in addition, they pluck continuously and mercilessly at the vitals of their own race." Affirming the mythology of black retrogression, Bowen asserted that "the sudden transition from a state of strict discipline as was found in slavery to one of democratic liberty was too much for the recently liberated slave."[85] These perspectives shared a very real concern that the unrestrained manhood symbolized by the image of the black rapist would reflect poorly on African Americans and fuel calls for black disfranchisement and renewed violence against the black community as a whole.

At one level, these expressions can be read as the tactical moves of black elites like Davis or Bowen to head off white reprisals for the alleged crime wave. On another level, they can also be read as an attempt by black elites to retain their hard-won class privileges in the face of a wave of antiblack sentiment voiced by white Atlantans unwilling or unable to see these distinctions. However, neither of these understandings can account for the extremity of the language used in these statements. The concerns voiced by Davis and others fed off a common early twentieth-century notion of manhood that men were inherently sinful creatures and that to grant power to black men who lacked "the strict discipline" and manly self-restraint needed to contain these passions would lead to the release of these sins and passions in socially destructive ways.[86] These black men grounded their standing as responsible citizens in an understanding of themselves as respectable members of the middle class, capable of restraining these savage and sinful impulses inherent in every man, black or white. What differentiated them from their white counterparts was that they believed this capacity for self-restraint was not a racial trait enjoyed by whites only. What alarmed them most was that their apparent inability as race leaders to restrain the black "crime wave" undermined their own position of authority in the eyes of both black and white Atlanta.

The "unrestrained manhood" of the black working class damaged elite black claims on political authority by destabilizing the black household, effective mastery over which sustained male claims to political power in the late nineteenth and early twentieth centuries. The disorder of black households—exacerbated by the transformations wrought by urbanization—undermined the claims of black men to political authority, especially in the face of disfranchisement. One month following Smith's electoral victory, on the very day that the 1906 race riot would erupt, the *Atlanta Independent* urged Atlanta's black middle class to "be practical" and admit that black lawlessness is "not a theory" but "a fearful condition threatening the very perpetuity of our institution[s] and the peace and happiness of every fireside."[87] Identifying the sites of working-class entertainment along Decatur and Peters Streets—the "Negro dives, [and] 'dago' joints"—as sources of instability for the black family, Ben Davis repeatedly called on the city fathers to take action.[88] In particular, Davis was concerned about the protection of black women and children. To defend both their physical safety and their moral integrity, he called on the city to pass a curfew that would "clear the streets of women and children not employed after 9 P.M." Davis lamented the common sight of "a dozen or more drunken colored women in the streets . . . made drunk with liquor sold them by white saloon keepers and borne to them by Negro bums and whiskey heads who do errands for a drink." This nefarious combination of unscrupulous white men, shiftless "Negro bums," and loose black women posed a dire threat to "public morals and the safety of our homes," and Davis pressured the city to put these saloons out of business.[89]

This was more than a threat to the morals of women; it was a concrete and very public demonstration that respectable black men were not masters of their households and did not have control over their women and children. As a result, "every night in the week you can find thousands of Negro women who do not work in the day prowling through the streets unaccompanied at night. . . . These women hang around . . . , drinking beer in the pool rooms and restaurants until the bars close, and when they close they go upstairs to the dance halls and club rooms." Finally, describing these barrooms as "cess pools that *breed* criminals," Davis suggested that the drunken license freely exhibited along Decatur Street was not just a threat to the black families of today but to those of the future as well. Davis urged the respectable men of the city to have the "moral courage to face the situation" and reassert paternal authority, noting that "nothing substantial will be accomplished until some man who has the courage to face the racket appears on the scene."[90]

The week before, Davis wrote that "the fight for our rights in American strenuosity [*sic*] is one of survival of the fittest and it is up to us to make good or go down in ignominuous [*sic*] defeat. We must quit petitioning for our rights and earn them. We must deport ourselves as men."[91] Citizenship was not a universal birthright, but rather it was rooted in manly endeavor and strict conformity to a shared ideal of bourgeois manliness. Davis feared that if black men did not discipline their families, white men would. Should that happen, this struggle would not be over the morality, progress, and civilization of the race, but could result in the brutal annihilation and exile of black people in America. The most extreme rhetoric of the disfranchisement campaign not only wanted to push black people to the bottom of society, it called for their elimination. In June 1905, in a widely reprinted pamphlet, Populist leader Tom Watson asked, then answered his own question: "What does Civilization owe to the negro? / Nothing! / *Nothing!!* / NOTHING!!!"[92] Two letters written to the *Atlanta Georgian* in August 1906 even advocated straightforward genocide, calling for the sterilization of black boys and girls at birth.[93] In response to this eliminationist sentiment, Davis thought it vital to police the morals of the black family and other black men in order to better fit African Americans for citizenship. These exhortations aside, nobody could prevent the violence that would shortly ensue.

The Atlanta Race Riot of 1906

Saturday, 22 September 1906, was a muggy, overcast day. The threat and promise of rain hung low over the city.[94] Following the election, the newly elected leaders of the state had done absolutely nothing to dissipate the escalating racial tension in the city. Though it ultimately did not rain that day, the violence that was to convulse the city for three days broke like a thunderstorm. The city's white newspapers had not ceased their sensational reporting of the alleged rape scare. If anything, Atlanta's four white dailies intensified their coverage, and hardly a day went by when a "black brute" was not committing "outrages" on some white woman right on page one. Among whites, the panic was so great that minor incidents were telescoped into all-out assaults on white womanhood. For example, after an evening of drinking, a black man stumbled off a streetcar and accidentally brushed against a white woman, drunkenly mumbling, "Hello, honey." The woman screamed and ran off. Shortly thereafter a would-be lynch mob cornered the man in a nearby boardinghouse, and only a vigorous appeal by the woman's father, a court bailiff, spared the man's life.[95]

On the day of the riot, all four newspapers issued extras describing a veritable siege on law and order allegedly being perpetrated by out-of-control black men.[96] Beginning at 5:00 P.M., the *Atlanta Evening News* issued the first of five extra editions of the paper with escalating headlines proclaiming "TWO ASSAULTS," "THIRD ASSAULT," and "ALL POLICE CALLED OUT."[97] The rest of the city's daily papers soon issued their own extras, each decrying the "fiendish" crimes perpetrated by savage and shiftless black men. That

evening, with the strident calls of the press to protect their women still ring-
ing in their ears, crowds of white men converged as usual near the Decatur
Street entertainment district that the *Atlanta Independent* had earlier that
day castigated as a "cess pool of vice and shame."[98]

The riot began when an unidentified man climbed a soapbox and exhorted the white men on their duty to protect their white women from black
rapists. He "harangue[d] the city and its white inhabitants for tolerating the
black brutes, for allowing a single perpetrator of assault to escape immediate
retribution . . . the time to strike back is NOW!" The crowd echoed back, "Kill
the niggers!"[99] He challenged the crowd: "Are we Southern white men going
to stand for this?" The crowd yelled back: "No! Let's kill all the Negroes so
our women will be safe." Despite this escalating rhetoric, thousands of unsuspecting African Americans remained in the downtown area—drinking,
carousing, working.[100] Interracial altercations were not uncommon on Decatur Street, so most black men and women simply steered clear of the angry
white man yelling atop his box. Shortly after 9 P.M., small groups of white
men, drunk on vitriol and whiskey, began to peel off and assault black men
and women who had been unlucky enough to be in the immediate vicinity.
The violence escalated quickly, and soon a throng 5,000 strong swarmed
the streets in and around Decatur looking for targets. Too late, Mayor James
Woodward appeared before the crowd in a vain attempt to calm the situation. He then ordered the fire department to turn its hoses on the seething
mass, but that did little but drive the crowd up nearby streets and out of the
reach of the hoses.[101]

By 10:00 P.M., the mob had doubled in size, and by midnight thousands
more were still pouring into the central business district, some having
returned home to retrieve their pistols and rifles.[102] Others armed themselves from the stock available in Decatur Street pawnshops, the windows
of which one observer described as veritable "arsenals" of "cheap revolvers
and knives."[103] (One nearby establishment reportedly sold $16,000 worth
of guns and ammunition.)[104] And those without weapons or the cash to
buy them simply stole them. The Penson and McCartey Hardware store,
which lay in the path of the mob as it marched on Peters Street, was looted
of its entire stock of guns, ammunition, hammers, and crowbars. For the
next four hours, this armed mob surged through the downtown district and
attacked every black person they saw. James W. English, the president of
Fourth National Bank and arguably one of the most powerful white men
in town, stood before the posh Piedmont hotel and tried to calm the mob.
Perhaps fearful that the white mob would turn their attention to the banks,

hotels, and other establishments owned by the city's white elite, he rang the fire bell ten times, calling on every active-duty policeman and firefighter in the city. Nevertheless, he watched on helplessly, unable to prevent the mob from plunging their knives repeatedly into the bodies of their hapless black victims.[105]

As the violence escalated, the police—largely sympathetic to the rioters— did little to calm the situation. While a few policemen attempted to rescue black victims from the mob, it soon became apparent that they would not use force against the rioters. A grand jury would later charge that "had the police department [presented] a determined front to the mob at the inception of the riot, all serious trouble could have been averted."[106] Free to act with impunity, the mob's beatings quickly gave way to murders.[107] Early in the evening, James N. Reeves, a black chaplain's son, was killed on a streetcar after being stabbed in the forehead. Frank Smith, a messenger, was stoned to death on the Forsyth Street viaduct. The bootblack Henry Welch was gunned down in a barbershop on Marietta. Will Marion, another bootblack, was shot and killed while polishing a white man's shoes on Peachtree. Leola Maddox was beaten and stabbed while shopping on Mitchell Street. Milton Brown, having just escaped the mob downtown, was caught by the mob near his home on Peters Street. He was shot more than forty times.[108] When the killing finally ended, at least twenty-five black citizens and two whites lay dead, with dozens injured.[109]

The mob also targeted black-owned businesses. Alonzo Herndon, the wealthiest black man in Atlanta, had a barbershop on Peachtree Street that catered to the city's well-heeled white elite.[110] In less than twenty minutes, his shop was ransacked by the mob, and two of his employees were beaten to death. Their bodies were piled at the feet of the statue of Henry Grady, a grisly and ironic tribute to the famous Atlanta booster who, though still a committed white supremacist, once claimed that "the future, the very existence," and the prosperity of the South depended upon extending "the fullest protection of our laws and the friendship of our people" to black southerners as well as white.[111] On nearby Peters Street, a crowd of white men attacked Mattie Adams's restaurant. Though she was able to hold them at bay for a few minutes, the crowd quickly pushed their way inside. They beat her into submission with a heavy wagon spoke, while taking turns shooting at her grandson, just missing him as he ran around the room. Before they left, they broke every piece of furniture and smashed her glass display cases, effectively putting her out of business. Mattie Adams recognized her neighbor's son, the owner of a competing restaurant down the street, in the crowd that attacked her.[112] Throughout the evening, the mob targeted restaurants, lunchrooms, and saloons owned by black entrepreneurs, financially devastating small business owners who aspired to middle-class respectability.

Another target for the mob's fury were the city's streetcars, a relatively new urban space where it was notoriously difficult to draw the color line.[113] As the journalist Ray Stannard Baker observed: "In almost no other relationship do the races come together . . . on anything like a common footing. In their homes and in ordinary employment, they meet as master and servant; but in street-cars they ride as free citizens . . . the white not in a place of command, the Negro without an obligation of servitude. . . . The colour line is drawn, but neither race knows just where it is."[114] For more than a decade prior to the riot, Atlanta's streetcars had been sites of friction between black and white commuters as both groups attempted—with their voices, their fares, and their very bodies—to demarcate precisely where that color line lay. Significantly, it was almost unavoidable for white women and black men to stand near one another in this crowded and confined space, making streetcars key arenas for acting out the pyschosexual drama that underlay Jim Crow.[115] Mob attacks on the streetcars were an attempt to impose through violence a racial order that had been undone by Atlanta's rapid urbanization.

At 10:30 P.M., a streetcar bound for Grant Park was surrounded by rioters at the corner of Marietta and Peachtree. After lifting the car from its guide wires and disconnecting the power, they gave the white passengers time to get off before they smashed through the windows to attack the remaining black passengers. Armed only with umbrellas and hat pins, two black women toward the front of the car attempted to hold back the assailants, but they were roughly shoved to one side as the mob descended on the four black men hiding in the back. Before the police could drive off the attackers, three of the men lay dead from multiple stab wounds.[116] Throughout the night, crowds of white men waited at streetcar stops to attack unsuspecting victims who were passing through downtown. However, it took until well after midnight for the transit company to suspend service to downtown. By that time at least nineteen additional cars had been attacked, resulting in the deaths of at least ten black riders.[117] The streetcars became targets for the wrath of the mob because they had disordered the geography of white supremacy. As a new civic right to which black Atlantans could assert equal access, the very act of riding on a modern streetcar eroded traditional hierarchies that assured white southerners that they were indeed superior to black people.

At about 12:20 A.M., Governor Joseph Terrell finally summoned the state militia to the city to restore order. An hour and a half later, the first of nine companies of infantry and artillery would arrive in the city to restore order. By 3:00 A.M., most rioters had returned to their homes, driven from the street by the arrival of the militia and a heavy rain that prompted all but the most committed to seek shelter.[118] This, however, did not end the violence. After having been pushed out of the city's central business district by the state militia the night before, the mob reassembled the next day and attempted to march on outlying black neighborhoods.[119]

On Sunday afternoon, 23 September, rumors reached "Darktown," the city's roughest black slum, that a mob was gathering to "clean out the niggers" and fire the neighborhood. Preparing themselves for the worst, the residents of Darktown shot out all of the streetlights to slow down the assault, took up positions in the brick buildings that commanded the street, loaded their rifles, and waited. Shortly after midnight, the first wave of attackers reached the edge of the slum. The boyhood home of Walter White, thirteen years old in 1906 and destined to lead the NAACP, lay directly in the mob's path. Though his father held down a well-paying job as a letter carrier for the post office, residential segregation had prevented the Whites from moving to a nicer part of town. Nevertheless, they still owned the nicest house on the street. They were prepared for the worst when they heard someone in the crowd yell, "That's where that nigger mail carrier lives! Let's burn it down! It's too nice for a nigger to live in!" White recalled in his 1948 memoir that as he lay on the floor in the living room, alongside his father, rifles aimed out the front windows, his father told him not to shoot "until the first man puts his foot on the lawn and then—don't you miss."[120] Fortunately, a group of armed black men barricaded in a house down the street scattered the oncoming mob with a hail of gunfire, repulsing the attack on Darktown.[121] The organized defense of Darktown likely saved countless black lives, including those of Walter White and his family.

The black residents of the middle-class neighborhood of Brownsville were not so lucky. According to one contemporary description, Brownsville was "a large settlement of Negroes . . . bearing the best reputation among white people who knew them." With three churches and no saloon, practically every resident "owned his own home, some of the houses being as attractive without and as well-furnished within as the ordinary homes of middle-class white people."[122]

Despite this law-abiding reputation, the all-black enclave at the edge of town bore the brunt not only of the redirected fury of the mob but of the state militia as well. President John Wesley Edward Bowen of Gammon Theological Seminary had barely slept since the riot began, and when he did he slept in his clothes, "expecting the mob at any moment."[123] When news of the violence reached them, many of the residents of Brownsville had crowded into the seminary's chapel, seeking safety in the house of the Lord.[124] Wealthy enough to have a telephone, President Bowen repeatedly phoned for police protection on Sunday, but none came.[125] When the authorities did come on Monday evening just after dark, they arrived in the neighborhood with orders to disarm and arrest any black man with a gun. Indistinguishable at night from the mob that had savaged downtown Atlanta two days previously, the black residents of Brownsville exchanged gunfire with a motley crew of seven county police officers and three white vigilantes. Several men fell wounded on both sides, and the commander of the police contingent, Officer James Heard, was shot from his saddle and died instantly. Outgunned, the police retreated downtown.[126]

Following this skirmish, rumors began circulating that 500 students from nearby Clark University had armed themselves and were preparing an assault on city.[127] Though the university was not yet in session for the semester and only two male students were in residence, the report was sufficient to bring the full might of the state militia into Brownsville.[128] Tuesday morning at dawn, with the residents hiding behind locked doors, three companies of infantry and the governor's horse guard marched into Brownsville with a machine gun and enough ammunition to kill every person in the village. One squad of soldiers reportedly adopted as their marching song the grim chant, "We are rough, we are tough, we kill niggers and never get enough." These troops then went door to door and arrested the majority of the enclave's male population. In the process, they gunned down or bayoneted four men, all of whom would have been placed among the ranks of the most respectable citizens: a grocer, a seventy-year-old Civil War veteran, a brickmason, and a carpenter. Upon encountering a bedridden man, one squad placed their revolvers against his chest and shot him several times in bed as his family watched in horror.[129] By the end of the day, the chapel had proven no sanctuary. President Bowen himself was clubbed in the head with a rifle butt, charged with Officer Heard's murder, and arrested along with 250 others.[130] Despite the brutality of the militia, the arrival of troops in the city and the consequent invasion of Brownsville meant the end of most of the violence.

In the immediate aftermath, black elites were forced to come to terms with their dependence on those whom they perceived to be the criminal class. Some even armed themselves should the mob return. In the days following the violence, W. E. B. Du Bois of Atlanta University bought a double-barreled Winchester shotgun, promising that "if a white mob [should step] on the campus where I lived I would without hesitation have sprayed their guts over the grass."[131] William H. Crogman, the president of Clark University, believed that Darktown's resistance averted a second massacre.[132] In a letter written to Mary White Ovington in New York City shortly after the riot, he reflected on the irony: "Here we have worked and tried to make good men and women of our colored population and at our very doorstep the whites kill these good men. But the lawless element in our population, the element we have condemned, fights back, and it is to these people that we owe our lives"[133] As Lugenia Burns Hope remembered, the fear of this lawless element ultimately would force elite white Atlantans to forge a postriot alliance with black middle-class leaders like herself. "No one person could have brought those people to terms. They felt they had stood as much as any man could—They were prepared for every eventuality."[134] After the riot, the politics of respectability would ultimately reassert itself through the establishment of the interracial Atlanta Civic League, which brought together representative leaders of black and white Atlanta in the interests of harmony.[135] However, what compelled white elites to embrace interracial cooperation was their fear of those armed black men, the "lawless element" who were "prepared for every eventuality," rather than their willingness to see their black counterparts as equals in a civilizing mission to uplift the masses.

The unrest demonstrated that even Atlanta, widely believed to be immune to mob violence, was susceptible to the sorts of racial pogroms that had rocked cities across both the North and South. At least temporarily, this anger shook black confidence in the leadership of Booker T. Washington's policy of race uplift and building alliances with influential whites, which he launched in his famed 1895 Atlanta Compromise. In the final years of her life, just after World War II, as Lugenia Burns Hope was making notes for her memoir, the rage she felt still resonated. She wrote that the "Negroes were quite unsuspecting that their white friends had planned to destroy them. The Negro will never forget or forgive the shock of realizing that their white friends had betrayed them."[136] On the most visceral level, the indiscriminate violence also directly challenged the ability of middle-class men to defend their families, threatening one of the ideological underpinnings of the right to vote. One young black man writing to a friend from exile after the riot asked, "How would you feel, if . . . after speeches and papers and teachings you acquired property and were educated, and were a fairly good man, it were impossible to walk the street (for whose maintenance you were taxed) with your sister without being in mortal fear of death if you resented any insult offered her?" The inability of the author to defend his sister reflected the growing understanding of black middle-class Georgians that the strategy of race uplift would not defend the integrity of black households in the face of white assaults. The author continued his line of questioning: "How would you feel if you saw a governor, a mayor, a sheriff, whom you could not oppose at the polls, encourage by deed or word or both, a mob of 'best' and worst citizens to slaughter your people in the streets and in their own homes and in their places of business?"[137] Not only could black people not depend upon the friendship of the "best citizens" of Atlanta, these white leaders would head the savage mob that hunted African Americans in the streets of Atlanta—the streets "for whose maintenance you were taxed." The bloodshed in Atlanta revealed the hard limits that Progressive Era development placed upon black aspirations.

For their part, the white city fathers were worried that the riot had permanently damaged Atlanta as a destination for northern investment capital. According to the journalist Ray Stannard Baker, the riot had "paralysed" the city. "Factories were closed, railroad cars were left unloaded in the yards, the street-car system was crippled . . . , hundreds of servants deserted their places [and] bank clearings slumped by hundreds of thousands of dollars."[138] The immediate aftermath of the violence had cost the city $200,000 in business, and the continuing acts of black and white retaliation threatened to deepen these losses.[139] Jesse Max Barber estimated that in the weeks after the bloodshed, some 5,000 African Americans had left the city.[140] Additionally, at least thirty families—"all of them good workers"—were forced to abandon their homes as they fled Brownsville.[141] The day after the assault on Brownsville, Charles T. Hopkins of the Atlanta Chamber of Commerce told a meeting of concerned businessmen, "Saturday evening at eight o'clock, the credit of Atlanta was good for any number of millions of dollars in New York; . . . today, we couldn't borrow five cents."[142] To staunch the bleeding, they offered an olive branch to the city's black leadership, promising a partnership and negotiations that held significant promise for the black community. Over time, these negotiations developed into a permanent biracial civic league, which Rev. Henry Hugh Proctor, Benjamin Davis, and other black leaders hailed as a significant concession.

This organization was able to achieve some victories, notably a fair trial for at least some African Americans facing riot-related charges as well as attaining the city's cooperation in preventing a second antiblack pogrom rumored to be planned for Christmas.[143] In addition, about a quarter of the police force was fired for either participating in the riot or dereliction of duty.[144] However important these concessions were, they were still very limited. Even though a report issued by the Atlanta Chamber had bluntly asserted that "several hundred murderers or would-be murderers" were at large following the mob violence, the police arrested only twenty-four members of the white mob, sentencing them to the chain gang.[145] Although two dozen black people perished on the streets of Atlanta, not a single white man was tried for murder. Nor did these postriot negotiations address the underlying vulnerabilities of black Atlantans in the face of white efforts to drive their fellow black citizens into a subordinate class of citizenship. To demand equal access to the fruits of urban development, as had the GERC in the weeks prior to the riot, was no longer possible. This point was driven home when the white members of the Atlanta Civic League remained either unable or unwilling to deliver on promises to place black police officers in black neighborhoods or put black jurors in the city's courtrooms.[146] Those white leaders willing to reach out to Atlanta's black elite were not willing to accord men like Ben Davis or Rev. Henry Hugh Proctor status as equals. What Atlanta's black middle class might describe as negotiations across the color line, their white partners in those negotiations viewed as benevolent white paternalism. In describing the role of white men in the Atlanta Civic League, Hopkins proclaimed "the Negro race . . . a child race. We are a strong race, their guardians. . . . It is our Christian duty to protect him."[147] Despite these limitations, those black leaders who used the Civic League as a forum for negotiating racial peace after the riot did so in a way that made the prevailing politics of middle-class respectability seem successful. Following the bloodiest clash on the streets of Atlanta since the Civil War, this cooperation allowed the leading citizens of both races to legitimately take credit for establishing the basis for negotiating a lasting peace.

Unlike the young refugee described above, most established black leaders anxiously sought to reestablish the working relationship between black and white elites that they had spent their lives building. However, the price of doing so was to disavow the momentary unity forged across class lines in the heat of the riot. The historian David Fort Godshalk has argued that biracial cooperation in Atlanta came at the expense of these "newly discovered bonds with working-class and socially marginalized African Americans."[148] Making explicit both his own fear of an idle black working class and the fear of black retrogression that lay at the heart of Hopkins's paternalism, *Atlanta Independent* editor Ben Davis claimed that "the Negro committed no rape in slavery because their masters kept them busy and the best preventative now for crimes of all characters . . . is to keep the Negro busy. If he won't keep busy on his own initiative, make [him] stay busy by force."[149] Echoing these sentiments, the white leaders of the biracial Atlanta Civic League acknowledged that "there were two classes of Negroes—the intelligent and the ignorant, the criminal and the non-criminal," and called for cooperation between black and white men "to separate the lawless from the law-abiding" in order to create a "better, more law abiding Atlanta."[150] The conventional wisdom that was beginning to solidify into historical truth held that the riot was the work of "the ignorant Negro and the uneducated white." According to Ray Stannard Baker, "it is in these lower strata of society where races rub together in unclean streets. Decatur and Peters streets, with their swarming saloons and dives, furnish the point of contact." It was this criminal class that had disgraced the "respectable, law-abiding, good citizens, white and black," of Atlanta.[151] Framed in this way, the major activity of the Civic League comprised efforts to control black crime and enlist black support for these law-and-order campaigns rather than address the underdevelopment that plagued black neighborhoods.[152] Even though the willingness of the city's black working class to take up arms had checked the advance of the mob, saving the homes of many "respectable" black families, the black middle-class alliance with the city's white elite required them to distance themselves from this "lawless element."

"A Wilderness Called Peace": The Exile of Jesse Max Barber and the Limits of Protest

To fully understand the road not taken by the majority of the city's black leadership following the riot, it is useful to examine the fate of *Voice of the Negro* editor Jesse Max Barber. Barber had been deeply involved with the establishment of the GERC eight months prior to the riot and had initially participated in the postriot negotiations with the city's white elite. At the first of these meetings, Dr. William F. Penn, a prominent black physician, took pains to offer the "support of the educated Christian members of his race . . . in protecting white women from the crimes committed against them by the criminal negro classes."[153] By contrast, Barber wanted firmer assurances that during the city's investigation and the prosecution of those found guilty, the law would be applied equally to all Atlanta's citizens, black and white. "All we want," Barber said, "is to be able to carry to them the assurance of protection . . . and to know that it will be carried out." In many ways, this was an extension of the GERC's work in attempting to ensure that the power of the state was exercised in a way that did not further fragment citizenship into racially segregated categories. Though reassured personally by Robert F. Maddox, a white banker who headed up the interracial committee, Barber's doubts persisted.[154] And with good reason. Those black leaders who chose limited progress within the biracial Atlanta Civic League also felt compelled to distance themselves from the earlier militancy of the GERC.[155] The postriot call for interracial unity among the city's elites sidelined any serious investigation into the culpability of the Hoke Smith campaign and the editorial decisions of the city's white newspapers in provoking the riot. Instead, remaining willfully blind to the full causes of the violence, this interracial elite would lay full responsibility for inciting the violence on the shoulders of the city's black working class.

The chain of events that led to Barber's exodus from Atlanta began with his response to an article written by *Atlanta News* editor John Temple Graves for the *New York World* and reprinted widely by the Associated Press. Written as the riot was still in progress, Graves's account opened with the bald statement that "the Atlanta race riot is due to the cumulative provocation of a series of assaults by negroes upon white women, which . . . are without parallel in the history of crime among Southern negroes." Broadcasting for a national audience the propaganda that helped spark the riot, he repeated the charges that black "fiends" had carried out eleven assaults in the preceding seven weeks, and "in almost every case the woman victims have been mutilated and disfigured monstrously." Among other things, Graves blamed "the cocaine habit among the negroes," "the revolutionary harangues of a local newspaper" (most likely Barber's *Voice of the Negro*), and the Decatur Street "liquor dives" for this "horrid carnival" of rape. As a result of these accumulated outrages, "the lid of the volcano blew off. Monstrous things were done in the name of retaliation. Old and young negroes, negroes good and bad, innocent and guilty, were cut and stabbed and killed." Skillfully, he acknowledged the brutality of the mob as "a blot on our civilization" while simultaneously exonerating white men who were driven to such extremes of violence "to protect the lives and chastity" of white women.[156]

Graves also employed metaphors of inevitability in order to justify the twin projects of disfranchisement and segregation. While never directly linking the predilection to rape to a racial trait of black men, he did ascribe it to medical pathology. He wrote that "we are studying rape now as the scientists have studied yellow fever and smallpox; we are looking for the germ." However, until a "cure" for this germ is found, "wherever there is provocation, there will be the mob." This "rape germ" brought white men seeking to defend their households into inevitable conflict with (ostensibly infected) black men. Reframing the causes of the riot as biologically determined allowed Graves to both assert that there was little common ground to be had between the races and justify the segregation and disfranchisement of African Americans as a medical necessity. "Separation of the races is the only possible, logical, inevitable solution. These two opposite, antagonistic races can never live together in the same government under *equal laws*— never."[157] Following Graves's logic to its ultimate conclusion required the acceptance of one set of laws for white men, whose loss of self-control only came following the most horrific of provocations, and another set of laws for diseased black men, whose supposed lack of sexual restraint threatened to overturn the sanctity of the white household and the foundation of Anglo-Saxon democracy.

Jesse Max Barber only loosely embraced the idea that the leading black men of Georgia could negotiate a just and peaceful coexistence with white elites like Graves without fatally compromising black demands for full inclusion in the benefits of Progressive Era development. Prior to the riot, his paper, the *Voice of the Negro,* consistently pierced this ideology of race uplift and criticized "respectability" as a strategy for ensuring equal protection under the laws. In a 1905 *Voice* editorial, for example, he commented sarcastically that "justice to the Negro means that which a certain class of white men think he ought to have, *nothing more.*" Barber, however, was not consistent. Though he had long been a trenchant critic of African Americans' place in the emerging Jim Crow social order, he was not able to articulate a solution consonant with his critique. Thus, on the same page, Barber also editorialized that the solution to the problems faced by black Americans was not to address the injustices of a white supremacist political and economic system, but rather to strengthen the black family. "Home life is the supreme need of the hour. A vagabond and predatory people are a dangerous people; they produce the vagrants and the law-breakers of the day. An intelligent citizenry is made in a good home." He even went so far as to blame the chain gang system on poor parenting, rather than the need of Georgia's entrepreneurs for a cheap and pliable labor source: "Drive the Negro boys and girls from the streets into good homes for twenty years and the Southern iniquitous chain gang system dies."[158] Bound to his opponents by a common language of respectable manhood and the family, Barber remained at a loss how to frame an alternative politics.

However, Graves's attempt to pin the blame for the riot on black rapists without acknowledging the role his own newspaper played in fanning the flames demanded a response. Three days after the *New York World* printed Graves's article, Barber sent an anonymous telegraph to the paper refuting Graves on every point. This time, he did not frame his critique using the language of hypocrisy; Barber no longer considered the *Atlanta News* editor as sharing with him a common standard of ethical judgment. Instead, Graves had devolved into a mere liar, seeking to use "high-sounding phrases" to make excuses for "a mob which has been as lawless and as godless as any savages that ever shocked civilization." Directly contradicting Graves, Barber asserted that there had been no "carnival of rapes," but rather "a frightful carnival of newspaper lies." For Barber, the behavior of both Hoke Smith and the white press that supported him during the election represented the utter failure of the politics of respectability. Barber had witnessed Smith, formerly "a Christian and liberal man," transform himself into "a human moccasin" in order to win election to the highest office in Georgia by abusing "the Negro to the snarling riff raff of this state." In a further attack on Smith's campaign, Barber cited a "prominent banker" of Atlanta who confessed that the newspapers generated a rape scare as a coordinated "trick" to get Smith elected "on his Negro hating platform." Although no evidence survives to sustain the claim that Smith campaign workers "blacked their faces [and] knocked down a few white women," Barber was insistent that of the eleven assaults Graves claimed occurred in the weeks prior to the riot, only one had any basis in fact.[159] Directly contradicting what was rapidly congealing as the conventional wisdom on the cause of the riot, he laid the blame at the feet of "sensational newspapers and unscrupulous politicians." In opposition to the proto-*apartheid* that Graves advocated, Barber insisted that the only thing that would prevent future race riots was not separation but rather "an impartial enforcement of the laws of the land." "The authorities," Barber concluded, "must protect all of the people."[160]

With this letter, Barber had given up entirely on appealing to the manhood of elite southern white men, correctly understanding that they would never negotiate in good faith with African Americans unless compelled to do so. He had also put his life at great risk; Barber's days in Atlanta were numbered. His attack on the character of these white men brought on calls in the white press for the name of the author to be made public, so he could be arrested or lynched.[161] The young editor was summoned to the office of James W. English, the president of the Fourth National Bank, the owner of the infamous Chattahoochee Brick Company, and one of the white elites who had taken a leading role in the postriot negotiations. Barber instantly knew that his letter was no longer anonymous, and he would later surmise that the telegraph office had revealed his name. According to Barber's own account of his parley with English, he faced representatives of the most powerful white men in the state. Besides English, present at the meeting were both a member of the board of police commissioners and the chief of staff of outgoing governor Joseph M. Terrell. They were unconcerned with Barber's charges that the press exaggerated the crime wave to assist Smith, especially since the city newspapers had already been criticized by a grand jury for their sensational reporting.[162] In any case, the disfranchisers who backed Smith would likely argue that it was defensible to use any means necessary to rid politics of the corruptible black vote, even if this entailed using the press to create a "tissue of misrepresentations" about black crime in which to wrap Smith's campaign victory.[163] Among Barber's accusations, the one that most concerned the assembled men was the allegation that white men had willfully "blacked their faces" in order to terrorize white women for the sake of Smith's campaign. English demanded that Barber publicly recant these allegations before a grand jury and print a signed retraction of his charges in both the local and national press. Should Barber refuse, the men assembled suggested that Barber leave the city within the next twenty-four hours or they would not "be responsible for the consequences."[164] Rather than recant, Barber chose exile. By October, he was publishing his newspaper from Chicago.

Following his departure, Barber became increasingly strident in his criticisms of the "best white men" of Georgia. In its first Chicago issue, the *Voice* opened with an editorial discussing the reasons for his flight from Atlanta. Without yet revealing the identities of the leading white men who threatened him, he unequivocally stated that "it was not the hoodlums" who drove him from Atlanta, but rather its "wealthiest men," who gave him the choice of exile or suffering "any penalty the community might see fit to inflict." The complicity of the city's white elite in driving him from Atlanta made Barber fear "not a mob but a legal lynching."[165] Having criticized the men to whom he was supposed to turn for protection, Barber's flight demonstrated the limits of protest and dissent within the bounds of the politics of respectability. His subsequent analysis of the causes of the riot described a newer politics defined by a sharp critique of the role of progressive white elites in establishing Jim Crow. Published in the November issue of the *Voice*, "The Atlanta Tragedy" provided a useful counternarrative to the notion that the riot was the work of white hoodlums who lacked the middle-class virtue they needed to restrain themselves in the face of a seemingly unstoppable tidal wave of black crime. Barber's evocative account of the riot told precisely the opposite story that Ben Davis, John Temple Graves, and others were broadcasting to the nation.[166]

Barber gathered several white sources to sustain his contention that the white press bore a significant responsibility for the violence, directing most of his ire at "the man who deliberately fomented and precipitated the riot . . . the Editor of the *Atlanta News*."[167] Additionally, he ably deflated the myth of the black rape scare, demonstrating in detail that of the eleven assaults reported in the papers, only two had any basis in reality.[168] Following the riot, police systematically disarmed black citizens citing concerns over black counterattacks, but this had only deprived black Atlantans of the means necessary to defend themselves from mob terror. Barber concluded that "all the soldiery and police of the city at once bec[a]me agents for Negro intimidation and white protection."[169] Or, as Barber put it, "if the mob were a pyramid, we would find hoodlums at the base but white politicians and newspaper editors at the apex. Tho[ugh] launched by the rabble, the creative force of this mob was the upper class."[170] The mob's leaders comprised precisely those white elites to whom black Atlantans were to turn for protection.

However, it was not just the betrayal by the Gate City's white elite that so alarmed Barber. The young editor noted that the riot's fury was directed not at black vagrants and law-breakers, but primarily at the "intelligent citizenry" who had established respectable homes. The white secretary of the Atlanta Chamber of Commerce corroborated these observations in a report that characterized the victims as "honest, industrious, law-abiding citizens and productive members of society." Among the wounded and dead, there was "not a single vagrant"—all were employed and responsibly supporting themselves and their families.[171] According to Barber, the object of this "organized ruffianism" was to "humiliate the progressive Negro." As the riot made clear, the strategy of race uplift and respectability did nothing to defend "progressive Negroes" against September's antiblack pogrom. In fact, the opposite happened. The apparent interracial harmony that emerged after the riot did not represent the ultimate victory of a civilized black elite reasserting control over a lawless black underclass. By contrast, Barber asserted that there was "no peace in Atlanta," but rather only "a wilderness called peace," which had emerged from "the inevitable logic of an anti-Negro campaign carried on for nearly two years by dishonest, unscrupulous, ambitious politicians and conscientiousless [*sic*] newspaper editors." Barber reported that even though "the Negroes *may* be humbler and more polite," there remained "extensive and deep-seated dissatisfaction" and continuing "discontent as long as present conditions prevail."[172]

Silencing the *Voice of the Negro*: Manhood, Race Leadership, and Its Discontents

In the bifurcated world of negotiations between leading black and white citizens, white elite men were (in theory) responsible for policing the morals of white men and women, while black elites were responsible for the morals of black men and women. Barber violated this unspoken boundary with his allegation that white men working for the Smith campaign "blacked their faces" in order to terrorize white women. This directly contradicted the underlying myth that justified the media's fabrication of the "carnival of rapes" and excused the riot as an inevitable reaction of white men acting in defense of their women. Rather, Barber was calling white men outright scoundrels of the worst sort—those who would "knock down" their *own* women in the pursuit of political office. And it was this that ultimately drove Barber into exile.[173] According to the historian Crystal N. Feimster, in order for the rape/lynching narrative to remain coherent, four things were necessary: chaste and pure white women, criminal and violent black men, immoral and depraved black women, and honorable and civilized white men.[174] Barber's critique of the riot took aim at all of these, making his expulsion from Atlanta all but inevitable. His critique also took aim at those black leaders who continued to embrace the politics of respectability and who had long given up on the state as a guarantor of equal protection under the laws. As long as they could work out an arrangement with the James W. Englishes and John Temple Graveses of the South, they were willing to suspend their claims for full citizenship. Even worse, it compelled them to accept publicly the rape/lynching narrative even as they tried to write themselves into that story as the honorable and civilized heroes rather than the depraved villains.

Barber rested his notion of the state and its responsibilities on a different notion of gender than did Graves—or even Ben Davis and Booker T. Washington. This, he thought, entitled him to criticize the political behavior and question the manhood of the white men involved in Smith's campaign. When Barber charged them with "black[ing] their faces," he was not calling upon them to hold up their end as politically virtuous men in negotiations between leading representatives of two different races. He was calling them criminals. By contrast, *Atlanta Independent* editor Ben Davis, whose rhetoric was every bit as truculent as Barber's, only ever criticized white elites for failing to hold up their end of the bargain, and rarely did he call them out on their moral behavior. When he did, it was in a manner that reaffirmed the notion that black and white authority must operate in racially separate spheres. Critical of those white postriot pundits whom he derided as "problem solvers," Davis asserted that they could make some real progress if only they "would pay some attention to the faults of the whites as well as the crimes of the Negroes." The faults enumerated by Davis echoed the language used by Barber and the GERC earlier that year. These included a "double standard of justice in the courts" as well as removing the means "of political self[-]defense from the Negro" by means of the white primary.[175] However, what distinguished Davis from Barber were the solutions he offered. In reaction to a city proposal to shut down black- but not white-owned saloons, Davis accused the "solvers" of settling this issue "on a white man's basis." Even though he called this proposal "unjust," the most vigorous demand Davis could make was "to appeal to the stronger race to give us a square deal." Compelled to reassure Georgia's white elites that they had nothing to fear from "the ignorant and poverty-stricken Negro masses," he could not really demand justice. Rather, he could only ask them to "unfetter us . . . and let us [have] a chance to prove our worth and usefulness."[176] This appeal to the "White Man's Burden" was one reason that Davis was able to stay in Atlanta and establish a new politics of respectability, while Barber had been forced to flee.

After Barber's letter appeared in the *New York World,* Davis took pains to distance himself from the still anonymous author. In an editorial entitled "Among Our Enemies We Are in the Midst of Our Friends and They Predominate," he criticized those white people who "charge the entire race with the sins of the vicious" as "manifestly unfair." Further, he added that it would also be unfair "to charge [white] Atlanta as a unit with mob violence." In demanding "fairness" rather than "justice," Davis implicitly disavowed any claims on reparations for damages done before, during, and after the riot. This language of "fairness" was at least partially rooted in the notion that the positions of Atlanta's white and black elites were somehow equivalent. By contrast, as Barber confronted the white power structure, he moved decisively beyond claims for simple fair play. Although Davis seemed to echo Barber when he said that it "makes no difference what the mob does, we must stand for law and order," he was not demanding that white men respect black claims on equal protection of the laws, but rather was urging *black* Atlantans to obey the law and refrain from retaliatory violence. With the "future of Atlanta . . . endangered by irresponsible whites and criminal Negroes," Davis refused to criticize the city's elites for their role in precipitating the violence, instead reaffirming the role that black and white elites were to play separately in policing the working classes of their respective races. As a result, he repeated the claim that Graves had made in his initial letter to the *New York World*, charging black criminals with responsibility for the riot: "We will have an occasional loss of life and property here as long as the provocation exists." Marking again the boundary that Barber had crossed, Davis reiterated his "abiding faith in the friendship and love of law and order of our white neighbors" and advised his readership to "keep the peace and appeal to their reason and sober judgment for protection from the irresponsible mobs."[177]

It was not enough to criticize Barber's ideas; it would also be necessary to disavow the man himself. Summarizing the sentiment in much of the conservative black press, Booker T. Washington criticized Barber's flight as an act of cowardice. In an anonymous letter to the *New York Age*, Washington expressed concern that Barber fled Atlanta because of "some threats" against him. According to Washington, "dozens" of the city's black leaders had faced similar threats, some having been led "very near death's door," all of whom nonetheless "stood their ground." Speaking on behalf of an imagined community of black Atlantans, he concluded, "We will all be disappointed in Mr. Barber's bravery and sense of loyalty to the race if he deserts us in this trying hour."[178] Ben Davis concurred. In a general attack on black "northern agitators" published in the *Atlanta Constitution*, Davis wrote that in "nine cases out of ten the colored man who flees from the south . . . by 'force' . . . has no real cause for flight." These men invariably sink into "insignificance," once white northerners tire of their "threadbare story of martyrdom to the cause of liberty."[179] While Davis was possibly unaware of the extent of the intimidation Barber faced, it is likely that Washington understood. Ten days before sending his letter to the *Age*, Washington wrote his friend Oswald Garrison Villard asking him to refrain from sending or receiving any telegrams about the riot, citing Barber's exposure by the telegraph office in Atlanta, which had "caused serious trouble" for "one of Atlanta's leading colored men."[180] However, rather than applauding Barber for having the nerve to speak the truth, Washington instead joined the chorus of black leaders condemning him for lacking the courage to stand his ground.

Despite the fact that Washington privately called Barber's letter to the *New York World* "perhaps the most correct account of the Atlanta disgrace of anything that has been published," he felt compelled to punish Barber for his indiscretion.[181] Indeed, Washington viewed Barber as such a threat that he took pains to drive Barber from politics entirely. Following the failure of the *Voice,* Barber briefly became editor of the *Chicago Conservator* until Washington used his connections in the black press to get him fired. After Barber moved to Pennsylvania, he took a position teaching in a vocational school until the trustees heard from Washington that Barber was a failure and troublemaker who sought to teach "colored people to hate white people." He did not escape the "Wizard's" reach until he worked his way through dental school and opened a dentist's office in Philadelphia.[182] Barber would not be able to return to the fray until the founding of the NAACP gave him a political home, in which he eventually become the president of the Philadelphia branch of the association.[183]

Why did Washington go to such great lengths to destroy Barber? Washington's biographer Louis T. Harlan points out that Barber's magazine had become the unofficial mouthpiece of the Niagara movement, and Washington may have found it irresistible to strike a blow against one of his most vocal opponents.[184] But Barber also represented an alternate vision of manhood that competed with Washington's own. Like Ben Davis, Washington rooted his identity in his ability to act as a "responsible" race leader. Both men attempted to take advantage of the crisis caused by the riot to reestablish and strengthen their roles as mediators between the white power structure and the needs of the black communities they served. As masters of the "art of the possible," they really did help black Atlantans weather the aftermath of the riot; however, in so doing they also reaffirmed the power of the advocates of white supremacy. By contrast, Barber had given up on the interracial alliance between Atlanta's black and white elites and was willing to directly challenge the pretensions of men like Graves and English. Freed from the gender conventions of "responsible" leadership, he found the independence necessary to speak truth to power. However, when Barber exposed the limitations of postriot interracial cooperation, he threatened the fictions upon which this progress depended, as limited as it was. This endangered the gains made through these negotiations and compelled Washington to go to considerable lengths to silence the *Voice of the Negro.*

Not everyone sought to distance themselves from Jesse Max Barber. Some responses to Barber's flight highlighted a growing critique of those black leaders whose political vision remained bounded by the politics of respectability. Yale graduate and prominent black educator William Pickens published a lengthy biographical sketch of Barber in the November issue of the recently relocated *Voice.* In it, he concurred with Barber's analysis of the riot, placing the onus for the turmoil on the shoulders of the city's white elite. "Georgia white politicians talked race-war; Georgia white hoodlums and 'best citizens' started race-war,—and blacks died and whites died. . . . The mob used bricks and bullets, and the overzealous officers of the law fought this mob with numerous drops of liquid from a certain city fire hose." In response to the attacks on Barber's character, Pickens praised the young editor for his courage in "openly and unequivocally defend[ing] the Negro" in the "heart of the South," and asserted that "there was a higher order of bravery than subjecting one's physical head to the axe . . . the editor of *The Voice* is a moral paladin." Piercing the ideology of manly responsibility and independence behind which Davis and others attacked Barber, he proceeded to contrast Barber's "moral courage" with that "large number of Negro leaders . . . unable to resist the temptation of catering to public sentiment in reference to their race. This is the easiest way in the world for a Negro to win the appellatives of 'wise' and 'level-headed.'"[185] By no means was Barber was a representative black leader in 1906; neither was Pickens nor many of the other participants in the Niagara movement. However, the support that Barber was able to garner for the stand he took in Atlanta indicated that Barber's notion of manhood resonated with a significant though still marginal segment of the black intelligentsia.[186] As these men defended Barber's manhood against the charges of cowardice leveled by the Tuskegee crowd, they played an important role in articulating an alternate notion of black courage and manliness, one that had the potential to form the basis of an alternative black politics untethered from the politics of respectability.

A sense of what this manhood comprised can be seen in a cartoon by Hardy Keith entitled "Locked!" published in the *Voice* several months before the riot. Keith's cartoon depicted a young Booker T. Washington, his lips sealed with a lock labeled "Diplomacy, Politics, Tact, Tuskegee Needs, Ambition," while a key tied around the lock is labeled "Southern white sentiment" (see figure 2). This correctly implied that only through understanding this "white sentiment" will "Diplomacy, Politics, [and] Tact" have any chance of succeeding. But the terms of this understanding suggested that Washington would be unable to speak unless his voice was unlocked by approving "white sentiment," which would then support his "Tuskegee Needs" and "Ambition." Though this seems a harsh indictment of Washington, it nonetheless put him in the position of being a race leader and offered him an alternate model of leadership. In the background of the cartoon Keith drew a key rack bearing the caption: "Where Moth & Rust Doth Corrupt" and from which hang three more keys labeled "Courage," "Manhood," and "Race Loyalty."[187]

FIGURE 2. "Locked!," *Voice of the Negro* (April 1906).

Rather than relying on "white sentiment," these keys could instead be used to open the lock, releasing Washington's powerful voice. In being both critical of Washington's policy of accommodation and holding out the hope that he could begin to embrace an alternate model of leadership, Keith's cartoon subverted the vision of manliness that Washington performed and supplanted it with another understanding of black manhood here portrayed as fully compatible with the political role that the Wizard had already carved out for himself.

In a similar vein, immediately prior to the riot, Barber published a pro-Niagara editorial that explored the same themes. In it, he responded to criticisms that the Niagara movement opposed the work of Washington's National Negro Business League (NNBL). Although responding in the negative, Barber still wrote that "we need education, money, land, business and the good opinion of the whites; but if these things are to be had only by the hush-mouth policy and the dumb driven cattle attitude, we declare openly that we would rather be ignorant and in the poorhouse [for] adhering to and proclaiming our principles of equality before the law." He succinctly described this new manhood in his desire to not just earn the title of "good Negro." Instead, Barber wrote, "We want a man's chance in a man's world."[188] Most black leaders would probably have agreed with this description of manly competition between the races. Nonetheless, it still represented an inversion of black Victorian manhood in which one's reputation with powerful whites was the most important weapon in the arsenal of ambitious black Americans. Barber's sacrifice, although it nearly ruined him, provided a model of manly independence that would be necessary in order to construct an autonomous black politics capable of contesting the prerogatives of erstwhile white allies.

Several historians have used the history of the riot to distinguish Du Boisian radicalism from Washingtonian accommodation, with most commentators using the riot to demonstrate the "extent to which the Bookerite bargain had become a fatal trap."[189] It is easy in retrospect to understand Barber and Du Bois as the true heroes of the day, the ones with the foresight to understand the future course of events, whose radical stance would be justified by the history that was to come. But in 1906, conventional wisdom had it that the folks who participated in the postriot interracial Civic League would be history's "winners." Both Du Bois and Barber were too radical to be considered responsible leaders, with the result that Barber was forced into exile and a demoralized Du Bois largely sat out the fight against disfranchisement in Georgia and was unable to hold together either the GERC or the Niagara movement. As Dominic J. Capeci and Jack C. Knight have argued, after the riot "Georgia's race men en masse abandoned Niagara tendencies, profoundly aware that their terra firma had become a bloody battleground."[190] The rapidity with which the city's black and white elites reestablished the status quo following the riot suggests that it was not the turning point that led to the emergence of a new form of politics.[191] What did change was that a new understanding of the political role of black women had begun to emerge and would ultimately alter the course of Atlanta's political history.

3

"Respectable Militants"

The Neighborhood Union
and the Transformation of the Politics
of Respectability, 1908–1913

Through the vehicle of the biracial Atlanta Civic League, the politics of re-spectability reasserted itself in the aftermath of the riot. While this allowed black elites to reestablish a relationship with the city's leading white men, critics of the new dispensation were forced to choose between silence and exile. Fearing for his life, Jesse Max Barber chose exile. Du Bois remained politically quiescent until he departed Atlanta to join the staff of the NAACP in New York in 1910.[1] Rev. William Jefferson White returned to his work in the church, and Bishop Henry McNeal Turner fell from grace following a sex scandal that savaged his reputation in the eyes of black Atlanta.[2] Without the leadership of these men, the Georgia Equal Rights Convention (GERC) col-lapsed. The next convention in February 1907 would adjourn in disarray and prove to be its last.[3] Finally, Ben Davis—after a last-ditch effort to prevent the passage of disfranchisement—retreated from local politics altogether. With the 1908 Republican National Convention coming up, he instead fo-cused his efforts alternately fighting for patronage and contesting the rise of the "lily-whites" within the GOP.[4]

As former militants retreated into a policy of accommodation and more radical voices were silenced, the cultural foundation upon which these black men had built their authority eroded significantly. The rhetoric of the 1906 gubernatorial campaign and the violence of the riot that followed had im-posed severe limits on public declarations of self-assured political black manhood. And once the disfranchisement amendment passed with a solid majority in favor, it decimated what remained of the black electorate, bar-ring black men from asserting themselves at the polls. In 1904, there were approximately 68,000 black registered voters in Georgia; by 1910, just prior to the first election following disfranchisement, there were only 11,285—a decline of 83 percent.[5] Despite the work of the Atlanta Civic League, the gendered identities black men now had to embrace were so severely constrained that it would be difficult (if not impossible) for elite black men to voice the kinds of demands that the GERC had tried to make.

Subsequently, it would fall to the city's black women to redefine the political agenda of black Atlanta. In July 1908, Lugenia Burns Hope led a group of black women reformers to found the Neighborhood Union. Under Hope's capable leadership, the Union soon became the first genuinely city-wide organization of black Atlantans, and by 1914 it was a presence in every black neighborhood in the city. Although these women still participated in the politics of respectability, the "nation of neighborhoods" they envisioned revealed new forms of black solidarity that were grounded in the fight to extend the benefits of Progressive Era urban development to black citizens. In contrast to the men who had led the fight against disfranchisement, the women of the Union were able to draw on different sources of cultural authority rooted in the duties of black mothers to defend the health and virtue of the home. This gave them the ability to reconstitute the politics of respectability in such a way as to make stronger claims on the benefits of economic and urban development than black men ever could have. It also provided a new foundation for black political solidarity that was not simultaneously a site for conflicting interpretations of the meaning of manhood.[6] By focusing on development rather than disfranchisement, the women of the Neighborhood Union were able to sidestep the conflicts over the terms of black manhood that had long fragmented black Atlanta and which had stoked white anxieties over politically aggressive black men.

As the Neighborhood Union grew, it also began to challenge the gender ideology that informed the politics of respectability, which depended upon a narrative in which heroic black men defended imperiled black women. In their charge to black patriarchs to keep their wives and daughters "at home and support them there," the GERC cast black men in the role of defending virtuous, but endangered, black women.[7] And when Ben Davis called on the city to impose a 9 P.M. curfew on women and children in order to both protect their physical safety and preserve their moral purity, he, too, was reiterating the gender ideology behind the politics of respectability.[8] By contrast, Lugenia Burns Hope and the other women who founded Atlanta's Neighborhood Union saw themselves as the protagonists in this narrative, rather than as mere symbols of potential racial decline or endangerment.

Following the example of Jane Addams's Hull House, the Union began a series of regular and systematic neighborhood surveys. On every doorstep in every block, the Union heard from the city's black women that they lacked access to modern city services such as running water, sewer lines, electricity, and public schools. These women, castigated as "depraved" by the city's white supremacist elite, were trying to keep hearth and home together on a domestic worker's income and without access to all of the amenities that made it easier for white women to assume the role of virtuous mother (amenities that, by the way, included access to the low-wage labor of black women). Atlanta's progressive black leadership had long known these facts, but it was not until they had the results of these neighborhood surveys that they understood the full extent of the crisis. The Neighborhood Union came to see the difference between the respectable and the unrespectable not solely as a moral distinction but also the result of having little access to city services and no decent employment.[9] The Union's surveys revealed that urban development not only created new public goods, it also created new forms of inequality. As Atlanta became a modern twentieth-century city that offered its white citizens access to amenities such as streetlights, running water, public schools, and municipal parks, city leaders tried to relegate black citizens into bleak nineteenth-century ghettos. On the flip side, this process also created a whole new range of "civic rights," benefits attached to urban citizenship such as libraries, parks, and schools. These stood alongside the earlier array of formal civil rights—such as the right to vote or the right to trial by jury—for which African Americans had long contended. Asserting equal access to these new urban amenities increasingly became a new vehicle for asserting racial equality.

These questions of access to public goods were much more easily answered by women's activism that was grounded in the idea of "municipal housekeeping" than it was by agitation for the right to vote. This notion, which had emerged from the settlement house movement, extended women's moral mission to defend the health and virtue of the home to encompass the broader neighborhood outside its four walls. By embracing what the historian Elisabeth Lasch-Quinn has termed an "activist womanhood," black women in the Union carved out a space in the public sphere where they were able to become more than symbols of racial advance or decline.[10] Expansively interpreting their mandate to defend the home, they became agents of racial uplift and began to assert a greater measure of control over the meaning of respectable black womanhood. While they still operated within the framework of the politics of respectability, the Union's uplift work among the working-class women of the city forced it to engage with the effects of decades of racially stratified urban development on the lives and labors of the city's black women. And as the Union incorporated more and more working-class women into the leadership of the organization, the language of respectability they used shifted from one that ranked and judged the black community on a scale of worth to one that described respectability as a right to which all families should have access.

"Future Citizens for the Race": The Gate City Kindergarten Association

Shortly after moving to Atlanta from Chicago in 1897, Lugenia Burns Hope received an invitation from W. E. B. Du Bois to attend a conference at Atlanta University on the "welfare of the Negro child."[11] The invitation allowed her to pursue her interests in reform work, which were kindled through her earlier involvement with Jane Addams's Hull House. Married earlier that year, she followed her husband, John Hope, to Atlanta, where he would eventually become president first of Morehouse College and then, later, of Atlanta University. The conference also allowed her to address her concerns for the safety of her own family. On her first night in the apartment provided by Morehouse, she heard the sounds of fighting and gunfire just beyond her bedroom window. The college, like most of the rest of the city's black institutions, was located in a neighborhood without streetlights, water mains, or even paved roads. As she looked forward to starting a family with her husband, she grew increasingly alarmed about the conditions of the city in which she would raise her children. Following the conference, her first step was to reach out to the other mothers in the neighborhood, whom she found to be similarly worried. She also discovered that the vast majority of these mothers worked full time and lacked access to day care and playgrounds for their own children. Eight years later, in 1905, now the mother of two sons, Hope helped organize the Gate City Kindergarten Association, establishing five kindergartens for children of working black mothers across Atlanta.[12] This experience of women from across the class spectrum working alongside one another to safeguard the health and happiness of their children would later help lay the foundation for the Neighborhood Union's broadly egalitarian vision.

However, Atlanta's black reform community would not even begin to articulate that vision for at least another decade. In the meantime, the reformers who gathered at Atlanta University in 1897 sought to attack the causes of urban poverty and black mortality by addressing the perceived moral flaws of impoverished families. Settlement house workers who worked among the black urban poor often ascribed the weaknesses of the black family all to the legacy of slavery and racial discrimination. These included the high incidence of single-parent households, alarming rates of infant mortality, as well as criminality. Though many of these reformers sought to overcome a biologically deterministic view of racial differences, many—whether black or white—still viewed the black urban poor as a "problem" to be solved.[13] As Hull House founder Jane Addams warned in a 1911 article, segregation had created "in every large city . . . a colony of colored people who have not been brought under social control."[14] The demoralization of the black family rooted in their relegation to the most squalid of neighborhoods not only put entire generations of African Americans at risk of moral degradation, it also carried with it the potential for racial strife that threatened to engulf entire cities.

These same sentiments were also shared by a good number of black settlement house workers, who viewed their work as a combination of uplifting black communities and purging them of unsavory elements. A 1906 review of the work of Philadelphia's Eighth Ward House in the *Southern Workman* expresses this duality. Anxious that it was only the "weaker element in the Negro race that comes drifting into Northern cities," the Eighth Ward House acted "as a disinfecting agency to the community . . . striving by the radiation of such spiritual power as lies within its command to make a purer, sweeter atmosphere for the more normal growth of all who respond to its influence." Some black settlement house workers were willing to write off some of those who did not respond as irredeemable. A 1908 conference of black philanthropists and educators in Clifton, Massachusetts, similarly concluded that no "legislation can ever shape this granite of African origin for its appropriate place in the temple of civilization."[15] Effectively powerless to address the full extent of the crisis faced by black urbanites, these frustrated black reformers used the language of race uplift to draw a distinction between themselves and their downtrodden brothers and sisters, lest they, too, be ejected from the temple of civilization. The women who would ultimately found the Neighborhood Union were not immune to expressing this sort of condescension toward the objects of their charity. Just like other black middle-class reformers, they used their uplift work both to distinguish themselves from the unrespectable and to establish a public role for themselves as race leaders.[16]

The proceedings of the 1897 Atlanta University conference reveal how the black elite established their superiority over the objects of their reforming zeal. Seeking to examine the causes of high mortality rates among black

Americans—especially children—the attendees concerned themselves extensively with questions of nutrition, dental health, sanitation, and hygiene. Despite their careful attention to the grim facts of urban poverty, the strategy of race uplift through the pursuit of "respectability" made it hard for them to disentangle the material causes of mortality from their moral judgments of the poor communities they sought to elevate. They concluded that the "excessive mortality" of African Americans was not caused by "unfavorable conditions of environment," but rather by the "ignorance of the masses" and their "disregard of the laws of health and morality." The introduction appended to the published conference proceedings even argued that "if poor houses, unhealthy localities, bad sewerage and defective plumbing" were the only causes of black mortality, "there would be no hope of reducing the death-rate until either the colored people became wealthy, or philanthropic persons erected sanitary houses, or municipalities made appropriations to remove these conditions." Such a statement highlights the appeal of moral uplift strategies. Lacking the political or economic power to compel Atlanta to safeguard the health of the city's black population, these reformers instead pursued a strategy of race uplift. As one participant observed, "If we are to strike at the root of the matter, it will not be at sanitary regulation, but at social reconstruction and moral regeneration."[17] Nevertheless, so long as African Americans continued to bear an inordinate share of the social and economic costs of Progressive Era development, black *mortality* rates would remain distressingly high, regardless of the state of black *morality*.

The focus of this anxiety over black morality centered on the upbringing of black children and was intimately connected to the cultural dynamics that would culminate in the Atlanta race riot. In 1904, a series of short articles published in the *New York Independent* explored the "Negro Problem." One author ascribed the criminality of black men to the depraved nature of black women, stating that "when a man's mother, wife and daughters are all immoral women, there is not room in his fallen nature for the aspiration of honor and virtue."[18] According to the gender ideology that undergirded the culture of Jim Crow, the ultimate responsibility for the threat posed to white women by beastly black male rapists lay at the feet of their morally depraved black mothers. The GERC's call to defend black women was in part a response to these slurs against black womanhood. Its demand for black men to assert patriarchal authority over the family would serve to defend both the reputation of black women and the race as a whole. However, such calls for male authority over the black family were not simply the result of black and white men jockeying for power; black women also frequently demanded that men fulfill this patriarchal and protective role. The women assembled at the 1897 Atlanta University conference passed a resolution criticizing those black men who "in failing to care for [their] family," proved themselves "unfit to be called husband or father." According to the resolution, the "large majority" of black men who were supported by their wives hindered women from "performing their higher duties, such as the careful training of families along moral and spiritual lines."[19] Eight years later, Nannie Helen Burroughs castigated black men in the pages of the *Voice of the Negro* for failing to protect the virtue of black women, accusing them of permitting "many encroachments upon the moral life of the race by not entering manly protests against all who insist on having social equality of the wrong sort." Attempting to shame them into defending the virtue of their wives and daughters, she charged that "white men offer more protection to their prostitutes than many black men offer to their best women."[20] Until black men were willing to "defiantly stand for the protection" of black womanhood against the sexual aggressions of white men, black women would continue to be seen as easy prey and lacking in virtue.[21] Burroughs concluded that "our women need the protection and genuine respect of our men; if not unto them, unto whom shall we go?"[22] The uncertainty at the heart of this concluding question reveals how the violence directed against assertive black manhood and the structure of the urban labor market had placed strict limits on the ability of black men to provide for and protect their families. The defense of the black family would have to rest on the shoulders of black men and women alike.

Women's role in defending the family was reflected by the conference's overriding concern with the health and moral development of black children, especially those left to their own devices while their mothers were at work. Selena Sloan Butler, a teacher from Atlanta, decried the plight of children whose parents must "toil from early dawn till a late hour to keep the wolf from the door . . . left alone during that most important period of their lives when good or evil principles will, by cultivation, become the[ir] ruling passion through life."[23] In the absence of the sort of moral training that parents could provide, these children were left "in the hands of chance, to be brought up . . . among the weeds of vice and sin, going from bad to worse, until they become a menace to society." Responding to the widespread notion that African Americans were retrogressing into barbarism without the supposedly civilizing influence of slavery, Butler advocated the establishment of day nurseries in order to safeguard the "physical, mental and moral natures" of these children, allowing them to develop the character necessary "to lift humanity onto a higher plane, instead of degrading it."[24] For these advocates of day nurseries for black children, the stakes were quite high; future generations of African Americans would either remain within the charmed circle of civilization or they would degrade it and be cast out as barbarian influences.

For the women assembled at Atlanta University, civilization was no abstract ideal. It was the yardstick along which the progress of the race was judged by most white Americans. Even though Charles Darwin's theory of natural selection had begun to displace Jean-Baptiste Lamarck's notion that acquired characteristics were inheritable, Lamarckian ideas of evolution remained incredibly influential in explaining race and racial difference throughout the late nineteenth century.[25] To say that acquired characteristics were inheritable was to say that children of those living in vice and squalor would be born vicious and squalid. By contrast, virtuous and prosperous parents would produce children born with biological characteristics conducive to virtue and wealth. If these ideas were correct, then immoral families would not only raise immoral children but would breed an entire race of miscreants. It was not just the moral character of working-class black children that caused such anxiety. These kindergarten advocates were also alarmed about these children's children, who would genetically inherit the vices their parents learned in their formative years. In a short speech on "prenatal and heredity influences," Adella Hunt Logan of Tuskegee presented the conference with the story of a boy who took "his large nose from his grandmother, the small mouth from his father, and a quick temper from his mother." However, unlike his "upright" father and his mother, "a model of purity," this young man seemed "prone to the social sin" (masturbation, fornication, or adultery). She explained that his grandfather had "sowed wild oats," and "a hundred years past" one of his great-great-grandmothers had been "born out of wedlock." Drawing from Lamarckian theories of heredity, Logan asserted that it was these seemingly distant moral transgressions that were to blame for the "downward grade" of this poor child's "social tendencies." Though his parents could easily have "kept the family skeleton in the closet and spare[d] their son the humiliation of such ugly tales, they could not so easily change the blood that coursed in their veins." He did not simply inherit the shape of his mouth and the size of his nose from his ancestors, but their morals as well. Logan concluded that this "force of heredity cannot be checked by a [single] generation" and warned that "we are to-day reaping what was sown, not by our fathers, but by their fathers and grandfathers."[26] Should black Americans not act vigorously to check this moral degradation, they would doom future generations to being murderers, thieves, and adulterers.

This perspective encouraged the elite black men and women at the Atlanta University conference to take seriously working black mothers' day care needs. Several speakers pressed the assembled leaders to make the welfare of black mothers and children their top priority through the immediate establishment of day nurseries and kindergartens. While white supremacists had often described "the Negro race" as a "child race," needing the firm hand of white benefactors to secure their progress and avoid slipping into barbarity, Lucy Craft Laney, the founder of Haines Normal and Industrial School in Augusta, Georgia, turned this language on its head.[27] In her speech before the women's meeting of the conference, she placed women at the vanguard of black civilization, relating how "a little more than a quarter of a century ago this American Republic, after much painful travail, brought forth the youngest child of civilization—the Negro citizen." She followed this with an explicit dismissal of the fruitless efforts of "politicians, honest and dishonest, ignorant and wise, [who] struggled in vain to bring about . . . true manhood in our race," which would seem to place her in Booker T. Washington's accommodationist camp. However, both ministers and (subtly) the Washingtonian model of education ("the Bible and the spelling-book") also came under attack as an "*ignis fatuus*," or a will-o'-the-wisp leading African Americans into "dangerous places." Her criticisms of the leadership provided by male institutions such as formal electoral politics and the ministry allowed her to claim a space to proclaim the public authority of black women. Laney asserted that motherhood gave black women "not only [an] interest in the home and society, but also authority [over] the welfare of her own and her neighbors' children [as well as] . . . the responsibility of making the laws of society [by] making environments for children." There was "no nobler work entrusted to the hands of mortals." According to Laney, it would fall to the women of the race to grant that "youngest child of civilization" entrance to a "glorious future."[28]

Following Laney's speech, the assembled women asserted this authority through a series of resolutions. Earlier in the day, Adella Hunt Logan had insisted that the moral regeneration of black Americans would call for more than individual acts of righteousness. The entire race would have to pull together to see to the material needs of black mothers. "Should the material wants of the mother be denied her to such an extent that she feels the necessity and yields to the temptation of supplying them by theft or prostitution," she asked, "who shall think it strange that her child should be a thief or prostitute?"[29] Thus, the women's section of the conference formally resolved that since "a race cannot rise higher than its women, and the home is the great school for the molding of character, and mothers are the most important factors in these schools," that mothers' meetings be held "for the uplifting of the motherhood of our race along practical, moral and spiritual lines." The women readily recognized that the primary obstacle to the uplifting of black motherhood and the fulfillment of their moral duties to their children was that too many women "being thrown upon their own resources for a livelihood for themselves and families" were compelled daily to work outside of the home, leaving behind "uncared for, their little ones." In response, they urged the "immediate establishment" of day nurseries and kindergartens to care for and educate the children of women who lacked the resources or paternal support to do so themselves.[30] Through establishing kindergartens, the women believed they could create an environment in which the children of their children could inherit the qualities necessary to prosper and uplift the race. It also placed them at the heart of the struggle against Jim Crow, presenting them with an awesome responsibility and power over any question relating to the health and education of children.

Although their language was shot through with condescension toward the objects of their charity, not a single participant in the Atlanta conference blamed working black women for choosing participation in the workforce over the care of their children. Given the economic realities faced by most black families, the vast majority of black women could not have chosen to remain at home and devote all of their energies to raising children. Even middle-class black women (unlike their white counterparts) regularly worked for wages. The tenuous financial position of all but the most successful black families made their prosperity dependent on women's wages. Though they had managed to escape domestic service and agricultural toil, many, if not most, of the wives and daughters of the elite men who organized and attended the Atlanta University conferences worked as teachers.[31] Thus, rather than trying to enforce an unattainable Victorian ideal for working-class black families, this group of middle-class reformers sought instead to create institutions that would help working mothers maintain respectable households. In some ways, this had the effect of partially displacing black men from their idealized role as the sole providers and protectors of the black family. The advocacy of free kindergartens placed the interests of the race above the interests of private households.[32] To augment the ability of working mothers to provide for the moral education of their children, black women reformers still reaffirmed "respectability" as a goal. However, by expanding the choices available to working-class black mothers, they did so in such a way as to unsettle the gender categories of Victorian morality, opening the door for a rearticulation of the gendered basis for black solidarity.

Though the perceived moral failings of working-class black mothers made them symbols of racial decline, by placing this responsibility on their shoulders, they also become potential agents of change and protagonists in the struggle against Jim Crow. As reported by the 1909 Atlanta University conference, through the "*heroic* efforts of [these] noble and self-sacrificing women" black communities across the nation were able to have access to "hospitals, homes for orphans and the aged, reformatories, kindergartens [and] day nurseries."[33] As the kindergarten movement spread rapidly throughout the nation, the Atlanta University conference repeated its call for the establishment of kindergartens in 1898 and 1905, and this call was echoed by the National Association of Colored Women at its biennial meetings in 1897 and 1899.[34] Black clubwomen in nearly every city with a sizable black population responded. As early as 1893, the women's auxiliary of the Central Congregational Church in Topeka, Kansas, opened that city's first kindergarten. Three years later, the Colored Women's League in Washington, D.C., opened its first kindergarten, and by 1898, drawing on the resources of D.C.'s black community, the league had established six more across the capital.[35] There were also kindergartens or attempts at kindergartens in cities as far flung as Anderson, South Carolina; Columbus, Georgia; Gainesville, Texas; Brooklyn, New York; and Philadelphia and Harrisburg, Pennsylvania.[36] By May 1905, Lugenia Burns Hope and several other women who had been regular attendees of the mothers' meetings that had become a regular feature of the Atlanta University conferences opened their first kindergarten in "Johnson's Row," a notorious neighborhood on Cain Street.[37] In addition to being kept off the streets, the children served by this kindergarten received fresh milk, wholesome meals, and a bath each day. Those over the age of six were given instruction in reading and other subjects. Within three years, the women had established four additional kindergartens operating in the poorest areas of the city, attending to the health and moral education of approximately 200 children every day, who would otherwise "have become the wayward and criminal element" of the city.[38] Atlanta's Gate City Kindergarten Association had finally become a reality.

Among the things that made Atlanta's kindergartens unique was the extent to which they were funded and controlled by the black community. Lugenia Burns Hope, chair of the fund-raising committee, worked hard to solicit the support of every successful black business leader and institution in the city. She convinced Atlanta University to donate the office space for the association's headquarters, while Rev. Henry Hugh Proctor's elite First Congregational Church paid for the Cain Street facility.[39] Heman Perry, the founder of Standard Life Insurance, donated $40 per month for the rent on another kindergarten and paid to connect the building to the city's water and sewer mains.[40] Hope also approached Alonzo Herndon, who as the founder of the Atlanta Life Insurance Company would become the city's first black millionaire. Impressed and not wanting to be outdone by his competitor Heman Perry, he purchased a building and lot for the Gate City Kindergarten Association valued at $10,000 to use as a school and playground. For several years, he subsidized the $480 annual salary of one teacher and covered the cost of the daily milk delivery for all five kindergartens.[41] His wife, Adrienne Herndon, served on the board of directors as did David T. Howard, the owner of Atlanta's most successful black mortuary.[42] In order to meet an annual operating budget that eventually reached $1,200, the Gate City women held an annual Thanksgiving bazaar, raising as much as $250 selling needlework, canned fruits, cakes, and handmade clothing. They held lawn parties, egg hunts, and baby contests, and sponsored track meets, which could net as much as $100 in gate receipts. Though the kindergartens remained free, supporters of the association paid $1 a month in dues, often collected from the same populations it served.[43] Until 1924, when funding the Gate City Kindergarten Association was assumed by the Atlanta Community Chest, the women who ran the kindergarten raised approximately $190,000, nearly all of which came from black sources.[44] The organizers of the annual Atlanta University conferences considered these kindergartens so important that they set aside an entire session of each daylong meeting between 1906 and 1917 devoted specifically to childhood development, during which the attendees would be treated to a demonstration of songs, games, and exercises by Gate City's kindergarten students as evidence of black progress.[45]

The moral vision and class origins of Gate City's founders did little to distinguish them from those who led the GERC or from men like Rev. Henry Hugh Proctor and *Atlanta Independent* editor Ben Davis. The women who ran the Gate City Kindergarten Association were a relatively elite group, the wives and daughters of the city's black business elite, many of them college graduates.[46] And at the outset, they shared the attitudes of their male counterparts toward the working-class objects of their uplift work. In speeches about her community organizing efforts in Atlanta, Lugenia Burns Hope frequently argued that "every slum child [was] a probable consumptive and a possible criminal."[47] However, unlike the men who led the GERC, they were unwilling to leave "the shiftless, worthless class of the race . . . behind in the great procession."[48] According to a short history of the kindergarten association written in 1925, the purpose of the association was "to furnish as far as possible a mother and home life for the underprivileged children whose mothers were away earning a support for them." In a turn of phrase that sums up the connection between Lamarckian ideas of human evolution, access to the full benefits of citizenship, and the hope for racial progress, this anonymous historian emphasized the role that Gate City played "in producing *future citizens for the race.*"[49]

Whereas the men in the GERC had used the language of class, gender, and respectability as markers of difference between those worthy of citizenship and those who were not, the women who founded the Gate City Kindergarten Association sought instead to carry as many black children across that barrier as they could. While they still used the language of respectability as a yardstick to measure the progress of the race, as the moral guardians of the home, the concern these women felt for the "future citizens" of the race provided a more broadly universal notion of black citizenship than that held by their husbands, brothers, and fathers. In the hands of the women who led the Gate City Kindergarten Association and the Neighborhood Union that followed it, "respectability" became the ideological basis for a much broader conception of black citizenship.

"Thy Neighbor as Thyself": The Founding of the Neighborhood Union

Lugenia Burns Hope and the women who founded the Gate City kindergartens established the Neighborhood Union in 1908 following a young woman's tragic death. She had recently moved with her family into the west-side neighborhood near Morehouse College. With her "shrinking disposition," she had difficulty making friends and spent her days alone while her father and husband worked hard trying to earn the money they needed to buy the house they had been renting. One day she fell ill, and the two men in her life, not thinking her condition serious, left the city in search of work, leaving her at home. It took several days for her neighbors to realize that they had not seen her at her usual place on her porch, so they paid her a visit and found her near death. They stayed with her and did their best to comfort her until she died a few hours later. Horrified that a poor woman could fall ill and die alone and friendless in their midst, these women vowed this would never happen again. Taking as their motto "Thy Neighbor as Thyself," they established the Neighborhood Union, whose purpose was to organize "Negro women to improve the social conditions of the city—particularly of their neighborhood."[50]

As a founding parable, this story reveals a lot about the race-building vision of these women and how this vision differed from that of their fathers, husbands, brothers, and sons. While the Union never explicitly defined itself in opposition to the patriarchal household, the death of this woman was due in part to the failure of the men in her life to protect her. In most retellings of this founding parable, it is unclear what the husband and brother did for a living.[51] However, given the relative lack of work for black men in Atlanta in 1908, it is probable that these men were not merely brutes insensitive to the poor woman's suffering. Rather, they were likely compelled to leave the city in search of work. This story was not so much a condemnation of the irresponsibility of these men as it was an acknowledgment of the limitations they faced as they tried to maintain a home within the constraints of a Jim Crow political and economic order. Nevertheless, this story conveyed a subtle critique of men's leadership. In highlighting this failure of patriarchal protection, the women of the Union stepped forward to claim public authority over the material conditions of black life in Atlanta.

According to the charter the Union filed with the city in 1911, the Union explicitly sought to address the exclusion of African Americans from the benefits of Progressive Era urban development, such as sanitation and streetlights. In addition, the Union charter laid out goals that both the GERC and the earlier reformers had pursued for decades, such as the abolition of "slums and houses of immorality," and the Union promised to cooperate with city officials in order to suppress "vice and crime."[52] Building directly upon the work begun by the Gate City Kindergarten Association, the Union also established youth clubs to provide "wholesome recreation and cultural education" and offered classes in home hygiene, nutrition, as well as prenatal and infant care. Where these women differed from the majority of the city's black male leadership was in their expansive, universalist vision for expanding the Neighborhood Union throughout the entire city, region, and even nation. Grounding their appeal in women's special moral mission to defend the health and morals of the black family, they called on black Atlantans to unite and "develop a spirit of helpfulness among the neighbors and to cooperate with one another in their respective neighborhoods for the best interest of the community, city and race."[53] Their efforts to spread this "spirit of helpfulness" helped establish new grounds for constructing a black solidarity that could transcend the contested notions of black manhood that had driven the intraracial conflicts of the preceding decade.

The Neighborhood Union fostered a notion of civic engagement and citizenship that had its roots in the defense of the neighborhood, rather than in access to the levers of state-sanctioned power, whether that be the ballot or a patronage position in the local Republican machine. It was also part of a longer tradition in Atlanta of the "women's work" of home visitations to care for those who were sick, impoverished, or terminally ill.[54] At the 1898 Atlanta University conference, Minnie Wright Price urged those in attendance to visit their "poor neighbors" in order to "give them hope, courage and strength to toil on," as well as lessons on "purity, cleanliness and economy." Whether or not these poor neighbors welcomed such instruction, this imperative to care for the less fortunate held the potential to bring these women together across the class and status barriers that divided black Atlantans. As Price addressed the aversion of some women to check in on the strangers around them, she granted them permission to enter the lives of and homes of people much different than them. "[Do not] withhold yourself," she urged, "because they are a little lower on the social scale than you are, or if they are higher, you fear that they will think you are seeking their recognition. How much better off we would be if we would cease to draw these lines of caste and each of us as we climb the ladder reach down and assist a struggling sister!"[55] The Union built on this tradition, which granted these women the ability to work outside of the networks of male political solidarity (including its attendant conflicts and contestations). This allowed the Union to establish a more egalitarian space in which the payment of the poll tax or mastery over a household was not a prerequisite for political engagement. Focusing on the health and welfare of black children granted these women public authority as defenders of the household as much as men.[56] They used this power to redefine the terms of "mastery" over a household as well as who deserved political standing in the community.

This is clearly expressed through the choice for the Union's slogan of "Thy Neighbor as Thyself," a phrase taken from the tale of the Good Samaritan as told in Luke 10:25–37. This parable begins with the story of a man who had been assaulted by thieves, robbed, and left for dead on the road between Jerusalem and Jericho. A priest came upon him and passed by, refusing to answer his pleas for help. A Levite, whose role it was to assist the priests in the temple, also passed by, ignoring the plight of the wounded man. Finally, a lowly Samaritan came upon the injured man, bound up his wounds, took him to an inn, and paid for his room and board until he was well. What the women of the Union sought to convey with this slogan went far beyond a generic moral proscription to be kind to strangers. The significance of this story resides in the contrast between the behavior of the well-to-do religious travelers who were too busy, too important, or perhaps too scared to aid a stranger in distress and the actions of the Samaritan, who hailed from a people widely despised in ancient Israel. It was necessary to reach across the social gulf that separated rich from poor, the respectable from the morally suspect, in order to establish an effective safety net for black Atlantans. When the Union urged African Americans to love their neighbors as themselves, it challenged them to expand their notion of who their neighbors were. By adopting this parable, the Union was not asking black women to reach out to white people as their primary allies in reform, but rather to other black people. Rooted in Christian universalism and a growing race consciousness, this slogan suggested that equality among African Americans was a critical element in the struggle for equality between black and white Americans. This stood in stark contrast to the limited terms of political solidarity articulated and defined by earlier attempts to seek inclusion into the racially stratified Progressive state.

"To Develop Group Consciousness and Mass Movements"

While politically engaged black men were fighting one another over the meaning of black manhood in the wake of the Atlanta race riot, the black women who participated in the Gate City Kindergarten Association were taking steps to unite black Atlantans. The historian Anne Firor Scott has defined the work of black women's voluntary associations such as these in terms that effectively describe an alternate state-building project led by black women themselves. These women established "homes for the aged, for working women, and for unwed mothers; hospitals in towns where white hospitals refused admission to black patients; neighborhood clinics; employment services; kindergartens where there had been none for children of either race, along with training programs for kindergarten teachers; libraries; settlement houses; and so on and on."[57] At the nadir of African American history, when black southerners were rigidly excluded from the vast array of newly established civic rights, the work of the Union was crucial to black Atlantans. Viewed in these terms, the work of black women in securing health care, education, housing, and sanitation for their communities created a sort of volunteer welfare state nested within the racially exclusive whites-only Progressive Era state.[58]

To give a sense of the sort of activity that comprised this "grassroots welfare state," Louie Shivery's history of the Neighborhood Union is invaluable. Shivery, for many years the corresponding secretary of the Union, recorded its story in 1936 while a student of Du Bois at Atlanta University.[59] Her master's thesis gives a year by year account of the development of the Neighborhood Union from its roots in the kindergarten movement all the way through the New Deal. Much as Jane Addams and Florence Kelley had done in Chicago for the areas surrounding Hull House, the first project the Union undertook was an exhaustive survey of every household in the First Ward neighborhood surrounding Atlanta University.[60] According to Shivery, these surveys not only made visible the full extent of the crisis caused by racially stratified development, they also revealed "an astounding need for better and more highly integrated home life."[61] This latter observation echoed earlier reformers who had a tendency to blame the poor themselves—especially the instability of their families—for the conditions in which they found themselves. Although the Union echoed these critiques, the way it chose to address them refocused black reform efforts on the structural factors that undermined black "home life." This initial survey revealed that the failure to lead respectable lives was not just the result of flawed moral characters; it was also the result of the morally hazardous urban environment where most black Atlantans were forced to live: "unsanitary conditions, poor housing, lack of recreation" as well as "streets badly in need of improvement, insufficient lights . . . little or no sewerage facilities and [a] water supply consist[ing] mostly of surface wells." The Union concluded that "the municipal authorities of Atlanta had not assumed the responsibility for their citizens, not only Negroes but white as well."[62]

Of particular concern were the fates of the thousands of black women who migrated to Atlanta. In the first two decades of the twentieth century, the black population of the city nearly doubled as almost 30,000 black migrants moved from the countryside to call the Gate City home.[63] Though the city offered women profoundly greater opportunities than those available to them as sharecroppers, it also presented an array of dangers they did not face in the countryside. The relative lack of employment for black men in Atlanta drew black women as domestic workers into white homes of white men, where they risked sexual assault and rape at the hands of their male employers. Segregation displaced the environmental costs of rapid development onto black neighborhoods, compounding the impact of the diseases of urban poverty and overcrowding. The relative ease of access to consumer goods in the city presented its own dangers. With the cash wages that they rarely saw in the countryside, black women could just as easily purchase a new cotton dress as a bottle of corn liquor. In the eyes of Atlanta's female reform community, all of these presented grave dangers to the morality of black women and their families. The woman whose death sparked the founding of the Neighborhood Union may very well have been a recent migrant from the countryside who suddenly found herself separated from the extended network of kin and community that had once secured her against the uncertainties of life under Jim Crow.[64] One of the Union's primary goals was to ensure that these women did not fall to illness or moral depravity.

In order to effectively address the scope of this urban crisis facing black Atlantans, the Union had to build relationships with a broad segment of the city's black population, especially its women. To facilitate this, Union members ambitiously divided the entire city into zones, which were further divided into neighborhoods, overseen by a neighborhood president. Each neighborhood was further subdivided into several districts, under the responsibility of a director chosen from the ranks of "key women" identified during house-by-house surveys.[65] Besides carrying on the work of the Union at the most local level conceivable, the director's job was "to know everyone in the district, every child, and what to expect of every one and how to meet [their] problems."[66] The management of the Union's work would be in the hands of a board of directors comprising the director of each district of the city and a board of managers that consisted of the zone chairpersons and the presidents of each neighborhood.[67] And, at all levels, the membership elected these leaders. What the historian David Fort Godshalk calls the "microscopically local" orientation of the Union's organization made it incredibly attentive (for better or worse) to the lives of individual women.[68] At its most elaborate, this structure permitted the Union to reach 42,000 of Atlanta's 63,000 black residents in a matter of two or three days.[69] It enabled, in the words of Lugenia Burns Hope, the creation of a genuine community and not merely "a group of houses or families"—a community of "families knowing one another, assisting and ever loving one another."[70] Such an ambitious plan of organization guaranteed that the Neighborhood Union would have to be in some measure broadly representative of the interests of Atlanta's women, encouraging solidarity across the divides of class, religion, and faction that had long split the black community.

Fortunately, they did not have to build an organization from the ground up. Over the course of their initial surveys, the Union's canvassers unearthed a foundation that had already been laid by Atlanta's working-class black women. As domestic servants and washerwomen, they already possessed informal networks of solidarity rooted in the communal nature of much of their work. For decades prior to the arrival of the Neighborhood Union, they had organized mutual aid and benevolent associations to help them weather the uncertainties of low-wage urban life in the late nineteenth century.[71] As the Union incorporated these preexisting networks, domestic workers assumed key leadership positions within the organization, profoundly shaping its agenda.[72] This is evident in an early campaign to address the dismal state of the rental housing available to African Americans that arose out of the complaints of Atlanta's black washerwomen. With no laws regulating the construction or maintenance of rental housing for African Americans, the poorer sections of the West Side looked "as if they had been dropped out of an airplane." The haphazard construction of these dwellings often meant that outhouses were located much too close to the house, often with a door off the kitchen opening into a room containing what was effectively a pit toilet that bred "flies and germs . . . and sickness." These were the dismal working conditions of most washerwomen, who traditionally worked from home to avoid exposing themselves to the surveillance and sexual predation of their white employers. A common complaint was the prevalence of poorly constructed and seldom maintained chimneys. Improperly vented, the fires needed to heat water for washing clothes filled their work spaces with smoke, making some women seriously ill. Additionally, the clothes sometimes became "so smoked" that washerwomen often lost work because of it. As Hope described it, "poor people paid vastly more for the rest of their shanties than do the better class for better homes, yet the greed of the landlords . . . makes them slow to repair." According to Shivery, these grievances over their living and working conditions encouraged the Union to make "a big fight" to correct some of these evils, forcing landlords to repair these houses.[73]

Beyond specific campaigns, these working-class women had a profound impact on the entire perspective of the Neighborhood Union. As domestic servants traveled to work, or washerwomen picked up soiled laundry, they also crossed the line that separated underdeveloped black neighborhoods from the rest of the city, a commute that highlighted the contrast between their lives and those of their white employers. They daily faced the indignity of toiling to clean someone else's house and to feed and care for someone else's sons and daughters, while their own families survived without them. How must it have felt for one of these women to give the best hours of her days to maintaining the integrity of a white household, while her own waited until evening? How must it have struck her to see her white employers' children reading at a table lit by electricity and drinking a cold glass of water from the tap on a hot August day only to return that night to her cramped two-room house with no lights, no running water, and no access to city services? The Union's ongoing campaign to extend city services to black neighborhoods was rooted in precisely these sorts of experiences. From the women they sought to organize, Lugenia Burns Hope and the other elite women who founded the Neighborhood Union learned about the ways in which the city's development undermined the ability of black mothers to keep good homes. Their engagement with working-class women over the city's development helped them link the project of race uplift to the expansion of the range of civic rights available to black families.

As black neighborhoods in Atlanta were excluded from the expansion of basic city services, the Union mobilized black residents to voluntarily provide these services for themselves rather than wait for the city to extend development into black neighborhoods. Building upon the original mission of the Gate City Kindergarten Association, a good number of these programs revolved around the health and welfare of youth. Volunteers working with the Union offered vocational classes for high school–age boys and girls, who did not have access to a public high school. They also established boys and girls clubs to keep black teenagers off the streets and out of trouble and offered young mothers courses in nursing and home hygiene.[74] One of the Union's most important early efforts resulted in the establishment of a number of health clinics. Beginning in 1908, these clinics, staffed by volunteers, offered health classes that taught the basics of nutrition and hygiene, and, perhaps most important, the facts about tuberculosis (TB), a disease that had long ravaged poor communities around the world.[75] The volunteers at these clinics also conducted regular neighborhood surveys to track the spread of the disease. These surveys were so valuable in combating the spread of TB in Atlanta that the Red Cross built directly on the work with the Union in its antituberculosis campaign of 1914–17. Another example was the Union's annual Clean-Up Day. When the Union was founded, the black West Side neighborhood was where the city dumped the trash collected from the rest of the city. Beckwith Street, which now runs through the heart of Atlanta University, was so full of trash that it was impassible for both automobiles and horse-drawn wagons until 1914.[76] It had long been difficult to get the City Sanitation Department to remove trash and rubbish from the city's black neighborhoods. However, the burgeoning population of Atlanta had transformed these festering heaps of trash dotting the city into a looming health crisis. In response, the Union won the city's cooperation with its annual citywide Clean-Up Days by exploiting white fears of black disease. Each year, beginning in 1917, teams of volunteers would encourage black tenants and homeowners to remove the trash from their basements and backyards for removal by the city.[77]

While progress, these were not necessarily victories. After all, while the city readily provided these services to its white residents, the Union had to organize black Atlantans to take out their own garbage, saving the city the expense of providing trash collection in black neighborhoods. But if this is understood as part of a voluntarily organized grassroots welfare state, these activities take on a different meaning. A case in point is the Union's campaign to provide playgrounds and parks for black children. The campaign began when Union organizers sought locations to provide "wholesome recreation" for the "hundreds of children on the streets after school hours."[78] In September 1908, the Union was able to secure the use of the playground at Spelman College. As the scope of the organization expanded, the children served by the Union soon filled Spelman's playground as well as the homes and backyards of volunteers living nearby. Ultimately, the Union decided to appropriate vacant lots in the city, which it cleaned up and transformed into playgrounds, supervised by neighborhood women. To defend "helpless little children" against the vice, crime, and other evils of "sidewalk education," the women in the Union reclaimed blighted areas of the city and made them their own. Black children could be protected from the hazards and chaos of public space in turn-of-the-century Atlanta and given a domesticated space to play overseen by responsible black matrons.[79] The Union never asked permission to use these empty lots; it simply cleaned them up and took them over regardless of who actually owned the land. This spirit of direct action that moved the Union to appropriate privately owned urban space for supervised play areas spoke to a capacity to look beyond the limits of a politics constrained by the realities of Jim Crow.

However inspiring, direct action would remain insufficient to contest the racially discriminatory dynamic of Progressive Era development. The Union would have to challenge the marginalization of black Atlanta from the city's growing network of streetlights, sewers, paved roads, and public schools. Early protests against the exclusion of black people from Atlanta's urban development were nothing dramatic. Lacking any real political power, the Union was limited to petitioning the city council and the mayor, framing its requests in the language of respectability. In 1911, the Union used the pretext of a crime wave to press the city's Health and Sanitation Departments to not only address the lack of police protection available in black neighborhoods but also the dilapidated housing stock, the lack of paved streets, the prevalence of "surface toilets" (latrines) rather than sanitary indoor toilets connected to the city sewer system, and the lack of streetlights, parks, and schools. The Union argued that all of these conditions had fed the rash of murders, assaults, and burglaries that plagued Atlanta that summer.[80] Several years later, during World War I, the Union employed a similar strategy, appealing to the War Department to have arc lights installed on several streets in order to drive away "loungers and vicious people." This managed to bring streetlights to some black neighborhoods for the first time.[81] In making such requests, however, the Union transformed respectability into something much bigger than the common set of cultural beliefs and practices with which black reformers had both established common ground with white reformers and distanced themselves from the immorality of the black working class. By framing development in language that linked it to expanding the ability for the black working class to lead respectable lives, the Union began to transform respectability from an exclusionary marker of status to a human right to which every citizen of Atlanta was entitled regardless of race.

Much of the work the Neighborhood Union did in its first decade placed it squarely in the tradition of the settlement house movement; however, several factors distinguished the Neighborhood Union from most settlement houses serving black communities. Most significant, the Union, like the Gate City Kindergarten Association before it, was funded and controlled entirely by the city's black community.[82] From its inception, the Union's leadership decided that they would not "beg" for funding. Instead, they would raise the money through ten-cent monthly dues to be collected from a membership expansively defined as every person living in the neighborhood. In addition to the array of fund-raising activities (bake sales, track meets, baby contests) that had been used to sustain the Gate City kindergartens, they also organized classes in cooking and dressmaking for which the charge was also ten cents per lesson.[83] Because of the decision to rely on the economic resources of black Atlanta, it took until late 1912 to purchase a building for $1,200 to serve as the Union's first community center. The bulk of this money came either from the women served by the Union or through donations by the city's black businessmen. In the meantime, the Union used the private homes and the donated facilities of Atlanta Baptist College, Spelman, and Atlanta University to run its ever-expanding array of programs.[84] Being able to draw on the resources of Atlanta's black community granted the Union an autonomy that other social service organizations lacked.

Unlike the Neighborhood Union, many other social service organizations and settlement houses located in black neighborhoods were supported

FIGURE 3. Photo of Neighborhood Union house. (Neighborhood Union Collection, Box 14, Folder 48, Robert W. Woodruff Library, Atlanta University Center)

in part or whole by white philanthropy. The wide array of programs offered through Rev. Henry Hugh Proctor's First Congregational Church seemed to duplicate much of the work of the Neighborhood Union; however, domestic workers would never have the voice in his organization that they would with the Union. Founded by white missionaries affiliated with Yale University just after the Civil War, Proctor's church had long served as a site for demonstrating the respectability of its elite black parishioners. Following the riot, it had been one of the key institutions through which conservative black elites like Proctor attempted to revive the tenuous alliance with the city's white elite. As a result, Proctor became the beneficiary of a good deal of white largesse. Contributors to First Congregational included Hoke Smith, John Temple Graves, and Clark Howell, all avowed white supremacists whose incendiary rhetoric had helped spark the 1906 conflagration. On the strength of introductions given him by Booker T. Washington, Proctor convinced white philanthropists to fund a kindergarten, cooking and sewing classes for young women, public baths, a library, a gymnasium, and an employment bureau. By 1918, some 30,000 black Atlantans were taking advantage of the programs offered through First Congregational.[85] Though delivering crucial social services that the city refused to provide to its black citizens, the imperative to maintain working relationships with the white supremacist city fathers made it impossible for Proctor to speak out more forthrightly against racial injustice. By contrast, the Neighborhood Union, in relying on the support of thousands of small donors, was able to maintain a degree of independence.[86]

Another factor distinguishing the Neighborhood Union from other settlement houses was that it viewed its work as equal parts race uplift and racial self-defense. Continuing the work begun by Atlanta's kindergarten movement, the Union's women were not simply rescuing the downtrodden; they were securing the destiny of "future citizens" of the race. When Lugenia Burns Hope helped found the Gate City Kindergarten Association in 1905, she did so out of concern both for the health and welfare of her neighbors' children as well as for her own two sons.[87] Traditionally, most white settlement house workers were born into relatively comfortable circumstances and made the choice to leave their middle-class neighborhoods to make their homes among those whom they sought to uplift.[88] In an 1892 speech before the New York Ethical Society, Jane Addams herself described settlement houses as a means for "educated young people seeking an outlet for [the] sentiment of universal brotherhood."[89] By moving into a settlement house, they came into contact with the "other half" of humanity from which they had been separated by the yawning chasm of class in the late nineteenth century. By contrast, Lugenia Burns Hope and the other women of the Neighborhood Union opened their own homes to the reform movement they led. Housing segregation meant that most black settlement house workers already lived in the very midst of the poverty, vice, and disease they sought to correct, or at least down the street from it. The women of the Union—elite, working class, and poor alike—acted in defense of themselves and their own neighborhoods.

At its founding, with roots in the Gate City Kindergarten Association, the Neighborhood Union had sometimes used the language of charity to describe its work, especially when fund-raising.[90] However, within the space of a few years, it had evolved into something far more than a charitable organization. Though the official charter filed with the state of Georgia strategically omitted it, the draft of the charter in the Union's files explicitly aimed "to develop group consciousness and mass movements."[91] Despite their adoption of the often conservative language of race uplift, the women of the Neighborhood Union had begun consciously, if not publicly, to organize a black public sphere alongside and in opposition to the racially stratified Progressive state. As this grassroots welfare state expanded, the Union's organizers began to conceive of themselves as the leaders of a "mass movement" that went beyond the boundaries of individual neighborhoods to encompass the entire city. Echoing the aspirations of Frances Willard, who in 1891 described a "Republic of Women," the mission of which would be to revitalize American society, Lugenia Burns Hope saw the Union as a model for the transformation of black urban life.[92] Her dream was the utopia that stood opposed to the white supremacist vision of progress that sought to relegate African Americans to the ragged margins of civilization and the mudsill of society.

The kernel of this utopia must have been in the minds of the elite black women attending the 1897 Atlanta University conference, who encouraged each other to reach across class lines within the black community as they initiated their campaign of "social reconstruction and moral regeneration." To build an organization that incorporated the *entire* black community, it was necessary to reach out to non-elite black women as partners in reform and find leaders among women of all class backgrounds. As a result, the organizing work of the Union subverted earlier strategies that relied upon the leadership of black elites, most famously Du Bois's call for the development of a "talented tenth" of race leaders. In order to reach every black household in Atlanta, one of the main goals of the Union's periodic surveys was to identify "key women" in each neighborhood.[93] These were women who enjoyed the trust and commanded the respect of their neighbors. Among these key leaders were at least five domestic workers who took relatively important leadership positions in the organization, including Laura Bugg, one of the original nine women who attended the Union's first meeting in Hope's home in 1908. Hattie Barnett, another domestic worker, became a vice president in 1913 and served on the board of directors, as did Maggie F. Williams, Mary Brawner, and Ella N. Crawford, who were also cooks, washerwomen, or domestic servants.[94] The Union's ambitious agenda required it to involve these "key women" in the operation of the organization. Rather than simply remaining objects of charity, these working-class black women had to become equal partners in reform. This in itself would come to form a basis for the renegotiation of the relationship between the black elite and the black working class that had long bedeviled black attempts to resist disfranchisement and segregation.

This inclusivity was built into the initial constitution of the Union, which encouraged the members of the organization to "become acquainted with one another and to improve the neighborhood in every way possible."[95] No other specialized credentials were necessary. Casting such a wide net brought women from all walks of life into the Union and allowed the organization to serve as a site for uniting black Atlantans across class lines. This search for key leaders was both systematic and selective and could even exclude those who would formerly have been treated with deference on account of their status, rank, and position. In her history of the Neighborhood Union, Louie Shivery recounted the story of a Union organizer who in 1911 interviewed a preacher in West End. Upon discovering "he had no influence in his community at all," the organizer decided the Union did not need his services and chose not to reveal to the good clergyman the real purpose of her visit.[96] The organizer was seeking people capable of actually leading and not just acting as exemplars of respectability; despite his title, this preacher was no leader.

Lugenia Burns Hope and the other women involved in the Union did not understand the objects of their charity as belonging to a community other than their own. The stakes were simply too high. To neglect the education and moral development of black families and their children would be to write off the entire future of the race. They offered neither a hand-out nor even a hand up. Instead, they attempted to forge a real solidarity. It was precisely this notion of a shared fate that transformed respectability from a marker of status and difference to a basic right and allowed the Union to view itself as a "mass movement."

"To Organize and Purify"

Despite their inclusivity, there were decided limits to the democratic vision of the Neighborhood Union organizers. Compelled to include those they found "unworthy," the Union took pains to uplift them. Should they resist— as they often did—the Union did not hesitate to expel these resisters from the community. As one organizer put it, "the express purpose of the N.U. is to organize + *purify* communities [so] that the children of all classes may have a chance."[97] Although acknowledging that the lack of access to city services was holding black Atlanta back, the Union still emphasized the moral impurity of black communities as an obstacle to black progress. To "purify" their neighborhoods, the Union established an Investigating Committee, which was responsible for monitoring each household, and reporting on "everything that seem[ed] to be a menace to [the] neighborhood."[98] After a visit by members of the committee, those deemed "immoral" were encouraged to get right with God and, more immediately, to get right with the Union. Those households considered to be incorrigible were asked to leave, and if they refused, they were evicted from the neighborhood with the assistance of the city police.

This activity reached an early peak in the wake of the crime wave of 1911. Anxious that allegations of black criminality would reignite the fires of 1906 and undo all of the progress it had achieved since then, the Union "launched a campaign against vice so drastic that no limit was untried to rid the community of crime, undesirable families and individuals, dens of vice and deterrence to the moral welfare of the community."[99] During that year, the Investigating Committee discovered a father who had sexually assaulted his own daughter, and brought him into court to face rape charges. Less heinous transgressions also fell under the purview of the committee. In February 1911, Hattie Barnett was able to get two families to leave her district "who indulged in doing things that were immoral such as breaking the Sabbath and gambling."[100] This eviction of "immoral" families became so common that the Union found it useful to develop a standardized form for submitting the names of such troublemakers to the police.[101] One of the prime reasons for the Union's aggressive vigilance was to control the kinds of negative attention black neighborhoods often attracted.

The activities of the Investigating Committee were part of the Union's attempt to interpose itself between the black neighborhoods under its protection and the often brutal and arbitrary actions of the city police force. In the decade prior to the 1906 riot, some 150,000 arrests were made by the Atlanta police, and, despite representing less than 40 percent of the population, about 53 percent (80,000) of these arrests were of African Americans. The overwhelming majority of these were men between fifteen and thirty years old, seized by the police for disorderly conduct, drunkenness, idling, and the nebulous category of "suspicious activity." While most arrests resulted in fines rather than jail time, it was not uncommon for unemployed black men to be arrested for vagrancy, incarcerated, and then sold into the convict-lease system.[102] Alongside the Union, other black elites also attempted to serve as a buffer between the police and working-class black neighborhoods. Established black churches, organizations like the Colored Co-operative League, and the black members of the postriot Atlanta Civic League all encouraged working-class black Atlantans to bring any legal issue to them before going to the police. The Neighborhood Union also sometimes intervened on behalf of black men and women who had received unjust treatment from the courts. In 1913, following the Union's intervention, one convict won a release from jail while another received a shorter sentence.[103] According to the historian Allison Dorsey, these sorts of advocacy allowed the city's black elite to limit the exposure of black neighborhoods to the power of the courts and police.[104] It also limited violent altercations between black communities and the police should black people choose to confront the police physically as sometimes happened when officers attempted to make an arrest.[105] Standing between working-class African Americans and the police, respectable black elites sought to avert another riot.

The Neighborhood Union's Investigating Committee, however, took this one step further. The committee sought to use the police to impose respectability upon a frequently unwilling populace in order to disprove the racist allegation that African Americans were retrogressing toward barbarism and had no place in the modern city. However, in policing the transgressions of the black community themselves, they also sought to wrest this power away from the city's police and courts, taking for themselves the power to name the causes and solutions of perceived black immorality. If the Union could explain crime and backwardness in the black community as the responsibility of a few deviants, it became possible to define these phenomena as something other than permanent racial traits. Thus, the Investigating Committee members positioned themselves as mediators between the police and the black community and used that position to enforce the committee's moral agenda. This is why their targets were not only criminals but also vagrants, gamblers, drinkers, immoral women, and other people they deemed hazardous to the black community's morals and reputation. This was evident in a two-year campaign that succeeded by 1912 in driving a Sanctified Church from Atlanta's West Side neighborhood as a "nuisance" on grounds of "disorderly conduct."[106] The emotional, ecstatic, and frequently loud worship of these "Holy Rollers" did not comport with the ideal of respectability and the race uplift strategy put forward by the Union. Distancing themselves from religious traditions, such as the "ring shout" and other "heathen" practices that had their roots in slavery, most black elites embraced a restrained style of worship in which the congregation silently absorbed the lessons of the weekly sermon. A good number of the city's black elite—among them several active in the Neighborhood Union—were members of Henry Hugh Proctor's First Congregational Church, the only one of Atlanta's major churches that prided itself on *not* having its roots in black religious traditions inherited from slavery. By contrast, the vast majority of working-class black Atlantans belonged to the relatively exuberant Baptist congregations, rejecting the notion that black Christians ought to worship like "white folks."[107]

The Neighborhood Union's moral uplift campaign encouraged the repression of certain expressions and articulations of working-class culture deemed immoral or unrespectable. From the very first door-to-door canvass, the Union members targeted sites of perfectly legal working-class entertainment such as dance halls and saloons that they believed put young people—especially girls—at risk of falling in with bad company.[108] As a result, the Investigating Committee was not always welcome in the communities they sought to "purify." Following the opening of a community center on Leonard Street in 1915, the building was vandalized by local toughs who apparently resented being uplifted.[109] And some women, despite being "worthy," refused to join the Union or cooperate with its efforts. It is also clear that its efforts to eliminate immorality from Atlanta's black neighborhoods did not eradicate cultural practices deemed antithetical to the Union's civilizing mission. Those driven from one neighborhood by the efforts of the Union could easily relocate their activities to another part of the city.[110]

By linking urban development with moral development, the Union reinforced Victorian norms of respectability and attempted to suppress some working-class articulations of early twentieth-century black urban culture. Through cooperating with the repressive arm of city government, the Union sought to bring police protection to the city's black neighborhoods in ways that were sensitive to the needs of the community. At the same time, the Union was in effect "borrowing" the police power of the state to help enforce its vision of the communities' needs.[111] Even though the police enforced Jim Crow, the Union's Investigating Committee was still willing to use its coercive power to assist the Union's moral surveillance of black Atlantans. This can be understood as a *nested hegemony*. That is, the Union collaborated with and contested the broader Jim Crow social and political order in order to advance its own race-building agenda. This nested hegemony was fully in place by 1911, when the city handed over all of its welfare activity among black Atlantans to the Union.[112] It was also manifest in the cooperation between the Union and the police. By 1916, members of the Union reported that "the police department has backed us when we have called on them. They say they are glad to assist us in our efforts to have a clean community."[113] Through this relationship with the city's welfare and law enforcement authorities, Union members were able to influence the terms on which the black community would be policed and thus avert another riot. While this strategy emerged from deeply held beliefs about racial progress and respectability, it also stemmed from their relative powerlessness in relation to the real sources of power within Atlanta. In order for the grassroots welfare state they envisioned to succeed, they needed to simultaneously share and contest the power of the white city leaders. So long as this granted them at least a limited measure of influence over the city's development agenda, the Union would not directly challenge the exclusion of African Americans from the full benefits of citizenship.

The organizing work undertaken by Hope and others was no value-free campaign for access to city services. Rather, the Neighborhood Union sought to use these city services to augment a social and cultural agenda of race uplift. In so doing, it positioned itself as a mediator between the goods and services provided by a rapidly expanding metropolis, while at the same time using its position to enforce and reinforce a particular constellation of gender and class identities. This mediator/enforcer activity defined black citizenship by providing a path, however limited, to inclusion in the Progressive Era state-building project, while at the same time defining the "unrespectable" out of the magic circle of citizenship. To do so, the Union's leaders employed all the strategies of the politics of respectability discussed in previous chapters. This included seeking to build an alliance for reform with like-minded white elites, grounding their requests for infrastructural improvements and city services in their shared practice of Victorian morality, and agreeing to police the morals of the black working class. The language they used to describe this program drew heavily on the discourses of respectability evident in Davis's, White's, and Turner's earlier derogatory language about the black working class in the face of disfranchisement. Nonetheless, the Union's early work laid the groundwork for an unprecedented level of unity among Atlanta's black residents. They would not draw on this unity to challenge the broader political and economic power structure of the city until their ability to mediate between the development agenda of Atlanta and the needs of its black residents began to wane after the city's fiscal crisis in 1913.

"Yeoman" to "Citizen"

The Neighborhood Union's work provided an alternate source for the meanings of gender, class, and race that could potentially form the basis for a new understanding of black solidarity. The semiautonomous black institutions it established created a notion of citizenship far more inclusive than the one possible within the bounds of the "whites-only" Progressive state. The Union rejected the strategy of seeking black inclusion as second-class citizens within a Jim Crow social and political order, distinguishing themselves from the backers of both the 1895 Atlanta Compromise and the signatories of the 1899 Hardwick memorial. Rather, these women defined, defended, and expanded a black public sphere in which black citizens could be more equal to each other than was possible between black and white citizens in the Jim Crow state. Even as they continued to wrestle with the cultural and social divisions caused by the discourse of respectability, they were able to avoid the internecine battles over the meaning of black manhood that had occurred in the face of disfranchisement.

Part of the reason they were able to do so was because the women in the Union understood citizenship in collective rather than individual terms. The men who led the GERC were so focused on "qualifying" for the ballot that their political discourse was centered on individuals' particular virtues and vices. By contrast, the women of the Neighborhood Union and the Gate City Kindergarten Association had come to understand citizenship in broader terms than the ballot—as a set of "civic rights" rooted in access to public infrastructure and city services. This allowed them easier access to a collective understanding of citizenship, based in the neighborhood and not just the individual household.[114] While this by no means signaled the Union's abandonment of respectability, the linkage between the material condition of black life and the ability of black people to lead respectable lives set the Union and the city on a collision course. Ultimately, this would radicalize the politics of respectability and transform the dynamics of Progressive Era urban development in Atlanta.

The ambition of the Union to unite all black Atlantans was apparent not only in its organizing plan and its 1911 charter, which promised to encourage "mass movements," but also in its original 1908 constitution, which extended membership to "any worthy family" residing within the territory covered by the Union's activities. This radically inclusive commitment was particularly evident in a 1909 speech given by Lugenia Burns Hope during a fund-raising drive for the establishment of the Union's first neighborhood center. While the main thrust of Hope's speech was her criticism of the city fathers for failing to extend adequate water services, lighting, police protection, and paved roads to the city's black neighborhoods, she also directed a significant portion of her speech to the city's black elite. She urged these prosperous black citizens to "become better acquainted with the conditions of the poor and vicious" and to recognize their "struggle . . . to preserve their independence and self[-]respect." The fact that most working-class black families were unable to organize their family life along Victorian lines did not mean they had no desire to lead respectable lives. Hope asked her audience to recognize that the black yeoman ideal that had once been held out as a model by the GERC was impractical for the vast majority of black Atlantans. She focused instead on the conditions that made it more difficult for black families to lead respectable lives rather than simply blaming the "unrespectable" for keeping the race down. In doing so, Hope shifted the object of black uplift work from the "poor and vicious" to the discrimination at the heart of Progressive Era urban development. This shift, combined with the recognition of the struggles of the black working class, paved the way for a real cross-class black alliance that could "seek to better and improve the conditions of all."[115]

In asking her audience to build an alliance with the "poor and vicious," Hope also subtly shifted the terms of intraracial political solidarity, unsettling the category of the black yeomanry and articulating a newer category of black citizenship. African Americans had contended for *citizenship* rights since before the end of slavery, but the idea of who ought to receive these rights had long been constrained by a notion of a prototypically male "black yeomanry" capable of protecting and providing for a household and the dependents therein. Although black leaders like Frederick Douglass and Bishop Henry McNeal Turner had been advocates for woman suffrage since the Civil War, it was not until large numbers of black women began to establish women's clubs, kindergartens and day nurseries, church auxiliaries, and other institutions in the black community that the gender ideology behind the "black yeomanry" began to change.[116] From the 1880s to the 1920s, this work subtly shifted the ideological basis of political standing from the possession of "yeoman" status to a more modern understanding of "citizenship." While unable to assert equal standing as citizens within the broader Progressive Era state-building project, black women were able to do so within this semiautonomous black state-building project that they themselves led. This grassroots welfare state built by the women of both the Neighborhood Union and the earlier Gate City Kindergarten Association helped black Georgians constitute themselves as a "black citizenry," providing a basis for black political unity that transcended the limits of the patriarchal yeoman household.

This was explicitly evident in the ways in which at least one of its organizers conceived of the work of the Neighborhood Union, as seen in her 1920 notebook, which has been preserved in the Neighborhood Union Collection at Atlanta University. The notebook was divided into lessons, and from the context provided by the notes toward the back, it is clear that this belonged to someone responsible for training new community organizers. The first lesson centered on the importance of the "fusion of individualities in one common *whole,* so that we forget self and think only of the purpose of the group."[117] The role of the organizer was not merely to create a community of interest but rather to help identify and forge new forms of deliberately chosen solidarity among strangers. In the rest of the notebook, the organizer spent a great deal of time navigating the potentially creative and sometimes destructive tension between the family (one of the most basic forms of solidarity) and the community or neighborhood (a basis for solidarity, which, given the upheavals of rapid urbanization and development, must have seemed almost as accidental as the arrangement of homes on the black West Side that looked as though "they had been dropped from an airplane").

In her lessons, the organizer contrasted a mythic primeval unity in which "savage tribes lived in communities [and] did not jump from one place to another," against modern forces of division. These modern forces are listed as "religion, industry, government [or the state], school," and, perhaps most surprisingly, "family"—all of which had the potential to "divide the community." The contemporary black family, which had been disorganized by migration, urbanization, and Jim Crow, left women and children with little recourse in the face of abuse or neglect, an analysis that was consonant with the Neighborhood Union's founding myth. Even though the women of the Union may have desired and called for the patriarchal protections of the family, they were also keenly aware of the limitations that "family" imposed on black women. The answer to this crisis was to organize these families into a *community* and not "simply a group of houses or . . . families."[118] While certainly not antipatriarchal, the message was clear: an organized community was imperative for black family survival—even if it meant overriding the prerogatives of a black yeomanry. The Union understood the tensions between older forms of organizing black solidarity via individual, often patriarchal families and a collective understanding of black community life. Rather than drawing on established sources of cultural and political authority (class status, patriarchal families, or alliances with white elites), these women created through their own community organizing efforts a new foundation of social power that could contest and displace older forms— even though it was constructed from the same discursive building blocks.

As the dislocations of Progressive Era urban development unsettled the notion of a "black yeomanry," the Neighborhood Union provided an alternate understanding of the gendered basis of black political mobilization. The understandings of gender and class held by the women of the Neighborhood Union were different than those held by men like Ben Davis or those who had led the now defunct GERC. As white southern progressives built a more rational and humane state for white citizens at the expense of black ones, the Union's women were forced to engage directly with the power of the state in the defense of their households. By reframing respectability as a community goal for which every family was responsible and which the progressive state was obliged to support, respectability became a *unifying dis-*

course rather than a *stratifying discourse.*[119] As a result, the notion of gender they helped articulate through their organizing efforts assisted the mobilization of black *citizens* rather than merely a black *yeomanry* dominated by respectable middle-class black men. This notion of a black citizenry made it easier for black women to make direct claims on the state, especially when acting in defense of the integrity of the household and the morality of black boys and girls.

The Neighborhood Union, excluded by the dual disfranchisement of black women throughout most of the Progressive Era, was also at least partially excluded from the gender system of formal electoral politics. Though the membership of the Union certainly did not exist entirely outside this gender system, their relative distance from it allowed them the flexibility to avoid the conflicts over manhood that had crippled the ability of both the GERC and the Republican Party to serve as vehicles for the defense and expansion of black civil rights. Furthermore, the Union's grassroots welfare state allowed it to change the rules that granted political standing only to men, black or white, who exerted mastery over their households. One did not have to pay poll taxes or vote in order to support a kindergarten or a neighborhood health initiative. Black women could wield political power in an alternate gender system that existed outside the rules of "normal" politics, which ordinarily required people to be able to "qualify for the vote" before they had any say in how the world was run. Through their grassroots organizing and uplift work, the women in the Union demonstrated that respectability was not always premised on the accumulation of wealth or power. Even the poorest families could lead respectable lives if given access to the benefits of clean water, decent housing, and—most important—public education. In effect, the Union used this understanding of respectability to articulate an alternate black political sphere that could potentially unite rather than divide black Atlanta. And the campaign that would unite them would be the fight for equal access for free public education.

The 1913 School Survey and the Radicalization of the Neighborhood Union

Adequate public schools for Atlanta's black students had long been a desperate need. Those schools that did exist had either been established by northern missionaries during Reconstruction or had originally been built through African American efforts and later taken over by the city. The first two permanent schools for African Americans in the city, Storrs School and

the Summer Hill School, were established in 1867 by the American Missionary Association (AMA) and the Freedmen's Aid Bureau, respectively, and
the salaries of their teachers were paid through donations raised among the
black community. During Reconstruction, Georgia's elected black officials
took the lead in instituting taxpayer-supported public education throughout
the state. James Porter, a black member of the state legislature, introduced
the 1870 legislation that authorized cities, counties, and other municipalities
to establish public schools. Two years later, a campaign led by the two black
members of the city council resulted in the establishment of the Atlanta
Board of Education and the passage of a $100,000 bond. This bond, over-
whelmingly supported by the city's black voters, established Atlanta's public
school system, including seven new schools for white students and incorporating Storrs and Summer Hill to serve the city's black population (roughly
45 percent of the city).[120]

This outcome established two patterns that would be repeated well into
twentieth century. First, the city was willing to provide funding for black
public schools so long as it could be done cheaply. Often the city did not have
to provide the buildings, but would instead subsidize the pay of teachers and
administrators who worked in facilities owned by the city's black churches
or organizations like the AMA.[121] This was an arrangement that held
throughout the South as black communities were forced to build the schools
that local governments would provide to white communities at taxpayer expense.[122] Compounding these inequities, Atlanta's black public schoolteachers earned $200 less per year than did their white counterparts.[123] Most of
these schools were utterly dilapidated and located on marginal land. One
was even nestled between the city stockade, a slaughterhouse, and a pest
house.[124] As a result of this chronic underfunding, throughout the 1880s
only 43 percent of the city's school-age black population attended school
as compared to 74 percent for white school-age Atlantans. By 1890, there
were only four public schools for black students, but twelve for white students.[125] Ten years later, the tally was five and fifteen, respectively, and by
1903 there were twenty schools for 14,465 white students and still just five for
8,118 black students.[126] As late as 1913, only half of Atlanta's black children
had schools to attend.[127] Second, by the twentieth century, in response to
the rapid growth of the city's population, black Atlantans would periodically
push for the expansion of the public school system. The city—unwilling to
raise taxes—would respond by proposing a school bond referendum to fund
this expansion. In exchange for the promise of new black schools, Atlanta's
black voters would invariably provide a significant proportion of the margin

of victory. However, following the sale of these bonds, the bulk of the money raised would be spent on the construction and maintenance of schools for white students with little to nothing going toward the education of the black community. In 1903, black voters went to the polls to provide the winning margin in support of a $400,000 bond referendum, most of which went to fund the construction of five new schools for the city's white students.[128] Seven years later, in 1910, only $38,200 of the funds from a $600,000 bond were dedicated to black public education.[129]

To pick up the slack, black women periodically ran small private schools out of their homes. Spartan and undersupplied, these grassroots educational initiatives were funded by monthly tuition payments ranging from fifty cents to a dollar.[130] Additionally, Atlanta's four black colleges assumed the burden of educating the city's black children, providing the instruction that the white city fathers would not. By 1910, Atlanta Baptist (Morehouse), Atlanta University, Morris Brown, and Spelman collectively enrolled 604 high school students and 1,111 grammar school students—a student body that dwarfed the city's entire black college cohort, comprising only 147 students.[131] Even though these institutions were heavily supported by northern white philanthropy, black tuition dollars comprised a significant portion of their revenues. Between 1898 and 1907, the tuition paid to these four institutions totaled more than $210,000, a significant sum from a population whose financial security was so tenuous.[132] However reasonable they may have been, these tuition payments made education inaccessible to most working-class African Americans. As Atlanta grew, it became less and less tenable for the city's black colleges to provide the desks that the city would not.

In 1913, the Neighborhood Union established the Women's Civil and Social Improvement Committee to "better the conditions of the Negro in the public schools in Atlanta."[133] The committee's first campaign was a comprehensive survey of the Atlanta public schools. According to Louie Shivery, this project marked the first time that the civic activities of the Union became truly citywide in scope, demonstrating to the city that the Union's efforts were not "spasmodic" but rather "permanent and relentless."[134] Though the number of black grammar schools had grown from five to eleven over the preceding decade, the six-month investigation still revealed critical shortages of classroom space, teaching materials, as well as qualified teachers.[135] In 1913 and 1914, the Union determined that while there were 6,163 black children enrolled in Atlanta's public schools, there were only 4,102 desks available. In order to accommodate all the students, about two-thirds of the black student population attended "double sessions," in which the same teacher daily taught two full classes—one in the morning and one in the evening.[136] The school buildings themselves were in wretched physical condition with poor lighting, sanitation, and playground facilities. In essence, the learning conditions of black students in Atlanta's public schools were a microcosm of the living conditions of black citizens in the city more generally. Just as black neighborhoods were denied sewers, paved sidewalks, and other improvements that black taxpayers had supported, so also were black parents barred from sending their children to quality public schools, despite the taxes they contributed to their construction and maintenance.[137] By 1913, black Atlantans' taxes had helped pay for thirty-eight grammar schools, two high schools, and five night schools, none of which were open to black students.[138]

The Union tabulated the results of its survey and, once again rehearsing the politics of respectability, presented them to "every influential white woman in the city that could be visited," seeking their assistance in the fight to improve school conditions for Atlanta's black and white children. The women of the Women's Civil and Social Improvement Committee met with the mayor and every member of the city council. With the assistance of the city's black and white clergy, they held several mass meetings and were able to get considerable press coverage of the condition of the city's schools. Finally, on 13 August 1913 the committee formally petitioned the Board of Education to address the deplorable state of the city's black public schools as well as to build two additional schools for black students. The text of the petition explicitly linked the desired improvements to the moral development of black children. The conditions of the bathrooms were not only unhealthful, but in two schools they were also "indecent and tend[ed] towards immorality," since only a wooden partition separated the boys' section from the girls' section. One of the biggest grievances outlined in the petition was the widespread use of double sessions. Besides harming the quality of the education these children received and putting the health of the teachers at risk, they also put children at moral risk from "sidewalk education." Children who could only attend a half-day of school were frequently on the streets until their parents returned from work. This, the committee members believed, enforced "idleness, and thereby promote[d] shiftlessness" in their children. Although the petitioners twice referred to themselves as "residents and tax-payers of . . . Atlanta," they did not emphasize equal access to quality public education as an entitlement of citizenship. The only place the word "citizen" appears in the text is toward the end in which the petition reassured the Board of Education that the "ultimate aim" of the petition was "to reduce crime, and to make of our children good citizens."[139] In its negotiations with the city's white elites, the Union, much like the GERC a few years earlier, still framed "citizenship" as something black people could earn through demonstrating respectability rather than as a set of rights they could unequivocally assert.

The Neighborhood Union's agitation sparked a citywide campaign for school reform. The *Atlanta Constitution* ran exposés on the condition of the public education system, warning at the beginning of the 1913 school year that a parsimonious city council was handicapping the city's ability to incorporate the record-breaking 26,000 students enrolled that year.[140] The paper decried the overcrowding and the "poverty of the facilities . . . such that 'instruction' degenerates into a burlesque." Even in the white schools, some classrooms held between eighty and ninety students, and the paper described the condition of the black schools as "barbarous."[141] By "barbarous," the editors of the *Constitution* were not only referring to the conditions under which black children were forced to learn, but—echoing the critique of the Neighborhood Union—they also feared the impact of these conditions on these children. They made this clear when they called for the amelioration of overcrowded conditions in black schools, contending that "the care of the negro. . . was a matter not for the philanthropic endeavor of the white people, but one sheerly of self-preservation, since the unfit negro is a menace to the white."[142] Despite the Union's damning revelations, James L. Key, one of the more influential members of the Board of Education, declared that school conditions were "not as bad as they have been painted," and actively lobbied against increased funding for the schools.[143] As a result, although the Board of Education requested $897,000 at the opening of the 1913 school year for the maintenance and expansion of the city school system, the city council only approved $513,000.[144] In response, with the support of the City Federation of Women's Clubs, the State Parent Teacher Association, and other civic organizations, school superintendent William Slaton urged the city to pass a school tax or a bond issue for the construction of four new schools for white students and one new south-side school for black children.[145]

Unfortunately, the additional money was not forthcoming. The city council had historically proven unwilling to raise the necessary funds for the construction of new schools in order to keep up with the growth of the student population. Ever since the first public school opened in 1872, Atlanta had been so resistant to the idea of publicly funded education that on several occasions even the city's white high schools faced closure.[146] So, on 24

October 1913, when the members of the city council finally acted, they did little more than release $5,000 in previously raised bond money left over from an earlier school construction project. This was to be put toward the construction of a small school for black students on a lot in South Atlanta donated by Clark University and the purchase of two lots for the construction of white schools.[147] On the same day of the city council's action, the Board of Education assembled a committee of twelve to formulate a secondary plan to address the needed expansions of the education system. A month later, this committee recommended the construction of eight new grammar schools and four new high schools for white students as well as five new grammar schools for black students. Though the Board of Education may have desired to embark on a somewhat more equitable dispensation of school funds, the political and fiscal constraints it faced compelled the board to perpetuate an earlier pattern of racially stratified development as it responded to the school crisis. In order to help pay for this, the committee once again urged a bond issue, but also recommended eliminating the literary course after the sixth grade for all black schools and replacing the seventh and eighth grades with vocational training.[148]

The Union's reaction was fierce. In an open letter to the *Atlanta Constitution,* the Women's Civil and Social Improvement Committee condemned the plan to eliminate the seventh and eighth grades for black children. Not only would such action damage black children "morally and economically," it was also "fundamentally undemocratic and unjust." Although they embedded their condemnation in an appeal "to the fair-minded citizens of Atlanta," this nonetheless marked a drastic shift in the Union's public language. As the city made preparations to expand the white school system, the Union demanded that "Negro public schools should be given *more* facilities rather than less. . . . [F]or Atlanta to limit the school facilities of the children of Negro citizens to . . . six grades, and to allow the children of white citizens a course of eight grades and a high school course at public expense, cannot in the 'opinion of mankind' be anything but unjust." Despite their visible ire at the board's decision, the Union's leadership still tried to contain this anger within the language and rituals of respectability, asserting that "we express the sentiments of the great majority of Negro citizens, and we cannot believe that our friends of the white race will think us unreasonable in our appeal." However, having reached the limits of what the politics of respectability were capable of, they grasped for another language through which to assert a right of equal access to public education. The open letter concluded that "the public schools are supported by the taxes of all the people and to confine the Negro population to a peculiar type of education against their will would evidently not be a fair deal and no fair-minded citizens wish to be a party to such discriminations."[149] They felt compelled to ground their "appeal" in their standing as *taxpaying citizens* rather than solely in their relationship with the better class of white Atlantans.

This response was remarkable for several reasons. First, they were willing to risk their carefully cultivated relationships with the city's white elite on behalf of public education for all black Atlantans. The children of both the black elite and the upwardly mobile members of the working class could easily have escaped the limitations of Atlanta's public schools by attending any one of the city's four black private schools. Indeed, they often framed their campaign over the condition of the black public schools as a way of enlisting the city government in support of their "civilizing" mission to the masses. The open letter protested the elimination of the literary course, arguing in part that doing so would make Atlanta's black population "even less morally and economically efficient than they are now."[150] Nevertheless, their moral uplift campaign forced them to begin building real bridges of solidarity with the city's black working class, obliging them to make real sacrifices on behalf of the entire black community of Atlanta. That they took a public stand in favor of public education and against the history of racially discriminatory urban development stands as compelling evidence of the strength of the cross-class alliance the Union had built in the five years since its founding. Also significant here was that, even though the Union had once called for the expansion of vocational training in the schools (and even organized to provide this), it also wanted to ensure that those black students who wanted to attend college could. The elimination of the seventh and eighth grades and the lack of a public high school for black students threatened to doom the majority of Atlanta's black youth to a servile position in the economy. The city's willingness to continue to provide any black public instruction whatsoever indicated that the deal worked out by the signatories of the 1899 Hardwick memorial still held—that African Americans would be guaranteed some place in civilization, even if only at the bottom. However, the women of the Union fought hard to ensure that African Americans in Atlanta could aspire to much more than being the black mudsill of white civilization, that they and their neighbors could become first-class citizens.

This assertion of their rights as citizens marked another shift in Atlanta's black political discourse. In 1899, when a group of leading black citizens presented a memorial to the state legislature in opposition to the Hardwick disfranchisement bill, they described public education as a gift "thankfully received [and] generously tendered." In 1913, the Neighborhood Union was demanding the equitable distribution of education funding as a just return on the investments made with their tax dollars and describing citizenship in terms of rights to be exercised rather than privileges to be won. Just as the Union's earlier work had begun to displace the "black yeomanry" with a "black citizenry," these "taxpaying citizens" had come to replace "worthy families" as the Union's constituency. Shorn of its moral baggage, this definition of citizenship meant that the Union could simply demand access to public goods and services in exchange for the tax dollars paid by black families.

The *Atlanta Constitution* chose not to publish the Union's open letter in full, and instead noted the women's protest on page nine of Friday's newspaper.[151] As a result, it is difficult to gauge the full impact of the protest. In the short term, the Union was only partially successful. The city did not impose a vocational curriculum, but as a cost-saving measure, it ultimately decided to eliminate the eighth grade for black grammar school students.[152] While the protest may have failed to influence the city council, it had a profound impact on the Union. Years later, the Union's corresponding secretary, Louie Shivery, recalled 1913 as a significant turning point for the organization. She opined that the "fierce controversy" surrounding the school "rather than harming the movement" was a "decided triumph for the Negroes."[153] After completing its school survey, the Union relied upon the hope that by simply revealing the facts to their supposed white allies, the Union's leaders would be able to count on the politics of respectability to make reform happen. Just the opposite happened: the city used the Union's work as a pretext for cutting funding to the black schools. The politics of respectability, born of a position of relative powerlessness, had limited the political and strategic imagination of black Atlantans. After spending five years uniting a significant portion of black Atlanta behind an agenda of respectability, the Union was now suddenly unable to use its position to mediate between the power of the city's white leadership and the black community. This had the effect of mobilizing and reinforcing the racial solidarity that the Union had assiduously developed through its organizing efforts. As this spirit grew, it allowed the articulation of gender identities outside those bounded by the tactics of accommodation or an earlier politics of respectability. Coincident with this shift from yeomanry to citizenship, respectability became less a theory of interracial political solidarity and more an explicit goal for all black people.

This allowed the reconstitution of the politics of respectability on different (and much more autonomous) grounds—one presaged on a more explicitly contentious relationship with the state. The failure of the 1913 campaign for black schools made these limitations evident and ultimately forced the Union on the path toward the articulation of a more confrontational strategy in pursuit of first-class citizenship for all black Atlantans.

4

"Close Ranks"

World War I as a Crucible
for Black Solidarity, 1913–1919

In 1917, the Neighborhood Union would recall its bittersweet victory as it fought off another attack on black public education. That year, facing unprecedented growth in the size of Atlanta's school-age population, the city abruptly announced that it would abolish the seventh grade in the city's thirteen black grammar schools in order to pay for the construction of a new junior high school for white students.[1] Since the Neighborhood Union had launched its first campaign to improve the city's black public schools, the number of students enrolled had steadily grown, placing impossible demands on an already underfunded school system. At the beginning of the 1917–18 school year, 30,000 students enrolled in classes—up from 26,000 in 1913, an increase of 15 percent.[2] However, the city once again proved unwilling to fund public education. The resulting budget shortfall led to considerable tension between the Board of Education and the city council, which held the purse strings.[3] During the 1917–18 school year, Atlanta spent a paltry $31.45 per pupil, ranking last among the nation's major cities; by contrast, the national average was $56.60, nearly twice that amount. Although the total budget for the school year had risen to $905,000, this sum was still only $7,000 more than the minimum deemed necessary by the Board of Education during the last budget crisis four years earlier.[4] Without the money to provide classrooms, books, and teachers for all of Atlanta's school-age children, the city opted instead to cut support for black education in order to accommodate the city's rapidly expanding white student body.

No longer pulling any punches, the *Atlanta Independent* condemned this move as a plan "to keep one half of the people intelligent and the other half ignorant." The paper's editors reasoned that since "the Negroes are taxpayers and citizens of Atlanta in common with the white people," they "ought not to stand silently by and allow this wrong to be perpetrated."[5] This was a far cry from the paper's previous editorial position in which its editor, Ben Davis, asserted that rights had to be earned by "the individual as he rises in the estimation of his neighbors and becomes useful and helpful in the community where he lives."[6] The esteem of white neighbors rooted in the shared cultural practice of respectability now seemed to matter much less than establishing standing as taxpaying citizens, an identity shared by all adult Atlantans regardless of race. Davis used this new attack on the black seventh grade as a pretext to

> demand as citizens, as taxpayers, as men and women, not only the return of the eighth grade, but a High School for our boys and girls. . . . We are tired of paying taxes for white boys and girls to have High Schools, Junior Schools, Technical Schools, and every other kind of school, [while] our children grope in ignorance. There is no need of parleying, no need of yes-sir, boss with hat in hand. . . . [We will] stand upon our rights . . . and ask that we be given what the law provides for us.[7]

This transformation in the language Davis used to describe African Americans' claims on the benefits of citizenship was nothing short of remarkable, representing a seismic shift in the broader social and cultural world in which he formed and articulated his opinions.

By 1917, Davis's earlier commitments to the politics of respectability had been eroded by the twin forces of rapid urbanization and America's impending entry into World War I. Urbanization had given Davis a language that permitted him to insist that black men and women were entitled to the enjoyment of their civic rights in proportion to their contribution as law-abiding taxpayers. As the substantive benefits of citizenship expanded for white Americans at the expense of black Americans, the city's black leadership increasingly used this language to vocalize their opposition to the second-class status reserved for black Atlantans. Building upon the framework laid by the Neighborhood Union over the previous decade, they simply claimed their rights to the public schools, garbage collection, and other fruits of urban development as benefits they had paid for with their taxes. Davis's strong words also challenged the connection between citizenship and mastery over a household and its dependents. The fight to preserve the seventh grade announced the emergence a more modern notion of citizenship—one that displaced the archaic prerogatives held by the "yeomanry" and privileged the claims of individual tax-paying citizens on the largesse of the state. This provided a new framework for black political solidarity that challenged the limits imposed by an older politics of respectability.

Also crucial in creating the space for Davis's newly militant language was the impact of World War I, the preparations for which provided black men a means through which to reenter political life after disfranchisement had decimated the black electorate. This path was articulated most famously by W. E. B. Du Bois in his July 1918 editorial "Close Ranks," published in the *Crisis*. Du Bois argued that German militarism "spells death to the aspirations of Negroes and all darker races for equality, freedom and democracy," and urged his black readers to forget for the duration of the war "our special grievances and close our ranks shoulder to shoulder with our white fellow citizens."[8] This call for patriotic unity was controversial, especially among those who balked at setting aside "special grievances" in order to serve in a Jim Crow army and defend a Jim Crow nation.[9] Nonetheless, the language of military service would soon dovetail with language that described access to public goods and services as an entitlement due to law-abiding, patriotic black taxpayers. Du Bois later asserted that the overseas service of African American men was a "deposit in the bank towards full citizenship."[10] Following the war, African American men could be expected to make their withdrawals.

This linkage between the language of patriotic service and the language of simple economic exchange also demonstrated a significant shift in the understanding of black Americans' relationship to the state. World War I made it possible to articulate claims on first-class citizenship that were less burdened by the moral baggage of respectability. Expressions of patriotic loyalty and military service had made available to the respectable black men of Atlanta a new repertoire of manly behavior. As a soldier writing to Du Bois from the front in 1918 put it, black soldiers would "make the world safe for democracy and America especially by being men in the truest sense of the word compelling a reluctant recognition from both friend and foe."[11] Likewise, black women used the war to establish a new framework for the assertion of their demands that was less constrained by the cultural limits imposed by the politics of respectability. In the midst of the war, the Neighborhood Union described this newly assertive women's politics in an open letter "to the President, the Cabinet, the Congress of the United States, the Governors and the Legislatures of the Several States of the United States of America." Openly expressing their "cumulative intolerance" for Jim Crow, the women in the Union set aside the constraints of respectability and promised to "exert our righteous efforts until not only every eligible black man but every black woman shall be wielding the ballot proudly in defense of our liberties and our homes. . . . We are loyal and will remain so, but we are not blind. . . . What think you will be the effect on the morale of black men in the trenches when they reflect that they are fighting on foreign fields in behalf of their nation for the very rights and privileges which they themselves are denied at home?"[12] Finally, wartime nationalism made the terms of black solidarity considerably more expansive. Through valor and service, those formerly deemed "unrespectable" could establish common ground with both white Atlantans and respectable black elites. This was especially true for those who served in the armed forces. Samuel Blount, upon arrival at Camp Upton, was astounded at the broad diversity of the hundreds of black men he encountered: "Heavens! what a collection and assortment of men . . . rogues, 'pimps,' cut-throats, longshoremen, hod carriers, tramps, thieves, students, professional men, business men and men who were just plain nothing."[13] Even though class and status hierarchies would continue to shape soldiers' experiences, military life often served to undermine those divisions, making it easier for "pimps," "longshoremen" and "business men" to find common ground. In the aftermath of the war, black men and women drew upon these new class and gender identities to lay the foundation for a new black politics. Black patriotism provided a new basis for claims on first-class citizenship, displacing respectability as the bridge discourse through which African Americans asserted equality with both white Americans and one another.

This new black politics and the confidence that drove it provoked a brutal white supremacist reaction. During and immediately after the war years, black Americans endured some of the most extreme violence since the imposition of Jim Crow in the 1890s. In 1918 and 1919, there were 147 lynchings nationwide, 39 of which took place in Georgia.[14] As African Americans took advantage of the wartime labor shortage and migrated north in search of better employment, they were met with a wave of antiblack urban pogroms. In 1919 alone, twenty-five towns and cities across the nation exploded in riots that rivaled or surpassed in intensity the violence of the 1906 Atlanta riot.[15] Among the myriad things that struck fear in the hearts of those white supremacists determined to restore the prewar racial order, one of the most terrifying was the return of tens of thousands of black veterans. Even before the war ended, black men in uniform had been targets for white vigilante violence, and in the year following the war, no fewer than eleven black veterans were killed by white mobs, several while in uniform.[16] According to the

NAACP's James Weldon Johnson, at least one was lynched "because he was wearing his uniform."[17] As black men filled those uniforms with their war-tested bodies, they also filled them with new meanings for black manhood. During the Red Summer riots in Chicago and Washington, D.C., black veterans used their military training both to defend their neighborhoods and to organize retaliatory violence.[18] This sort of organized black resistance to white violence was not unprecedented; during the 1906 Atlanta riot, the "lawless element" of Darktown armed themselves, checking the advance of the mob. Before the war it was the "lawless element" to which black Americans had to turn for the defense of their communities; after the war the military service of thousands of black veterans had made armed self-defense respectable. Whereas the black elites in Atlanta had been embarrassed to admit their dependence on the hoodlums of Darktown for their defense, the nation's black press now applauded the role that black soldiers had played in defending their communities against the mob. Following the violence in Chicago, the *Chicago Defender,* reflecting on how "the younger generation of black men are not content to move along the line of least resistance as did their sires," announced that "a Race that had furnished hundreds of thousands of the best soldiers that the world has ever seen is no longer content to turn the left cheek when smitten upon the right."[19] World War I had temporarily provided both the cultural space for black men to employ violence in defense of their homes and families (a prerogative previously reserved for white men only) and a new model for black manhood drawn from outside the limits of the politics of respectability.

Despite its impact on ideas of black manhood, it remains important to resist describing the emergence of the New Negro in the postwar period as a remasculinization of black politics. The uncritical acceptance of any narrative of postwar New Negro militancy driven by a heroic male vanguard threatens to obscure decades of difficult work done by both the politicians of respectability and the efforts of women like Lugenia Burns Hope to challenge the limits imposed by Jim Crow. While the experience of war and military mobilization did represent a significant turning point, it would be inaccurate to suggest that it transformed a generation of humble black accommodationists to spirited postwar militants.[20] The path that black politics in Atlanta took from the 1899 campaign against the Hardwick bill through World War I shows that the fight for first-class citizenship had not vanished with the imposition of Jim Crow; it had simply adopted different strategies. Additionally, the timing of these radical transformations in African American political discourse in Atlanta—all preceding America's entry into World

War I—suggests that Ben Davis's exchange of the accommodationist politics of respectability for New Negro militancy had been powerfully influenced by decades of unacknowledged organizing on the part of Atlanta's black women. Their organizing efforts helped create both the political moment and the cultural preconditions necessary for Davis's seemingly sudden conversion to occur. By the time Ben Davis demanded to "be given what the law provides for us," black politics had already been profoundly transformed by the organizers of the Neighborhood Union. When the NAACP came to town in 1916, it soon became the most dynamic and successful branch in the entire association, because it was built directly atop the networks of solidarity created by a decade of organizing by the Union and the women who led it. While World War I made it possible for black men to assert the less deferential attitude toward Jim Crow associated with the idea of the "New Negro," they did not do so unaided.

"Back-Bone Enough": The Founding of the Atlanta NAACP

The NAACP had been trying to establish a branch in Atlanta with little success since 1913. However, in December 1916, a young and energetic graduate of Atlanta University named Walter White was able to convince the city's black middle-class leadership to support forming a branch.[21] A survivor of the Atlanta race riot, Walter White had been born in 1893 into a relatively affluent family. His mother, born into slavery in the middle of the Civil War, ultimately graduated from Clark University to become a schoolteacher in Atlanta. His father, also born into slavery in 1856, had struggled to earn a living as a laborer for much of his early life; however, by the time Walter was ten he had been a postal carrier for two decades. With steady, year-round employment, White's family was able to ascend into the ranks of the black middle class. They were wealthy enough to own the nicest house on their block and enjoy a line of credit at Rich's Department Store in downtown Atlanta. His parents did all they could to shield him and his siblings from the indignities of Jim Crow, even going to the extent of purchasing a horse-drawn carriage for the family to use as they traveled through town, thus avoiding having to travel on the city's segregated streetcars. In addition to their elite status, the White family was incredibly fair-skinned, with some of the children—Walter especially—light enough to pass for white. While this somewhat mitigated the harshness of Jim Crow, there were still sharp limits to the tolerance of white Atlanta for even the most elite, fair-skinned, and respectable black families. Though White's father may have been able to purchase a hat on credit from Rich's, neither he nor his family was permitted to use the restrooms or eat in the store's restaurant. Indeed, their status and skin color had made them targets in 1906.[22]

Walter White first attempted to form a branch of the NAACP at Atlanta University as early as 1910, writing an old family friend, W. E. B. Du Bois, for advice. However, unwilling to expend scarce resources on the ephemeral passion of a brash young man, the fledgling NAACP did not encourage White. Six years later, in the midst of the fight to preserve the seventh grade, White tried again.[23] This time James Weldon Johnson, the NAACP's new field secretary, responded with much greater enthusiasm. Drawing on his connections at the Standard Life Insurance Company, where he had been employed since graduating college, White brought together the organizational nucleus of the new branch. The first branch president, Harry Pace, was an executive at the firm, and Heman Perry, the founder of Standard Life and one of the wealthiest black men in the city, became one of the branch's founding members.[24] White himself was chosen as branch secretary. Building on this base, White recruited leaders representing a broad cross section of black Atlanta. The most significant among these new recruits were Atlanta University president John Hope and the ever-tempestuous Ben Davis, editor of the *Atlanta Independent*. Both were among the nine men elected to the branch executive committee.[25]

Davis's willingness to support the new branch is significant, because it signaled that the fights over black partisan loyalty that had crippled black Atlantans' response to disfranchisement had moderated somewhat. In the minds of stalwart black Republicans like Davis, the NAACP was inextricably linked to its most famous black leader, W. E. B. Du Bois. Davis had opposed Du Bois's call to punish the GOP following the 1906 "Brownsville Affray" and had never forgiven Du Bois, now a prominent leader in the NAACP, for his support of Democrats Bryan in 1908 and Wilson in 1912.[26] Davis's willingness to support the local branch despite his disagreements with the NAACP's national leadership made it easier for much of the rest of the city's black leadership, all loyal black Republicans, to join. Even though White was able to assemble these men under the banner of the NAACP, what kept them together was their decision to continue the Neighborhood Union's fight for school equality.[27] The presence of John Hope, the husband of Neighborhood Union founder Lugenia Burns Hope, helped ensure that the Union's agenda would also be the NAACP's agenda.

Walter White's account in his 1948 autobiography of the fight to preserve the seventh grade for Atlanta's black schoolchildren omits any mention of

FIGURE 4. Officers of the executive committee of the Atlanta branch of the NAACP,
April 1917. Standing, left to right: Peyton A. Allen, George A. Towns, Benjamin J. Davis
Sr., Rev. L. H. King, Dr. William F. Penn, John Hope, David H. Sims. Seated, left
to right: Harry H. Pace, Dr. Charles H. Johnson, Dr. Louis T. Wright, Walter F. White.
(NAACP Papers, Group I, Series G, Box 43, Library of Congress)

the groundbreaking work that the Union had accomplished since its founding in 1908. The way he narrated the story described African Americans
in Atlanta as "voteless, outnumbered, [and] helpless" until the men of the
NAACP came to town. However, without the organizing framework established by the Union's door-to-door canvass, the success of the NAACP
would have been inconceivable.[28] By 1919, in conjunction with their work
with the Atlanta Anti-Tuberculosis Association, the Union's organizers
could reach as many as 42,000 people in the space of just a few days.[29] Despite the fact that no women were invited to the founding conference of the
Atlanta branch of the NAACP, the unity among the black men who established the Atlanta NAACP was built directly upon the solidarity created by
the organizing work of the Neighborhood Union.[30]

Even before the branch was granted its official charter, the executive
committee appointed a team of six men, including Hope and Davis, to "present the views of the thinking Negro and the tax-paying Negro" before the
Board of Education.[31] Two days after meeting with the city, the *Atlanta In-*

dependent reprinted the text of their formal presentation. In contrast to the language used in the 1899 Hardwick memorial, the NAACP men asserted their rights as "both citizens and taxpayers" to quality public education. Carrying this argument even one step further, the delegation insisted that not only were they entitled to public education, but that it did not matter whether this would result in black Atlantans "receiving more money than we contribute as taxpayers." Instead, they insisted that "public funds" ought to be administered "in the interest of all of the people. . . . [T]he city of Atlanta owes the black child the same opportunity to himself for usefulness and helpful citizenship that it owes the white child, and it cannot do less and serve the interest of humanity and good government."[32] Demanding equal access to the benefits of urban development gave these men new grounds upon which to assert equal rights as citizens.

Grounded in something other than appeals to a fleeting white paternalism, the delegation placed four requests before the board that went beyond the initial demand that the board leave the seventh grade alone. First, they called on the board to take the necessary steps to relieve overcrowding in black grammar schools. Second, they called for the introduction of a modern vocational training program for black students that would train young men to become "shoemakers, carpenters, [and] brick layers" and young women to become "stenographers, bookkeepers, trained cooks and laundresses." Third, in addition to this vocational training, the NAACP delegation wanted the public schools to institute a curriculum that would prepare black students for high school. Finally, they requested the provision of "a high school to prepare our boys and girls to enter the colleges of the city, state and country, in like manner as you provide high schools for your boys and girls." Even though they insisted on equal standing as citizens, the use of the second person here acknowledges that there are two categories of citizens—white first-class citizens and black second-class citizens. An earlier appeal would have elided this difference and referred to *our* children, as did the Georgia Equal Rights Convention (GERC) when it reached out to the white elites of Georgia as "common children of a common state"—a phrasing that complicated the possibility of articulating an autonomous black position toward the Progressive Era state. In closing, the delegation reiterated that "these betterments we ask because they are justly [and] fully ours, because we are citizens and taxpayers, and because the state instituted this system for our benefit in common with yours."[33] Although the language by the delegation was polite, it was never deferential. Indeed, had the delegation possessed any real leverage over the board members, these additional "requests" could very easily have been demands.

Following the presentation of the memorial, a member of the Board of Education protested that the city lacked the money to address the deficiencies in Atlanta's black schools. According to White's account, Dr. William F. Penn, a member of the delegation, responded to these concerns in a "straight-from-the-shoulder manner" that the city could "obtain the money from the same sources that they had gotten money to build fifty fine schools for whites."[34] The board then made the outrageous suggestion that the city's private black schools pick up the slack and adjust their curricula to incorporate black students deprived of a public seventh grade education—something the city's black private schools had been doing for decades.[35] The committee responded that the Board of Education "had no authority to dictate" curriculum to the city's black private schools and refocused the discussion on the original grievance: "to grant what they as citizens and tax-payers were justly entitled."[36] The members of this delegation, unlike those that had come before, no longer felt the need to demonstrate that they were worthy of the full benefits of citizenship. Instead, after clearly identifying that white first-class citizenship had long depended upon the existence of a vast number of disfranchised black Atlantans, the delegation asserted what they, too, were entitled to their rights as first-class citizens.

After the meeting, Walter White wrote NAACP field secretary James Weldon Johnson that upon hearing the NAACP testimony, the Board of Education had agreed that the seventh grade "was not to go." White added that board member James L. Key went on record as "being against every move that will take away the rights that belong to the colored men and women of Atlanta, and that my vote is for every move that will give them what is theirs. . . . We have not given them a square deal and I do not propose to do anything that will any longer keep them from a square deal." Most members of the board concurred with Key, and even the mayor, Coca-Cola magnate Asa Candler, who was no friend of public education, agreed that "what these dear colored brethren said is true."[37] With the approval of President R. J. Guinn, the school board even appointed a committee to devise a plan to relieve understaffing and overcrowding in black public schools.[38] Justifiably proud of their victory, White concluded his report to Johnson that "we have just begun to fight."[39]

White's brash account was, however, secondhand and colored by his desire to impress Johnson. A more accurate description of the meeting comes from Ben Davis, who was a member of the delegation. Davis reported on the board's response in the pages of his paper, providing more context for Key's apparent liberality, which would have been a sharp reversal of his previous stance against additional funding for black education.[40] As the *Independent* reported, Key responded to the petition by declaring that "we, the white people, . . . control the government; we have the money; we spend the money; we run the courts; we control the country. . . . We cannot afford to be less than fair." White's report that Key promised to give to black Atlantans "a square deal" may have been accurate, but Davis's account suggests that this generosity was framed in the language of white paternalism that spoke to a progressive version of the "White Man's Burden." Although board president R. J. Guinn told the delegation that the board was prepared to substantively respond to their suggested reforms for black education, including building "a vocational training and junior high school . . . just as soon as it is financially possible," if this burden got too heavy to bear for white voters interested in taking care of their own children, it would be set aside.[41]

While the black men who assembled before the Board of Education in order to save the seventh grade no longer viewed public education as a gift from well-meaning white progressives, this was not true for men like Key.[42] So long as the strongest white allies in the fight for equal access to public education believed that this access was a gift, that gift could easily be taken away. The future strategy of both the Union and the NAACP in Atlanta would be determined by this disjuncture between black and white visions of Progressive Era development. As shared notions of respectability failed to establish an interracial solidarity that respected black claims on the city's education budget, African Americans in Atlanta would be obliged to compel this respect from their erstwhile allies. However, the relative ease of this victory did not give the NAACP a chance to force a debate with Atlanta's white progressives that would raise the question of whether African Americans would be understood as citizens entitled to justice or simply as the objects of white benevolence.

Regardless of its limitations, the NAACP's victory in Atlanta served as a powerful demonstration of what black unity could achieve. The demand for patriotic unity during World War I was not just a call to "close . . . ranks shoulder to shoulder with our own white fellow citizens," it also gave African Americans the language to close ranks with one another as well. Downstate, the *Savannah Tribune* editorialized that the victory in Atlanta had taught African Americans a valuable lesson, "indispensable for race

advancement—an unselfish subordination of purely local and individualis-
tic interests to those of the great group, and an unwavering and fearless unity
for simple justice everywhere." The *Tribune* added that "the sympathies of
our people—one group for the other, one individual for the other—are becoming as broad and as acute as among any other people through a growing
nationalism and national unity." Though tempting to attribute this appeal to
the rising tide of black nationalist sentiment that accompanied World War
I, in March 1917, this would be premature. Instead, less than a month before the United States entered World War I, the *Savannah Tribune* appropriated the hyperpatriotic language associated with the military preparedness
movement in order to describe the terms of racial unity. Furthermore, this
call for black patriotic unity demanded black unity across class lines as well.
Speaking directly to the state's wealthy black elite, the *Tribune* insisted that
"no Negro, however blest locally, can be truly emancipated so long as the
humblest and most ignorant Negro of the back woods, is denied ordinary
opportunity and simple justice."[43] This aspect of the *Tribune's* commentary
was revealing. Any of the men who comprised the delegation to the Board
of Education were wealthy enough to send their children to private acade-
mies and could easily exempt themselves and their families from the fight
for equal schools in Atlanta. The wartime shift away from the interracial
politics of respectability enabled this new black unity to express itself across
class lines.

Walter White's next move was to expand the fight. Two weeks after the
memorial to the school board, he organized a "monster mass meeting" of
the Atlanta branch of the NAACP to be held at the Odd Fellows auditorium, with James Weldon Johnson as the featured speaker.[44] According to
the *Independent*, 1,500 people attended the meeting, making it one of the
largest black political meetings in the state for many years. In his speech,
Johnson portrayed two futures for black Americans: "One is for American
citizenship and the other is a state of almost servitude." He warned that the
forces arranged against black Americans would "force the Negro down into
permanent secondary standing in this country . . . unless we took steps to
prevent it," and challenged his audience to "ask for bigger things." Preserv-
ing the black seventh grade was a significant victory, but so long as Atlanta's
school system failed to serve African Americans as citizens fully entitled to
quality public education, this fight was far from over. The black citizenry
of Atlanta, especially those wealthy enough to mitigate the more destructive elements of Jim Crow, had to admit that "the Negro could not solve

his problem individually and that the Negro should get together with one object in view, that the humblest Negro get the same protection the white man receives." In response to Johnson's call, 211 people joined the NAACP that night.[45]

White used this momentum to encourage each of the 300 members of the Atlanta branch of the NAACP to write "a letter of protest" over school conditions to each member of the Board of Education as well as to the mayor in advance of a meeting with the Board of Education planned for 26 April 1917.[46] White explained his next step in a letter to NAACP executive secretary Royal Nash written shortly after the Board of Education's decision to back down on eliminating the black seventh grade: "the psychological effect of three hundred letters . . . every one of which expresses the same idea is planned to show . . . that our protest was not a mere 'flash-in-the-pan' performance on the part of a few self-appointed men, . . . but that they are the representatives of the thinking men and women of the race."[47] Although White encouraged them to use their own words, he nonetheless usefully provided four talking points for NAACP members to use in crafting their letters. These demands, which mirrored those voiced by the Neighborhood Union following its 1913 survey, were:

> 1. We want the absolute elimination of all double sessions in all the public schools.
> 2. We want better school buildings, the destruction of all the unsanitary fire traps called schools. . . .
> 3. We want a Junior High School, commercial and industrial, for the training of those of our youth who cannot afford a college education. . . .
> 4. We want high schools for our boys and girls. Atlanta is the only city of her size that has so great a Negro population that does not at least pretend to have high school facilities for Negroes. Colored people pay taxes on over a Million and a Half Dollars worth of property in Atlanta, and yet have a smaller pro-rata share . . . expended on them in . . . schools . . . than any city in the country.[48]

Significantly, the first two demands spoke to the conditions of all the public schools and not just those reserved for black students. Just as Johnson asked black parents at the recent mass meeting to ask for "bigger things," Walter White sought to challenge white parents to do likewise. Rather than trying to argue for inclusion into the city's reform agenda, White thought that the city's black leadership could actually drive that agenda under the auspices of the NAACP.

"Unity Is the Rock Bottom of Our Rights"

The fight for school equality faced almost insuperable intransigence from white school authorities. The degree to which the city's white political leadership disregarded black education is evident in comments made by the school superintendent three weeks before the start of classes in 1917. Facing a budget shortfall and yet another spike in enrollment, school superintendent J. C. Wardlaw assured white parents that double sessions would not be necessary, except possibly for black schoolchildren. To add insult to injury, Wardlaw boasted that the city had been able to rent a sufficient number of rooms to accommodate the overflow of white students for the Girls' High School as well as to construct a ten-room annex for the (white) English Avenue School. All in all, including the construction of modern biology laboratories, improvements and expansions were made to some thirty school buildings for white students, while little or nothing was done for black education.[49] In spite of the work of both the Neighborhood Union and the NAACP in bringing the wretched state of Atlanta's black schools before the public, the city refused to take seriously the needs of its black citizens.

Although he took extensive measures to prevent overcrowding in the white schools, Superintendent Wardlaw was nonetheless compelled to float the idea of temporary double sessions for white students in the first, third, and fourth grades of the Tenth Street School until new white schools could be built. In stark contrast to the city's response to the much more serious overcrowding facing every single black school in the city, the public outcry against the plan to institute double sessions in just three grades of one white school was ferocious. The *Atlanta Constitution* condemned the suggestion as "inhumane, barbaric and wholly out of place with Atlanta's place and pride" and demanded that the city rent enough space "so as to accommodate every child who has a right to a seat at reasonable school hours." Outraged, the city's white parents joined the *Constitution* in its call for Atlanta to take immediate steps to relieve the crowded conditions in the city's white schools. Before a mass meeting of hundreds of angry white citizens, school board president R. J. Guinn stated that he was doing everything in his power to avoid the necessity of double sessions, adding that, even though it would be "very expensive," he had "looked at several houses . . . which could be used for classrooms."[50]

The ferocity of this reaction stemmed in part from the fact that whiteness had increasingly become defined by access to the full range of Atlanta's civic rights. The city's two-tiered educational system was not only the result of racial discrimination, it also shored up white identities. Double sessions would deny white children access to a quality public education and threaten to erode the racial standing of white families, prompting fierce resistance. A little more than a week after the idea of double sessions for white students was first floated, the Board of Education was compelled to scrap the idea.[51] At its meeting on 17 September, the city council passed a $750 emergency appropriation for the rental and modification of a building to serve as an overflow annex for the students of the Tenth Street School.[52] Within four days of the council's vote, double sessions for white students had been eliminated.[53] Although this was a major victory for progressives who sought to ensure that the city made a real commitment to expanding public education, it represented a significant setback for Atlanta's black citizenry.[54] As long as the city's white progressive leadership was unwilling to embrace a racially inclusive reform agenda, their actions would do little more than reinforce a stratified understanding of citizenship that relegated African Americans to a permanently inferior position.

Although members of the local branch of the NAACP had been relatively quiet over the summer, they immediately sprung into action and assembled another delegation to the Board of Education.[55] Their two-hour discussion—at times acrimonious—with the members of the board ultimately proved fruitless. Commissioner W. H. Terrell, who was a member of the committee specifically appointed to examine ways to abolish sessions in black schools, rebuffed this second delegation and openly declared his hostility "to giving one nickel more for the education of the Negro children as they were already getting more than they deserved."[56] According to Walter White, the "members of the board had been attacked . . . and ridiculed by many of their friends for being 'whipped into line by niggers.'" Other members of the board were less polite than Terrell, and informed the delegation "with brutal frankness and considerable profanity" that nothing would be done for black schools in Atlanta.[57] In response to these broken promises, Walter White wrote James Weldon Johnson that he was planning to organize a "monster silent protest" modeled on the one recently held in New York to protest lynching "in order to make some tangible move toward the abolishing of double sessions."[58] While these and similar responses would prove more difficult to execute than White initially imagined, they reveal a willingness on the part of at least some of the local NAACP leadership to embrace a far more confrontational array of tactics than previously had been possible.

Ben Davis, who had been a member of the original delegation to the Board of Education to discuss overcrowding in black schools, publicly excoriated the hypocrisy of this outcry over double sessions. He denounced Wardlaw's willingness to tolerate double sessions for black schools even as he took pains to prevent them in white schools as "un-American and inhuman." As the city committed the necessary funds to ensure that every white student could obtain a quality public education, Davis demanded to know "how many of these improvements have been among the Negro schools" and insisted that "these conditions . . . be remedied."[59] Following the *Atlanta Constitution*'s praise for the city's "indignant protest" that eliminated the "menace" of double sessions, against which "any community [had] the right to revolt," Davis reminded them that double sessions had by no means been eliminated.[60] He used the *Independent* to provide an angry counternarrative to the *Constitution*'s account of progress and victory for public education, which had completely written African Americans out of the story. Asserting that "the Negroes' cause is equally as just as the white man's cause," the editorial argued that this progressive victory for quality public education would remain incomplete so long as it failed to address the educational needs of black children as well as white children.[61] Davis consciously fought against the attempt of Atlanta's white progressives to construct a hegemonic narrative of universal progress that disregarded the welfare of their black neighbors. Progressivism had to include black citizens if it was to be worthy of the name.

Davis did not just challenge the *Constitution*'s claims of progress; he categorically rejected "the argument that the Southern white man is the Negro's best friend, unless he demonstrates it by his actions."[62] Coming from a man who once argued in the wake of the 1906 Atlanta riot that "among our enemies we are in the midst of our friends and they predominate," sentiments such as these mark a sea change in African American attitudes toward interracial alliances.[63] Davis's response to the *Constitution* was yet one more sign of the decline of the politics of respectability as a theory of interracial political solidarity and marked the rise of a new set of black political identities in the wake of World War I.[64] Given the willingness of white progressives not only to pursue but also to celebrate a vision of progress that excluded their African American allies in reform, it was increasingly difficult for men like Davis to view their primary allies as supposedly sympathetic whites. More important, in arguing that "friendship is what friendship performs," Davis's understanding of the basis of interracial politics shifted from a solidarity forged through the shared practice of respectable manhood to a more baldly transactional exchange contingent on the full inclusion of African Americans in the benefits of Progressive Era reform. This transformation would open the way for more creative uses of black political solidarity and the black community's increasingly fraught relationship with their erstwhile white allies.

Walter White offered a somewhat more restrained response to the city's campaign to eliminate double sessions from the city's white schools. Although fully supported by Davis in the pages of the *Independent,* White's rhetorical strategy differed from the editor's. Rather than outright condemning the motives of the city's white progressive leadership, White first attempted to reach out to white parents in search of common ground over double sessions. In a letter published in the *Atlanta Constitution* ten days after the initial editorial that stoked Davis's ire, White praised the paper's position opposing double sessions as "unanswerable." However, repeating the *Constitution*'s words that overcrowded schools were "intolerable viewed from any . . . angle," he reminded them that double sessions existed in every one of the city's fourteen black public schools, "yet not a single word of protest has been uttered against this condition." Affirming that "the colored people of the city do not begrudge the white children any advantages they may have," White asked only that black children be given "the same opportunity" as white children to get a quality education. However conciliatory, White nonetheless firmly declared that "the Negroes of this city are not asking for favors nor are they pleading for patronage at the hands of the school board. . . . [T]hey are only asking for those things which are rightfully theirs as taxpayers and law-abiding citizens."[65] Building on the organizing work done by the Neighborhood Union in changing the discourse around black public education, White was able to describe equal access to quality schools not as gift "generously tendered" to deserving African Americans as it had been described in 1899, but rather as a right to which black citizens were entitled. At the same time, this appeal allowed him to strategically reach out to white constituencies that should be natural allies—other parents of school-age children. However, this attempt to reach out to white parents would fail. Jealously guarding the privilege of sending their children to superior and segregated schools, white Atlantans secured their own racial identities against the disorder of urban life by excluding their black neighbors from the circle of their concern. White's efforts to build an interracial school reform movement would fail, ultimately forcing the mobilized black community of Atlanta to pursue a far more aggressive strategy.

Nevertheless, the *Constitution* reprinted White's letter, even going so far as to accompany it with an editorial agreeing that Atlanta's black citizens "have not had a fair showing in the matter of educational facilities provided for them."[66] In addition to this endorsement, both R. J. Guinn, the president of the Board of Education, and city councilman James L. Key acknowledged the crisis and reiterated their desire to address the issue.[67] Despite these promising developments, the city took no steps to address overcrowding in black schools; white progressive leaders lacked both the will and leadership to do so. The promised committee on the abolition of double sessions never materialized, and board president Guinn, who had been responsible for the earlier abolition of the eighth grade, had become embroiled in several controversies over his autocratic management style and busied himself trying to find a way to reintroduce the idea of double sessions for *white* schools.[68] If men like Key and Guinn lacked the political will to address the shortcomings of black education, black Atlantans in 1917 still lacked power to force them to do so.

For months, Walter White struggled to keep the issue of double sessions alive in the black community, but without a real plan to force the city to invest in black education, he was met by widespread apathy. In several public exhortations printed in the *Atlanta Independent*, he urged black Atlantans to take a stand for the "things that are rightfully theirs" and "awaken to the fact that by not protesting . . . they are pushing their own selves deeper into the mire." In an editorial printed on the front page of the *Atlanta Independent* on 6 October 1917, White directly addressed black parents and advised them to raise their expectations, arguing that "it is not a question of what the white man will do for us but what we will do for ourselves." He urged the "eighty thousand Negroes of Atlanta [to solidify] into one compact unit fighting for those things which are theirs. . . . [I]f ever they hope to be free in reality as well as in name, they must learn the value of racial unity."[69] While White was vague on the precise strategy his "compact fighting unit" would employ, he was nonetheless beginning to articulate publicly the terms of a new and openly contentious relationship between African Americans and the city's development agenda. A month after this editorial appeared, White again attacked black apathy in the pages of the *Independent*, encouraging black Atlantans to "put aside the curse of continually being afraid of what might happen to us if we express an honest man's opinion."[70] White was as much up against the long shadow cast by the riot of eleven years earlier as he was up against the politics of respectability. Many black leaders had carved out a space in which they could exist and exert a limited form of power rooted in their relationship to powerful white allies. When White intimated that the full inclusion of African Americans into the prerogatives of Progressive Era citizenship had to be based on a "racial unity" that may require politically assertive and aggressive action against these erstwhile allies, he was unable to bring the NAACP Atlanta branch leadership with him.

The available evidence also suggests that there were internal divisions within the Atlanta branch of the NAACP over how to continue the fight against double sessions after the initial delegation to the Board of Education. When White wrote his letter to the editor of the *Atlanta Constitution* protesting the premature declaration that double sessions had been eliminated from the city's public schools, he signed it as the cashier of the Standard Life Insurance Company—as a private citizen rather than as the secretary of the Atlanta branch of the NAACP.[71] Although the language of the letter that was eventually published was relatively tame, the original draft may have been somewhat more confrontational. White complained to James Weldon Johnson that although Clark Howell, the editor of the *Constitution,* saw fit to use White's letter, "reproducing it almost as was written," he nonetheless edited out "some paragraphs which did not exactly conform to his Southern White ideas."[72] That his employer, NAACP Atlanta branch president Harry Pace, allowed him to use the company's name on the letter but not the NAACP's name suggests that the members of the branch were split as to the best way forward and were perhaps afraid of putting at risk the relationships they had built with their white allies over the years. Even Pace himself may not have been 100 percent behind White's efforts. James Weldon Johnson encouraged Pace to attend the NAACP Mid-Winter Conference to speak about the successes of the Atlanta branch. After repeated attempts to contact Pace, the branch president finally replied that he was too ill to travel to the meeting.[73] Despite its size and recent successes, the Atlanta branch failed to send a single delegate to the meeting—definitely not a sign of a branch both excited and unified behind its plan of action.[74]

In a final attempt to reinvigorate the branch, White, Davis, and other NAACP leaders renewed their membership drive. As part of these efforts, George A. Towns, the chairman of the Atlanta NAACP's Committee on Education, published an appeal for new members in the *Atlanta Independent.* He specifically addressed the divisions in the black community, proclaiming that the NAACP was "one movement we all ought to join, regardless of our differences. . . . This unity is the rock bottom of our rights." He directly attributed the failure of the recent drive to end double sessions to the failure of black solidarity. The authors of the appeal contrasted the efforts of black Americans to gain full access to publicly funded education with the experience of recent immigrants from Europe. There was no outcry over spending "the public money for Jewish schools, Irish schools, Italian schools, and

Greek schools" primarily because these new immigrants "have the ballot and because we have it not." Towns appealed to black Atlantans to unite as citizens, for "in a country like this, there is no middle ground; we are either real citizens or we are not."[75] However eloquent, his appeal ultimately failed. Without a real plan to move the campaign for equal schools forward, the local branch fell into disarray.

Despite its early successes, the NAACP experienced difficulty in uniting the city's black leadership behind its work in Atlanta. Although the successful recruitment of Ben Davis to the NAACP was initially a coup for the organization, he had nonetheless brought with him a great deal of controversy, which frequently interfered with the effectiveness of the branch.[76] These divisions came to a head over the question of the location of the Atlanta NAACP offices. At its founding, Davis had offered the use of a room in the Odd Fellows' lodge, of which he had long been a leader. As White reported to the national office, this posed two significant problems. First, the women of the Neighborhood Union refused to attend an NAACP meeting held in "a lodge room," an indication that White understood the vital importance of bringing these women into the branch. Second, as White wrote Johnson in December 1917, "an element antagonistic to Mr. Davis [would] not attend any sort of meeting in the Odd Fellows Building."[77] The most significant member of this antagonistic element was Rev. A. D. Williams, the pastor of the influential Ebenezer Baptist Church (and grandfather of Martin Luther King Jr.), who at the outset had been "violently opposed" to the NAACP and whom White described as one of its "worst opponents."[78] As a result, White wrote, the branch's work had been "considerably handicapped as we have no place to hold our meetings."[79]

Without the ability to bring these two groups fully into the leadership of the local branch, the NAACP in Atlanta could never become self-sustaining. With his determination to keep the association on "absolutely nonpartisan grounds" and unite black Atlanta behind its program, Walter White confronted the predicament of removing the NAACP offices from the Odd Fellows' lodge while at the same time not alienating Ben Davis.[80] White, however, never got the chance to solve this dilemma. Impressed with the young Atlanta leader, NAACP field secretary James Weldon Johnson offered him a job as his assistant in the national office, and in January 1918 White and his family moved to New York City.[81] Although White would continue to take an active interest in the development of the Atlanta branch, he would no longer have the influence he had previously enjoyed in the city.

This left the branch in the hands of men like Davis, Towns, and others, whose appeals to black Atlantans to unite as *citizens* were as yet incapable of overcoming the fragmentation of Atlanta's black community. In 1917, the language of citizenship was compelling enough to describe the outline of a new form of black political solidarity, yet still not powerful enough to unite the still fractious black leadership of Atlanta. But the surging chorus of patriotism following American entry into World War I altered the logic of racial solidarity and helped a new generation of branch leaders overcome the fragmentation, fear, and isolation that had stalled the movement.

"The Negro's Duty in Case of War"

Two fires scarred the city of Atlanta in 1917. The less destructive of these began on 21 May in an alley off Auburn Avenue and ultimately destroyed seventy-three square blocks, causing millions of dollars in damage and leaving nearly 10,000 people without shelter, representing more than 5 percent of the city's population.[82] While the Great Atlanta Fire sliced right through some of the city's toniest white neighborhoods, the majority of the 1,900 homeless families came from the ranks of African American renters and homeowners living between Auburn Avenue and Old Wheat Street.[83] The disaster compelled the city's black leadership to turn their full attention to providing relief for the thousands of African Americans displaced from their homes.[84] Alongside the rest of the city's black institutions, both the NAACP and the Neighborhood Union focused their energies on organizing relief efforts for the fire's black victims.[85] Even though the destruction miraculously left all four schools in the fire-swept area unscathed, it nonetheless sparked a crisis in city finances, placing any of the NAACP's suggested reforms well beyond the city's ability to pay. It took a full three weeks for the last embers to be extinguished; by the time the last fire guttered out, the school campaign had come to an abrupt end.[86]

The second conflagration began thousands of miles away in Sarajevo, after an assassin's bullet took the life of Archduke Franz Ferdinand on 28 June 1914. Within days, the entire continent was preparing for a war that would last nearly five years and kill more than nine million combatants and cripple seven million others.[87] The hot cinders from this inferno would reach Atlanta on 6 April 1917, when the United States officially entered the war against Germany. The city responded enthusiastically to Wilson's call to raise an army of at least a half a million men as the front page of the *Atlanta Journal's* evening edition commanded its readers to "WAKE UP" and "be patriotic at any price."[88] Following the passage of the Selective Service Act, more than 19,000 of the city's young men answered these calls to duty by registering for the draft on the first day, a total far in excess of the number of the city's registered voters.[89] The city's black men also filled out their draft cards with enthusiasm. Twenty-seven clerks were required to process thousands of registrants at a special registration precinct for black men established under the aegis of Ben Davis's Odd Fellows, Heman Perry's Standard Life Insurance Company, and Alonzo Herndon's Atlanta Life.[90] Though often dismissive and even distrusting of any expressions of black patriotism, the Atlanta Journal's expansive praise for "the youth of America, millions strong," who registered "to fight for civilization and humanity," described a cultural space for black political assertion that was unimaginable just a decade earlier.[91] When the first 150 black draftees were called up, they and 3,000 of their friends and family members were fêted with a barbecue and personally sent off to nearby Camp Gordon with speeches by Mayor Asa Candler, along with Rev. Henry Hugh Proctor and other black leaders.[92] World War I had transformed the terrain upon which black Atlantans fought for their place in the city's development by burning away much of what remained of the older politics of respectability. The war seemed to have made possible a new foundation for interracial politics rooted instead in a shared, though contested, patriotism.

With hopes that supporting President Wilson's call to "make the world safe for democracy" would bring democracy to Georgia as well, most African Americans heeded Du Bois's famous call for African Americans to "close ranks."[93] Atlanta's black leadership put aside the fight for black schools and called on African Americans to unite with white Americans in support of Wilson's war effort. On the first Sunday that April, black ministers delivered patriotic sermons. James Bond of Rush Memorial Congregational Church echoed Theodore Roosevelt, advising that all "differences . . . be forgotten and [that] there should be no hyphenated Americans, black or white. Let us have one flag and one people."[94] Rev. Henry Hugh Proctor of the elite First Congregational Church stated that he would display the American flag above his pulpit until the war was over.[95] Asserting that no "black anarchist has ever raised his hand against the flag," Proctor insisted that "in a crisis like this, there are two classes only—Americans and traitors [and] Negroes are Americans!"[96] The following Sunday, nearly 5,000 parishioners at several Atlanta churches ratified a prowar resolution, which declared that black Georgians stood "squarely behind the President . . . ready to live or die for the country," and called on every branch of the armed services to be opened to any black American who wished to serve.[97] In addition to these efforts, the NAACP and other groups of African Americans across the state planned several patriotic mass meetings. The earliest of these meetings, held just four days after the United States' entry into the war at the Allen Temple African Methodist Episcopal (AME) Church, drew more than 1,000 black men and women. In a notice about the meeting that Davis printed in his *Atlanta Independent,* he could justifiably brag that "every denomination and organization will be represented."[98] The patriotic fervor was not limited to Atlanta alone; black patriotic meetings of similar size were held across the state in several cities, including Albany, Augusta, Macon, and Waycross.[99]

That same month, at its regular monthly meeting, the NAACP's Atlanta branch passed a resolution reaffirming its loyalty to the United States, offering its "unqualified support" for the war effort, and denouncing as "without foundation the newspaper reports to the effect that the Negro is in sympathy with Germany. . . . The Negro is American first, last and all the time; that he neither entertains nor tolerates any division in his allegiance to the American Constitution."[100] As the United States deepened its involvement in the war, Walter White laid plans for a "great patriotic meeting" sponsored by the NAACP to be held in the middle of May.[101] The published agenda included addresses by NAACP branch president Harry Pace encouraging "Loyalty to the President and Government in this Hour of National Crisis," which was followed by two speeches advocating the constitution of a black fighting regiment and an exhortation to all black men of draft age to volunteer for military service. The meeting was to open with the song "America" followed by the "Negro National Anthem," an inclusion suggesting that, despite the demand to reject "hyphenated Americanism," black patriots could not necessarily submerge their entire identity in the patriotic fervor of the times. As much as the organizers of the event wished to equate the victory for democracy abroad with the progress of African Americans on the home front, it was still impossible to completely lay aside the "special grievances" of even the most fervently patriotic black Americans. Several speakers used the war effort to argue for expanding the opportunities available for black patriotic service, including a call to open the National Guard to African Americans. While these sorts of calls were predictable, what stood out are the two speeches linking redress of long-standing domestic "grievances" to the success of the war effort. Drawn almost directly from the platform of the Neighborhood Union, these speakers argued that the lack of playgrounds and parks for the enjoyment of black Atlantans as well as the poor conditions of black school facilities undermined morale and military preparedness.[102] Although the war effort had seemingly brought black aspirations into harmony with patriotic aspirations, the medley of "America" and the "Negro National Anthem" proved difficult to sustain in a martial mood. The disarticulation between these two ideals would slow the tempo that would nonetheless play on, dragging its blue notes behind.

Nonetheless, the number of African Americans attending the NAACP's "great patriotic meeting" was Atlanta's largest black gathering in recent memory, surpassed only by the number attending the Atlanta Cotton States and International Exposition in 1895 and the Negro Young People's Christian Congress in 1902.[103] With 5,000 African American men and women in attendance, the turnout for the patriotic meeting dwarfed that of the 1,500-person "monster mass meeting" the NAACP had held just two months earlier concerning overcrowded black schools.[104] This patriotic meeting also marked the first time that the city of Atlanta permitted its black residents to use the city auditorium.[105] Even a year into the war, these public demonstrations of patriotic fervor did not flag. In April 1918, an estimated 10,000 black Atlantans marched through Five Points in an all-black parade headed by a contingent of Spanish-American War veterans and 600 black soldiers from nearby Camp Gordon.[106]

Perhaps drawing on their experiences during the Atlanta race riot of 1906, the organizers of these patriotic assemblies also sought to preempt the doubts that many white Georgians may have held about black loyalty.[107] Days before the official declaration of war against Germany, NAACP field secretary James Weldon Johnson declared that "the bald truth is that the Negro cannot afford to be rated as a disloyal element. Imagine the results if he should for an instant arouse against himself the sentiment . . . now directed against the pro-German element."[108] As the United States prepared to enter the war, rumors abounded that German agents were attempting to incite African Americans against the government.[109] The *Atlanta Journal* claimed that foreign infiltrators, disguised as Bible salesmen, were encouraging black workers to abandon their jobs and migrate to Mexico.[110] The *Atlanta Constitution* cited unnamed "local federal agents" who claimed that imperial German spies were working throughout the Black Belt from North Carolina to Alabama "to induce the negroes to rise against the whites," even blaming them for the exodus of black farm laborers to the factories of the North.[111] While reports of German espionage were certainly exaggerated, some black southerners were in fact disaffected from their government. Less than a week after the *Constitution* published these espionage rumors, Coleman Akins, a thirty-two-year-old carpenter, was arrested for treason for allegedly fomenting racial discord. In order to prevent a lynching, federal agents were compelled to transport Akins nearly forty miles to the city jail in Atlanta.[112] Even relatively innocuous expressions of discontent were dealt with punitively. Howard Wright was a black prisoner serving thirty days. After one of his supervisors had stuck a flag in his cap, he removed it, threw it to the ground, and exclaimed, "I don't care a d—n for the old thing!" For "showing disrespect for the American flag," he had twenty-one days added to his sentence and was fined $10.75.[113] In order to ensure that expressions of frustration by black men like Coleman and Akins did not come to publicly define black responses to the war effort, it was vital for the city's black leadership to aggressively promote black patriotism.

These expressions of black patriotism were more than just defensive; demonstrations of black loyalty also powerfully served to buttress black claims on full citizenship. However, these fervent expressions of support for the war effort also threatened to submerge black particularity into a de-racialized notion of American citizenship, placing hard limits on the sorts of rights claims that could be made. In July 1916, with the certain prospect of war looming on the horizon, President Wilson gave an address before the Bureau of Naturalization on the "American spirit." Referring primarily to German Americans and other recent immigrants, his words constrained the ways in which African Americans could articulate their citizenship claims. Beginning with the premise that ethnic and (presumably) civil rights organizations were "absolutely incompatible with the fundamental idea of loyalty," he carefully distinguished between two ideas of loyalty, one based on "sacrifice" and the other based on "selfishness." That is, the state had the legitimate power to demand a loyalty from its citizens, requiring them to "be ready to sacrifice every interest, [even] life itself, if [the] country calls upon you to do so." Wilson's speech was deemed so important to the naturalization of new Americans that it was included in the textbook given to new immigrants applying for citizenship.[114] Extending these ideas and echoing Roosevelt's famous diatribe against "hyphenated Americans," Wilson personally drafted a platform for the 1916 Democratic National Convention promoting 100 percent Americanism and denouncing "hyphenism."[115] It was within these strict limits that African Americans would continue to press their claims for first-class citizenship.

Just prior to American entry into the war, the *Atlanta Independent* ran two editorials on the same page that wrestled with the terms of black loyalty to the United States. The first of these, entitled "With the President Right or Wrong," urged black Americans to "forget that Wilson is a white man and a Democrat; . . . forget that his party is dedicated to segregation, disfranchisement . . . and Jim Crowism when the flag is assailed and the integrity of this nation is insulted."[116] Statements such as these demonstrate that assertions of black patriotism were inseparable from the "special grievances" that had to be laid aside in order to close ranks. The affirmation of one seemingly entailed the negation of the other, but this negation was impossible without the explicit invocation of the "special grievances" that had to be set aside.

The most stunning example of this can be seen in an editorial Davis penned two weeks prior to the beginning of direct American involvement in the war. In the course of detailing "the Negro's duty in the case of war," Davis laid bare the distance between the ideal and the reality of black patriotism. Answering his own rhetorical question, "What position will Negroes take in case of war between this country and Germany?," Davis recited the record of loyal black soldiers in every U.S. conflict from the Revolution to, most recently, the Battle of Carrizal in Mexico during the previous year. However, despite Davis's protestations of black patriotism, it was impossible for him to ignore the "special grievances" of black Americans. Rather, he had to explicitly set them aside and in the process name them all. Davis assured readers that the African American soldier will

> do just as he as always done—fight for Old Glory. It matters not whether he has always been treated right; it matters not that he has not had meted out to him all the rights of an American citizen; it matters not that he has been discriminated against in his native towns, cities, and states; it matters not that he has been regarded as an inferior, with few rights that other races were bound to respect; it matters not that even the Government, for which he has fought and bled, has connived and condoned this mistreatment; it matters not that he has been segregated in the Governmental Departments in Washington, where he has a right to expect equal and exact justice; it matters not in courts that his word has very little weight, and in many instances he has been lynched by mobs without due process of law; yet, it is his pride and glory to fight for the country that has given him birth, and which has given him only a few crumbs that have fallen from the Government's table. When the tocsin of war has been sounded, he will not be found wanting.[117]

Rather than a call to arms in defense of the United States, what Davis offered was essentially a long train of grievances.[118] It was impossible to forget them entirely, and they formed the central contradiction of black patriotism during World War I—the imperative to forget "special grievances" served as a reminder that they must be addressed after the war.

Nevertheless, President Wilson, in declaring Germany a "foe to democracy," gave African Americans a foundation upon which to build a new relationship between black Americans and the U.S. nation-state. Reprinting in the *Independent* Wilson's recommendation before Congress that the United States enter the war, Ben Davis appended a brilliant exegesis that emphasized the contingency of black patriotism. He could not help but compare German despotism with the way in which "Negro people are treated in this country. . . . When we reflect that black men have no voice in this government and are mistreated in the courts, on railroads and nearly everywhere else, we are inclined to ask: 'What about this great doctrine as applied to the[se] ten million American citizens in his own country?'"[119] By highlighting the contradictions between Wilson's professed ideals of popular government and America's treatment of its black citizens, Davis articulated a discourse of black patriotism in which the fulfillment of black America's "special grievances" became a patriotic exercise in itself. He exploited this contradiction to link the goals of the NAACP and the Neighborhood Union to the success of the war effort. For example, in a speech delivered in Athens in July 1917, the feisty editor explicitly linked the fight for equal schools to Wilson's war aims, declaring that any "distribution of public funds that provides ample and modern school houses for . . . white children and affords starvation salaries for Negro teachers and provides no [school]house at all for the Negro children is . . . inconsistent with the democracy for which we fight."[120] As Davis's fellow Republican Roscoe Conkling Simmons concisely framed this tension in the pages of the *New York Age:* "Let us help in the world battle for liberty. The white man can't break his own shackles without loosening mine."[121]

Despite Wilson's insistence that loyalty to the state ought to be based on "sacrifice" rather than "selfishness," World War I marked a very important shift away from an obligation-based vision of citizenship in which the politics of respectability made a certain cultural sense. Replacing the perception that black and white elites held certain obligations toward one another was a reaffirmation of the notion that access to the full benefits of citizenship was rooted in the possession and exercise of certain rights.[122] The betrayals of Reconstruction had long since made it clear those rights meant nothing without the power to defend them, thus any conception that citizenship was a right and not a reward also compelled a rethinking of the sources of African American political power. The prewar understanding that citizenship was based on mutual obligation grounded that power in strategic relationships with white elites. However, by the time the war had ended, the guarantee of African Americans' civil and civic rights would be found in the social and political power generated by black racial solidarity.

The resulting synthesis of race consciousness and patriotism significantly augmented the role of the war as a crucible for black unity. This is reflected in an editorial from the *Savannah Tribune* reprinted in the *Independent* on the same page that Davis penned his avowal to stand by Wilson, "right or wrong." As a counterpoint to Davis's avowals of patriotism, the *Tribune* spoke to the need for racial consciousness. These appeals to racial consciousness differed from those offered in the past by emigrationists like Bishop Turner, who asserted that full racial consciousness was only possible outside the bounds of an irredeemably racist United States. By contrast, the *Tribune's* notion of race consciousness was fully congruent with U.S. patriotism. In order to close ranks during World War I, it was necessary to "rid [those] ranks of malcontents, fomenters of discord and promoters of confusion." However, black patriotic unity was not just necessary to defend the United States against its foes; it also was vital for racial self-defense as well. Rather than acting as "individuals, or disorganized nuclei," the author of the *Tribune* editorial urged racial unity as a defense against exploitation by "designing and unfriendly interests, [who] count on racial dissension" in order to "capitalize on the practice of putting one individual and class of us against the other." He urged black Americans to "go on record before the state and nation as a united people, differing in matters becoming to us, but solidly together on matters which affect our status as a people and as a class of the citizenry of the United States."[123] What is interesting about the *Tribune's* invocation is how closely it equated racial consciousness with black citizenship. In fact, it is through patriotism that this race consciousness is articulated. This helped complete the transformation of black yeomen into citizens and helped make patriotic citizenship a powerful tool in mobilizing an independent and unified race-conscious black polity.

"Work or Fight"

Even though nearly 400,000 black soldiers served in the U.S. Army over the course of the war, black Americans had plenty of reasons to withhold their support for Wilson's crusade.[124] Initially, the brutal stories of the rape of Belgium that filled the pages of American newspapers in the summer of 1914 failed to move the black press. Writing in the *New York Age,* James Weldon Johnson minimized German atrocities in the Low Countries, arguing that "nothing [Germany] did in Belgium can surpass what the Belgians themselves did in the Congo." The editors of the *Norfolk Journal and Guide* even went so far as to suggest that the Belgians deserved what they got as just retribution for their own actions in Africa. Calvin Chase, of the *Washington Bee,* said it plainly: "The Belgians are reaping what they have sowed."[125] More to the point, many black Americans heard demands to fight for democracy as sheer hypocrisy, drawing direct parallels between German atrocities and white supremacist violence in the United States. In February 1916, the *Chicago Defender,* reflecting on the sixteen African Americans lynched in Georgia in the preceding month, opined that "as disgraceful and degrading as these occurrences are, the 'best citizens' appear to have developed a pride in this hideous work. . . . As ghastly as are the horrors of the European war, man's inhumanity to man is not confined to our brethren across the sea."[126] The *Baltimore Afro-American* noted that black men and women would be hard-pressed to distinguish "German ruthlessness on the high seas" from that at home. By contrast to the Germans, who were supposedly killing for the sake of national survival, "Negroes [were] killed in the South . . . for stealing a pig, swearing in public, for wanting to vote."[127] Before the United States entered the war, it was difficult for many African Americans to understand why it was important for the nation to stop German aggression in Europe when they could not stop white aggression against African Americans at home. In October 1915, the *Atlanta Journal* printed an editorial criticizing white hoodlums who had recently attacked white tourists who used black chauffeurs. Warning that "the community that tolerates such a spirit has a perilous future," the editors reverently claimed that "Georgia is a state founded on law and humanity, not a place for Turkish deviltry and persecution."[128] However, by comparing these hoodlums to the perpetrators of the Armenian genocide, they obscured Atlanta's own history of "deviltry and persecution." Not only did the *Journal's* editors omit any mention of the Atlanta race riot of nine years earlier, they also overlooked more recent attacks against black Atlantans. Responding to the *Journal's* editorial, the *Savannah Tribune* pointed out that the *Journal* had ignored a much more serious incident in which an armed mob of white men had invaded an adjacent black neighborhood, forcing the residents to move out, tenants and homeowners alike. The *Tribune* rejected the *Journal's* false piety, advising the South to "stop blaming Germans for the alleged ill treatment of the Belgians, the Turks of the Armenians, and have a house cleaning first."[129]

Nonetheless, this did not stop black Atlantans from exploiting the opportunities opened up by the war to improve their lives. Thousands migrated to Chicago, Detroit, Pittsburgh, and other northern cities in search of employment in the rapidly expanding defense industry. Others took advantage of the labor shortage in the South to hold out for better wages and working conditions.[130] Even prior to the United States' entry into the war, between April and December 1916 the NAACP claimed that an estimated 118,000 African Americans had already left the city.[131] Thousands more joined the army, which not only allowed them to stake their claim on the fruits of Wilson's "democracy," it also came with a paycheck of $30 per month—a sum far in excess of anything they could earn otherwise.[132]

As black Georgians seized these opportunities, they exacerbated longstanding white anxieties over black social and economic mobility that had been present since the end of the Civil War. As Walter White described this exodus from the South, "The once seemingly inexhaustible supply [of black labor] has poured out of that section . . . in a manner that suggests the plunging of a sharp scalpel into a human vein."[133] Desperate to regain control over their workforce, white employers and their allies attempted to use the war to extend the coercive power of Jim Crow. Using the exigencies of the mobilization as a justification, the *Columbus Ledger* in November 1917 called on the federal government to round up all black men fit for service and send them off to France, and advised that the remaining black population be placed under guard and forced to work on southern farms.[134] However, the most common way for securing and disciplining black labor was through manipulating the draft classifications of military-age black men. Some draft boards used their authority to remove unwanted black men. In Fulton County, the draft board approved the exemptions of just 6 of 202 black applicants, while approving the exemptions of 526 of the 815 white applicants.[135] This abuse of the system was so egregious that by February 1918, the Fulton County draft board was closed by the secretary of war.[136] Civil authorities in Atlanta attempted to rid the city of "excess" black men; by contrast, throughout rural Georgia local draft boards manipulated the registration rolls to ensure that planters would not lose the labor of their black tenants. Unmarried, childless, draft-age black men working in cotton production found themselves arbitrarily classified III-A ("a man with dependent children"), ensuring that they would never be drafted until all of the men in classes I and II had been called up.[137] Illiterate black men found themselves at the mercy of their employers, who often also controlled their access to the mail, withholding draft notices until after the harvest. In collusion with local sheriffs, these planters would then collect the reward for turning in their now delinquent tenants for failure to report for duty.[138] Even those who managed to make it into the army did not always escape the reach of Georgia's cotton farmers. To feed the planters' voracious appetite for labor, black soldiers stationed in Georgia were furloughed to local farmers to bring in the 1918 cotton harvest.[139]

Even more menacing was the passage of compulsory work laws throughout the South. Federal legislation in 1918 authorized local registration boards to immediately draft men who did not have any visible means of support. The resulting "work or fight" laws gave draft boards throughout the South new powers with which to discipline black labor.[140] Following the lead of Maryland, New York, New Jersey, and Delaware, the Georgia Chamber of Commerce responded with calls for statewide compulsory work laws. Initially passed in Savannah, Augusta, and Macon, these municipal laws required every able-bodied male to carry a work card that had to be punched at least five of every seven days by their employer. Those unable to present an adequately punched card when challenged by a police officer risked a sentence on the chain-gang.[141] While the *Atlanta Constitution*'s editorial page officially praised such supposedly race-blind legislation for "weeding out loafers, driving hoboes to other pastures and putting the habitual idlers to the task of . . . helping to win the war," another columnist extolled the "work or fight" laws for the effectiveness in disciplining "colored laborers, [who] work for three or four days and lay off the remainder of the week."[142] As the *New York Age* warned, these laws were designed to "bring about an absolute stop [to] the free movement" of African Americans "in search of better employment."[143]

Beginning on 1 September 1918, Georgia's "work or fight" law required every able-bodied male citizen between the ages of sixteen and fifty-five to be "regularly engaged in some . . . useful . . . employment" or join the armed forces.[144] Despite assurances that its "enforcement will be impartial, applied to white and black alike," the enforcement of the state's new compulsory labor laws aggressively targeted black men.[145] Though based on vagrancy statues that had long been used to railroad poor and unemployed African Americans into the convict-lease system, Georgia's new "work or fight" laws vastly expanded the reach of the law. Formerly, men who had been able to demonstrate their possession of wealth, property, or income had been able to escape prosecution under the vagrancy statutes. Georgia's "work or fight" laws endeavored to close this loophole.[146] According to testimony gathered by the NAACP, the authorities did not use these laws "to molest the criminal type of Negroes, the 'blind tigers,' gamblers, runners for immoral houses and the inmates of these houses," but instead targeted members of the respectable working and middle classes. Downstate, in the town of Pelham, the $225 monthly income of Rufus G. McCrary, the agency director for the Standard

Life Insurance Company, did not prevent his prosecution under the local law. Although he employed twenty-five men, the town marshal ordered him to change jobs, since selling insurance was not an essential wartime occupation, especially for a black man. The marshal also harassed McCrary's employees. Frank McCoy, who cleared $150 each month in commissions, also worked part-time as a laborer in Pelham's fertilizer plant. The town marshal ordered him to quit selling insurance in order to put more hours in at the factory. On the other side of the state, local officials in Columbia County grew suspicious that local black men of means were hiring black workers in order to protect them from the "work or fight" laws. In response, county authorities amended the law and made it illegal for black employers to hire other black people.[147] Even though the material success of these men made them targets of white suspicion, their wealth and respectability had once served to shield them from the worst of Jim Crow. Now, in the face of the expanded coercive powers of the state during the war, the black bourgeoisie could protect neither themselves nor their communities.

Black women who took advantage of the new opportunities presented by the war to leave domestic service also became targets of Georgia's "work or fight" laws. Each month, in addition to the $30 paycheck each soldier earned, the dependents of black draftees also received an allotment ranging from $15 to $50—far more than the $4 to $8 monthly wage most of these women could earn working as domestic servants.[148] Additionally, over the course of the war, the wages of most of Georgia's workers, black and white, hit an all-time high.[149] Consequently, cooks, maids, and nannies throughout the state quit jobs that paid as little as $6 per month for employment in war-related industries that paid regular wages ranging between $9 and $15 per week.[150] As a result, black women with expanded employment options or with husbands and fathers who earned enough to support them left domestic service in record numbers. By the war's end, the percentage of black wage-earning women working as domestic servants had fallen from a prewar figure of 84 percent to just 75 percent, prompting widespread alarm over a "servant crisis."[151] The women's pages of the *Atlanta Constitution* warned white women to "prepare for domestic emergency" as their maids and nannies quit to find higher-paying work.[152] Employers dependent on low-wage women workers demanded that action be taken. J. Lee Barnes, the president of the city's Hotel Men's Association and manager of the Majestic Hotel even went to so far as to advocate the passage of a law making it illegal for his black housekeepers and kitchen staff to quit their jobs.[153] To address this crisis, the authors of the state's "work or fight" laws attempted to broaden

their scope to encompass African American women as well.[154] On the pretext of freeing white women for war production, draft boards attempted to
drive black women into work as servants in white homes, regardless of their
ability to demonstrate sufficient income or a means of self-support.[155]

These abuses led black Georgians to write to the NAACP's national office
seeking its assistance. A black tailor from Wrightsville protested that the
"work or fight" laws passed in that town "apply to the white women as well
as the black one but they are only enforcing it on the black women. What I
want to [know] is this law legal?"[156] On the basis of these complaints, Walter White crisscrossed the South for seven weeks in late 1918 investigating
the extremes to which white employers were willing to use the compulsory
work laws to force African Americans, especially black women, into domestic and agricultural labor.[157] In his inquiry into the laws, White related the
story of a woman in Macon who was ordered to find employment suitable
for a "Negro woman." When she protested that her husband made enough
to support both her and their children, city authorities fined her $25.75 and
ruled that she would have to find work as a domestic, face arrest, or leave the
city.[158] In Thomasville, several black women were arrested for vagrancy and
given ten-day sentences during which local authorities put them to work
cleaning the streets for a dollar a day.[159] Acting independently of the elected
city government, the Valdosta chief of police issued an edict ordering all
black domestic servants to carry work cards or risk arrest, specifically ex-
empting white women from this requirement.[160] An ordinance passed in
Bainbridge targeted black housewives who had chosen to remain outside
of wage labor. Dozens of married black women were ordered to appear in
court, charged with vagrancy and fined $15. After being told that "taking
care of their homes was not enough work for them to be doing," they were
ordered to find paid work. This harassment only ended after an indignation
meeting demanded they stop, promising a "race riot" and darkly warning
that should the harassment of black women continue, the black men of Bainbridge would resist "until the last drop of blood in their bodies." Throughout
his investigation, White found no record "of any able-bodied white women
being molested" in this manner.[161]

Over the course of 1918, resistance to these "work or fight" laws became
the top agenda of the NAACP throughout the state. Prior to the release of
White's exposé, the Atlanta branch contacted the national office for advice
on how to proceed in the fight against these laws. In his response, NAACP
national secretary John Shillady cautioned against any outright assault on
the law "lest the organization be characterized as disloyal," advising instead

that the branch fight for a racially equable application of the "work or fight" statutes.[162] However, just three weeks later, as White was concluding his initial investigations into the abuses of the "work or fight" laws throughout the South, the NAACP reversed its position. White's report to Shillady dispelled all doubts as to "whether the practice of conscripting Negro labor was extensive." According to the young, energetic NAACP investigator, it had become a "full grown development."[163] Rather than constraining their protests by concerns over maintaining inclusion in a Jim Crow patriotism, White's efforts against these laws revealed a determination to change the terms upon which black people would seek inclusion into the war effort. At its heart, the struggle against these laws was a contest over the meaning of patriotic service. White Georgians were desperate to prevent their black neighbors from using the war as a means of asserting racial equality. And black Georgians like Walter White were as equally determined to bring democracy into the fields of Georgia as Wilson was determined to establish it on the fields of France.

The campaign against "work or fight" laws bolstered the membership of the NAACP throughout the South. Local organizations founded during the war to protest the abuse of the Selective Service Act became branches of the association after the war.[164] In Atlanta, the campaign against the persecution of black women by draft boards brought the local branch face to face with Governor Hugh Dorsey just as he was preparing to sign the state's compulsory work measures into law. Led by Rev. P. J. Bryant, the NAACP delegation warned that the application of the law to women would be in the hands of prejudiced white sheriffs and police officials who would enforce it "with undue severity against the colored people," and that it was "unreasonable to believe that white women" would be prosecuted under the law. They urged the governor not to sign the law or risk accelerating the vast northward migration of black workers that had begun before the war.[165] Swayed by this logic, the governor pressured the conference committee resolving the House and Senate versions of the state's "work or fight" law to strike the provision covering women despite complaints by state legislators that "the negro women would not work and that the cotton in south Georgia would remain in the fields." In addition to the pressure from the governor, the committee explained that there would be no way for the measure to "hit at the idle negro women, a distinction could not be drawn between the two races, and was sure to be trouble."[166]

Not to be derailed by the state's inaction, two days before the end of the war the Atlanta City Council attempted to pass its own version that included men and women alike.[167] However, the NAACP managed to defeat it as well.[168] In his remarks before the 1919 NAACP annual meeting in Cleveland, Ohio, Rev. Peter James Bryant of Atlanta's Wheat Street Baptist Church described the confrontation between Mayor Asa Candler and a delegation from the local branch: "We went up before His Honor, the Mayor, looked him squarely in the face and told him that the bill meant simply humiliation to black women and that black men had the same respect for their women as white men had for theirs." They castigated the law as unconstitutional "class legislation," since the only group of people to whom it would apply were black working-class mothers, wives, and daughters.[169] The most striking thing about Bryant's description of this confrontation is how similar in tone it is to the earlier confrontation between the Atlanta NAACP and the Board of Education. Two years previously, before the United States' official entry into the war, the Atlanta NAACP had demanded in a "straight-from-the-shoulder manner" that the city improve the educational offerings available to taxpaying black citizens.[170] In addition to the bold confidence of the NAACP's delegation, Bryant also attributed the success of the branch in keeping black women beyond the reach of the "work or fight" laws to the cross-class unity within Atlanta's black community. Though his comments remained tinged with condescension, he remarked that "it is one thing to talk about the laboring people, and it is another thing to talk to them. It is one thing to work for the laboring people and it is another thing to work with them. The reason many of us cannot help these people we talk about is because we stand too far from them and feel ourselves so far above them."[171]

It is a commonly held notion that the war remasculinized black political discourse, allowing this transformation of black political consciousness. However, the ability of the NAACP's Rev. P. J. Bryant to stand manfully before the mayor and governor with the strength of a broad cross-section of black Atlanta behind him was a direct legacy of the Neighborhood Union's previous organizing work *before* the war. It was in defense of the Union's agenda to protect and expand public education for black students that the men who led the NAACP branch initially found the confidence to push back against cuts to the seventh grade. Before the war, it was this fight that shook Atlanta's black men from their self-imposed political quietude following the 1906 riot. And it was also from the Union, which first sought to organize all of city's black women regardless of class or creed, that Bryant and the NAACP learned to "work with" and "talk with" the city's black working class. In Atlanta, the rejection of accommodation and its attendant embrace of the politics of respectability began prior to the war and was built directly atop the foundation laid by the city's organized black women.

"We Have No Duties Where We Have No Rights"

In 1917 and 1918, 2.3 million black men had registered for the draft; 367,000 of these men served in uniform.[172] The widely shared experience of military service and the fervor of wartime patriotism provided these men the opportunity to publicly express gender identities that challenged and destabilized the politics of respectability. One of these soldiers, Asa H. Gordon, wrote to his former teacher at Atlanta University from Fort Des Moines, the segregated training camp established in Iowa for black officer candidates. In his letter, Gordon explained that "on the question of the color line, men's minds have been changed out here, and when the men here . . . get back home a mob in their vicinity will be in a danger zone without doubt." Military training, he concluded, would serve "as an antidote to mob rule and lynch law in the South."[173] Sentiments like these encouraged the camp's commanding officer, Colonel Charles Ballou, to complain to the adjutant general's office that the men under his command were trying to "ram social equality down the throats of the white population, [when they] must *win* it by their modesty, patience and character." In an attempt to contain this newly assertive black manhood, Colonel Ballou issued an order forbidding the officer candidates from defending themselves or responding in any way to racist insults of the hostile white citizens of nearby Des Moines. Compelled to comply with Ballou's order, trainee Charles Hamilton Houston recalled in 1940 that from the moment Ballou issued his order, "morale at Fort Des Moines died."[174] The war had undermined the effectiveness of these appeals to "modesty, patience and character." During and especially after the conflict, black veterans like Asa Gordon and Charles Houston would refuse to wait patiently for their rights, insisting that through military service and patriotic loyalty, they had already won them.

Although segregation kept most African American troops relegated to labor battalions, black men who entered the military nonetheless entered a cultural milieu that equated manhood with martial discipline, leadership, and courage under fire—all of which transformed the meanings of respectability and heightened race consciousness.[175] Such was the case for Horace Pippen of Goshen, New York, who signed up with Company K of the 369th Colored Infantry. Pippen remembered his military service with pride, since "every man in that co[mpany] were a man."[176] Likewise, Harry Hall joined the Eighth Illinois Infantry in early 1917 explicitly to be part of a unit that was "officered by Blacks from the colonel on down." The Eighth Illinois had been created in 1898 in response to the overwhelming desire for black men to fight in the war against Spain and had black commanding officers since its inception.[177] Its members had seen service in Cuba during the Spanish-American War and had fought in the "punitive expedition" against Mexico in 1916, following Pancho Villa's raid on Columbus, New Mexico.[178] Though Hall's decision to enlist was motivated by patriotism, he also longed to join an organization where he was free to assert a different sort of black manhood. As he reflected in his autobiography, "I didn't regard it as part of a U.S. Army unit, but as some sort of big social club for fellow race-men." These "race-men" would use their patriotic sacrifices to establish a new foundation for asserting equality with white Americans. As a black lieutenant who served in the Eighth alongside Hall put it: "if we can't fight and die in the war just as bravely as white men, then we don't deserve an equality with white men, and after the war, we had better go back home and forget about it all."[179]

World War I shifted the terms of the contest over the place of black people in American civilization as black men in uniform began to assert claims to full and equal citizenship, prompting a fierce reaction from the defenders of white supremacy. Two years before the United States entered the war, the image of the black soldier as a savage beast hell-bent on raping white women was burned into the minds of millions of white Americans by D. W. Griffith's epic 1915 film *Birth of a Nation*. With its portrayal of Reconstruction as an unmitigated disaster for the South and its heroic depiction of the Ku Klux Klan as the guarantors of honest government, it provided ideological justification for Jim Crow and helped inspire the establishment of the second Klan atop Stone Mountain, just outside of Atlanta.[180] Not only did Griffith characterize black political power as corrupt and ignorant, he also directly made the connection between black military service and threats to white womanhood. In one of the pivotal scenes in the movie, Gus, a black captain in the Union army, pursues a young white woman named Flora through the woods, pressuring her to marry him. Refusing his ardor, she chooses to jump off a cliff to her death in order to preserve her purity. In his grief, the girl's father, Confederate veteran Ben Cameron, founds the Ku Klux Klan to avenge his daughter's death. Within two weeks of the film's arrival at the Atlanta Theater on Peachtree Street, more than 35,000 people had seen the movie, which had an electrifying effect on white audiences. Ward Greene of the *Atlanta Journal* reacted to the film's depiction of Reconstruction: "Loathing, disgust, hate, envelop you, hot blood cries for vengeance." Ned McIntosh of the *Atlanta Constitution* applauded the film's portrayal of the Reconstruction "South crushed under a Black heel . . . a period of ruin and destruction. . . . You could shriek for a depiction of relief and—yes, retribution."[181]

Tapping this wellspring of white racist anxieties, in a diatribe against black conscription into the armed forces Mississippi senator James K. Vardaman warned of

> the deleterious effects of the "melting pot" of war, the merging of the races, and the enforced equality and solidarity of citizenship. The suggestion is monstrous. . . . Let it not be forgotten Mr. President, that political equality in a country where the races are practically equal in number means ultimately social equality; social equality is universally followed by race amalgamation; race amalgamation means race deterioration, and with race deterioration will come the final disaster, the . . . downfall and death of our civilization.[182]

These sentiments were not just confined to the ravings of a notoriously intemperate senator. Other white commentators were equally alarmed at the potential consequences of the "enforced equality and solidarity" of wartime citizenship. A U.S. Army communiqué sent to the French military command in August 1918 warned of the "menace of degeneracy" presented by the arrival of thousands of black troops and urged the French to adopt a policy of strict segregation in order to contain and repress "the vices of the Negro." Citing no evidence, the missive claimed that that "black American troops in France have, by themselves, given rise to many complaints for attempted rape as all the rest of the army." Although the black U.S. troops were "the choicest with respect to physique and morals," even these men were unable to control themselves when presented with the opportunity for intimacy with white women.[183] At the close of the war, Colonel Allen J. Greer, chief of staff for the Ninety-Second Infantry Division (Colored), wrote to Tennessee senator Kenneth McKellar about plans for reorganizing the army following demobilization, offering his evaluation of the performance of black troops. He reported that black soldiers were incompetent soldiers, "rank cowards," and "dangerous to no one except themselves and women." While citing several instances of accidental shootings and self-inflicted wounds, at the heart of Greer's unease was the same fear that Vardaman had articulated on the floor of the Senate, namely, that unrestrained black manhood, empowered by military service, would present a grave threat to the sexual purity of white women. Repeating the myth that black soldiers were more prone to committing rape than white soldiers, he nonetheless endorsed the continued use of black soldiers, but only if led by white officers capable of restraining them. By contrast, he asserted that "Colored officers neither control nor care to control the men. They themselves have been engaged very largely in pursuit of French women, it being their first opportunity to meet white women who did not treat them as servants."[184] As the war offered new ways for African Americans to articulate their relationship to the state, it shook the cultural foundations that assured white men of their supremacy. In their fevered rehearsals of the myth of the black beast rapist, Griffith, Greer, and Vardaman were desperate to change the terms of this relationship from what a grateful nation owed its black veterans to an older one in which the white hero saves the white damsel from the black monster.

Drawing upon the newly expanded meanings of wartime citizenship, African Americans offered a counternarrative to this story of black savages and white heroes by recounting the long history of black military service. These history lessons soon became a common feature of the defense of black loyalty and valor during and immediately after the war. In the pages of the *Atlanta Independent,* Ben Davis responded to accusations of black disloyalty by reciting the long record of black servicemen in every U.S. conflict since the Revolution.[185] Echoing Davis, the *Savannah Tribune* reminded its readers that "Negro blood was among the first which was spilled in the Revolution and his was the blood that stained the hot sands at Carrizal."[186] In the preface to his *Official History of the American Negro in the World War,* Emmett J. Scott, special assistant to the Secretary of War for Negro Affairs, wrote that this was not the "first instance in the Nation's history that this ever-loyal racial group rightly and cheerfully responded to the tocsin of war." African American men had "made a military record of which any race might well be proud. In the Revolutionary War, in the War of 1812, in the Mexican War, in the Civil War, and in the War with Spain,—the American Negro soldier has always distinguished himself by bravery, fortitude, and loyalty."[187] In June 1917, the *Crisis* reminded its readers that "this country belongs to us even more than to those who lynch, disfranchise and segregate. . . . It rightly demands our whole-hearted defense as well today as when with Crispus Attucks we fought for independence." Another editorial in that same issue demanding that black men be allowed to enlist and fight asserted that "the American Negro more unanimously than any other American has offered up his services in this war as officer and soldier. . . . Up to the present his offer has been received with sullen and ungracious silence. . . . Nevertheless, the offer stands as it stood in 1776, 1812, 1861 and 1898."[188]

During the war, expressions of patriotism began to displace respectability as the primary vehicle for cultural self-defense against racist stereotypes of black criminality and perversity. Black soldiers in government-issued khaki completely upended the gender ideology of Jim Crow; rather than beastly black rapists, the uniforms these men wore defined them as noble, heroic, and disciplined defenders of the nation, usurping the role reserved for white men in the pyschosexual drama of white supremacy. With celebrations of black martial manhood at their heart, these recitations of the record of black military service served as much as a rebuke to the black beast rapist myth as they were a way to assert equality with white men. Whereas the politics of respectability often compelled black elites to publicly accept the rape/lynching narrative, patriotism gave them a language that allowed them to dispense with this narrative altogether. Just weeks before the United States officially entered the war against Germany, the *Baltimore Afro-American* printed an editorial directly comparing the political choices faced by African Americans being asked to defend a Jim Crow nation with those faced by the first generation of American patriots. "England disfranchised her colonies, so to speak, and treated them in much the same way as Uncle Sam treats his colored citizens," and in the face of this, the revolutionaries proclaimed, "We have no duties where we have no rights, it were cowardly to believe otherwise." The *Afro-American* concluded that "in the spirit of those same patriots, whose children we are, we say the Negro who speaks of duties where he has no rights, places himself in the position where he may deserve the name—a moral coward." Though carefully acknowledging duty to the government in time of war, the paper insisted that "until we have won the political, economic and social freedom that any other citizen of the United States enjoys," black Americans "had but one duty . . . to fight the battle for inner freedom. Our greater enemies are within."[189] The patriotic fervor of the war years allowed the *Baltimore Afro-American* to reach back to the American Revolution for the language it needed to assert a new black politics and reject the old.

Nevertheless, even as this new discourse of patriotic manhood challenged the politics of respectability, it continued to be shaped by it. White racial anxieties that had arisen during the mobilization for war compelled Atlanta's black leadership to assume a defensive posture. For the nineteen months of active U.S. participation in World War I, expressions of black patriotism became a basis of interracial solidarity, functioning much as the politics of respectability had earlier. This was evidenced by the friendly exchange of opinions regarding black loyalty between Clark Howell of the

Atlanta Constitution and Ben Davis of the *Atlanta Independent*. On the same day that Congress voted to commit U.S. troops to the war in Europe, Howell printed an editorial responding to rumors that German agents were circulating among black southerners "to incite them against the American government." Dismissing these concerns as "preposterous," Howell asked his readers to recall the "loyalty, homage, service and devotion" that enslaved African Americans displayed during the Civil War. Drawing heavily on the myth of the loyal slave, the white editor explained that "the white women and children, cripples and old men were dependent largely upon the negroes for protection in their homes, while most of the white able-bodied [men] were at the front fighting for the right to continue in bondage those who were at home taking care of the women and children and the helpless! . . . During that entire period . . . history does not record an instance in which a negro as much as lifted his finger in violation of the honor . . . of [those] in their keeping."[190] According to Howell's logic, since African American slaves did not take advantage of the chaos of war to violate the sanctity of their masters' households, their descendants could be trusted to defend the flag that ultimately gave them freedom. With a brazen confidence born of holding all the aces, Howell affirmed that African Americans would remain loyal to their country regardless of the conditions under which they were forced to live.

Ben Davis, rather than reject this argument, reprinted it in full on the front page of the *Independent* on the following day, accompanying it with glowing commentary. He took pains to agree with Howell's central assertion that if "we proved loyal, true and patriotic to the trust that imposed in us then by our masters who were fighting to preserve slavery, it is unthinkable now . . . that any condition would lead the Negro to rise against his country."[191] This commentary, along with similar letters written by J. W. Davison, the *Independent*'s managing editor, and H. R. Butler, a prominent black doctor, were themselves printed in the *Constitution*.[192] Howell's fairy tale of black loyalty to the Confederate family gave Davis the ability not only to reassure white Atlantans that black Americans would remain loyal to the United States but also to assert that the war would not unsettle the patriarchal authority of white men over their households. This was meant to reassure white Atlantans that black men—especially those in uniform—would not pose a threat to white women. Using patriotic language, this exchange between Davis and Howell articulated what was essentially a defensive alliance with white men rooted in a shared patriarchal mastery of racially segregated households. The potential for violence sparked by white wartime racial anxieties over black disloyalty compelled black men to retool the politics of respectability for use during wartime.

Likewise, the moral vigilance of the home front during World War I gave black women reformers like Lugenia Burns Hope a vast new field of endeavor. These women expanded their patriotic *obligation* to participate into a *right* to shape the impact the war had on their communities, transforming the war effort into a vehicle for the moral uplift of black citizens.[193] A good part of this work served to defend black communities against attacks on their moral character. The Selective Service Act of 1917 had made it a federal offense to sell alcohol or operate houses of prostitution within five miles of any training camp. This gave military police the power to extend their jurisdiction over vice-control efforts in the neighborhoods, towns, and cities adjacent to the nation's expanding network of military bases.[194] By adopting a very expansive definition of vice, this law effectively made policing young women's sex lives a federal policy; throughout the South, this invited unwanted intrusion by white military authorities into black neighborhoods. The war work of organizations like the Neighborhood Union was an attempt to renegotiate this relationship between the wartime state and its impact on black communities. As they mediated between federal power and local black populations, they enforced a still influential agenda of respectability and race uplift.

One of the primary vehicles through which black clubwomen exerted their influence over the war effort was through the establishment of "hostess houses" for black soldiers in camp. A joint project of the National Association of Colored Women and the YWCA, these hostess houses were modeled on the settlement houses of the day and enabled the women who ran them to protect the health and morals of black men who had volunteered to serve. The first of these houses opened at New York's Camp Upton in early 1918, and within six months hostess houses had been established at most camps with large black garrisons.[195] Barred from local restaurants, bars, and places of entertainment by Jim Crow laws and local white sentiment, these hostess houses provided much-needed recreation and escape from the rigors of camp life. While still inferior to the camp facilities available to white troops, black soldiers could write letters home, socialize with members of the opposite sex, and find refuge from the rigors of camp life. Despite their limitations, these houses were incredibly popular. At Camp Funston in Kansas, more than 4,000 black people (including 1,200 women) visited the house over the course of a single month.[196] These hostess houses created a space in which the interaction between young black enlisted men and black women could be confined within the bounds of respectability, deflecting the charges of sexual licentiousness and immorality that often served to stoke white fears of black men in uniform.

By linking respectability and patriotism, Atlanta's Neighborhood Union was able to significantly expand the scope of its work. Even as it sought to deflect the coercive power of the state to police the lives of black people, the Union also drew on the shared language of patriotic citizenship in order to tap into the newly expanded powers of that state to bring much needed improvements into the city's black neighborhoods. The patriotic work of the Union included organizing educational and recreational activities for black troops stationed at nearby Camp Gordon as well as adapting the organizing structure of the Union to the establishment of patriotic leagues to shore up black support for the war. While this work was certainly more than a mere means to an end, the Union nonetheless used its support for the war to expand and advance its prewar agenda. Early in the war, the Union wrote the War Department that its patriotic work was being hampered by the vice and crime that were enabled by a lack of proper street lighting in Atlanta's black neighborhoods. Of particular concern were "the loungers and vicious people" who were disrupting the work of the Union's neighborhood center on Leonard Street. To remedy the situation, the Union requested the installation of two arc lights on that block. In its memo to the War Department, it made the case for installing arc lights throughout the city in order to protect the virtue of black women from the very real threat posed by the large number of male soldiers, black and white, stationed near Atlanta. It usefully provided a map that outlined the "districts in which Negroes lived [and] where lights were needed as a deterrent to War vice."[197] In using patriotic language to link its long-running campaign for streetlights in black neighborhoods to the war effort, the Union leveraged military mobilization to advance its moral uplift and development agenda.

In 1918, the Union organized the Atlanta Colored Women's War Council, and sent another series of recommendations to the War Department. In addition to its earlier request for arc lights, the Union also called for the "rigid enforcement of sanitary laws" regarding surface toilets and garbage disposal in black neighborhoods. It encouraged military provost guards and city police to show "more consideration towards colored people," and recommended that these officers of the law fairly administer the segregation laws in public parks and streetcars. The Union also called on the city to crack down on "the colored prostitute [as well as] the white" and on employers to allow women workers to return home before dark—both measures intended to protect the moral and physical well-being of black women. Finally, and most significant, it urged the War Department to "use its influence" to induce the daily press "to evince a keener sense of fairness" in its coverage of black Atlantans. In "suppressing the good and commendable qualities of the race" in favor of "glaring headlines," the city's newspapers "inflame reciprocal race intolerance and [do] death to the spirit of race co-operation. Such utterances . . . should be regarded in their proper light, as . . . treasonable acts against the government."[198] For stating sentiments similar to these about the white press in the aftermath of the Atlanta race riot, *Voice of the Negro* editor Jesse Max Barber had been driven from the city just twelve years earlier. However, the overarching national imperative of patriotic unity gave the Union a language that safely allowed it to mark as treasonous the sort of racially inflammatory reporting that sparked the riot in 1906. As such, patriotism served as a far more powerful restraint on arbitrary white behavior than had the discourse of respectability.

Will Alexander, a white southern liberal who headed the War Work Council of the Young Men's Christian Association (YMCA) in Atlanta, interpreted these moments of interracial cooperation as the dawn of a new era in race relations. It was his fervent hope that the patriotic unity he had witnessed in Atlanta would endure. Although this shared language of patriotism may have served to cement a wartime interracial alliance in Atlanta, once the war ended it collapsed in the face of white anxiety over the place of returning black soldiers from a war meant to make the world safe for democracy. Just days before the end of the war, Alexander mused about the seeming progress in race relations: "We'll never go back to our old ways. If we behave this way during a war, we can behave this way all of the time."[199] However, he bitterly recalled decades later that "within forty-eight hours after the Armistice was signed . . . the morale and spirit that had existed began to disappear."[200] The end of hostilities in Europe unleashed an unprecedented wave of antiblack violence throughout the country. During the war there had been violent racial altercations in East St. Louis, Illinois, and Houston, Texas, but this violence paled in comparison to the "Red Summer" that followed the war.[201] In 1919, between the end of May and the beginning of September, there were race riots in twenty-six cities across the nation; the most infamous of these occurred in Washington, D.C., and Chicago, during which dozens of black and white citizens perished.[202] Throughout Georgia, these urban clashes were reproduced on a smaller scale. In retaliation for the deaths of two white police officers following a disturbance at a church in Millen, white townsmen killed five African Americans and burned down seven black churches and fraternal lodges. A dispute in Milledgeville over class colors between black and white high school seniors led black parents, fearing an assault by whites, to post over 100 armed guards outside the church where the graduation ceremonies were held. An attempted lynching in the town of Berkeley prompted an armed response from the black community, which led to the deaths of four white men. The lynching was averted.[203] Other African Americans were not so lucky; during 1918 and 1919 white mobs murdered thirty-nine black Georgians—an average of one lynching every nineteen days.[204]

Measured against its promise to create a foundation of interracial cooperation rooted in a shared patriotic citizenship, World War I was an utter failure. Thomas W. Hardwick, one of the architects of disfranchisement in Georgia, had moved from the House to the Senate in 1915 and used his position to rail against the menace proposed by returning black troops. He predicted that these black veterans would comprise an unstoppable menace once they returned home: "What will be the result when . . . hundreds of thousands of Negroes come home from this war with a record of honorable military service? I can conceive that a new agitation may arise as strong and bitter as the agitation for Negro suffrage which swept the North after the Civil War."[205] In a 1919 letter to Secretary of War Newton D. Baker, J. W. Sammons, another white Georgian who was deeply concerned that black veterans would seize their rights by force of arms, predicted "war between the negroes and the white people before the year was out."[206] Laying aside Sammons's fantasies of a race war, he was nonetheless responding to a very real assertiveness on the part of returning black veterans. In 1917, at the age of twenty-two, a black farmer named Daniel Mack signed up with the 365th Infantry and served overseas. After returning home to south Georgia's Worth County two years later, Mack donned his uniform and joined his friends for a day on the town in Sylvester, the county seat. That Saturday, 5 April 1919, was market day, and the streets were very crowded. In the crush, Mack accidentally brushed against a white man, who struck the veteran, knocking him off the sidewalk and into the street. Before the war, Mack may have kept his anger in check, but having recently returned from France, he chose instead to strike back and was promptly arrested. On Monday morning, before the judge, he pleaded not guilty to assault, arguing that "I fought for you in France to make the world safe for democracy. I don't think you treated me right in putting me in jail and keeping me there, because I've got as much as right as anybody else to walk on the sidewalk." The judge, unmoved by Mack's appeal, reminded him that "this is a white man's country," and sentenced him to thirty days on the chain gang.[207] In the months following the Armistice, encounters like these grew increasingly common on the streets of southern towns and cities, where the "right" of white men to assault black men had previously gone unquestioned.

Apprehensive about the place of African Americans in the postwar order, returning black soldiers like Daniel Mack became targets of white violence throughout Georgia. On 3 August 1919, Charles Kelley, recently discharged from Camp Gordon, was killed in Woolsey for not turning his car out of the way of a white boy who was coming down the street. Incensed at this violation of racial etiquette, the boy's father confronted Kelley and shot him in the back as he attempted to flee. Two weeks later, a white mob hung Jim Grant in Pope City for allegedly killing two white men as they attempted to arrest another man. After forcing him to watch the lynching of his son, the crowd publicly whipped Grant's father and ordered him to leave town immediately.[208] Ben Herne, a wounded black veteran, was savagely beaten with a baseball bat in an Atlanta drugstore for having the temerity to ask for a glass of soda water. In Blakely, 200 miles south of Atlanta, black veteran Wilbur Little was killed for wearing his uniform.[209] The lynching of black veterans in their uniforms represented not only the ultimate symbol of contempt for black citizenship, it was also a desperate attempt to reinforce the gender ideology of white supremacy.[210] Military uniforms signified authority, leadership, courage, and self-respect along with manly restraint and the capacity for disciplined violence—all traits reserved for white men in the cultural drama of Jim Crow. The visibility of black veterans in uniform on the streets of postwar Georgia contradicted the cultural signposts that assured white men that they were of the superior race. The resulting brutality directed against black veterans in uniform had become so dangerous that the Neighborhood Union repeatedly petitioned the War Department, asking it to take steps to prevent the lynching of black soldiers. In response, the government enlisted the Union in enforcing its rule forbidding the wearing of campaign ribbons and decorations for valor after demobilization.[211] Unable to restrain white violence, the Union worked hard to get black veterans *out* of uniform so that they did not put themselves in danger.

In or out of uniform, the war had wrought a profound transformation in the political consciousness of black veterans, their families, and their communities. In a lengthy letter to the *Washington Bee* describing the travails and triumphs of black soldiers in France, Sergeant Greenleaf Johnson, a veteran of the 372nd Infantry, demanded to know: "Will [the Negroes'] country, after admitting them to *full brotherhood* in labor, sacrifice, suffering and death, continue to deny them full *heirship* in the unmolested enjoyment of the pursuits of peace, happiness and the protection of its laws and guidance in the governing affairs of the nation?"[212] By invoking the metaphors of family, Sergeant Johnson echoed the rhetorical strategies of the 1906 GERC, which once described black and white Georgians as "the children of a common state" in an attempt both to deracialize citizenship by drawing the circle of family around all of Georgia's citizens, black and white, and to recast paternalism as brotherhood.[213] However, postwar violence had limited the effectiveness of such familial metaphors and made untenable any promise of interracial solidarity rooted in a shared patriotism. Nonetheless, family was only one of the languages of solidarity invoked in Johnson's letter. More powerfully, the martial sacrifice of black men now permitted claims on full and equal citizenship that were not available in 1906. Invoking the history of the French Revolution, Greenleaf demanded that African Americans "oppose and denounce" all "Negro men who sit in high places, whether by unanimous choice of their fellows or those . . . hand-selected to fill a position of apologist and unction for the insufferable wrongs inflicted on their race."[214] For Sergeant Greenleaf and thousands like him, it was no longer sufficient for black leaders to draw their power from strategic interracial alliances with influential white men and women. A new standard of race leadership had emerged from the war and with it a return to Reconstruction-era articulations of the true sources of political power.

In a *New York Age* column published less than seven months following the Armistice, James Weldon Johnson described how the "idealistic war dreams" of interracial patriotic unity—"a new world, a new order, a new South"—had vanished "one by one" as the "solid outlines of the old, pre-war conditions loom[ed] up clearer and clearer." Embittered, disillusioned, and profoundly wizened, Johnson asked:

> Why is it that these war dreams, not only of the Negro but of humanity the world over, have been dissolving ever since the Germans acknowledged defeat? It is the old, old story; as old as the history of civilization. The people dream dreams of a changed and a better world, but generally without paying attention to the machinery necessary for making those dreams come true. Those in control dream no dreams, but use all of their intelligence and energy and power in keeping hold of the machinery by which the established order is maintained. . . . The Negro should learn that he will never be able to make any of his dreams come true until he is

able to get his hands on some sort of machinery. Dreams floating around in the air come to nothing; they must be run through a machine to be realized. The machinery for the Negro is organized and united power in all of his efforts for economic, industrial, political and civic advancement.[215]

It was precisely to this task that the Atlanta branch of the NAACP would bend all of its energies in the months following the end of the war.

5

"A Satisfied Part of Our Composite Citizenship"

The Fight for Booker T. Washington High School, 1918–1924

The end of World War I meant a renewal of the fight for equal schools in Atlanta. Given the inability of Atlanta's black progressive leaders to persuade the city to address the overcrowded and unhealthy conditions in black schools, they took advantage of the city's postwar fiscal crisis to shift their strategy from defense to offense. Since 1900, the city had relied increasingly on bond issues to fund the expansion and maintenance of the public school system—a decision that allowed elected city officials to break ground on projects for their constituents while distributing the tax burden to future generations.[1] When combined with the rapid growth of the city during the war years, the postwar economic downturn made a bond issue to fund urgently needed expansions to the public schools even more attractive. Building upon the massive organizing work of the Neighborhood Union, the NAACP attempted to compel the city to invest in black education by mobilizing black voters to defeat all municipal bond referenda until Atlanta took steps to address the crisis in the black schools.

This strategy was possibly suggested by the failed attempt of the city in 1915 to pass a $3.3 million bond issue meant to improve the schools, Grady Hospital, streets, and sewers.[2] The biggest obstacle to the passage of these bonds was the constitutional requirement that any bond issue be approved by two-thirds of *all* registered voters and not simply those voting in the referendum.[3] As the *Constitution* editorialized, "not only is it necessary to marshal the approval of two-thirds of the voters who can be relied upon to vote at the election, but it is necessary to enlist the sympathy and assurance of support of enough voters in addition to the voting two-thirds to outweigh the dead men, the living absentees and the other non-voters who were registered a year ago—and many of who cannot, or will not, vote now."[4] According to state law, all registered nonvoters would be counted as voting against any bond proposal even if indifferent to the outcome of the election.

This requirement made it incredibly difficult to fund most major development projects, and the situation had become so untenable by 1915 that the city had unsuccessfully tried twice to change the rule.[5] Walter White and the officers of the local NAACP sought to take advantage of these hurdles to compel the city to invest in black education.[6] Despite the passage of disfranchisement nearly a decade previously, African Americans could not be barred from participation in municipal referenda by means of the white primary. Should enough African Americans succeed in running the gauntlet of the poll tax, the literacy test, and the understanding clause, they could determine the outcome of the election.

"The White Man's Love Passeth All Understanding": The July 1918 Bond Election

During the summer preceding the 1917–18 school year, white parents organized to stop the introduction of double sessions in the schools for their children. White fathers adopted the slogan "Wake Up, Daddy," and using their status as both voters and taxpayers, they took the fight to the state legislature.[7] Pledging "to take the schools out of politics," they demanded an amendment to Atlanta's city charter that would force the city to permanently dedicate a portion of its annual tax revenue to the schools.[8] Though unsuccessful, they nonetheless got the city's attention.[9] While the operating budget for the public schools would remain tight, the "Wake Up, Daddy" movement raised the idea of floating a bond issue in order to construct new schools. One "daddy" invoked the peril faced by their children and insisted that bonds were necessary in order to "build a new high school for girls before the one we have burns up and kills a lot of our daughters."[10] When the city proved unwilling to raise the money for school construction, the agitation by white parents would not die down. Facing record enrollments, the specter of double sessions for white students led to a renewal of hostilities between white parents and the city. These tensions did not subside until the Board of Education successfully appealed to the city finance committee to appropriate the money necessary.[11] The 1918 city budget was enlarged to include $140,000 for the construction of three new schools as well as a further $37,500 for additional improvements to white schools.[12] With the white "daddies" appeased, Atlanta's politicians could sleep well now that the anger of white parents at the threat of double sessions would not likely become an issue in the upcoming elections.

However, not everyone was satisfied. For nearly a decade, the ongoing crisis of double sessions in black schools had gone unaddressed, the city council protesting that the city was too poor to remedy the situation. The board's decision to provide "three new schools for white children and no new schoolhouses for black children" was the final straw for *Atlanta Independent* editor Ben Davis. The man who in the aftermath of the 1906 riot sought to reassure an anxious and terrified black public that "we are in the midst of friends and they predominate" now denounced the "white man's love . . . for the Negro" as "peculiar. . . . It is an article that 'Passeth all understanding.'" Invoking and inverting the meaning of Philippians 4:7, Davis castigated the bad faith of the city's white leadership. The original Epistle to the Philippians was a letter from Paul thanking the Christians in the Roman city of Philippi for their considerable sacrifices on behalf of the early church, the reward for which will be "the peace of God, which passeth all understanding."[13] By contrast, the sacrifices made by black Atlantans as "citizens, taxpayers, soldiers and human beings" had been for naught; Davis had lost all faith in a religion that will "starve a human being because he is black; that will take from the poor and needy and give to the rich and plenteous." The shattering of his faith in "the white man's love of the Negro" also shattered Davis's illusions regarding what it would take to achieve justice for black Americans. No longer would it suffice to appeal to the better angels of white conscience; rather, it was "up to the Negro to organize politically for the purpose of bringing about a better day." Denouncing the lack of consideration given Atlanta's black schoolchildren as "barbarous" and "outrageous," the editor called on his African American readership to "march on the white people," but do so "within our rights." He urged "every Negro citizen . . . to vote against every bonded issue; it matters not whether it is for water, street improvement or what not," until the city agreed to "build up-to-date modern school houses for Negroes."[14]

The bonds that Davis called on black voters to defeat had nothing to do with the public schools; they were originally proposed following the Great Atlanta Fire of 1917 to fund a sorely needed modernization of the waterworks and fire department.[15] The initial request in October was for $250,000, but by the time that the city council finally approved a date for the bond election four months later, this total had risen to $800,000, comprising four different bond issues.[16] Initially, Mayor Asa Candler and several city councilmen were reluctant to get behind the bond issue both out of fear that the issue would fail at the polls as well as out of a fundamental fiscal conservatism.[17] Despite the tripling of the initial bond request, it was still so small that the ordinarily prodevelopment *Constitution* initially urged the voters of the city to oppose the bonds, maintaining that the amount to be voted upon represented a mere "drop in the bucket."[18] Given the mayor's belated approval and the *Constitution*'s ambivalent endorsement, few in the city were willing to take up the fight to pass the bonds, with the result that the election was postponed twice.[19] Finally, in the hopes of achieving a turnout high enough to win the approval of a majority of the city's registered voters, the bond election was scheduled for 10 July 1918, the same day as the city's Democratic white primary.[20]

For the boosters of the bond issue, this was good news since it also became an issue in the city's mayoral race, with all four candidates turning out their supporters to vote for the bonds.[21] Two weeks before the election, the supporters of the bonds launched their campaign with a mass meeting at city hall. On the rostrum were the mayor, several city councilmen, the head of the Atlanta Federation of Trades, as well as the editors of the *Atlanta Constitution,* the *Georgian,* the *Atlanta Journal,* and the *Journal of Labor.*[22] These civic leaders resolved to hold mass meetings in every ward and concluded with a vote committing each and every attendee to work for the success of the bond issue.[23] In addition to the political rallies held by the four candidates for mayor, the bond committee held meetings every night of the week preceding the election, culminating in a heavily attended mass meeting two nights before the election.[24] Following these efforts, "every candidate for [every] office, every newspaper . . . and every labor organization [and] business organization" in the city of Atlanta declared themselves "heartily in favor of the bonds."[25]

With thousands of doughboys still fighting in Europe, the bond campaign committee employed baldly patriotic appeals, urging "every loyal and patriotic citizen" to vote for the bonds. Using the term usually reserved for draft dodgers, the committee condemned those who would fail to vote as "slackers of the worst sort."[26] These appeals to patriotism were reinforced by several cartoons printed on the front page of the *Atlanta Journal* during the week before the election. One of these cartoons portrayed Atlanta as Joan of Arc facing a stereotypical dagger-wielding "Hun," representing "DANGER from Lack of Vital City Improvements" (see figure 5).[27] Referring to a giant sword labeled "BONDS" at Atlanta's side, the cartoon's caption commanded its viewers to "Give Her This Weapon" in order to defeat the advancing foe.

GIVE HER THIS WEAPON

FIGURE 5. "Give Her This Weapon," *Atlanta Journal*, 5 July 1918.

Just as France was being menaced by Germany, so was Atlanta by those who would oppose the passage of the bonds.[28]

By every indication, the bonds were all but guaranteed to pass. The weather was fair, the bond commission had decked out dozens of cars with banners urging registered voters to go to the polls, the Chamber of Commerce phone bank had already contacted 1,500 voters before noon, and the commander of nearby Camp Gordon had even given those soldiers registered as voters in Atlanta permission to leave the base in order to vote.[29] However, by 2 P.M. on Election Day only 3,881 votes had been cast in the bond election, leaving them well over 5,000 votes short with only five hours left before voting was finished.[30] When the polls finally closed, Atlanta had failed to pass the four bond issues, each of which needed 9,230 votes to pass.[31] Despite predictions of a record-breaking turnout, support for the four bonds fell short of the two-thirds majority of *registered voters* required for passage by 786, 813, 855, and 892 votes, respectively.[32]

Though black voters only comprised 5.4 percent of the city's electorate, their absence from the polls contributed heavily to the defeat of the bonds. Reviewing the returns, W. Tom Winn, the chairman of the bond commit- tee, noted that of Atlanta's 742 registered black voters, "only a small number voted."[33] Prior to the election, the selection of the white primary for the date of the bond election had raised enough concern over black turnout to prompt Winn to make a special effort to reach out to black voters. At a meet- ing held at Friendship Baptist Church two days before the election, the bond commissioners reassured the black voters in the congregation that although they were excluded by their race from the primary, they were still entitled to vote in the bond election.[34] They even arranged to have the black clergy in the city speak about the bond issue the Sunday before the election and made sure that two additional polling places were located in black neighbor- hoods. The arrogance of the city's white progressive leaders blinded them to the possibility of defeat at the hands of the black voters, whose stake in the development of the city they had repeatedly dismissed. Despite repeated calls in the pages of the *Independent* for the defeat of the bonds, the *Atlanta Journal* blithely declared that "no one is against the proposed issue."[35] The fact that one of the polling sites was located in the Odd Fellows' lodge, where Ben Davis, an outspoken opponent of the bond issue, had his offices, sug- gests that the city could neither anticipate nor comprehend black opposition to the bond issue.[36]

Though the bonds had been defeated, it remained difficult for the NAACP to translate this into leverage over the city's budget priorities. White hubris, combined with the caution and secrecy with which the NAACP had chosen to proceed, effectively prevented the NAACP from taking credit for the defeat of the bonds. In addition to the city's registered black voters, the chairman of the bond commission attributed the votes' failure to three ad- ditional groups of people, each notable for their absence from the city: 1,500 men serving overseas in the military, 800 "railroad men . . . absent on their runs," and the 1,000–1,500 mechanics who had left the city that month for work in other areas of the state.[37] While it is difficult to know what the three absentee groups of citizens would have done had they been in the city to vote (the ranks of which undoubtedly included black voting-age men), their absence from the city obscured the impact of the nearly 750 missing black votes on the outcome of the election. The problem was that the NAACP's

efforts were not public enough to be legible to the city's white elites as organized black opposition to the bonds. As a result, the role of the black vote
in defeating the bonds was made invisible by the overriding narrative of the
war.[38] Within two days of the bonds' defeat, the *Constitution* was reporting
that their failure to pass was due not to the opposition of black voters but
rather to "the large number of voters who have moved away from the city
since registration," including "several thousand men . . . now away from the
city in the military and naval service."[39] Because of this developing media
narrative, the NAACP was unable to parlay this defeat into actual political
leverage, even though black voters had opposed the bonds almost to a man.

Another issue that prevented the NAACP from using the defeat of the
bond issues as a demonstration of its political power was fear of white retaliation, which undoubtedly played a role in crafting a strategy that did not
require black voters to openly oppose Jim Crow. Georgia's stiff constitutional
requirements for passing municipal bond referenda provided a very low bar
for black voters to participate in the campaign. If all that was necessary to
defeat the bonds was to register to vote and then stay home on Election
Day, it might be possible to put the brakes on Atlanta's racially stratified
development. Even given such a low bar for participation, Atlanta's recent
history of racial violence freighted this sort of electoral collective action with
considerable risk. The white "daddies" who mobilized to demand that the
city educate their children could easily become a lynch mob, targeting those
black "daddies" who dared used their ballots to compel the city to educate
their children as well. Although on the eve of the election Ben Davis repeated his exhortation that "every Negro who is qualified to vote ought to
stay away from the polls," he could be easily dismissed as an outspoken and
opinionated black editor.[40] It was quite another thing to organize the city's
black registered voters to publicly undermine the development plans of the
city's most powerful white men. That black participation in the boycott of
the election was nearly universal meant that some amount of organizing
went into convincing black voters to stay home from the polls. Nevertheless,
fear of retaliation and the desire to proceed clandestinely undermined the
ability of the NAACP to pressure the city to fund black schools.

Despite the failure to convince the city to invest more of its budget in
black schools, the 1918 bond election made visible the weaknesses in the
funding mechanisms of Atlanta's racially stratified development that a more
organized black electorate could exploit. Not only would this require increasing the number of black voters on the rolls, it would also be necessary
to make explicit the role that black voters played in the defeat of any future

bond issue. The city's recurring fiscal crises ensured that another opportunity would soon arise, allowing black voters to emphatically make the case that Atlanta's urban development was only going to progress *with* black support and would fail *without* it. In order to take advantage of this opportunity, it would first be necessary to significantly expand the NAACP's organizing base in Atlanta by signing up new members and recruiting new leaders. To do so, the leaders of the branch would make appeals using the language of both racial solidarity and patriotism, helping bring these two discourses into articulation with one another and forming the foundation for an unprecedented black political solidarity.

The Challenge of Black Solidarity

The lessons of the 1918 fight were easier to learn than apply. Part of the problem was that Walter White, the creative force behind a good number of the branch's early successes, had joined the national staff of the NAACP in January 1918 and was no longer in Atlanta. Even more significant were the limitations of the branch leadership that remained following White's departure. That these leaders may not have been up for the fight ahead is suggested by a letter from James Weldon Johnson sent to branch president Harry Pace just days before the 1918 bond election. Voicing his "disappointment in Atlanta," the NAACP field secretary expressed regret that Pace was stepping down as president. The national office expected the branch to lead the South in terms of membership, but its efforts had stalled at a couple hundred members.[41] This stagnation resulted from the fact that this membership derived mostly from the supporters of Ben Davis in the Odd Fellows and the Republican Party; the leadership of the branch did not accurately reflect the leadership of black Atlanta. This fact became apparent during the campaign to defeat the bonds in July when the sizable congregations of two of Atlanta's largest black churches had held rallies *in support* of the bonds. Friendship Baptist Church welcomed city attorney James L. Mayson and bond commissioner Claude Ashley to a meeting the Sunday before the election, and at Big Bethel African Methodist Episcopal (AME), the influential Rev. P. James Bryant of Wheat St. Baptist Church and Rev. E. R. Carter of Friendship Baptist Church shared a platform with city council president A. J. Orme and the chairman of the city bond commission.[42] At the two polling places reserved for black voters in the First and Fourth Wards, a total of 127 votes were cast, with only one in opposition.[43] Assuming these were all black voters, this meant that nearly one in six of the approximately 750 registered black voters refused to boycott the election. Even though the NAACP could take encouragement from the fact that five in six black voters were willing to defeat the bonds by their nonparticipation, these defections prompted Walter White to return to Atlanta on the eve of the bond election to bring these dissident ministers into the organization and put the local branch "on a firm basis."[44]

The efforts to reorganize the Atlanta branch reveal how much the terms of black solidarity had changed since the establishment of the Georgia Equal Rights Convention (GERC) in 1906. In preparation for White's visit, Harry Pace sent out 250 invitations welcoming every black leader of significance in the city to attend a reorganization meeting to be held at the Atlanta offices of the YMCA on 9 July 1918, the night before the election.[45] Pace's invitation frankly admitted the failure of the branch to include every black citizen of Atlanta. As he diplomatically phrased it, "in the beginning there was some difference which crept in through misunderstanding on the part of some our citizens." The language here is telling: misunderstanding "crept in," an ideological usage that sought to portray the relationship between the powerful black personalities in Atlanta as normally harmonious when they were frequently the opposite. Anxious "to eradicate all differences and to bring everybody into the branch, regardless of affiliation, in church, society or business," Pace took pains to reach out to religious and civic leaders who had originally opposed the NAACP. His stated goal was to make the NAACP "one place where all factions . . . can unite." Drawing on the lessons of almost two decades of organizing that had been tempered by disillusionment over the possibility of interracial cooperation and refined by the work of the Neighborhood Union, Pace believed that even in fractious Atlanta, this unity would be possible because of the "principles for which the N.A.A.C.P. stand[s] . . . its sole object, the advancement and welfare of the whole race."[46]

What differentiated this call for racial unity from previous calls was its emphasis on the welfare of the whole race without the explicit invocation of respectability or the need to uplift a morally suspect working class. This was not the result of a profound transformation in the class composition of Atlanta's black leadership; the same "respectable" black elite that had led earlier attempts to unite black Atlanta behind "the advancement and welfare of the whole race" still led the local NAACP. What had changed were the perspectives of these leaders. Since 1906, they had experienced the imposition of disfranchisement and rapid urban development that had widened the gulf between black and white Atlantans. America's entry into a war to "make the world safe for democracy" had only intensified white supremacist violence against black men in Georgia and brought about the passage of "work or fight" laws targeting black women and extending white control over the labor of black families. In none of these instances did the politics of respectability effectively shield black Atlantans from a resurgent white supremacy. As respectability failed as a strategy, older discursive cues describing black solidarity in terms of race uplift dropped from the NAACP's appeal for racial unity. Taking their place was a language of self-reliance. This reflected the drastic shift in the relationship between Atlanta's black and white elites as interracial cooperation founded on the shared embrace of respectability gave way to a more oppositional relationship.

In laying aside "respectability" as an organizing principle of black solidarity, the terms of the contest between Atlanta's black leaders had to be explicitly renegotiated. This is reflected in Pace's assertion to this leadership that at the reorganization meeting, "we are all going to start anew and we are all going to start on the same basis of equality."[47] A few days after the meeting, Pace explained to James Weldon Johnson: "In order that no one might feel that any advantage was taken of them, I made the concession that our Branch had gone defunct" and was in need of reorganization.[48] Pace made his concession "in order that those who had not hitherto been members could pay their membership fees and join and feel that they were on the same footing with the old members." The "equality" that Pace emphasized was not interracial equality, but rather equality between African Americans themselves. Pace asked the city's black leadership to set aside all their other identities ("church, society or business") through which they jockeyed with each other for power and instead privilege their identities as black men and women in struggle against "the things . . . which we must continually fight, right here in this community."[49]

According to White's account, Pace's appeal for racial solidarity in the struggle against a Jim Crow school system made the reorganization meeting a "splendid" success.[50] One of the major reasons for this excitement was the election of Rev. Adam Daniel Williams, the pastor of the influential Ebenezer Baptist Church, as the new president. Initially described as one of the "worst opponents" of the Atlanta NAACP, the recruitment of the powerful and ambitious Rev. Williams seemed to augur well for the future of the branch.[51] A slave preacher's son, he ran away from home at an early age and eventually assumed the pulpit of a heavily mortgaged church in Atlanta's Summerhill neighborhood, which had only thirteen members and was facing imminent foreclosure. Rising to the challenge, Rev. Williams aggressively began to recruit new members to what was to become Atlanta's famous Ebenezer Baptist Church. He soon had more than 100 members, and by 1900 Ebenezer was able to move into a much larger building. By the time he assumed the presidency of the local NAACP, Williams had served as the head of the Atlanta Baptist Ministers' Union and was the national treasurer for the National Baptist Convention.[52] Under Williams's leadership, the branch expanded from the small core of leaders initially recruited by Walter White to well over 2,000 members. Much as the participation of prominent Republican Ben Davis assuaged concerns of the city's black residents that the NAACP was not merely a front for black Democrats, Rev. Williams's national stature as a Baptist leader played a crucial role in bringing the congregations of the city's fifteen major Baptist churches into the fold.[53] These churches included the congregations of the aforementioned Reverends Bryant and Carter, who had led the drive in the black community *for* the bonds in the 1918 election.[54]

The reorganization also brought into office a new executive committee that, according to Harry Pace, represented "all shades of differences and local factions."[55] Significantly, two women joined the leadership of the branch. Cora B. Finley, the principal of Yonge Street School, became treasurer, while Mrs. P. J. Bryant was elected to the position of assistant secretary.[56] Both women had been active in the campaigns of the Neighborhood Union, and their inclusion would ensure that the branch would continue to build on both the organizing base and the ideology of racial solidarity that the Union had come to embrace.[57] However, this ideology was not powerful enough to convince Rev. A. D. Williams to stay in Atlanta to lead the next stage of the fight for equal schools. Midway through the campaign, the new branch president made the decision to take a lengthy trip to Detroit with plans to move his church there from Atlanta.[58] Fortunately, Rev. Williams left behind Truman K. Gibson, a black insurance executive who had been elected to the office of vice president. A Republican Party activist, Gibson frequently found himself opposing Ben Davis in the internecine battles within the state GOP.[59] Unlike Williams, he was willing to lay aside his personal agenda and make the sacrifices necessary to advance the fight for school equality. Reflecting on this new spirit of unity, Gibson reported to James Weldon Johnson in early March, "You know that Atlanta has its full share of groups and circles, ofttimes hostile to each other, yet in this fight we have for this purpose at least welded them together and voted once, altogether."[60] Gibson's readiness to work alongside his political foe speaks to the overwhelming power of this race-conscious language in uniting black Atlantans behind the banner of the NAACP.

"If We Do Not Have a Vote We Are at the Mercy of Those Who Do Have It": The Changing Meaning of the Poll Tax

The first goal of the reorganized branch was to expand the effective reach of the Atlanta NAACP. Thus, a week after the election of new officers, the branch launched an ambitious membership drive, with an initial goal of 1,000 new members.[61] Within ten weeks the branch had attracted nearly 700 new members, prompting it to double its initial goal.[62] By December, this membership had climbed to 1,200, and by the end of February 1919 the Atlanta NAACP was nearly 1,700 strong and growing.[63]

A good deal of this growth was driven by a sense of urgency that stemmed from a change in the law governing bond elections. The July defeat of four bond issues that each received the support of more than 90 percent of those voting handed the city a compelling argument that convinced the state legislature to revise the bond election law. As of 7 August 1918, the city of Atlanta would no longer require two-thirds of registered voters to pass bond issues. Instead, the passage of any future bonds would now require two-thirds of those voting *and* only a simple majority of registered voters.[64] This change in the law required the NAACP to adjust its strategy. Boycotts would no longer be sufficient to defeat future bond issues. It would now be necessary to go to the polls and actively vote against the bonds, a significantly greater challenge that would require a sizable increase in black voter registration.

The branch had little time to lose. Although the bond issue was dead for the remainder of Mayor Candler's term, when James L. Key took office in January 1919, one of his first acts as mayor was to reintroduce the bonds that had been defeated the previous July. Pledging cooperation with the Board of Education, Mayor Key promised to raise the necessary funds to both increase teacher salaries and build new schools. Although Key was well regarded among the black citizens of Atlanta for his previous stand on school equality, his initial plans to expand Atlanta's school system made no mention of the needs of black schoolchildren.[65] It would be up to the NAACP to remind him. Thus, concurrent with its membership drive, the branch kicked off what was to be Atlanta's most successful black voter registration drive since Reconstruction. During the seven months between the defeat of the bonds in July 1918 and the date that the registration books closed prior to the next bond election, which would be held the following March, the branch was able to increase the number of registered black voters in Atlanta from 600 to more than 1,000.[66] And by April 1919, before yet another bond election, the NAACP was able to expand the total number of black voters in Atlanta to nearly 3,000.[67] Contributing to the success of this voter registration drive was the relative affluence of the war years. Not only did black men command higher wages generated by wartime labor shortages, black soldiers received $30 each month plus a dependency allowance.[68] Taken together, these two factors provided a broadly shared financial security that loosened ordinarily tight family budgets just enough to afford paying poll taxes.

Just because black Atlantans had the ability to pay their poll taxes did not mean they would do so without encouragement. Built directly atop the groundwork laid by the Neighborhood Union's organizing efforts over the preceding eleven years, the NAACP "started a house-to-house campaign through the third and fourth wards and on the west side where the Negro population was segregated."[69] Not only did the NAACP become heir to the Union's agenda, it also inherited a "co-optable network" of black neighbors connected through the structure of the Union.[70] In an era before television, email, or even the widespread adoption of telephones, this network was vital in forging a political community of interest. According to Lugenia Burns Hope, at the height of the Union's reach during World War I, its organizers could speak to as many as 42,000 people in any given week.[71] This remarkable claim is supported by reports of the Union's success in its health education efforts. Working with the Atlanta Anti-Tuberculosis Association in 1919, the Union was able to visit 5,406 homes, communicating with 23,771 residents.[72] Two years later, during the course of the organization's annual Clean-Up campaign, organizers from the Union visited 2,500 homes twice each.[73] The ability to mobilize hundreds of black women not only helped weave together an incredibly tight-knit community, but their periodic neighborhood surveys were able to establish whether the men of the household had paid their poll taxes. In fact, it was a regular question on the Union's surveys.[74] This sort of information proved invaluable in helping the NAACP identify black voters throughout the city who could be eligible to vote in the next referendum. In his memoir, White recalled the excitement when one of these men, "none-too-prosperous . . . paid [his] back poll taxes . . . for thirty-two years—a sum he could ill afford—in order to vote, even though all his children were long past grammar or high school age."[75]

The response to the voter registration drive was so overwhelming that the NAACP was forced to pace and even limit its registration efforts. Should a crowd of new black registrants appear at city hall seeking to pay their back taxes, the organizers feared it could spark "a counter-campaign among the whites." Thus, the key to this strategy working was absolute secrecy. By the time its opponents realized what was about to happen, it would be too late to launch the traditional antiblack tirade against "Negro domination" and register "a large enough number of white voters to override the Negro vote."[76] Should it emerge that the black voters of Atlanta were conspiring to vote in a bloc to defeat the bonds, the city's white progressive leadership would either attempt to increase the turnout in favor of the bonds or withdraw them altogether, depriving black Atlantans the opportunity to flex their political muscle. That the NAACP was able to register so many black voters without sparking a backlash speaks as much to the hubris of white progressives as it did to the unity of Atlanta's black community. (It helped that the city's registrars had convinced themselves that the increased black voter registration was meant to *support,* and not oppose, the bonds.)[77]

More significant, the black community's response to the NAACP's voter registration drive signaled a revolution in the public understanding of the poll tax. Recall how in 1906 the poll tax was described by the *opponents* of disfranchisement as a means to eliminate the "shiftless, worthless element" from politics, a sentiment shared by those advocating further restrictions on the right to vote. The inability of men like Rev. William J. White or W. E. B. Du Bois to articulate a full-throated defense of universal suffrage hindered them as they sought to resist the disfranchisement amendment of 1908. The tumultuous history of the intervening decade had transformed the meanings of class, gender, and respectability, introducing alternate understandings of the poll tax. The NAACP's door-to-door registration campaign made it easier for Atlanta's black political leadership to describe the tax as a means to disfranchise poor and African American voters rather than as a tool designed to "improve the quality of [the] electorate." The ways in which the NAACP appealed to black voters to pay their poll tax in preparation for the bond election marked an important step toward the articulation of an independent black politics rooted in a changing understanding of who should comprise the black electorate.

The expansion of the idea of black political solidarity was further assisted by black participation in World War I. Military service had created a new way for African Americans to stake a claim on full citizenship rights that was not bounded by adherence to a narrow standard of respectability. The war gave the NAACP and its allies a language of manly patriotic sacrifice from which they borrowed freely in order to unite black voters behind the fight for school equality in Atlanta. This is reflected in various appeals that black men heard urging them to pay their poll taxes and in which the NAACP explicitly linked registering for the draft with registering to vote. Prior to the July 1918 bond fight, the *Atlanta Independent* published an editorial urging its readers to register and castigating those who did not as having "no patriotism." These "slackers" failed to appreciate "the great sacrifices and rivers of blood which have been [spilled] on battlefields to give them this inestimable right [to vote]" and would "desert the flag on the battlefield in time of war."[78] President Wilson's decision to enter the war in order to make the world safe for democracy made the linkage between military service and the right to vote even more apparent. In January 1919, the *Independent* made this connection explicit by insisting that every black man of voting age "owed it to the soldier boys who died on the battlefields of France . . . that we may enjoy the rights of American citizenship" to pay their poll tax and register.[79] These sentiments were echoed a month later in an NAACP notice announcing a voter registration drive begun on Lincoln's birthday "so as to be ready to get some of the things for which their brothers and sons died in France."[80]

This discursive strategy of manly sacrifice was related to another that shifted the meaning of the vote from a privilege that must be earned to a duty that must be performed. Whereas in previous wars the United States had been able to rely upon a largely volunteer army, World War I was the first war in America's history in which the military was compelled to rely almost entirely on the draft for the vast majority of its recruits. It was also the first war in which the military's manpower needs were successfully met through conscription. The passage and implementation of the Selective Service Act in 1917 transformed an earlier discourse that held the draft to be "forced conscription" to one that framed the draft as "voluntary service" to one's nation. As a result, military service—even if compulsory—became much easier to link with both the duties and prerogatives of citizenship.

Thus, in many ways, the duty of paying one's poll tax was simply an extension of the language of military service. As the *Atlanta Independent* phrased it, paying one's poll tax was "one of the most fundamental civic duties of every American citizen," akin to the "duty to repel invasion of the enemy" during wartime.[81] The shift from earned privilege to patriotic duty—though subtle—is quite significant for the role it played in undermining the earlier idea that potential voters must prove their manhood in order to qualify to vote. Instead, black men were being called upon to do just the opposite— prove their manhood *by registering to vote.* In a published appeal for new voters, the NAACP declared, "Let every young man in Atlanta and every taxpayer not think he is really a man until he has registered."[82] This sentiment was echoed by another voter registration appeal proclaiming that "we must acquit ourselves like men; we must do our full duty, and one of our paramount duties is to pay our taxes, register and do everything else incumbent upon good citizens."[83] Good citizenship was the path to manhood, rather than vice versa—an inversion that helped supplant a partially discredited politics of respectability as a means of asserting formal equality with white citizens. The oft-repeated descriptions of the poll tax "as one of the civic duties of all citizens, white and black," emphasized the role of the vote as a great equalizer.[84] This was made explicit in a voter registration appeal penned by Captain Jackson McHenry, who urged "the black man [to] value his [own] vote," especially since that vote "will be counted just as much . . . as Mr. Asa Candler's and . . . Mr. Inman's," two of Atlanta's most powerful white men.[85] Rather than accept a racially stratified notion of citizenship, the leaders of the voter registration drive reframed the right to vote as one of a universal set of duties expected of every patriotic citizen, regardless of race.

Though transformed by appeals to patriotic duty, manhood and voter registration were still as intimately linked as they had been in 1906. The Women's Registration Committee, organized by the Neighborhood Union in cooperation with the NAACP, encouraged black men to register and vote against the bonds as part of their role as protectors of the home. In a published advertisement, it appealed to "brothers, husbands, fathers and sons" to "exercise . . . the right to vote [and] secure for us that protection which is rightfully ours but which all the world knows is denied us simply because you do not vote. We urge you to register NOW and keep registered so that our homes and lives may be forever safe." The women of the Union mobilized the language of defense of the family during wartime to get men to vote the correct way, promising any "slackers" that registration shall become the "measure of your real manhood in this critical period."[86] Within the context of the voter registration drive, the Union and the NAACP were able to harness the language of patriarchal defense of the home to explicitly challenge Jim Crow. However, in doing so, they changed the role gender played in stratifying black men by class. If the "measure of real manhood" was participation in the fight for equal schools, then anyone willing to pay his accumulated taxes and vote could by his participation assert a formal equality with the wealthiest of black men. In the context of the school equality movement, then, the poll tax shifted from being yet another marker of class distinction to a means of unifying an African American voting bloc by increasing membership in the circle of "real manhood."

The poor man who paid off years in back poll taxes measured up equally alongside the wealthy few who had been able to keep their taxes paid and remain on the rolls. And both men were superior to the well-to-do men who, out of supposed selfishness or irresponsibility, failed to pay their poll taxes. With the pressure to register as many black voters as possible, this opened those members of the respectable black middle class who evaded the poll tax to harsh criticism in the pages of the *Independent,* where they were denounced as "drones and carbuncles on the body politic."[87] Ben Davis singled out for special abuse the "large class" of black men who had actually paid their poll tax but neglected to register as "more blame-worthy" than the tax dodgers, "for a man who has sufficient intelligence and pride to acquire property . . . has more at stake."[88] Although these men would never be considered *un*respectable, the schools fight had raised the bar for them to be considered leading members of the black community. The NAACP's campaign for equal schools had begun to transform the meanings of manhood, temporarily opening up new ways for building black solidarity across class lines.

A significant proportion of the 3,000 voters whom the NAACP added to the rolls were undoubtedly those members of the black middle class. These are men who had either kept up their registration previously (for example, the 742 black voters who participated in the July 1918 bond referendum) or were property owners who had paid up their poll taxes but failed to register until encouraged by the campaign to do so. Nevertheless, a good deal of these 3,000 people were neither middle class nor property owners and could not have been financially secure enough to easily afford to pay the accumulated back taxes they owed in order to vote in the upcoming referendum. In order to win in the fight for school equality, it was necessary to reach out to these voters and ask them to invest several weeks' or even months' worth of salary. The thirty-two years in back taxes owed by the poor man whom White described in his 1948 autobiography represented a significant sacrifice.[89] The extremity of his case is what made it notable nearly three decades later, but it would not be atypical to owe ten to fifteen years in back poll taxes. In his report to James Weldon Johnson on the progress of the voter registration campaign, branch vice president Truman K. Gibson reported that many people paid "as much as fifteen, twenty or twenty-five dollars in back taxes" in order to vote in the election.[90] For the woefully underpaid black teachers, whose husbands were a special focus of the voter registration campaign, just ten years in back taxes would represent an entire week's salary.[91] It was this that prompted the NAACP to declare that "the hour has struck for all of the Negroes in Atlanta, high and low, rich and poor, to drop everything and rally to this cause."[92] The ability of the NAACP to have such success with this sort of appeal rested upon the profound transformations that had occurred in African American understandings of class, gender, citizenship, and patriotism since disfranchisement in 1908. It also helped that they were able to rely upon the organizing networks established by the Neighborhood Union, which had long been working to bridge the class divide within Atlanta's black community.

The NAACP also inherited from the Neighborhood Union a race-conscious vision that helped the city's black political elite to expand their notion of who could and should stand with them in this fight. The need to register as many black voters as possible had transformed voter registration from an exercise in bourgeois manliness into a means whereby the black community could defend itself. In the midst of the voter registration campaign, Ben Davis made an uncharacteristically explicit appeal to racial self-reliance, urging black men to register and vote with the argument that "the remedies lie in the black man's hand—not in congress, the Republican Party or the white man."[93] It may be tempting to interpret this phrase as evidence of an incipient black nationalism. However, the sentiments that Davis expressed were not so much nationalist as they were a response to the explicit need to define a ground for black solidarity that resided outside loyalty to the GOP, the politics of respectability, or faith in the processes of democracy under Jim Crow.

As the local NAACP put it in its published appeal for new black voters, "Under a democracy, if we do not have a vote we are at the mercy of those who do have it." This characterization of democracy is as far from the politics of respectability as it is possible to get. It recognizes that a racially stratified democracy will allow white voters to displace the social, economic, and political costs of development onto voteless black Americans, regardless of any ties that black and white reformers had established previously. The NAACP followed this assertion with another, stating the "white people in Atlanta who are our real friends want to see us get a square deal . . . a high school, especially . . . but they cannot do for us the things we must do for ourselves. If we make no effort to get what in right belongs to us, they will conclude we do not want those things." However, these "real friends" had been aware since 1913 of the dismal conditions under which black teachers and students were forced to teach and to learn and had done little to address them. For the 3,000 black voters who had paid their poll taxes in 1919, it was increasingly clear that black Atlantans would continue "to be ignored and fed on fine words" until they threw their votes like monkey wrenches into the gears of Atlanta's municipal machinery.[94]

"The White People Would Receive the Benefits and the Negroes Bear the Burden": The March 1919 Bond Election

The gears of that machine were already beginning to grind due to a lack of revenue. The defeat of the bonds in July 1918 forced the city to make an emergency appropriation for the modernization and repair of the city waterworks. As a result, for the last half of 1918 there had been nothing left in the city budget for things like street repair and park maintenance.[95] Although money was tight, neither Key nor the city council was alarmed. The new law that only required the support of two-thirds of those voting in the election to pass a bond referendum made it seem a simple matter for Atlanta to raise additional money for modernizing the city's infrastructure, since each of the previous bonds had garnered the support of more than 90 percent of the voters. Thus, they passed a balanced city budget for 1919 and deferred the necessary improvements to the city parks and fire department as well as the construction of an electricity plant until the all but guaranteed approval of the bond issue scheduled for 5 March 1919.[96]

At the same time the city faced these challenges, the combination of wartime inflation and postwar recession had begun to squeeze the salaries of the city's teachers. Representing the city's 750 white educators, the Atlanta Public School Teachers' Association (APSTA) took advantage of the decision to hold a bond referendum to pressure the city to include pay raises for the teaching workforce as part of the bond issue.[97] Unlike other city employees, the teachers had gone several years without a raise and were paid so little that between September 1917 and December 1919, more than 450 had left the public schools in pursuit of wartime employment.[98] To make matters worse, following the defeat of the 1918 bond issue, the city had raided the school budget, with the result that the Board of Education had $18,000 less than the year before to spend on teachers' salaries.[99] According to the APSTA, teachers' salaries would have to increase by 30 percent just to keep pace with inflation.[100] In order to avert a potential strike, the Board of Education diverted $25,000 from its budget to cover a limited emergency pay raise through the end of the school year.[101] Both the board and the teachers' union were banking on the successful passage of the bond issue to make up for the resulting budget shortfall.[102] To increase the amount of these pay raises and make them permanent, the APSTA pressured Mayor Key to support a proposal placing a second bond referendum on the March ballot that would raise the city tax rate by 0.25 percent (from $1.25 per hundred dollars to $1.50).[103] By all measures, the fate of the schools—"the heart and hope of true civic progress," according to the *Atlanta Journal*—rode heavily on the passage of both the bonds and the newly added special school tax.[104]

The proponents of the bond issue reassembled the same coalition of supporters that had backed the 1918 bond issue, including the city's labor organizations, the Atlanta Parent-Teacher Association, the Board of Education, and the Chamber of Commerce.[105] As earlier, the members of this coalition explicitly drew the connection between support for the city's bond election and support for the Liberty Bonds that had been sold to support the war effort and urged the support of the bonds as a patriotic duty.[106] The *Atlanta Journal* urged all "loyal citizens" to support the referenda, an equation that—on the eve of America's postwar Red Scare—implied the unpatriotic disloyalty of their opponents.[107] The mayor declared the 5 March election date a city holiday and let all municipal employees off work, while the bond commission asked the city's business leaders to do likewise to ensure that everyone had the opportunity to cast a vote.[108] To make certain that these workers could qualify to vote, the city tax collector announced he would keep the registration books open until seven o'clock each evening until the election.[109] On the day before the election, the city's teachers sent 30,000 letters home with their students urging fathers to support the tax increase.[110] Even the city's utilities got behind the effort. Southern Bell provided volunteers and phone lines to call voters reminding them to vote, while the water company sent notices with the monthly bills urging its customers to support the bonds.[111] This campaign effectively duplicated the previous year's failed drive, the only difference being the repeal of the "archaic" bond law that had stood in the way of progress. In fact, Mayor Key was so confident of success that he left town the week of the election in order to attend a conference in Washington, D.C.[112] Key and the rest of the city's white progressive leadership were utterly convinced that both referenda were certain to pass.

This election resembled the earlier one in another crucial aspect as well. Throughout the entire campaign, the utterly dismal pay of the black teachers and the wretched condition of the black schools were all but ignored.[113] The one significant attempt to reach out to the black community was in response to an effort initiated by a delegation of black men who opposed the NAACP as too antagonistic. A group of black ministers, uncertain as to the wisdom of a political strategy that had yet to produce any concrete results, invited Mayor Key to meet with them at Big Bethel Church on the Friday before the election in order to "outline the benefits that all classes of citizens will derive through the success of both measures."[114] One of these men, Rev. Henry Hugh Proctor of the First Congregational Church, was reluctant to disturb the amicable relationships with powerful white funders that he relied upon for the success of the community programs he ran from his church.[115] Rev. Proctor and the other ministers who supported Key's bond referenda were not convinced of the need to abandon the politics of respectability and sought instead to exchange favors with the new mayor, rather than assert black political power. These calculations seemed to work, since after this meeting Key made a very strong statement in support of black education, insisting that Atlanta "should not be content until it has placed itself in a position to furnish a comfortable seat in a comfortable schoolhouse to every child. And by every child, I mean every child, black and white, high and low, rich and poor."[116] Following the mayor's speech, many white observers believed that Proctor and his allies spoke for black Atlanta and were convinced that the heavy black registration was being undertaken to *support* the tax and bond issue.[117] However, Neighborhood Union activist Cora Finley was also at the meeting and remembered a different exchange between Key and the black men and women assembled at Big Bethel. When asked by the mayor whether they would support the bond issue, Finley and other members of the NAACP in attendance replied that if the mayor could guarantee the abolition of double sessions, equal pay for black teachers, and the construction of a high school for black students, then they would "gladly vote for [the] bonds and taxes; if not, we will vote against [them]." However, the mayor ignored this threat and refused to give any concrete guarantees, offering instead his promise that their grievances would be addressed after the referenda passed.[118]

Events would prove, however, that most black voters were no longer in a mood to place any trust in promises such as these. To believe this would require the willful ignorance of the clearly stated demands of the NAACP. A week before the election, the branch's vice president, Truman K. Gibson, sent a letter to the black voters and taxpayers of Atlanta demanding to know "WHAT PROMISES HAVE BEEN MADE TO US FOR OUR SUPPORT?"[119] At a mass meeting held in Big Bethel AME Church on the eve of the election, the members of the Atlanta branch of the NAACP, "packed to the doors," voted unanimously to go to the polls and vote down both referenda. In so doing, they hoped to "serve notice upon the white people that after this they must reckon with the Negro when they are dealing with municipal affairs."[120] On 5 March 1919, the city's black voters would not only register their opinion on the ballot referenda, but the results of the election would determine who led black Atlanta. This was the moment of truth for the renascent branch.[121]

The effectiveness of the NAACP's organizing efforts were evident as the polls opened the next day. Armed with ballots that had been premarked in opposition to both the tax and bond issues, the NAACP managed to get the bulk of its supporters to the polls before noon.[122] Besides the danger posed by the black vote, the bonds were once again threatened by insufficient turnout. While the tax required only a simple majority to pass, the bond referendum still required the support of two-thirds of those voting in the election *and* the participation of a majority of registered voters, or at least 5,529 votes.[123] By noon, only 2,000 ballots had been cast, forcing the campaign workers to redouble their efforts to bring an extra 3,500 voters to the polls. Making matters worse was the torrential downpour through most of the afternoon that literally dampened turnout. This prompted Alderman John S. McClelland to issue a panicked statement urging white voters to the polls to save the propositions. These efforts were to no avail. When the polls closed, the special school tax lost by a narrow margin—with 2,411 for and 2,545 against—comprising a majority of 134 against the tax increase.[124] Since a considerable amount of the opposition arose from the city's two predominantly black wards, it was clear that black voters had defeated the school tax.[125] As for the bonds, City Attorney James L. Mayson initially ruled that they had passed; however, despite the overwhelming margin in favor of each issue, the election had failed to garner the participation of a majority of registered voters.[126] Although Mayson believed he could make a case for the legality of the bonds using an earlier voter list, he instead advised the city to hold a second election to pass both the special tax and the bonds without a doubt and avoid a costly legal battle.[127]

One of the reasons that the city attorney gave for repeating the election was that the "small margin of votes" against the school tax had been cast "by an element that failed to comprehend the true situation" rather than by any "willful plotting" on the part of black voters.[128] Although it was clear that black votes had effectively defeated both measures, long-standing racist characterizations of black voters as stupid and easily misled obscured the role that an organized black electorate had played in defeating the referenda. Initial Election Day rumors broadcast by the *Atlanta Journal* described the black vote against the referenda as a "plot" concocted by unprincipled white conservatives to "cast [the] Negro ballot against the issue." Not only did this deny the agency of the black voters, the *Journal* also refused to acknowledge that the black argument against the bonds was anything more than a nefarious "influence" designed to mislead black voters and "crush the bond issue." Rather, it was the result of "certain white people . . . lobbying around negro churches urging them to vote against bonds, and misrepresenting to them that the white people would receive the benefits and the negroes bear the burden."[129] In fact, the city went so far as to attempt to discount the black vote entirely. Acting with the support of the city attorney, Mayor Key, Alderman McClelland, and A. J. Orme, the chair of the bond committee, made an unsuccessful appeal to the state legislature to disregard the results of the election and approve the tax increase anyway. They reasoned that "white voters overwhelmingly supported" it and that the black voters who "flocked in droves to vote against the tax rate . . . may have been misinformed."[130] Despite years of agitation on precisely this point and the existence of a semi-public campaign to defeat the bonds in both July 1918 and March 1919, it was still difficult for most of Atlanta's white progressives to grasp what was going on as independent black political action.

For the NAACP to translate the defeat of the bond referenda into leverage over the city's budget, Atlanta's white leaders would have to recognize clearly the reasons for their defeat. Fortunately, the NAACP would have yet another chance to mobilize black Atlantans against the passage of any bond referenda until their demand for a black high school was met. On 21 March, the city council acted on the city attorney's advice and scheduled another election to be held on 23 April.[131]

"A Satisfied Part of Our Composite Citizenship": The Legibility of the Black Vote and Black Political Independence

The difficulty the city's white leadership had in comprehending the solidity of black opposition to the referenda stemmed from their failure to understand where the leadership of black Atlanta actually lay. While this is largely attributable to a long history of white condescension, it also resulted from the enduring fragmentation of black Atlanta itself. Despite a decade of building a real consensus around the struggle for educational equality, there were still significant public differences over how to pursue that goal, which were only partially resolved by the NAACP's appeal for unified black opposition to the referenda. Besides those who simply opposed the campaign, there were also black leaders who supported the campaign out of a deeply held fiscal conservatism rather than as an the attempt to demonstrate black political clout. In an interview following the election, Henry A. Rucker, one of the highest-ranking black Republicans in Georgia, told the *Atlanta Constitution* that the bulk of the opposition came from black tenants who feared that increased city taxes would increase their rents. He concluded that if the taxes currently raised were properly distributed, the city would have plenty of funds to meet its needs without additional taxation.[132] This fiscal conservatism was prevalent enough that the NAACP found it effective to appeal to these sentiments in its efforts to unite Atlanta's black electorate in opposition to the referenda. A letter sent out by the Atlanta branch a week prior to the second bond election questioned the city's need to issue bonds and raise taxes, describing both as a "subterfuge on the part of adroit politicians" to expand the size of the city government at the expense of "overburdened" black taxpayers, whose property was "already . . . at the mercy of the tax assessor."[133] Although still asking black voters to carefully evaluate whether the city would deliver on the promises that had been made to secure their support for the bonds, this appeal to fiscal conservatism helped obscure the significance of the election. With multiple competing narratives coming from Atlanta's black leaders, the reasons for the defeat of the bonds and the special tax were not immediately legible as an assertion of organized black political might.

It was not just men like Rucker whose public statements obscured the meaning of the vote. Even those intimately involved in the campaign voiced contradictory interpretations explaining why the referenda went down to defeat. In his response to the effort by councilmen Orme and McClellan to discount the black vote against the tax increase, Ben Davis accused them of trying to "make it appear that Negroes defeated the higher tax rate" in order to "stir up race strife and . . . hatred. . . . Out of a total vote of possibly 5,000 people, less than 1,000 Negroes voted. How do these eminent gentlemen reach the conclusion that the Negroes alone defeated their pet scheme?"[134] Davis reminded those who would disregard black votes that their action would entail throwing out a large number of white votes; however, in making this argument, it undermined the ability of the NAACP to argue that it was the *black vote* that "defeated their pet scheme" and the implicit promise that it would continue to do so until the city equitably allocated its resources among all of its citizens regardless of race. At the same time, he did not disavow the notion that black voters opposed both the bonds and the new taxes because the city "would spend all the money for white betterment in public schools, city improvement and . . . utilities," with the tax burden borne by the black citizenry for services they would not be allowed to use. Further confusing the matter was Davis's retreat into the language of fiscal conservatism from his earlier, much more aggressive declarations that black voters would continue to defeat all school funding referenda until the city began to take concrete steps to improve the city's black school system. De-emphasizing the role played by racially discriminatory development in shaping black opposition to the new taxes, he assailed the city's public officials as "inefficient and incapable of handling wisely and economically" the city's tax revenue, and any tax increase would do nothing more than "create additional opportunities for waste and extravagance."[135]

It might well have been the case that Davis's opposition to raising taxes came from his own deeply held fiscal conservatism. However, his ambivalence about the impact of the black vote on the March election may also have stemmed from his unease with an explicitly racialized voting bloc. Though unvoiced, fears of white retaliation could have animated Davis's equivocation, especially since this new strategy seemed to require the rejection of the politics of respectability. Recall that respectability served as a cultural form of self-defense that attempted to deflect white violence by removing race from politics, instead basing the qualifications for first-class citizenship on the appropriate class and gender practices. By contrast, racialized bloc voting not only admitted the permanence of race in politics, but explicitly elevated race to a position of primary importance. The articulation of a coherent and unified black balance of power capable of punishing false friends and avowed enemies required the acknowledgment that there were very few white people who would willingly sacrifice their own racial privileges to advance the cause of equal rights for African Americans. Instead, these black voters would have to *compel* these "friends of the Negro" to act in concert with their black fellow citizens. For Davis, this would certainly have seemed a risky a step to take. While offering "no apology" for the role that African American voters played in the election, he denied that black opposition to the bonds had arisen from anything clearly identifiable as "the black vote." Rather, the bonds were defeated by a group of voters who just all happened to be black. Davis insisted that the "Negro is a citizen, entitled to his own opinion, clothed with the right to exercise it as a free man. . . . When he votes he acts of his own free will and volition, expressing by his ballot his honest convictions, arrived at after due consideration of every municipal interest, just like the Mayor or any other white man."[136] Using the language of a shared manly independence, the editor argued that black opposition to the funding measures on the March ballot was equivalent to white opposition. In this reading of the results of the election, the interests of black voters were not racial. They were instead the result of the same sort of reasoned reflection that might have caused any white voter to oppose the bond measure as well.

In light of this, it is significant that two weeks prior to the April bond election, the *Independent* gave most of its editorial page over to Judge George Hillyer, a prominent white conservative, who used the space to argue against the upcoming bond and tax referenda without once mentioning the city's history of discriminatory development.[137] In granting so extensive a platform to Hillyer, Davis obscured the racial specificity of black voters' grievances in order to bridge the contradiction between the ideology of respectability (which implied that it was possible to have a nonracialized citizenship) and the results of the election (which sharply delineated the electoral contours of a polity deeply divided along racial lines). In other words, attempting to remain consistent with the politics of respectability, Davis sought to deracialize citizenship by mobilizing a black vote that did not itself act on racial grounds. Ironically, by thus obscuring identifiably black political interests, he made it easy for the white press to discount the black vote as no more than the tool of designing white men.

Despite Davis's apprehension, the NAACP prepared to use the black vote to coerce the city into extending the benefits of urban development into black neighborhoods. On 5 April, after a handful of black leaders purporting to represent the city's black electorate held a conference with Mayor Key, Councilman Orme, and other white progressives on plans to organize black support for the tax and bonds, the NAACP felt compelled to clarify the true "position of [the] Colored Citizens."[138] Explicitly invoking the organized power of the city's black voters, a delegation of NAACP members delivered an eight-point memorial to the mayor, the Board of Education, and the members of the city finance committee detailing the particular grievances that would continue to sustain the "solidarity of the Negro vote" in opposition to the referenda. Recapitulating the campaigns undertaken by the Neighborhood Union and its precursors over the previous fifteen years, the bulk of the demands addressed the dismal condition of black public schools. These included improvements to the physical plant of buildings for black students, the abolition of double sessions and the restoration of the seventh grade, the elimination of racial pay disparities among the teaching workforce, and a high school for black children that was "no sham or make-believe" but rather fit black children "for a useful calling in life" or "even higher and more complete training." In addition to school improvements, this manifesto called on the city to provide playgrounds and swimming pools for black children, a library, and the extension of paved streets, sewers, and regular garbage removal to black neighborhoods.[139]

The city responded by insisting that the NAACP endorse the referenda before making demands about how the revenue would be spent. Wary of a repeat of the March election results and anxious to win black support for the tax, every member of the school board loudly attested to their support for black education, even W. H. Terrell, who two years previously had responded to the NAACP's initial campaign to abolish double sessions that black schoolchildren "were already getting more than they deserved."[140] To blunt the force of the NAACP's demands, the Board of Education suggested that three underenrolled white schools could be turned over to black students and proposed $4,000 to install new bathrooms in some of the black schools.[141] Additionally, on the same day the NAACP delegation made their demands, the *Atlanta Journal* published a letter from the chairman of the Georgia State Library Commission offering to establish a branch library for black Atlantans dedicated to the "negro soldier of the South who fought and fell" in World War I.[142] An earlier generation of black leadership might have taken these offers as a sign of progress, but the NAACP was not looking to rehearse once again the rituals of respectability. Turning its rejection of these offers into a badge of manhood, the NAACP insisted that it was asking for "no special favors and want[ed] no exceptions made for us." Rather, it concluded that "these things which we desire are not immoderate. They are not unjust. They are not unfair. They are ours, every one of them, and we are entitled to them because we are citizens as all other men are." To ground African American claims to full and equal citizenship, the NAACP made special reference to the military service of black men, who "gave their blood and their lives that democracy might not perish from the earth."[143] They also emphasized black taxpayers' entitlement to the full benefits of the development their tax dollars supported.

While this patriotic rhetoric evinced a firmer foundation for the articulation of black solidarity outside of the bounds of the politics of respectability, these words would have come to naught had it not been for the extensive work done by the Neighborhood Union. In every single one of Atlanta's black neighborhoods, Lugenia Burns Hope's organization established a Women's Registration Committee to register voters and get them to the polls.[144] In the heat of the battle, the leadership of the local NAACP openly acknowledged the role that the Union played in the campaign to defeat the bond issue. Just days before the third bond election, NAACP member L. C. Crogman wrote to the national office that "a large part of the praise must be given to the women who have rendered inestimable service."[145] Appropriating the language of martial manhood, Ben Davis acclaimed the "earnest, hard-working women [of] the Women's Registration Committee," who proposed to "'go over the top' with their slogan of FIVE THOUSAND REGISTERED VOTERS before the next election." The organizing talents of Lugenia Burns Hope ensured that from "the rostrum of every service, sacred and secular, fraternal or social," women's voices would be heard "calling men forth to do their duty."[146] And despite his absence from the city for a considerable stretch of the campaign, Rev. A. D. Williams recalled that the women's committee did the bulk of the work in the registration campaign. At weekly meetings in every part of the city, "night after night, people came forward and paid their [poll tax]. That was done largely because the women were allowed to make speeches."[147] The leadership of Hope and the Neighborhood Union was indispensable in bringing black Atlantans together across class lines. Though his syntax denied the central role the Union played in leading the campaign, Rev. Williams praised Hope in an open letter to the Union for possessing "the faculty of being able to have all classes of women work together. . . . Whenever we have wanted the women of the city to work as a unit, we have always secured Mrs. Hope as a leader and . . . have never failed."[148] Each of these comments strongly suggests that the patriotic unity forged by black men in the context of the equal schools campaign was heavily buttressed by the solidarity among black women that the Union had established over the preceding decade.

Despite the unprecedented scale of these organizing efforts, the NAACP and the Neighborhood Union still had difficulty in getting the city's white politicians to notice their public, concerted opposition to the bonds. The trouble that black Atlantans had in simply making their dissent visible suggests a different reading of the notion of "hidden transcripts" and "infrapolitics" advanced by Robin D. G. Kelley and James C. Scott. Kelley defines these "hidden transcripts" as the "daily conversations, folklore, jokes, songs, and other cultural practices" through which oppressed groups challenge those in power despite maintaining overt appearances of consent. Taken as a whole, these everyday forms of resistance constitute an infrapolitics, or an entire system of politics that exists, "like infrared rays, beyond the visible end of the spectrum. That it should be invisible . . . is in large part by design—a tactical choice born of a prudent awareness of the balance of power."[149] Though a prudent strategy for survival in circumstances where this balance of power is extremely unequal, the success of these infrapolitical forms of resistance threatened to derail the entire equal schools campaign.

Sometimes, what kept the infrapolitical hidden from view was more the blinding racism of white men and women rather than any subterfuge on the part of African Americans. Atlanta's white progressive leadership were unwilling or unable to recognize organized black political activity as a challenge to their racial prerogatives to leadership. In their minds, white men were leaders, not black men. Additionally, infrapolitics sometimes worked a little too well, especially if one interprets the politics of respectability as a form of middle-class infrapolitics that rephrased black dissent in the language of moderation and compromise. Any deviation from that strategy through open defiance to Jim Crow was easily marginalized as the isolated ravings of an intemperate, immature, or hotheaded leader (as had happened to Jesse Max Barber in 1907). To make certain that Atlanta's white leadership both heard this dissent and acknowledged it for what it was, it had to be unequivocally stated as a position independent of the dominant transcript of respectability and race relations. By attempting to coerce Atlanta into extending the full benefits of urban development into black neighborhoods, the city's organized black electorate forced the hidden transcript to the surface of white consciousness and compelled the revision of the dominant narrative of interracial politics in Atlanta. For the equal schools campaign to succeed, its leaders would have to publicly reject the politics of respectability.

This is precisely what the NAACP did when it issued its April manifesto, a document that attempted to redefine the relationship between black and white citizens. To make its dissent visible, the NAACP was compelled to argue against the position of white newspapers such as the *Atlanta Georgian,* which claimed that in "voting against everything," black voters had acted "stupidly in the light of their own real interests" and were instead "led by shrewd white men ready to use them to the limit." The authors of the manifesto countered that no outside influence, "either corporate or individual, was in any measure responsible for the solidarity of the Negro vote in the last election," and denied that any white men—"expect maybe some small and unheard of ones"—had visited black churches to urge black voters to vote as they had. "Colored men," they argued, "are responsible for their own actions, which resulted from decisions arrived at after full, frank and free discussions among themselves and with themselves."[150] By denying the influence of white men in their decision to oppose the referenda, they defined an autonomous racial community capable of supporting a black voting bloc willing and able to use its strength to compel its erstwhile white allies to act on their behalf.

The contours of this political community were brought into sharper relief when the authors of the manifesto expressed their regret at the "necessity that compels us to assume any other attitude than that of a satisfied part of our *composite citizenship.*"[151] This particular choice of words reveals a new understanding of citizenship that is essentially fragmented into a composite of competing racialized voting blocs, which could perhaps be brought into a balance of contending racial interests, but could not reconciled any time soon. Though dramatically different than the earlier politics of respectability, this position still fell short of the nationalist politics that would emerge later in the 1920s. Rather, the composite citizenship described in the NAACP's manifesto had more in common with the sorts of ethnic urban machine politics that earlier commentators like T. Thomas Fortune had once celebrated.[152] This older vision for black politics, submerged by the rising tide of Jim Crow in the 1890s and the consequent ascendancy of the politics of respectability, had only resurfaced when the upheavals of rapid urbanization and World War I had made it possible to redefine the relationship between black and white citizens. For a time, this established a new basis for black politics in Atlanta, one that cast votes solely on racial interests as a right of citizenship.

No longer seeking to enlist white elites as partners in a mission to civilize both the black and white working classes, the black progressives in the Atlanta NAACP instead sought to establish an alliance with their white counterparts in order to build a progressive state that extended its benefits to all citizens without regard to race. As stated in the manifesto declaring the NAACP's opposition to the April bond issue, "the Negro wishes to move forward and not backward. We are willing to pay for these things." However, there was a price for black cooperation. In the conclusion to the manifesto, the NAACP signaled its willingness to support the bonds, but only if they contained "specific and unalterable provisions for a division of the funds so that the colored schools will be amply taken care of."[153] Unfortunately, the city was not yet ready to negotiate and pressed ahead with its plans to hold a third bond election. Dismissing the dissatisfaction of Atlanta's black voters, the bond commissioners underestimated the extent to which the black community had already committed to putting a halt to all urban development until they were included as full and equal partners. This final bond election gave the city's black electorate a clear opportunity to demonstrate the power of the black vote.

A New Basis for Interracial Politics: The April 1919 Bond Election

Though confident over the prospects of the passage of the bond and tax issues on 23 April, the city's progressive leaders nevertheless spared no effort in turning out the city's white voters, kicking off their campaign a full six weeks prior to the date of the next election.[154] In addition to the string of endorsements garnered during the March election, bond proponents added that of J. Epps Brown, president of the Southern Bell Telephone and Telegraph Company, despite his opposition to Mayor Key's plans for the municipal ownership of Atlanta's utilities.[155] Three weeks prior to Election Day, the mayor's office and the city council organized a series of mass meetings in favor of the tax and bond issues in every neighborhood on an almost daily basis, with ward committees promising to canvass every household in the city.[156] A group of white schoolchildren even staged a series of twelve short plays dramatizing the conditions of Atlanta's public schools.[157] Similar to the build-up to the March election, the campaign also linked support for the bonds with patriotism.[158] The teachers' union urged support for the school tax since "the spirit of nations is born in the classrooms where . . . children are taught."[159] Opposing the school tax would imperil the nation's future. A panel from a cartoon that ran on the front page of the *Atlanta Journal,* captioned "The Call of the Old Time Spirit!," depicted a World War I officer whose uniform was emblazoned with the words "Atlanta Spirit" (see figure 6). Holding aloft a banner entitled "The BONDS And The New TAX Rate," he is calling behind him to his men to "Fall In!" and go over the top in support of Atlanta's progress.[160] If this was trench warfare, the NAACP had dug in and fortified its position against the bonds, tripling the number of black voters in the city over the previous election. And if the "spirit of nations" was indeed born in the classroom, that spirit was about to express itself at the polls in the form of a contending vision for the future of the nation; out of the 15,665 voters who signaled their intent to vote in the election prior to the closing of the registration books, an astounding 3,000 were African American.[161]

Although some white public education advocates had started to raise the alarm about the city's failure to address black demands, most city leaders had once again convinced themselves that the large black registration was meant to support, and not oppose, the bonds.[162] The first sign of panic came as school board member W. H. Terrell reported from the First Ward that nearly all black voters who cast their votes in the first hour of polling either came with a preprinted ballot or openly made out their ballots in opposition to both the bonds and the tax increase. Terrell, despite his profession of concern over the conditions of black schools, huffed that "apparently the negroes do not appreciate our effort to give them better schools, and are satisfied with the schools they have." The openness with which black voters opposed the bonds at the polls was a function of the organizing efforts of the NAACP. Unable to comprehend this as organized black political asser-

FIGURE 6. Detail, "Brewerton's Billboard of Current Events,"
Atlanta Journal, 13 April 1919.

tion, Terrell instead framed it as the result of a conspiracy stemming from a "secret meeting" held by black voters the night before where they decided to "vote against everything."[163] If he and the rest of the city's white progressive leadership had been paying attention to the oft-repeated concerns of black voters, the results of the election would not have been such a surprise. Despite weeks of organizing in their favor and the fortuitously perfect weather for the election, each of the bonds fell significantly short of the 7,833 needed to pass, and the tax increase was defeated by a margin of 895 votes.[164] Although voter participation in each referenda significantly exceeded a majority of registered voters, the number of votes cast against each bond issue had roughly tripled since the preceding election, paralleling the increase in the number of registered black voters as reported by the *Atlanta Independent*.[165] Ultimately, 2,000 black voters cast ballots in April, convincingly contributing the bulk of the opposition to the referenda.[166]

The defeat of the tax and bonds pushed the city into a deep fiscal crisis. Since the annual budget for 1919 had anticipated the revenue derived from the success of the two ballot measures, the city was left with a shortfall of nearly $350,000.[167] Not only were the city's development plans put on hold, but the failure of the bond issue forced a radical retrenchment by the city finance committee. Compelled to make deep cuts across every city department, the committee proposed the removal of $32,500 from streets and bridges; $41,700 from health, sanitation, and sewers; $11,100 from the city hospitals; $16,500 from the city parks; $20,000 from the water department; and $17,650 from schools and libraries, the bulk of which was meant for the purchase of coal to heat the schools in winter.[168] In order to keep the city's swimming pools open, the city was forced to institute a ten-cent admission fee for each patron.[169] The city's finances were wrecked. As one contemporary white observer put it: "Atlanta faces a crisis. Our public school system is demoralized. Many of our school buildings are a disgrace. The teachers are underpaid. Our children come home asking if our schools are to be closed. . . . We are told that our swimming pools must be closed. Our streets are in awful shape. Every department is crippled. Something must be done."[170] However, until the city took real steps to extend the benefits of urban development to its black citizens, all it could do was trim the budget and hope to raise additional revenue by increasing various city fees as well as rates charged by city-owned utilities, such as the water department.[171]

Initially, the city's political leaders stubbornly refused to recognize that black voters had defeated the bond and tax issues. As accusations flew at city hall over who was responsible for the loss, Councilman J. R. Nutting of the Sixth Ward charged that Alderman Orme of the Eighth was unable to win the confidence of the well-to-do voters in his district, who for self-serving reasons had overwhelmingly rejected both proposals. In contrast to the selfishness of these wealthy white citizens, the opposition of the black voters was at least comprehensible; they "never had confidence [in the city government], because they were clamoring for further political recognition."[172] Even this oblique acknowledgment was too much for some white leaders. Nearly a month after the election, the Board of Education received a delegation of black leaders led by Henry Rucker protesting that a proposed 15 percent raise for public school teachers had excluded black teachers. Following their testimony, the board questioned Rucker as to "why the colored voters had opposed their own interests in defeating the tax increase and the proposed bonds in the recent election."[173] The elderly Republican leader responded that black Atlantans opposed the referenda "because they believed . . . that they would never get the [schools] they needed." Insisting without irony during a hearing on pay discrimination against black teachers, Commissioner Terrell and Councilman Orme explained to Rucker that the city had already promised to spend the bond and tax revenue on black education as well as white. They expressed "amazement that the colored leaders would permit members of their race to contribute to the defeat of a measure that would work for their own good."[174] Although black teachers ultimately got their 15 percent pay raise that day, their wages still lagged significantly behind those of white teachers. More important, this blunt dismissal of the testimony of one of the city's oldest and most conservative black leaders made it clear that the city's elected leadership was not yet willing to take seriously black demands for inclusion in their vision for Atlanta's future.

The first group of white citizens who understood that addressing black demands for inclusion was central to the success of future development plans was the leadership of the white teachers' union. Continued economic turmoil continued to undermine the viability of public education, prompting the APSTA to become Local 89 of the American Federation of Teachers and to affiliate with the powerful Atlanta Federation of Trades.[175] In response to the looming threat of a December school shutdown, the teachers' union used the resources provided by its affiliation with the local labor federation to successfully lobby for an emergency tax levy in order to keep the schools open through the spring semester.[176] Having averted that catastrophe, white teachers launched their own investigation of the schools in October 1919 in order to lay the groundwork for yet another bond issue. In the course of its investigation, the federation discovered 120 black schoolchildren crammed into a single basement classroom, which verified for white audiences what the NAACP and the Neighborhood Union had been arguing all along—that massive investment was necessary to eliminate double sessions and bring the city's black public schools into the twentieth century. Going one step beyond calls to relieve overcrowding in the city's black grammar schools, labor leader Jerome Jones opined in the pages of the *Journal of Labor* that African Americans were "entitled to better treatment." Thus, when the federation floated the idea of a $3 million bond issue as part of the solution to the long-term crises of public education in Atlanta, it specifically included a call for a publicly funded black high school in its plans.[177]

This was by no means an altruistic decision on the part of the white union leadership, but a calculated decision that they would need black support in order to pass the next school bond referendum. Indeed, Local 89 was strictly segregated and, for the duration of its existence, would represent only white schoolteachers.[178] And just a few months previously, the leader of the white teachers' union had supported the mayor's effort to lobby the state legislature to discount the black vote and overturn the results of the March referenda.[179] The APSTA and other education advocates would only work as hard as they had to in order to win enough black support to secure their votes in the next election. This is reflected in a speech given before a meeting of the APSTA on the eve of the April election. Urging the city to offer enough to the black community to win their support, the speaker declared to his white audience that "we have been hindered by the negro, or at any rate, have allowed the negro to hinder our progress. But if we withhold our means and our efforts in the selfish fear that the negro will benefit, . . . we are [only] starving the minds of all white children concerned, denying them their heritage."[180] Thus, in November 1919, when union members met to make preparations for the next salary fight, they included for the first time demands for raising the salary of black teachers. There were limits to this newfound interracial solidarity, however; they asked for only a $10 increase in the monthly salary for black teachers, while insisting on increases for white teachers ranging from $20 to $30. Although this sparked a protest from black leaders, the city council disregarded it and approved the pay scale presented them by the APSTA.[181]

Emboldened by their victory in the April bond election, Atlanta's black community would no longer settle for second-class treatment. The following month, when the Board of Education met to pass its annual budget, a black delegation over 100 strong, led by the NAACP's Harry Pace, demanded higher salaries for black teachers, asserting that black Atlantans were "learning to strike back . . . for [their] rights" just like white citizens did.[182] They threatened that if the board should adopt the APSTA's pay scale, "not ten negroes would support a bond issue."[183] The threat worked. With the assistance of the editor of the *Journal of Labor* and key leaders within the Atlanta Federation of Trades and the Atlanta Ministers' Evangelical Association, the Board of Education was compelled to raise black teachers' salaries by $15, finding the money for this increase by reducing the size of the raise granted to white teachers by $2.[184] Despite the dissension this caused among the white rank and file of the teachers' union, one of the leaders of the Atlanta Federation of Trades defended this position, stating that "the colored people of this city had stood almost solidly against bond issues and other public improvement measures. . . . This attitude would change if the negroes were shown a fair deal."[185] Though neither the teachers' union nor the city council challenged the racial stratification of teachers' wages by race, the position they took in response to the demand by black teachers for equal pay represented an open acknowledgment of the composite nature of citizenship during Jim Crow. That is, these white leaders recognized that the interests of black citizens and white citizens were opposed, forming the basis for honest negotiations across the color line and spelling out an alternate basis for interracial politics not bounded by shared notions of respectability.

Just two months after the failure of the April 1919 bond vote, Mayor Key took the occasion of the NAACP's annual conference in Cleveland, Ohio, to open these negotiations. Following a unanimous vote by the Atlanta branch in favor of hosting the next annual conference, former branch president Harry Pace convinced Mayor Key to publicly endorse the NAACP's efforts in the city.[186] As delegates to the convention wrangled over the location of the next convention, they received an unexpected string of telegrams from the Gate City. The first of these arrived from Mayor Key informing them that the "city of Atlanta would be delighted" to host the 1920 convention. Indicating that he finally understood that there would be no progress for Atlanta until he incorporated the NAACP's vision for the future of the city as well, he added that "we have a very large progressive citizenship among the colored people. . . . [T]here is a [distinct] harmony and cordial relation between white and colored."[187] This was followed two hours later by telegrams from the Atlanta Chamber of Commerce and Governor Hugh Dorsey urging the NAACP to bring the association's annual meeting to Atlanta.[188] Ironically, the basis for this newfound interracial harmony had only been made possible by the defeat of the mayor's bond issues at the hands of the city's black electorate. Had the NAACP not so thoroughly derailed Key's plans for Atlanta's development, Key, Dorsey, and the Atlanta Chamber of Commerce would never have endorsed the 1920 meeting. These three telegrams signaled that a significant faction of the city's white elite were ready to renegotiate the terms of interracial politics.

This new politics would be established with the assistance of the newly established Commission on Interracial Cooperation (CIC). Founded in 1920 by a small group of white moderates, this organization was an outgrowth of an effort after World War I to create a framework for interracial negotiations meant to defuse racial tensions and avert violence by substituting "reason for force." Initially funded by the YMCA, the organization eventually became the major conduit for northern philanthropy, funding both race uplift and civil rights campaigns throughout the South.[189] Ultimately, the CIC would become the arbitrator through which the NAACP would negotiate a final settlement with the city fathers over the direction of Atlanta's development.[190] To persuade the NAACP that the CIC would be a trustworthy intermediary, the CIC's leaders convinced the city's white evangelical leaders to donate seven acres of land to the city, with the proviso that it must be used "in perpetuity" for the construction of a "properly equipped and supervised" park and swimming pool "for the pleasure and recreation of our colored citizens."[191] Named Washington Park, this parcel of land became Atlanta's first city park for African Americans, fulfilling a long-standing demand of the Neighborhood Union.[192]

In a letter to commission chairman John Eagan thanking him for this generous gift, Mayor Key elaborated that "what is needed to establish correct relations between the races is a measure of simple justice to our negro citizens." By "justice," he meant concrete benefits delivered to Atlanta's black community that went beyond mere "expressions of good will, kind sentiment and social philosophy." Magnanimously conceding that, while all of these were "good in their way," the mayor insisted that "unless they lead to a point where justice is done, they amount to nothing." If Key was suddenly willing to enlist in the struggle, it was because the NAACP forced him to, since he needed to win black cooperation with his plans for Atlanta's future. As he frankly concluded in his letter to Eagan, "I am going to ask the negroes again to cooperate . . . and when I do I feel that I am in position to ask it and obtain it."[193] To signal Key's willingness to negotiate, he agreed to meet with the executive committee of the local NAACP and provided copies of his correspondence with Eagan. Reporting on these developments to the national office, Chairman Harry Pace explained his belief that the mayor was "honest in his statement and while we have opposed him politically, he has been consistently fair and outspoken both before white [and black] audiences."[194]

Key desperately needed the support of the city's black voters. As a result of a new compulsory attendance law passed by the state legislature, enrollment in Atlanta's public schools jumped 10 percent, from 32,682 students in the 1919–20 school year to 37,772 students in 1920–21.[195] The need to expand the number of schools in the city grew increasingly dire. Despite the pressing need for public investment, a third of the city's voters stubbornly continued to oppose any increase in the city's bonded debt.[196] To win black support for another bond issue, Mayor Key began to make notable concessions. In addition to welcoming the NAACP to Atlanta for its 1920 annual convention, Key wrangled Governor Dorsey and representatives of the Atlanta Chamber of Commerce to speak at the meeting, flanked by CIC leaders John Eagan, Emory professor Plato Durham, and Rev. Ashby Jones.[197] Then, moving beyond mere expressions of goodwill, the mayor invited black representation on the new city planning commission and established a black advisory committee that would consult with the Board of Education on the funding and staffing of black schools.[198] Finally, the mayor negotiated funding for an African American hospital to be built in facilities donated by Emory University, included $5,000 in the 1920 budget for the purchase of land for the construction of a library for black patrons, and increased the wages of the city's black sanitary workers, who had struck for higher wages the previous May.[199]

While significant, none of these concessions was enough to guarantee black support for another bond issue. This was made evident when H. R. Butler, who had long been an active supporter of the NAACP and the Neighborhood Union, was approached by several white politicians with an offer of three or four dilapidated buildings for use as black grammar schools in exchange for his support of the school funding referendum. Furious at this insulting offer, he denounced the bond issue in the pages of the *Independent*. To pacify Butler, whose outrage threatened to unravel the mayor's diplomatic efforts in the black community, the mayor, backed by a phalanx of white civic and political leaders, publicly promised Ben Davis that one-third of the $4 million in the bond issue earmarked for education spending would go toward the construction and financing of black schools.[200]

Finally, on 8 March 1921 the voters of Atlanta went to the polls to approve four separate bond issues, totaling an unprecedented $8,850,000. Since the previous bond election, the ratification of the Nineteenth Amendment had granted women the right to vote, effectively doubling the size of the electorate. Black voter registration since 1919 had doubled as well, with 5,905 African Americans qualifying to vote in the election. Had black voters decided once again to oppose the bonds, they stood a good chance of defeating them, since the initial base of agitation in the black community was precisely the black women who were members of the Neighborhood Union. Even though they would have to pay the poll tax, this would at most have been $2, since there had only been two years for it to accumulate. Thus, out of a record-breaking registration of 26,000 voters, more than 22,000 cast ballots. These ballots supported the bond issue by a margin of 21,170 for and 513 against.[201] By 1924, the city of Atlanta, compelled by the organized political might of Atlanta's black voters, had finally built for black schoolchildren four new grammar schools and a new publicly funded high school, christened Booker T. Washington.[202] As James Weldon Johnson, the executive secretary of the NAACP in 1924, wrote of the victory: "The five new Atlanta schools are a concrete example of the value of united action. Only through united action can the Negro exercise the power necessary to gain his due in America."[203] The lessons learned in Atlanta would provide a new framework for black politics in the South as well as the foundation for the NAACP's political strategy for much of the rest of the twentieth century.

Epilogue
"Self-Determination at the Ballot Box"

Despite the magnitude of the victory in the March 1921 bond vote, the gains for the city's black schools proved meager. Ultimately, Atlanta's black schools only received a fraction of the money that black voters were promised in exchange for their support of the 1921 bond issue. A budget crisis caused by the extra costs of eliminating double sessions in white schools left the members of the Board of Education with a deficit of nearly $800,000, forcing them to reapportion the school bonds in order to build a girls' high school that they had guaranteed to white parents.[1] Even before the city councilors once again diverted money away from black education to fund the expansion of white schools, they tried to back out on their pledge to build a black high school. The only thing preventing the city from breaking its promises to the black voters of Atlanta was the threat of a lawsuit by the Commission on Interracial Cooperation (CIC).[2] Though indispensable to the ultimate success of the campaign, the fact that black Atlantans had to depend on this alliance with powerful paternalistic white liberals to secure a victory that they had already won demarcated the limits of their power.

Despite the NAACP's efforts to establish a racially equitable school system, the schools built for black students out of the bond money remained underfunded, overcrowded, and far inferior to the facilities offered to white students at public expense. Three of the five grammar schools that were established in 1924 opened with double and even triple sessions.[3] And, even though black Atlanta was justly proud of Booker T. Washington High School, it was woefully inadequate to meet the needs of the city's black students. When it opened, it was not just the only high school for black students in Atlanta, but in the surrounding area as well. Students crammed into its classrooms from East Point, College Park, Decatur, and even distant Marietta. By 1935, Washington High had almost 6,000 students in facilities built to hold 2,000. Estelle Clemmons, who taught there between 1937 and 1947, recalled that one year she had a math class with seventy-five students who were forced to sit two to a seat. There was no gymnasium, no auditorium, and little in the way of athletic facilities or equipment. Even though the city provided textbooks for the students, these were all discarded and damaged books from the city's white high schools.[4] The construction of Booker T. Washington High School was a bittersweet victory. Without constant political pressure, it was not possible to maintain a separate but equal school system at public expense.

The sustained organizing necessary to ensure continued support for the black public schools would have been difficult to maintain under any circumstances. However, this was compounded by the demobilization of both the NAACP and the Neighborhood Union in the early 1920s. There are several reasons this happened. First, the leadership of the local NAACP fell into the hands of more conservative leaders such as Rev. A. D. Williams, severing its relationship with the grassroots militancy of the Neighborhood Union. This prevented the branch from building on its victories in the 1919 bond fight, and membership in the Atlanta NAACP declined precipitously.[5] Second, the victory of Warren Harding in the 1920 presidential election returned the White House to Republican hands for the first time since 1912, reigniting the struggle for patronage among the party faithful like Ben Davis. This had the dual effect of undermining the unity that had been established over the previous eight years and removing a good number of dynamic leaders from the local movement. Third, the work done by the Neighborhood Union itself changed over the course of the 1920s, leaving the realm of social movements to became a part of the professionalized world of social work. The Union's vision of grassroots community development was further sidelined as the organization was muscled aside by the arrival of the National Urban League, which quickly moved to take over most of the social service work that the Union had once performed.[6] In fact, the work of the Neighborhood Union had become so marginalized that when the local NAACP was reorganized in 1924, the national office had to remind the new branch leadership to "meet with as large a group of women as can be gathered, that they might be interested in certain concrete things that they might do for the Association."[7]

Finally, and most important, the immediate postwar years were marked by a rising tide of white supremacy and antiblack violence, the most visible manifestation of which was the rebirth of the Ku Klux Klan in 1915 on Stone Mountain, just outside Atlanta. Few people paid much heed to the organization prior to the war. The Atlanta Klan did not even make its first public appearance until October 1919, when Klan members marched down Peachtree in a Confederate reunion parade. However, the cultural and economic dislocations of the postwar period provided fertile ground for the rapid expansion of the Klan within Atlanta as well as far beyond the borders of the South, reaching the height of its influence in the early 1920s. By 1923, the Atlanta klavern was 15,000 members strong and counted three city councilmen among its ranks. One of these city councilors, Walter Sims, would ride this wave of Klan expansion into the mayor's office in 1922, capping an electoral wave that elected Klansmen to the U.S. Senate, the governor's office, and the superior court.[8] With Atlanta being the headquarters of the "Invisible Empire," the ascendancy of the second Klan made it much more dangerous for black Atlantans to assert their rights in as public a manner as they did during and just after World War I. The brief window of opportunity in which black Atlantans could flex their political muscle had closed.

Despite the limitations of the victory and the fragility of the black voting bloc that made it possible, the events of 1919 in Atlanta revealed new forms of black solidarity and changed the terms on which it could be achieved. The victory in 1917, when a delegation led by the NAACP convinced the Board of Education not to cut the seventh grade from black schools, was incredibly tenuous. Even though the delegation characterized themselves as "citizens and taxpayers" entitled to their rights, the strategy they employed was still bounded by the customary limits imposed by the politics of respectability. There was nothing that Atlanta's assembled black leaders could do to prevent the school board members either from breaking their promise to preserve the black seventh grade or from simply making these cuts in the future. It was not until the NAACP mobilized an effective black voting bloc that it was able to assume anything beyond a defensive posture in the fight for equal schools. Until black Atlantans had something to hold over the heads of their erstwhile white allies on the school board and the city council, they would perpetually be forced to defend their dwindling share of the city development budget.

When the NAACP decided to actively interfere with the city-building aspirations of Atlanta's white progressives by mobilizing black voters against municipal development bonds, this shift in strategy required a demonstration of independent black political power that required the rejection of the politics of respectability and the emergence of a new cultural foundation for solidarity and race leadership. This is explicitly described in an editorial published in the *Independent* the week prior to the April 1919 bond election. Borrowing from President Wilson's language of national self-determination, Ben Davis encouraged black Americans to change their "*modus operandi.* Let us stop petitioning, begging and truckling and redress our wants . . . through self-determination expressed at the ballot box." Using the experience of organized labor as a model, Davis explained that it does not "stand before the politician with uncovered heads and beg for what it wants, but . . . goes to the ballot box and registers its will." The *Independent* asserted that so long as black Atlantans are denied a "square deal as citizens of Atlanta," there would be effectively no common ground between black and white Atlantans. Neither "white friends" nor "compromising leadership . . . have brought us any nearer our rights as men and citizens . . . the remedy is plain and at hand—THE BALLOT."[9] The week following the election, Davis demanded electoral self-determination, announcing that the "ballot is the Negro's only defense. . . . We voted solidly as a race against every proposition, because the white man has acted solidly as a race against our best interest."[10] The victory in Atlanta revealed that in order to build black political power, it would be necessary to disrupt the plans of white elites with whom an earlier generation would once have sought to build an alliance.

This carried with it new risks. The abandonment of respectability as a political strategy destabilized the role played by Victorian ideas of gender and class that regulated interracial relationships. In the *Independent*'s first editorial following the April bond election, editor Ben Davis proclaimed that the election results proved that "the black man is as much the master of the white public servants at city hall as the white man and he is entitled to enjoy a part of the privileges [of citizenship]." However, he took pains to reassure white Atlantans that this mastery of black men over the white public servants at city hall did not extend into the white man's household. Even though black men wanted equal access to the fruits of citizenship, these fruits did not include white women. It was for this reason that Davis concluded his triumphant editorial paragraph that "when we refer in this editorial to social questions we do not mean social equality between the races. No self-respecting Negro or white man wants anything of the kind."[11] The ever-present possibility of violence directed against black men and women suspected of violating the racial norms imposed by a white supremacist political order was what made the politics of respectability necessary in the first place. On the eve of the infamous Red Summer of 1919, the implications of an idea of black citizenship not rooted in the correct performance of Victorian morality made Davis's qualification necessary.

The victory in Atlanta also played an important role in shaping the NAACP's political strategy in the first half of the twentieth century. Reflecting upon the lessons of the victory in Atlanta, *Crisis* editor W. E. B. Du Bois asserted that "the colored people of the United States are beginning to be assured within their own minds that there is one great thing for which they must strive and that is the ballot. But the ballot is, as you and I know and as another day did not realize, not the end but the means."[12] While this seems unremarkable for anyone born after World War I, this statement represents a sea change in the conception of the vote. Recall that in 1899, Booker T. Washington had described the ballot as the reward given to those "conservative and intelligent negroes" who had proven their fitness for citizenship and had cast their lot "more closely with the southern white man and cease[d their] continued senseless opposition to his interests."[13] Two decades later, black popular understandings of the ballot had transformed it into a means of collectively exercising black political power, often in explicit opposition to the interests of "the southern white man."

Based on this understanding, at the dawn of the New Deal ten years later, the fight in Atlanta inspired an ambitious campaign to defeat the nomination of Judge John J. Parker to the U.S. Supreme Court. At issue were comments Parker had made as a candidate for the governor of North Carolina, when he had denounced "the participation of the Negro in politics as a source of evil and danger to both races."[14] The NAACP worked alongside the American Federation of Labor (AFL), which opposed Parker for his previous anti-labor rulings, to successfully kill his nomination in the Senate by a vote of forty-one to thirty-nine. However, because of the AFL's clout relative to the NAACP's, few believed that the civil rights organization had played any significant role in the nomination fight, especially considering the number of Republican senators who voted to confirm President Hoover's nomination of Parker to the Supreme Court.

Using this as an opportunity to demonstrate the power that African Americans could wield, Walter White, as the acting executive secretary of the NAACP, and W. E. B. Du Bois, as the editor of the *Crisis,* promised to mobilize black voters—who were still largely Republican—to defeat these Republican senators. Between 1930 and 1934, they did just that. Out of the seventeen senators targeted by the NAACP, they significantly contributed to the defeat of twelve. In doing so, the NAACP foreshadowed the election of 1936 when black voters "turned Lincoln's picture to the wall" and cast their ballots for President Franklin Delano Roosevelt and the New Deal. Although there were many reasons for African Americans to support the Democrats in 1936, their ability to turn so decisively away from the party of Lincoln drew significantly on the cultural shifts in the understandings of gender, class, and nation seen in the fight for Atlanta's Booker T. Washington High School.

The Atlanta NAACP attempted to repeat its success in the 1919 bond fight throughout the 1930s and 1940s. Beginning in 1933, civil rights lawyer Austin T. Walden, Atlanta branch president since 1924, established a series of "citizenship schools" in conjunction with Lugenia Burns Hope's Neighborhood Union. In 1935, the NAACP threatened to mobilize black voters in Atlanta against a proposed bond issue for sewers and school improvements unless the city set aside a fair proportion of the funds raised for the maintenance of black schools. They were, however, out-organized by the mayor and his allies, and fewer than 1,000 of the city's 90,000 black citizens registered to vote in the bond election. Again, in 1936, John Wesley Dobbs, the influential founder of the Atlanta Civic and Political League, sought to register 10,000 black voters into a "simple, strong, separate voting organization" that would serve as a powerful black voting bloc. Two years later, Dobbs attempted to mobilize this league to defeat a school bond measure that was on the ballot that year with the same demand, but that attempt also failed, with only 830 votes cast against the measure.[15] The historian Tomiko Brown-Nagin attributes the failure of both of these campaigns to "black leaders' inability to inspire the sort of collective racial identity needed to cultivate mass interest in voting." In the midst of the Depression, it was just too difficult to convince the mass of poor and working-class black men and women that they had much to gain by participating in these campaigns. Additionally, the legal barriers to voting—especially the cumulative poll tax—were simply too great to overcome.[16] In the flush years of America's involvement in World War I, black families in Atlanta could afford to pay their poll taxes; however, after seven years of economic depression, this was no longer possible for the vast majority of Atlanta's black voters.

Despite these failures, the dream of a unified black voting bloc continued to captivate the imaginations of the city's black leadership. By 1949, after World War II had brought prosperity and a new spirit of militancy to the Gate City, black voters came to comprise 25 percent of the city's total voting population—roughly 25,000 voters. That year, in order to forge this quarter of the electorate into a solid mass of black voters, Dobbs, a staunch Republican, and Walden, now a Democrat, established the nonpartisan Atlanta Negro Voters League (ANVL). Bridging what were still fierce partisan divides within the city's black community, members of ANVL were free to vote how they pleased in national elections, but were pledged to support local candidates whom the organization deemed best for black Atlantans. In command of 25,000 pledged votes, Dobbs and Walden could throw a close election to the candidate that ANVL chose. The first test of this strategy came in the mayoral race of 1949, which pitted the incumbent, William B. Hartsfield, against Fulton County commissioner Charlie Brown. In exchange for its endorsement, ANVL presented a list of demands that echoed the earlier agenda of the Neighborhood Union and the NAACP: African American policemen and firemen, parks and playgrounds in black neighborhoods, public housing for low-income black renters, and tracts of land for the construction of homes for black families. For the first time in Atlanta's history, both leading mayoral candidates actively campaigned for the black vote. When ANVL decided to throw its support behind Hartsfield, he won reelection by a narrow margin provided by the city's organized black electorate. In the 1949 election, ANVL delivered victory to almost every candidate it endorsed.[17] Atlanta's black voters had finally won a place in the city's political life.

The protagonists of this book attempted several different strategies in their struggle to deracialize citizenship, a pressing necessity for African Americans who faced a Progressive Era Jim Crow regime that sought to restrict the full prerogatives of citizenship to "whites only," relegating African Americans to a subordinate caste. The ultimate strategy of the NAACP and the Neighborhood Union was to embrace a racially composite understanding of citizenship. The black voting blocs organized by the NAACP in Atlanta in 1919 and by ANVL in 1949, along with those organized to punish the pro-Parker senators between 1930 and 1934, had a deep impact on African American politics. Implicit in this strategy, however, was the contradiction between marshalling black voters to vote in a racially defined bloc to press for a deracialized understanding of citizenship. Ben Davis acknowledged this contradiction in the aftermath of the April 1919 bond election: "If the white man wants the racial question eliminated from public questions, he must not raise it."[18] Or, as C. L. R. James phrased it in a slightly different register: "The Negro . . . is a nationalist to the heart and perfectly right to be so. His racism, his nationalism, is a necessary means of giving him strength, self-respect and organization in order to fight for integration into American society. It is a perfect example of dialectical contradiction."[19] Even though today's appeals to white supremacy have been able to raise what Davis called "the racial question" without explicitly mentioning race, this contradiction endures—a deracialized citizenship was and still is utopian. What can and must be continued is the ongoing struggle to become "a satisfied part of our composite citizenship."[20]

Notes

Introduction

1. Michael R. Haines, "Population of Cities with at Least 100,000 Population in 1990: 1790–1990," Table Aa832–1033, in *Historical Statistics of the United States: Millennial Edition*, ed. Susan B. Carter et al. (New York: Cambridge University Press, 2006).

2. Doyle, *New Cities*, 147–49.

3. Du Bois, *Souls of Black Folk*, 41.

4. Ibid., 42.

5. An exception to this general trend can be found in the work of Howard N. Rabinowitz. See his *Race Relations in the Urban South*, and *Race, Ethnicity and Urbanization*, 61–89, 137–63. See also Hale, *Making Whiteness*, 121–97.

6. Excellent examples of newer scholarship sensitive to the broader contours of Jim Crow and local black resistance include Godshalk, *Veiled Visions*; Ortiz, *Emancipation Betrayed*; and Kelley, *Right to Ride*.

7. Meier and Rudwick, "Boycott Movement"; Kelley, *Right to Ride*.

8. Dittmer, *Black Georgia*, 146–48; Godshalk, *Veiled Visions*, 246–51; Rouse, "Legacy of Community Organizing," 124–28; Rouse, *Lugenia Burns Hope*, 74–79. The remarkable fight for Booker T. Washington High School is not even mentioned in the best of the most recent histories of the NAACP: see Berg, *Ticket to Freedom*; and Sullivan, *Lift Every Voice*.

9. Despite the later embrace of school desegregation as the signature struggle of the civil rights movement, some African Americans were concerned about losing black-controlled educational and cultural institutions. To turn away from these schools was also to turn away from a legacy of black collective action in pursuit of equality. See W. E. B. Du Bois, "Does the Negro Need Separate Schools?," *Journal of Negro Education* 4, no. 3 (July 1935): 328–35; and Cecelski, *Along Freedom Road*.

Tomiko Brown-Nagin argues that the Atlanta branch of the NAACP had long deviated from the national organization's focus on desegregation, an approach she terms "pragmatic civil rights." This approach "privileged politics over litigation, placed a high value on economic security, and rejected the idea that integration (or even desegregation) and equality were one and the same." Pursuing political power meant that black Atlantans would seek first to improve conditions *within* the system of Jim Crow rather than "devot[ing] all of their energies to directly challenging the legal regime of segregation in all of its breadth and depth." Though her story begins well after mine ends, I contend that the cornerstone of Atlanta's civil rights pragmatism was laid in the struggle for black education in 1919. See Brown-Nagin, *Courage to Dissent*, 1–58 (quotations on 2 and 19).

10. Du Bois, *Souls of Black Folk*, 62–72.

11. Peiss, *Cheap Amusements.*

12. Higginbotham, *Righteous Discontent*, 197.

13. Historians of respectability such as Victoria Wolcott, Tera Hunter, and Kevin Gaines demonstrate the ways in which respectability was a crucial discursive strategy that black men and women employed to combat racialized sexual and moral stereotypes. These understandings of respectability do play a role in this book, but my focus here is on how respectability is used to negotiate racial and interracial solidarity. This is similar to Evelyn Brooks Higginbotham's argument in *Righteous Discontent*, which shows how black women in the Baptist Church employed the politics of respectability to define and advance an ambitious reform agenda. Similarly, Glenda Gilmore's *Gender and Jim Crow* demonstrates how black women used the language of respectability to build alliances with white progressives in order to deliver crucial social services to the black community.

The definition of respectability used in this book is historically specific to the South before the northward migration of black southerners beginning in World War I. As the discourse of respectability moved north throughout the 1920s and 1930s, it changed dramatically. The best discussion of this is in Davarian Baldwin's *Chicago's New Negroes*. As Baldwin uses the term, "respectability" is a measure of social acceptance, a yardstick of status—akin to Bourdieu's concepts of social or cultural capital, social statuses that can be exchanged like currency for political power. The denominations in which this currency comes—the terms of respectability—change radically between Atlanta in the 1890s–1910s and the milieu of 1920s Chicago on which Baldwin focuses. Whereas the protagonists of *Schooling Jim Crow* contend with Victorian standards of moral behavior in the Jim Crow South, Baldwin's New Negroes recast respectability in response to migration to Chicago and the spread of 1920s black consumer culture.

For more on respectability, see Higginbotham, *Righteous Discontent*, 185–211; Hunter, *To 'Joy My Freedom*, 130–86; Gaines, *Uplifting the Race*; White, *Too Heavy Load*, 21–109; Hine, "Rape and the Inner Lives of Black Women"; and Gilmore, *Gender and Jim Crow*, 147–202. For respectability during and after the Great Migration, see Wolcott, *Remaking Respectability*; and Baldwin, *Chicago's New Negroes*.

14. Dittmer, *Black Georgia*, 131.

15. "An Analysis of the Race Problem by a Southern White Woman," *Independent* (New York), no. 56 (17 March 1904), 590.

16. Hale, *Making Whiteness*, 20.

17. "The Atlanta Tragedy," *Voice* (November 1906), 479.

18. Meier and Rudwick, "Boycott Movement," 758. See also Kelley, *Right to Ride*.

19. Rabinowitz, *Race, Ethnicity and Urbanization*, 61–89, 137–63.

20. Rosen, *Terror in the Heart of Freedom*, 122–26, 140–41.

21. Washington, *Up From Slavery*, 221–22.

22. *Savannah Tribune*, 17 February 1906, 4.

23. Higginbotham, *Righteous Discontent*, 187.

24. Singh, *Black Is a Country*, 47. Singh notes the strong antidemocratic cast of this sort of politics: "Early black public activism under Du Bois's leadership was built on the idea of substituting hierarchies of gender and education for those of race and accumulated wealth ('a dictatorship of character and intelligence across the color line')."

25. Higginbotham, *Righteous Discontent*, 187, 193.

26. Dorsey, *To Build Our Lives Together*, 9.

27. *Atlanta Independent*, 26 April 1919, 1.

28. Jones, *Labor of Love*, 110–51.

29. Ryan, "Gender and Public Access," 266.

30. Ibid., 278.

31. Kerber, *Toward an Intellectual History of Women*, chapters 1–5.

32. Hickey, *Hope and Danger*, 5; Hunter, *To 'Joy My Freedom*, viii.

33. Guy-Sheftall, *Daughters of Sorrow*, 41–42.

34. Ibid., 18.

35. Bayor, *Race and the Shaping of Twentieth Century Atlanta*, 7; Hunter, *To 'Joy My Freedom*, 45–46, 187–218.

36. Bayor, *Race and the Shaping*, 9.

37. Hickey, *Hope and Danger*, 136, 139–44.

38. Marion Talbot, *The Education of Women* (Chicago: University of Chicago Press, 1910), 31.

39. Lasch-Quinn, *Black Neighbors*, 113.

40. This does not mean it was safer or easier for black women to publicly contest the limits imposed by Jim Crow. As the sheer level of violence—particularly sexual violence—directed at black women attests, outspoken black women assumed the same risks as their male counterparts. Brown, "Negotiating and Transforming the Public Sphere," 63, n.63. See also Rosen, *Terror in the Heart of Freedom*; McGuire, *At the Dark End of the Street*; and Feimster, *Southern Horrors*.

41. Rouse, *Lugenia Burns Hope*, 16–17, 24–30, 57–90.

42. Feimster, *Southern Horrors*, 103.

43. Prather, "We Have Taken a City," 23–24.

44. Giddings, *Ida*, 221–25.

45. "Close Ranks," *Crisis*, 16, no. 3 (July 1918): 111.

46. Williams, *Torchbearers of Democracy*, 52.

47. Capozzola, *Uncle Sam Wants You*, 33. On black men's participation in World War I, see Barbeau and Henri, *Unknown Soldiers*; Kennedy, *Over Here*, 156–63; Nalty,

Strength for the Fight, 107–24; Astor, *Right to Fight,* 108–24; Slotkin, *Lost Battalions;* Shenk, *Work or Fight;* Lentz-Smith, *Freedom Struggles;* and Williams, *Torchbearers of Democracy.*

48. Brown, *Private Politics and Public Voices,* 67–72.

49. Breen, "Black Women and the Great War," 421–40; Salem, *To Better Our World,* 201–53; Morgan, *Women and Patriotism,* 101–26; Brown, *Private Politics and Public Voices.*

50. Rouse, *Lugenia Burns Hope,* 95–96.

51. Williams, *Torchbearers of Democracy,* 232–60.

52. Fortune, *Black and White,* 127.

53. Logan, *Betrayal of the Negro,* 55–57.

54. Lane, *Brownsville Affair;* Wynne, "Brownsville"; Thornbrough, "Brownsville Episode."

55. Wynne, "Brownsville," 155.

56. *New York Age,* 22 November 1906, 5; Thornbrough, "Brownsville Episode," 472.

57. *Atlanta Independent,* 10 November 1906, 4.

58. *New York Age,* 13 December 1906, 4.

59. Weiss, *Farewell to the Party of Lincoln;* Frymer, *Uneasy Alliances,* 49–86.

1. "Manhood Rights"

1. Bacote, "Negro in Georgia Politics," 279–80.

2. *Atlanta Journal,* 29 November 1899, 1.

3. Litwack, *Trouble in Mind,* 280–83.

4. After the lynching, Mrs. Cranford revealed that her late husband and Sam Hose had in fact quarreled over wages and that the black farmworker never laid a hand on her. Litwack, *Trouble in Mind,* 283.

5. Du Bois, *Autobiography,* 222; Lewis, *W. E. B. Du Bois: Biography of a Race,* 226.

6. Perman, *Struggle for Mastery,* 281–83.

7. Bacote, "Negro in Georgia Politics," 287; *Atlanta Constitution,* 6 November 1899, 2.

8. Brundage, *Lynching in the New South,* 270–80.

9. Quoted in ibid., 139.

10. Harlan, *Booker T. Washington: The Making of a Black Leader,* 291.

11. Washington, *Up From Slavery,* 221–22; Rabinowitz, *Race, Ethnicity and Urbanization,* 61–89, 137–63.

12. Kousser, *Shaping of Southern Politics,* 218.

13. *Atlanta Constitution,* 10 November 1899, 7.

14. Ibid.

15. Ibid.

16. Ibid.; "A Memorial to the Legislature of Georgia on the Hardwick Bill," Atlanta History Center, Long-Rucker-Aiken Papers (hereafter cited as "LRA Papers"), Series II, Subseries IV, Box 1, Folder 11.

17. "The Suffrage Fight in Georgia," *Independent* (New York), 30 November 1899, 3226–27.

18. "Memorial to the Legislature of Georgia."

19. *Atlanta Constitution*, 10 November 1899, 7.

20. "Memorial to the Legislature of Georgia."

21. Ibid.

22. Bederman, *Manliness and Civilization*, 23–31.

23. Anderson, *Education of Blacks*, 33–109.

24. "Memorial to the Legislature of Georgia."

25. Ibid.

26. Ibid. On literacy rates in Georgia, see Dittmer, *Black Georgia*, 141.

27. "Memorial to the Legislature of Georgia."

28. Through "second-taxing," black communities collected money for the maintenance of their own schools after paying their state, county, and municipal taxes. Dittmer, *Black Georgia*, 141–48; McMillen, *Dark Journey*, 79–82.

29. *Atlanta Constitution*, 29 November 1899, 1.

30. Goodwyn, *Populist Moment*, 158–63, 187–94, 227–28; Woodward, *Tom Watson*.

31. Bacote, "Negro in Georgia Politics," 289–90; Harlan, *Booker T. Washington: The Making of a Black Leader*, 292.

32. Woodward, *Origins of the New South*, 369–95.

33. Goodwyn, *Populist Moment*; Woodward, *Origins of the New South*, 235–90; Ayers, *Promise of the New South*, 214–309.

34. Quoted in Ayers, *Promise of the New South*, 282.

35. Woodward, *Tom Watson*; Ayers, *Promise of the New South*, 270–76; Crowe, "Tom Watson."

36. Woodward, *Tom Watson*, 190, 348.

37. Crowe, "Tom Watson," 105–7.

38. Hahn, *Nation Under Our Feet*, 364–411; Rachleff, *Black Labor in Richmond*.

39. Woodward, *Tom Watson*, 191.

40. Ibid., 204; Goodwyn, *Populist Moment*, 189–90.

41. Woodward, *Tom Watson*, 206–7.

42. Crowe, "Tom Watson," 107.

43. Woodward, *Tom Watson*, 232.

44. Ibid., 320.

45. Ibid., 320–21.

46. Perman, *Struggle for Mastery*, 283–90.

47. Ibid., 286–87 (Hardwick quoted on 286).

48. Prather, "We Have Taken a City"; Gilmore, *Gender and Jim Crow*, 61–146.

49. *Atlanta Constitution*, 12 September 1889, 5; 13 September 1889, 4, 8; and 14 September 1889, 2.

50. *Atlanta Constitution*, 5 September 1906, 2.

51. Grantham, *Hoke Smith*, 28–30, 125.

52. Ibid., 126.

53. Grantham, "Hoke Smith," 423–25; Grantham, *Hoke Smith*, 131–55.

54. Grantham, "Hoke Smith," 426–27.

55. Bacote, "Negro in Georgia Politics," 401.

56. Woodward, *Tom Watson*, 323.

57. Crowe, "Racial Violence and Social Reform," 235–37, 245–46.

58. Perman, *Struggle for Mastery*, 288; Woodward, *Origins of the New South*, 369–95.

59. Hale, *Making Whiteness*, 77.

60. Bartley, *Creation of Modern Georgia*, 149.

61. Bacote, "Negro in Georgia Politics," 421.

62. Robert A. Margo, "Monthly Earnings with Board of Farm Laborers, by Region: 1818–1948," Table Ba 4234–43, in Carter et al., *Historical Statistics of the United States*.

63. Perman, *Struggle for Mastery*, 288.

64. Bacote, "Negro in Georgia Politics," 401.

65. *Georgia Equal Rights Convention*, 2—pamphlet in the Papers of W. E. B. Du Bois, microfilm edition, Reel 1, frames 1017–25.

66. Donaldson, "New Negroes in a New South," 24–78.

67. On Du Bois in Atlanta, see Lewis, *W. E. B. Du Bois: Biography of a Race*, 211–387.

68. William J. White to H. A. Rucker, 28 November 1905; and Rucker to White, 9 December 1905, both in LRA Papers, Series II, Subseries II, Box 1, Folder 10.

69. This feud began after Du Bois, attempting to establish some basis of local cooperation between the Tuskegee machine and the fledgling Niagara movement, endorsed Rucker, who was Washington's point man in the state. Capeci and Knight, "Reckoning with Violence," 736–38. On Davis's criticisms of Du Bois, see *Atlanta Independent*, 5 August 1905, 4; and 19 August 1905, 4.

70. Dittmer, *Black Georgia*, 173; *Georgia Equal Rights Convention*, 2.

71. *Georgia Equal Rights Convention*, 2.

72. Rev. William J. White to W. E. B. Du Bois, 9 January 1906, Papers of W. E. B. Du Bois, microfilm edition, Reel 1, frame 1015.

73. *Georgia Equal Rights Convention*, 4–5.

74. White to Du Bois, 9 January 1906.

75. *Georgia Equal Rights Convention*, 12.

76. Capeci and Knight, "Reckoning with Violence," 737–38; Godshalk, *Veiled Visions*, 70.

77. *Georgia Equal Rights Convention*, 6–8.

78. Bacote, "Negro in Georgia Politics," 7.

79. *Georgia Equal Rights Convention*, 6–8.

80. Ibid., 12.

81. Ibid., 13.

82. *Voice of the Negro* (March 1906), 163–64; Donaldson, "New Negroes in a New South," 30, 34–35, 46–52.

83. Coon, *Public Taxation and Negro Schools*; Dittmer, *Black Georgia*, 143.

84. Mancini, *One Dies, Get Another*, 82; Blackmon, *Slavery by Another Name*, 54.

The most thorough history of the convict lease system in Georgia is Lichtenstein's *Twice the Work of Free Labor.* See also Curtin, *Black Prisoners and Their World;* and Shapiro, *New South Rebellion.*

85. Lichtenstein, *Twice the Work of Free Labor,* 46, 54.

86. Mancini, *One Dies, Get Another,* 85.

87. Quoted in ibid., 3.

88. Lichtenstein, *Twice the Work of Free Labor,* 112–13.

89. Blackmon, *Slavery by Another Name,* 91; Lichtenstein, *Twice the Work of Free Labor,* 105–25.

90. Blackmon, *Slavery by Another Name,* 91–92, 338–70.

91. *Georgia Equal Rights Convention,* 15–16.

92. Ibid.

93. Bauerlein, *Negrophobia,* 39. Ray Stannard Baker notes that in 1905, the city of Atlanta (population 115,000) had over 17,000 arrests. The $100,000 in fines paid by black men and women arrested for vagrancy constituted a significant portion of the 1905 city budget, which totaled only $1,879,000. Baker, *Following the Color Line,* 3; Cooper, *Official History of Fulton County,* 692.

94. Bauerlein, *Negrophobia,* 43.

95. *Georgia Equal Rights Convention,* 15.

96. Mancini, *One Dies, Get Another,* 72–73.

97. Ibid., 72. This may certainly be an exaggeration, and some of these liaisons were voluntary. In addition, women sent to prison sometimes brought their children with them, either because they could not bear to be separated from them or because there was nobody to leave them with. Curtin, *Black Prisoners and Their World,* 113–29.

98. *Georgia Equal Rights Convention,* 15.

99. Ibid., 15–16.

100. Hunter, *To 'Joy My Freedom,* 119–20.

101. Jones, *Labor of Love Labor of Sorrow,* 113.

102. Hunter, *To 'Joy My Freedom,* 105–6.

103. Jones, *Labor of Love Labor of Sorrow,* 150; Hunter, *To 'Joy My Freedom,* 106.

104. Guy-Sheftall, *Daughters of Sorrow,* 58.

105. "The Race Problem: An Autobiography by a Southern Colored Woman," *Independent* 56 (March 17, 1904), 588.

106. McGuire, *At the Dark End of the Street,* 131–55; White, *Ar'n't I a Woman?,* 164.

107. *Georgia Equal Rights Convention,* 16.

108. Jones, *Labor of Love, Labor of Sorrow,* 142.

109. Martin Summers has argued that the claims of these men to successful middle-class manhood frequently depended upon the existence of men who could not live up to these standards. Summers, *Manliness and Its Discontents.*

110. Brown, "Negotiating and Transforming the Public Sphere," 49–50.

111. Hickey, *Hope and Danger,* 26–27; Hunter, *To 'Joy My Freedom,* 120.

112. Bayor, *Race and the Shaping of Twentieth Century Atlanta,* 7.

113. Maclachlan, "Women's Work," 281–86; Hunter, *To 'Joy My Freedom,* 50, 57.

114. Jones, *Labor of Love, Labor of Sorrow*, 112, 114, 125–26.

115. Almost any form of work was preferable to domestic labor, especially where alternatives were available. While arduous, filthy, and often dangerous, black women's preference for these sorts of jobs led to shortages of domestic labor in towns with tobacco processing plants and coastal areas with active fishing industries. See ibid., 134–42.

116. Ibid., 124.

117. *Atlanta University Publications No. 7: The Negro Artisan: A Social Study* (Atlanta: Atlanta University Press, 1902), 118; Jones, *Labor of Love, Labor of Sorrow*, 143.

118. *Georgia Equal Rights Convention*, 9–10.

119. Williamson, *Crucible of Race*, 115–20.

120. *Georgia Equal Rights Convention*, 5, 9, 13–15.

121. Perman, *Struggle for Mastery*, 281.

122. *Georgia Equal Rights Convention*, 10–11.

123. Ibid.

124. On "best men and women," see Gilmore, *Gender and Jim Crow*, xix.

125. Kevin Gaines argues that elite versions of racial uplift ideology encouraged African Americans to retreat from more democratic notions of racial progress at the beginning of the twentieth century. Though he highlights the dissent of black thinkers like Jesse Max Barber from this conservative uplift ideology, Gaines does not fully explore the ways in which this dissent was itself articulated with the language of the politics of respectability. In overlooking these contradictions, it is difficult to understand how they were ultimately resolved. See Gaines, *Uplifting the Race*, 61–66.

126. *Voice of the Negro* (March 1906), 177; Washington, *My Life and Work*, 125–58; Gaines, *Uplifting the Race*, 16.

127. *Voice of the Negro* (March 1906), 163–64.

128. Godshalk, *Veiled Visions*, 72–73; *Voice of the Negro* (March 1906), 177.

129. *Voice of the Negro* (March 1906), 163–66.

130. *Atlanta Independent*, 20 January 1906, 4; Capeci and Knight, "Reckoning with Violence," 736–38.

131. *Atlanta Independent*, 20 January 1906, 4.

132. Ibid.

133. *Atlanta Independent*, 10 February 1906.

2. "To Humiliate the Progressive Negro"

1. *Atlanta Constitution*, 22 August 1906, 1.

2. Bauerlein, *Negrophobia*, 100–103; *Atlanta Constitution*, 22 August 1906, 7; and 23 August 1906, 6.

3. Perman, *Struggle for Mastery*, 289; Grantham, *Hoke Smith*, 154.

4. Bacote, "Negro in Georgia Politics," 452–53, 455.

5. Bauerlein, *Negrophobia*, 107–8.

6. Ibid., 81.

7. *Atlanta Independent*, 9 June 1906, 4.

8. Horne, *Black Liberation/Red Scare*, 17–22; Davis, *Communist Councilman*, 21–30.

9. Bullock, "Profile of a Periodical"; Gaines, *Uplifting the Race*, 60–66; Godshalk, *Veiled Visions*, 65–68.

10. *Voice of the Negro* (January 1904), 35.

11. *Voice of the Negro* (March 1906), 216–17.

12. *Voice of the Negro* (July 1906), 473–74.

13. *Atlanta Independent*, 16 June 1906, 4; *Voice of the Negro* (July 1906), 469–70, 473–74.

14. *Voice of the Negro* (July 1906), 473–74.

15. However, it does not follow that Smith believed he shared the same moral universe as Barber. Had he, the politics of respectability would have continued to function effectively.

16. *Voice of the Negro* (August 1906), 595–96. Barber, like most other black leaders, rejected mechanisms such as grandfather clauses as class legislation, disfranchising both the qualified and nonqualified through the mere accident of birth.

17. Ibid.

18. *Atlanta Independent*, 8 September 1906, 4.

19. Bacote, "Some Aspects of Negro Life," 194.

20. Jones, *Labor of Love, Labor of Sorrow*, 80. On white landlords' control of black tenants' lives, see Ransom and Sutch, *One Kind of Freedom*, 81–99, 149–50.

21. National white life expectancy at birth ranged between forty-six and fifty-six years over the same period. See Michael R. Haines, "Expectation of Life at Specified Ages, by Sex and Race: 1850–1998," Table Ab656–703, in Carter et al., *Historical Statistics of the United States*; Jones, *Labor of Love, Labor of Sorrow*, 92.

22. Jones, *Labor of Love, Labor of Sorrow*, 92.

23. Ransom and Sutch, *One Kind of Freedom*, 44–46.

24. By contrast, only 2 percent of white married women did so. See Jones, *Labor of Love, Labor of Sorrow*, 63.

25. Ibid., 82.

26. Baker, *Following the Color Line*, 76.

27. Ransom and Sutch, *One Kind of Freedom*, 120–25, 128–31.

28. Jones, *Labor of Love, Labor of Sorrow*, 83.

29. Hale, *Making Whiteness*, 172–73, 177–79.

30. Jones, *Labor of Love, Labor of Sorrow*, 84–92.

31. Hunter, *To 'Joy My Freedom*, 45.

32. Garrett and Martin. *Atlanta and Environs*, 426, 507, 559.

33. British Board of Trade, *Cost of Living in American Towns: Report of an Enquiry by the Board of Trade into Working Class Rents, Housing and Retail Prices, together with the Rates of Wages in Certain Occupations in the Principal Industrial Towns of the United States of America* (London: His Majesty's Stationery Office, 1911), 57. The best homes available to black Atlantans were two-story houses owned by graduates of Atlanta University, mail carriers, merchants, and other black professionals. These

typically had seven or eight rooms, indoor plumbing, gas, and electricity. See *Atlanta University Publications No. 13: The Negro Family* (Atlanta: Atlanta University Press, 1908), 58–59, 65.

34. Bayor, *Race and the Shaping of Twentieth Century Atlanta*, 46–48.

35. British Board of Trade, *Cost of Living*, 50; Hunter, *To 'Joy My Freedom*, 45.

36. British Board of Trade, *Cost of Living*, 49.

37. Hunter, *To 'Joy My Freedom*, 46.

38. *Atlanta University Publications No. 7: Mortality Among Negroes in Cities: Proceedings of the Conference for the Investigation of City Problems* (Atlanta: Atlanta University Press, 1896), 18–19.

39. British Board of Trade, *Cost of Living*, 50. Life in Atlanta was not that healthy for white people either: 5,714 white Atlantans died over the same period, and 1,003 (17.5 percent) were less than one year old.

40. Hunter, *To 'Joy My Freedom*, 47–49.

41. Ibid., 99–103.

42. British Board of Trade, *Cost of Living*, 54–55.

43. Bacote, "Some Aspects of Negro Life," 188.

44. British Board of Trade, *Cost of Living*, 54–55.

45. Hunter, *To 'Joy My Freedom*, 50, 52–53.

46. Jones, *Labor of Love, Labor of Sorrow*, 104–5.

47. Some female sharecroppers did participate in wage labor; however, the number who did remained relatively small in comparison to the number of urban women wageworkers. Ibid., 93–95.

48. James, "Policies of Organized Labor," 40–65.

49. Jones, *Labor of Love, Labor of Sorrow*, 111. This pattern was noted as early as 1897. See *Atlanta University Publications No. 2: The Social and Physical Condition of Negroes in Cities* (Atlanta: Atlanta University Press, 1897), 7.

50. Hunter, *To 'Joy My Freedom*, 52.

51. James, "Policies of Organized Labor," 22.

52. Maclachlan, "Women's Work," 281–86. In 1890, 46 percent of black wage earners in Atlanta were women. By 1900, that number had risen to 54 percent. A math error in the tables at the back of Tera Hunter's otherwise careful study of black working-class women overstates the severity of the gender disparity between black male and female wage earners. The figures she gives for the percentage of female wage earners as a proportion of the black population is correctly calculated for the years 1870, 1880, 1890, and 1920. However, her figures are incorrectly calculated for the years 1900 and 1910, when she mistakenly inserts the percentage of black women workers as the proportion of all *female* workers. Rather than 71 percent of all black wage earners being women in 1900, the correct figure should be 54 percent. For 1910, the correct figure is 50 percent. See Hunter, *To 'Joy My Freedom*, Table 2, 242.

53. *Georgia Equal Rights Convention*, 16.

54. Hunter, *To 'Joy My Freedom*, 88–97.

55. Ibid., 121–24, 134–35.

56. Bacote, "Some Aspects of Negro Life," 194.

57. Hale, *Making Whiteness*, 124.

58. Dittmer, *Black Georgia*, 13–14; Hunter, *To 'Joy My Freedom*, 104.

59. Garrett and Martin, *Atlanta and Environs*, 607–9; Hunter, *To 'Joy My Freedom*, 152–54.

60. Dittmer, *Black Georgia*, 124.

61. Hunter, *To 'Joy My Freedom*, 171–75.

62. Quoted in White and White, *Stylin',* 160.

63. Garrett and Martin, *Atlanta and Environs*, 542–43.

64. Hunter, *To 'Joy My Freedom*, 175; Garrett and Martin, *Atlanta and Environs*, 517. For more on Atlanta's black working-class entertainments, see Goodson, *Highbrows, Hillbillies, & Hellfire*, 166–72.

65. Hunter, *To 'Joy My Freedom*, 172–73.

66. Gordon, *Pitied, But Not Entitled*, 129–30.

67. *Atlanta University Publications No. 5: The College-Bred Negro* (Atlanta: Atlanta University Press, 1900), 57; Dorsey, *To Build Our Lives Together*, 103.

68. *College-Bred Negro*, 57.

69. *Atlanta University Publications No. 13: The Negro American Family* (Atlanta: Atlanta University Press, 1908), 41.

70. "Work for Backward Races," *Outlook* 72, no. 9 (1 November 1902): 482; Dorsey, *To Build Our Lives Together*, 104.

71. Bauerlein, *Negrophobia*, 1–109.

72. *Atlanta Journal*, 1 August 1906 (quoted in Godshalk, *Veiled Visions*, 50–51).

73. Woodward, *Tom Watson*, 328.

74. McCurry, *Masters of Small Worlds*, 5–129. It is important to note that late nineteenth-century black family structure was not always strictly patriarchal. Domestic order was frequently kept by women whose husbands had been killed in the war or lost during slavery. Ben Davis Jr., who grew up in Georgia, recalls his grandmother as a "father" who ruled over the family with "authority and responsibility . . . with iron discipline." See Davis, *Communist Councilman*, 24–25.

75. Kantrowitz, *Ben Tillman*, 105, 162–65.

76. *Atlanta Journal*, 1 August 1906 (quoted in Godshalk, *Veiled Visions*, 50–51).

77. Quoted in Dorsey, *To Build Our Lives Together*, 153.

78. *Atlanta Constitution*, 10 November 1899, 7.

79. *Georgia Equal Rights Convention*, 16.

80. *Atlanta Independent*, 1 September 1906, 4.

81. Black mobs did lynch black men for a variety of alleged crimes, including rape. Of 148 known cases of black men lynched by black mobs, 25 percent were accused of rape. Most of these accusations were for raping black women. The mob activity of black communities was a response to law enforcement's unwillingness to prosecute crimes committed against black people. Davis's call was unusual in that it called for an interracial lynch mob to defend white women against black rapists. Feimster, *Southern Horrors*, 103.

82. To clarify exactly with whom he was trying to forge an alliance, Davis reprinted an article by the *Atlanta Georgian*'s John Temple Graves on the same page as

this editorial. Responding to Davis's concern that the innocent not be punished along with the guilty, Graves asserted that history showed that "the mass must frequently suffer from the continued and unchecked outrages of a few of its representatives." Indeed, the "innocent must join with all their hearts and hands with the better element of the white race to terrorize and to intimidate the criminals of the Negro race." He made no mention of white criminality. See *Atlanta Independent*, 1 September 1906, 4. See also Godshalk, *Veiled Visions*, 74–75.

83. Godshalk, *Veiled Visions*, 75–76; Dorsey, *To Build Our Lives Together*, 155–58.

84. *Savannah Tribune*, 29 September 1906, 4.

85. Bauerlein, *Negrophobia*, 269.

86. Rotundo, *American Manhood*, 1–9.

87. *Atlanta Independent*, 22 September 1906, 4.

88. *Atlanta Independent*, 1 September 1906, 4.

89. *Atlanta Independent*, 22 September 1906, 4.

90. Ibid. (emphasis added).

91. *Atlanta Independent*, 15 September 1906, 4.

92. Woodward, *Tom Watson*, 328–29.

93. Dittmer, *Black Georgia*, 130.

94. *Atlanta Constitution*, 22 September 1906, 1.

95. Bauerlein, *Negrophobia*, 90; Baker, *Following the Color Line*, 8.

96. Bauerlein, *Negrophobia*, 144.

97. Dittmer, *Black Georgia*, 124; Bauerlein, *Negrophobia*, 144.

98. *Atlanta Independent*, 22 September 1906, 4.

99. Bauerlein, *Negrophobia*, 146.

100. Godshalk, *Veiled Visions*, 85, 88.

101. Dittmer, *Black Georgia*, 124.

102. Ibid., 125.

103. Baker, *Following the Color Line*, 10.

104. Dittmer, *Black Georgia*, 124.

105. Godshalk, *Veiled Visions*, 90, 95.

106. Ibid., 86.

107. Dittmer, *Black Georgia*, 125; Godshalk, *Veiled Visions*, 96.

108. Godshalk, *Veiled Visions*, 91–96.

109. Dittmer, *Black Georgia*, 129; Godshalk, *Veiled Visions*, 105–6.

110. Merritt, *Herndons*, 32–66.

111. Williamson, *Rage for Order*, 48; Dittmer, *Black Georgia*, 125; Henry W. Grady, *The Life and Labors of Henry W. Grady* (Atlanta: H. C. Hudgins, 1890), 110–11.

112. Godshalk, *Veiled Visions*, 95.

113. Hale, *Making Whiteness*, 133–38.

114. Baker, *Following the Color Line*, 30–31.

115. Kelley, *Right to Ride*, 33–50; Godshalk, *Veiled Visions*, 108–9.

116. Godshalk, *Veiled Visions*, 90–91.

117. Dittmer, *Black Georgia*, 125; Godshalk, *Veiled Visions*, 90–92.

118. Godshalk, *Veiled Visions*, 97.

119. Dorsey, *To Build Our Lives Together,* 160.

120. White, *Man Called White,* 11. This story is likely apocryphal. Biographer Kenneth Janken unearthed contradictory testimony from both Walter White's sisters and his mother, denying that Walter and his father were armed. Janken argues that White embellished his tale both to raise his national profile as the leader of the NAACP and to demonstrate that black men were manly enough to defend their women and children. Godshalk adds that this story also allowed the middle-class White to deny his dependence upon the working-class toughs who fired on the advancing mob. Janken, *White,* 14–19; Godshalk, *Veiled Visions,* 112–13.

121. Dittmer, *Black Georgia,* 127; Godshalk, *Veiled Visions,* 102.

122. Baker, *Following the Color Line,* 12.

123. Ibid.

124. Godshalk, *Veiled Visions,* 102.

125. Baker, *Following the Color Line,* 12; Dittmer, *Black Georgia,* 128; Godshalk, *Veiled Visions,* 102.

126. Bauerlein, *Negrophobia,* 194–99; Dittmer, *Black Georgia,* 128; Godshalk, *Veiled Visions,* 102–3.

127. These rumors were not unfounded. Prior to the riot, mortician David T. Howard received a shipment of guns from Chicago delivered in a casket. Lugenia Burns Hope also recalled shipments of guns arriving in the city in coffins. Dittmer, *Black Georgia,* 126; Rouse, *Lugenia Burns Hope,* 43.

128. Baker, *Following the Color Line,* 13.

129. Godshalk, *Veiled Visions,* 100–104.

130. Baker, *Following the Color Line,* 13; Dittmer, *Black Georgia,* 129; Godshalk, *Veiled Visions,* 100–104.

131. Du Bois, *Autobiography,* 286.

132. Dittmer, *Black Georgia,* 127–28.

133. Ovington, *Walls Came Tumbling Down,* 65.

134. Rouse, *Lugenia Burns Hope,* 44.

135. Baker, *Following the Color Line,* 20–22.

136. Rouse, *Lugenia Burns Hope,* 43.

137. Baker, *Following the Color Line,* 16–19. These sentiments were echoed publicly by Dr. William F. Penn at the first meeting of the biracial Atlanta Civic League, founded after the riot: "What shall we do? We have been disarmed; how shall we protect our lives and property? If living a sober, industrious upright life, accumulating property and educating his children as best he knows how, is not the standard by which a coloured man live and be protected in the South, what is to become of him? If the kind of life I have lived isn't the kind you want, shall I leave and go North?" Quoted in Baker, *Following the Color Line,* 19–20.

138. Baker, *Following the Color Line,* 17.

139. Godshalk, *Veiled Visions,* 101–2, 135. When the violence began, most black people who fought back did so in self-defense. However, by the second day, some began to organize retaliatory action as well. See Dittmer, *Black Georgia,* 126–27.

140. Gaines, *Uplifting the Race,* 64; Godshalk, *Veiled Visions,* 106.

141. Ovington, *Walls Came Tumbling Down*, 65.

142. Baker, *Following the Color Line*, 18.

143. Godshalk, *Veiled Visions*, 153–57.

144. Williamson, *Rage for Order*, 149.

145. Baker, *Following the Color Line*, 15, 18.

146. Godshalk, *Veiled Visions*, 153–57.

147. Baker, *Following the Color Line*, 19.

148. Godshalk, *Veiled Visions*, 135–62.

149. Quoted in Dorsey, *To Build Our Lives Together*, 163.

150. *Atlanta Constitution*, 30 November 1906, 1–2.

151. Baker, *Following the Color Line*, 17.

152. Godshalk, *Veiled Visions*, 155; Dorsey, *To Build Our Lives Together*, 165.

153. *Atlanta Independent*, 29 September 1906, 1, 8. The *Atlanta Independent* mistakenly ascribes this speech to "Garland S. Penn." Baker, in *Following the Color Line* (19–20), correctly identifies the speaker as Penn the physician. The journalist Irving Garland Penn fled the city shortly after the assault on Brownsville and would not return until late November. See Harrison and Harrison, *Life and Times of Irving Garland Penn*, 181–82.

154. *Atlanta Independent*, 29 September 1906, 1, 8.

155. Godshalk, *Veiled Visions*, 136.

156. *Washington Post*, 24 September 1906, 1.

157. Ibid. (emphasis added).

158. *Voice of the Negro* (January 1905), 695–96.

159. Barber would later change this estimate to two, which matches the estimate made by Ray Stannard Baker.

160. Reprinted in *Voice* (November 1906), 470. In November 1906, following its move to Chicago, Barber changed the name of his paper from to the *Voice of the Negro* to simply the *Voice*.

161. Godshalk, *Veiled Visions*, 118; *Atlanta Constitution*, 29 September 1906, 6.

162. *Atlanta Constitution*, 25 September 1906, 3; and 28 September 1906, 7. This part of Barber's charges were so uncontroversial that one section in Ray Stannard Baker's 1908 exposé was titled "How the Newspapers Fomented the Riot." Baker, *Following the Color Line*, 9.

163. Quotation from *Voice* (November 1906), 470.

164. Godshalk, *Veiled Visions*, 118. Though white elites like James W. English may have heroically confronted the mob on the night the riot broke out, he was not averse to threatening black men with violence. The only difference between the two situations was that he could not control the violence of the mob, whereas this violence he could.

165. *Voice* (October 1906), 391–92.

166. *Voice* (November 1906), 473–79.

167. Ibid., 475.

168. According to muckraker Ray Stannard Baker, there were fifteen accusations of rape leveled in the six months preceding the riot. Three of these were the respon-

sibility of white men. Of the twelve assaults allegedly committed by black men, "two were cases of rape, . . . three were aggravated attempts at rape, three may have been attempts, three were pure cases of fright on the part of the white woman, and in one the white woman, first asserting that a Negro had assaulted her, finally confessed attempted suicide." Without dismissing the real terror these women must have felt, it is clear that there was no "epidemic" of black men raping white women in the months preceding the riot. See Baker, *Following the Color Line*, 5.

169. *Voice* (November 1906), 473.

170. Ibid., 479. Godshalk's analysis shows that of the forty white men arrested during the riot, only two possessed criminal records. The arrests targeted the mob's most aggressive leaders, a group including a doctor, a dentist, a carpenter, a butcher, a college student, a clerk, "a nattily dressed white man," a wealthy Mississippian, a railway machinist, a cement worker, and an employee of the Georgia Railway and Electric Company. If these arrests are representative of the mob as a whole, the white rioters ran the gamut of class identities available in early twentieth-century Atlanta. See Godshalk, *Veiled Visions*, 98.

171. Baker, *Following the Color Line*, 15.

172. *Voice* (November 1906), 473–79.

173. That this was the single most damning accusation is further buttressed by the fact this is the only concrete detail mentioned in a letter describing Barber's exile written to the *Philadelphia Tribune* nearly three decades later. With no mention of the riot at all, the writer described how "some years ago, I paid a year's subscription to a magazine called 'The Voice of the Negro.' I received three copies . . . before . . . the plant was ransacked and burned to the ground. The editor was J. Max Barber. And he was told to leave town . . . because a release appeared in a New York paper setting forth the facts in some atrocious crime that had been committed and charged to a Negro but had . . . been committed by a white man who had blackened his face." *Philadelphia Tribune*, 21 September 1933, 4.

174. Feimster, *Southern Horrors*, 103.

175. *Atlanta Independent*, 20 October 1906, 4.

176. *Atlanta Independent*, 13 October 1906, 4.

177. *Atlanta Independent*, 29 September 1906, 4. Booker T. Washington made a similar point in an essay tellingly titled "The Golden Rule in Atlanta," *Outlook* 84, no. 16 (15 September 1906): 913–16.

178. Harlan, *Booker T. Washington: The Wizard of Tuskegee*, 105; Bauerlein, *Negrophobia*, 254–55.

179. *Atlanta Constitution*, 3 November 1906, 6.

180. Harlan, *Booker T. Washington: The Wizard of Tuskegee*, 303.

181. Ibid., 304.

182. Ibid., 104–6.

183. Barber also led campaigns to desegregate military mess halls, lobbied the Pennsylvania state legislature for civil rights legislation, and eventually returned to the press with a weekly column in Robert L. Vann's *Pittsburgh Courier*. In 1932, he became one of the earliest black leaders to support Franklin Delano Roosevelt and

became for a time a power within the local Democratic Party. This stands in contrast to Louis Harlan's history of Barber's fate after crossing Booker T. Washington, who claimed that Barber had been "driven completely out of work for his race." On Barber's post-Atlanta career, see the *Philadelphia Tribune*, 12 June 1915, 1; 30 December 1916, 4; 6 October 1932, 14; and 3 May 1934, 1. See also *Pittsburgh Courier*, 12 December 1932, A1; 8 October 1932, 3; 12 November 1932, 1; 10 December 1932, A3; and 21 July 1934, 2.

On the attempts of Washington to silence Barber, see Harlan, "Booker T. Washington and the Voice of the Negro"; Dittmer, *Black Georgia*, 165–66; and Bullock, "Profile of a Periodical."

184. Harlan, *Booker T. Washington: The Wizard of Tuskegee*, 105.

185. *Voice* (November 1906), 483, 486–87.

186. Barber also found an important ally in T. Thomas Fortune, the editor of the *New York Age*. As the *Voice* was beginning to fail, Fortune, who had recently broken with Booker T. Washington, tapped his personal savings to sustain the magazine in its final months. See Harlan, *Booker T. Washington: The Wizard of Tuskegee*, 105, 320–21.

187. *Voice of the Negro* (April 1906), 243.

188. *Voice of the Negro* (September 1906), 669–70. The inconsistency in the page numbers between the September and October issues can be attributed to the chaos of uprooting the magazine to Chicago. October's pagination begins at 390.

189. See, for example, Lewis, *W. E. B. Du Bois: Biography of a Race*, 337, 341–42; Dittmer, *Black Georgia*, 172; Harlan, *Booker T. Washington: The Wizard of Tuskegee*, 320–21. Quotation from Lewis, *W. E. B. Du Bois: Biography of a Race*, 341–42.

190. Capeci and Knight "Reckoning with Violence," 727–66.

191. Capeci and Knight, "W. E. B. Du Bois's Southern Front," 492.

3. "Respectable Militants"

1. Capeci and Knight, "W. E. B. Du Bois's Southern Front," 503–4.

2. Ibid., 500; *Atlanta Independent*, 7 December 1907, 1, 4; 28 December 1907, 1; and 11 January 1908, 8.

3. Capeci and Knight, "W. E. B. Du Bois's Southern Front," 497.

4. *Atlanta Independent*, 30 March 1907, 4; 6 April 1907, 4; and 12 April 1907, 4. On black Republicans in the South under Taft, see Sherman, *Republican Party and Black America*, 83–112.

5. Perman, *Struggle for Mastery*, 298.

6. Stephen Hahn makes a similar observation about how disfranchisement impacted the gender of black politics. I extend this interpretation, arguing that as black women stepped forward, they shifted the terms of solidarity in ways that redefined the black political agenda in Atlanta. See Hahn, *Nation Under Our Feet*, 463. See also Higginbotham, *Righteous Discontent;* Jones, *All Bound Up Together;* and Gilmore, *Gender and Jim Crow*, 147–76.

7. *Georgia Equal Rights Convention*, 16.

8. "Let Us Be Practical," *Atlanta Independent*, 22 September 1906, 4.

9. Lasch-Quinn, *Black Neighbors,* 120.

10. Ibid., 113.

11. Ibid., 122.

12. Rouse, *Lugenia Burns Hope,* 16–17, 24–30.

13. Lasch-Quinn, *Black Neighbors,* 13–14.

14. *Crisis* 1, no. 3 (January 1911): 22–23.

15. Lasch-Quinn, *Black Neighbors,* 27.

16. This becomes especially important as black men in Atlanta mobilized to defend their "manhood rights," using the image of the endangered black woman. This also had the effect of driving black women from the public sphere. To counter this, middle-class black reformers relied on another narrative of black working-class female endangerment to sustain their claims to public life. Brown, "Negotiating and Transforming the Public Sphere," 50.

17. *Social and Physical Condition of Negroes in Cities,* 3–4.

18. "Experiences of the Race Problem by a Southern White Woman," *Independent* 64, no. 2885 (March 17, 1904), 593.

19. *Social and Physical Conditions of Negroes in Cities,* 32–33.

20. Nannie Helen Burroughs, "Not Color But Character," *Voice of the Negro* (July 1904), 278.

21. Feimster, *Southern Horrors,* 117; Burroughs, "Not Color But Character," 279.

22. Burroughs, "Not Color But Character," 279.

23. Selena Sloan Butler, "Need of Day Nurseries," in *Social and Physical Conditions of Negroes in Cities,* 63. On fears of black retrogression, see Williamson, *Crucible of Race,* 115–20.

24. Butler, "Need of Day Nurseries," 63–64.

25. Reed, *W. E. B. Du Bois,* 119–20.

26. Adella Hunt Logan, "Prenatal and Hereditary Influences," in *Social and Physical Conditions of Negroes in Cities,* 37–38.

27. On Laney, see Dittmer, *Black Georgia,* 149–51; and Griggs, "Notes."

28. Lucy C. Laney, "Address Before the Women's Meeting," in *Social and Physical Conditions of Negroes in Cities,* 55–56.

29. Logan, "Prenatal and Hereditary Influences," 40.

30. "Resolutions Adopted by the Conference," in *Social and Physical Conditions of Negroes in Cities,* 32–33.

31. Lugenia Burns Hope supervised the dormitories at Atlanta Baptist. Lucy Laney was the head of Haines Normal and Industrial School. Adrienne Herndon, the wife of Alonzo Herndon, the wealthiest black man in the city, worked as an instructor at Atlanta University. By 1910, three out of four of Atlanta's largely female teaching force were middle-class black women who graduated from one of the city's four black colleges. Jones, *Labor of Love, Labor of Sorrow,* 142–46; Gordon, *Pitied, But Not Entitled,* 136; Dorsey, *To Build Our Lives Together,* 90; Rouse, *Lugenia Burns Hope,* 47.

32. Critics of kindergartens charged that they undermined the institution of motherhood by enabling working women to put their young children in the care of strangers. However, the experience of the women who established Gate City in bal-

ancing motherhood with their political commitments helped them find commonalities with the working-class mothers they sought to uplift. Gordon, "Black and White Visions of Welfare," 584–85. On the history of day care, see Rose, *Mother's Job*.

33. *Atlanta University Publications No. 14: Efforts for Social Betterment among Negro Americans* (Atlanta: Atlanta University Press, 1909), 48.

34. *Atlanta University Publications No. 10: A Select Bibliography of the Negro American* (Atlanta: Atlanta University Press, 1905), 7; Salem, *To Better Our World*, 81.

35. Salem, *To Better Our World*, 79.

36. *Efforts for Social Betterment among Negro Americans*, 119, 127.

37. "The Gate City Free Kindergarten," 1917, 2, Neighborhood Union Collection, Box 12, Folder 2, Robert W. Woodruff Library, Atlanta University Center.

38. "The Story of the Gate City Free Kindergarten Association," [1925], 2, Neighborhood Union Collection, Box 12, Folder 25, Robert W. Woodruff Library, Atlanta University Center; *Efforts for Social Betterment among Negro Americans*, 126.

39. *Efforts for Social Betterment among Negro Americans*, 31.

40. Shivery, "History of Organized Social Work," 9; Henderson, "Heman E. Perry."

41. Shivery, "History of Organized Social Work," 6–7; Rouse, *Lugenia Burns Hope*, 29; Neverdon-Morton, *Afro-American Women of the South*, 142–43; Dittmer, *Black Georgia*, 45–49.

42. Dorsey, *To Build Our Lives Together*, 90.

43. Shivery, "History of Organized Social Work," 8–9; Hunter, *To 'Joy My Freedom*, 142–43.

44. Shivery, "History of Organized Social Work," 11; *Efforts for Social Betterment among Negro Americans*, 126. This is how most black women, denied public monies, typically funded their reform work. See Gordon, *Pitied, But Not Entitled*, 114–15.

45. See *Atlanta University Publications No. 11: The Health and Physique of the American Negro* (1906), 109; *No. 12: Economic Co-operation among Negro Americans* (1907), 181; *No. 13: The Negro American Family* (1908), 6; *No. 14: Efforts for Social Betterment Among Negro Americans* (1909), 4; *No. 15: The College-bred Negro American* (1910), 4; *No. 16: The Common School and the Negro American* (1911), 4; *No. 17: The Negro American Artisan* (1912), 4; *No. 18: Morals and Manners among Negro Americans* (1914), 4; *No. 19: Economic Co-operation among the Negroes of Georgia* (1917), 4; and *No. 20: Select Discussions of Race Problems* (1916), 4.

46. Shivery, "History of Organized Social Work," 6.

47. Godshalk, *Veiled Visions*, 237.

48. *Georgia Equal Rights Convention*, 10.

49. "Story of the Gate City Free Kindergarten Association," 2.

50. *Neighborhood Union*, pamphlet, n.d., Neighborhood Union Collection, Box 2, Folder 1, Robert W. Woodruff Library, Atlanta University Center.

51. See also Hickey, *Hope and Danger*, 101; Godshalk, *Veiled Visions*, 230–31; Rouse, *Lugenia Burns Hope*, 65–66; Shivery, "History of Organized Social Work," 43; and *Neighborhood Union*, draft pamphlet, 1911 or 1912, Neighborhood Union Collection, Box 2, Folder 11, Robert W. Woodruff Library, Atlanta University Center.

52. "The Neighborhood Union's Aim Granted by The Laws Of Georgia Under

The Charter Of The State Of Georgia," 30 January 1911, Neighborhood Union Collection, Box 2, Folder 3, Robert W. Woodruff Library, Atlanta University Center.

53. Rouse, *Lugenia Burns Hope*, 68–72.

54. Dorsey, *To Build Our Lives Together*, 110.

55. Minnie Wright Price, "Friendly Visiting," in *Social and Physical Conditions of Negroes in Cities*, 58–59.

56. Gilmore, *Gender and Jim Crow*, 147–224.

57. Scott, "Most Invisible of All," 16–17.

58. Taken individually, the work of isolated black women's clubs is no more than charity, but taken in their entirety (which is how many of these women understood their efforts), it more closely resembles the construction of a black welfare state within a state that excluded or marginalized them. Gordon, "Black and White Visions of Welfare"; Salem, *To Better Our World*, 65–100; Muncy, *Creating a Female Dominion*.

Gerda Lerner commented that "in the 1890s, the long tradition of women's organized effort in support of some local charitable or educational institution was transformed into something new and different by the emergence of multi-purpose women's clubs, embracing a broad range of activities and interests. The immediate stimulus of their formation was political: the defense of the race against lynchings" (Lerner, "Early Community Work," 160). What transforms the Neighborhood Union in Atlanta was the additional imperative to address the exclusion of black people from the fruits of urban development.

59. Lewis, *W. E. B. Du Bois: The Fight for Equality*, 304–5, 383–84.

60. *Hull House Maps and Papers* (New York: Thomas Y. Crowell, 1895); Sklar, *Florence Kelley*, 277–79; Knight, *Citizen*, 326.

61. Shivery and Smythe, "Neighborhood Union," 150; Shivery, "History of Organized Social Work," 43.

62. Shivery, "History of Organized Social Work," 47–48.

63. Bayor, *Race and the Shaping of Twentieth Century Atlanta*, 7.

64. Jones, *Labor of Love, Labor of Sorrow*, 84–85.

65. Rouse, *Lugenia Burns Hope*, 67–68.

66. Shivery, "History of Organized Social Work," 47.

67. Rouse, *Lugenia Burns Hope*, 68.

68. Godshalk, *Veiled Visions*, 235.

69. Bayor, *Race and the Shaping of Twentieth Century Atlanta*, 7; Godshalk, *Veiled Visions*, 234.

70. Quoted in Godshalk, *Veiled Visions*, 235.

71. Hunter, *To 'Joy My Freedom*, 62–63, 70–72, 131–32.

72. Freeman, "On the Origins of Social Movements"; Hunter, *To 'Joy My Freedom*, 141–42.

73. Shivery, "History of Organized Social Work," 49; Hunter, *To 'Joy My Freedom*, 104.

74. Shivery, "History of Organized Social Work," 43–45; Lasch-Quinn, *Black Neighbors*, 124.

75. Shivery, "History of Organized Social Work," 45. On TB and black Atlanta, see Hunter, *To 'Joy My Freedom*, 187–218.

76. Shivery and Smythe, "Neighborhood Union," 151–53.

77. Shivery, "History of Organized Social Work," 138, 161, 191–93.

78. Shivery and Smythe, "Neighborhood Union," 150; Shivery, "History of Organized Social Work," 44.

79. Shivery, "History of Organized Social Work," 44.

80. Ibid., 79. On the crime wave, see *Atlanta Constitution*, 12 July 1911, 1, and 14 July 1911, 8.

81. Shivery, "History of Organized Social Work," 142.

82. Salem, *To Better Our World*, 97–100.

83. Neverdon-Morton, *Afro-American Women of the South*, 146–47; Salem, *To Better Our World*, 99.

84. Neverdon-Morton, *Afro-American Women of the South*, 148–52.

85. Godshalk, *Veiled Visions*, 77–78, 159, 210–12.

86. Salem, *To Better Our World*, 190; Dorsey, *To Build Our Lives Together*, 77–80.

87. Lasch-Quinn, *Black Neighbors*, 122; Rouse, *Lugenia Burns Hope*, 28–31.

88. Lasch-Quinn, *Black Neighbors*, 116–17; Davis, *Spearheads for Reform*.

89. Jane Addams, *Twenty Years at Hull House* (New York: Macmillan, 1981), 91.

90. A 1910 fund-raising letter issued by the Gate City Kindergarten Association solicited funds in order save black children "from growing up in ignorance and vice" and "from becoming a burden upon the State in after years." The *Atlanta Independent* also described the Gate City Kindergarten Association in much the same terms, emphasizing "the little ones" who needed to be rescued from neglect rather than the conditions under which mothers had to raise their children. Ben Davis assured his readers that the women in charge of Gate City would make no money off the kindergarten and that it represented "charity on the part of the ladies." See Mrs. Ida E. Wynn and Mrs. J. W. E. Bowen to Rev. E. T. Ware, 22 December 1910, E. T. Ware Papers, Box 33, Folder 7, Robert W. Woodruff Library, Atlanta University Center; and *Atlanta Independent*, 19 August 1905, 4.

91. *Atlanta Constitution*, 16 February 1911, 14; "Neighborhood Union's Aim Granted by The Laws Of Georgia."

92. *Transactions of the National Council of Women of the United States, Assembled in Washington DC, February 22-25, 1891* (Philadelphia: J. B. Lippincott, 1891), 27–31.

93. Shivery, "History of Organized Social Work," 46–47, 56.

94. Hunter, *To 'Joy My Freedom*, 141–42; Godshalk, *Veiled Visions*, 236.

95. Shivery, "History of Organized Social Work," 57.

96. Ibid., 80.

97. Untitled notebook pages, 1920, Neighborhood Union Collection, Box 1, Folder 18, Robert W. Woodruff Library, Atlanta University Center.

98. Rouse, *Lugenia Burns Hope*, 70.

99. Shivery, "History of Organized Social Work," 79.

100. Rouse, *Lugenia Burns Hope*, 70.

101. Shivery, "History of Organized Social Work," 80.

102. See Bayor, *Race and the Shaping of Twentieth Century Atlanta*, 7; Dorsey, *To Build Our Lives Together*, 147–48; Lichtenstein, *Twice the Work of Free Labor*, 168–71.

103. Salem, *To Better Our World*, 112.

104. Dorsey, *To Build Our Lives Together*, 163–64.

105. Hunter, *To 'Joy My Freedom*, 121–24.

106. Godshalk, *Veiled Visions*, 239; Rouse, *Lugenia Burns Hope*, 70; Hunter, *To 'Joy My Freedom*, 177–78.

107. Dorsey, *To Build Our Lives Together*, 70–74.

108. Shivery, "History of Organized Social Work," 55. Although Georgia had passed prohibition in 1908, Atlantans were still able to buy, sell, and consume low-alcohol beer. What made saloons sites of illegal activity was that they often sold moonshine under the table. See Kuhn, *Living Atlanta*, 172–73.

109. Kuhn, *Living Atlanta*, 117–18.

110. Godshalk, *Veiled Visions*, 242.

111. John Watson, the husband of one of the Union's leaders, spoke of a "Neighborhood Union game" in which Union organizers explicitly played on white fears of black criminality "to enlist law enforcement officials in its moral policing campaigns." Ibid., 238–39.

112. Shivery, "History of Organized Social Work," 70. This certainly allowed Atlanta to avoid the expense of providing for its black citizens; nevertheless, the city still expressed its confidence in the Union to police and reform the behavior of the black working class.

113. Hickey, *Hope and Danger*, 99.

114. Such a collective understanding of citizenship is not new. During Reconstruction, African Americans decided how to vote collectively and even went to the polls collectively. This understanding of politics created a public space in which black women enjoyed political standing. By the end of the century, after the most active black leaders were silenced or absorbed into the patronage networks of the GOP, this space vanished. Hahn, *Nation Under Our Feet*, especially 175–76, 224–29; Brown, "Negotiating and Transforming the Public Sphere."

115. Shivery, "History of Organized Social Work," 57, 60.

116. White, *Too Heavy a Load*, 26–40.

117. Untitled notebook pages, 1920, Neighborhood Union Collection, Box 1, Folder 18, Robert W. Woodruff Library, Atlanta University Center.

118. Ibid.

119. Kevin Gaines identifies a "historical tension between two general connotations of uplift. On the one hand, a broader vision of uplift signifying collective social aspiration had been a legacy of the emancipation era. On the other hand, black elites made uplift the basis for a racialized elite identity claiming Negro improvement through class stratification as race progress." While the Union manifested these deeply conservative tendencies, the Union's solution lay as much in uplifting the race as building a society in which race uplift was possible. Gaines, *Uplifting the Race*, xv.

120. Dorsey, *To Build Our Lives Together*, 83–85; Bayor, *Race and the Shaping of Twentieth Century Atlanta*, 7.

121. Bayor, *Race and the Shaping of Twentieth Century Atlanta*, 11; Dorsey, *To Build Our Lives Together*, 91–92.

122. *Common School and the Negro American*, 7–8, 58.

123. In 1894, the average salary for white teachers was $553. The average for black teachers was $369. Neverdon-Morton, *Afro-American Women of the South*, 80; Dorsey, *To Build Our Lives Together*, 94.

124. *Common School and the Negro American*, 63.

125. Bayor, *Race and the Shaping of Twentieth Century Atlanta*, 10–11.

126. Dorsey, *To Build Our Lives Together*, 93; Bayor, *Race and the Shaping of Twentieth Century Atlanta*, 198.

127. Bayor, *Race and the Shaping of Twentieth Century Atlanta*, 198.

128. Dorsey, *To Build Our Lives Together*, 95; Bayor, *Race and the Shaping of Twentieth Century Atlanta*, 203; Dittmer, *Black Georgia*, 147.

129. *Common School and the Negro American*, 63; Garrett, *Atlanta and Environs*, 560; Bayor, *Race and the Shaping of Twentieth Century Atlanta*, 203.

130. Dorsey, *To Build Our Lives Together*, 88.

131. *College Bred Negro*, 14–15.

132. *Economic Cooperation among Negro Americans*, 86–87.

133. Lerner, "Early Community Work," 163–64.

134. Shivery, "History of Organized Social Work," 92.

135. Dittmer, *Black Georgia*, 146–47.

136. Shivery, "History of Organized Social Work," 97–98.

137. In 1907, the state education budget for Georgia was a little over $3 million. If allocated strictly on the basis of race, the 46.7 percent of Georgians who were African American would have received $1.4 million in school funds. However, they only received $500,000—despite the $650,000 African Americans contributed to the school fund that year. Black taxpayers in Georgia paid $150,000 annually to subsidize a public school system from which their children were excluded. See Coon, *Public Taxation and Negro Schools*.

138. Dittmer, *Black Georgia*, 147.

139. Shivery, "History of Organized Social Work," 98–100.

140. *Atlanta Constitution*, 8 September 1913, 4.

141. *Atlanta Constitution*, 7 October 1913, 4.

142. *Atlanta Constitution*, 14 October 1913, 4.

143. *Atlanta Constitution*, 24 October 1913, 1, 3.

144. *Atlanta Constitution*, 7 October 1913, 4.

145. *Atlanta Constitution*, 14 October 1913, 4–5; 17 October 1913, 14; 14 October 1913, 5; and 22 October 1913, 11.

146. Cooper, *Official History*, 453.

147. *Atlanta Constitution*, 24 October 1913, 1, 3.

148. *Atlanta Constitution*, 27 November 1913, 1, 13; *Atlanta Constitution*, 24 October 1913, 1, 3; Shivery, "History of Organized Social Work," 103.

149. Shivery, "History of Organized Social Work," 104–5 (emphasis added).

150. Ibid., 104.

151. *Atlanta Constitution,* 5 December 1913, 9.

152. Toppin, "Walter White," 9; *Atlanta Constitution,* 6 December 1913, 5; Bayor, *Race and the Shaping of Twentieth Century Atlanta,* 201.

153. Shivery, "History of Organized Social Work," 92, 100.

4. "Close Ranks"

1. *Atlanta Independent,* 3 February 1917, 4; *Crisis* 13, no. 6 (April 1917): 285. The thirteen black grammar schools were Bailor Street, Storrs, Carrie Steele, Pittsburg, Dimmock, Houston, Wesley Avenue, Roach, Summer Hill, Mitchell Street, Gray Street, South Atlanta, and Yonge Street. Englehardt, *Survey of the Public School System,* 1:243.

2. *Atlanta Constitution,* 7 September 1917, 6.

3. *Atlanta Constitution,* 29 July 1917, C2.

4. Englehardt and Evenden, *Survey of the Public School System,* 2:72–92.

5. *Atlanta Independent,* 3 February 1917, 4.

6. *Atlanta Independent,* 20 January 1906, 4.

7. *Atlanta Independent,* 3 February 1917, 4.

8. *Crisis* 16, no. 3 (July 1918): 111.

9. Lewis, *W. E. B. Du Bois: Biography of a Race,* 555–58; Rudwick, "Accommodationist in Wartime"; Williams, *Torchbearers of Democracy,* 75–77.

10. Quoted in Grant, *Negro with a Hat,* 97.

11. Quoted in Williams, *Torchbearers of Democracy,* 3.

12. Salem, *To Better Our World,* 199.

13. Quoted in Williams, *Torchbearers of Democracy,* 84.

14. Brundage, *Lynching in the New South,* 228; Kennedy, *Over Here,* 283; Williams, *Torchbearers of Democracy,* 225.

15. Tuttle, *Race Riot,* 13–14.

16. Williams, *Torchbearers of Democracy,* 232.

17. *New York Age,* 7 June 1919, 4.

18. Williams, *Torchbearers of Democracy,* 248–57.

19. *Chicago Defender,* 2 August 1919.

20. Ortiz, *Emancipation Betrayed,* 178.

21. White, *Man Called White,* 30–32.

22. Janken, *White,* 1–28.

23. Walter White to Roy Nash, 16 December 1916; and Application for Charter, 31 January 1917, both in NAACP Papers, Atlanta Branch Files, Series I, Group G, Box 43.

24. Toppin, "Walter White," 8.

25. Walter White to James Weldon Johnson, 22 February 1917, NAACP Papers—Microfilm Edition, Part 12, Series A, Reel 9, frames 588–89.

26. Lewis, *W. E. B. Du Bois: Biography of a Race,* 340–34, 423–24. Davis's opposition to the young organization must have also been tempered by James Weldon Johnson, the NAACP's new field secretary. Davis and others suspicious of the Democratic leanings of the NAACP's national leadership were likely reassured by the presence of

such a prominent Republican on the association's staff. *Atlanta Independent,* 3 February 1917, 4.

27. Walter White to Roy Nash, 3 February 1917, NAACP Papers, Atlanta Branch Files, Series I, Group G, Box 43.

28. White, *Man Called White,* 28–38.

29. Godshalk, *Veiled Visions,* 234.

30. The absence of women from the Atlanta branch was also notable to James Weldon Johnson, who repeatedly encouraged White to incorporate the city's leading black women as charter members. See Janken, *White,* 23–24.

31. Toppin, "Walter White," 8; White to Johnson, 22 February 1917.

32. *Atlanta Independent,* 24 February 1917, 1.

33. Ibid.

34. Walter White to Royal Nash, 5 March 1917, NAACP Papers—Microfilm Edition, Part 12, Series A, Reel 9, frames 661–63.

35. *College Bred Negro,* 14–15.

36. White to Nash, 5 March 1917.

37. White to Johnson, 22 February 1917.

38. *Atlanta Constitution,* 28 September 1917, 8; Toppin, "Walter White," 14.

39. White to Johnson, 22 February 1917.

40. *Atlanta Constitution,* 24 October 1913, 1, 3.

41. *Atlanta Independent,* 24 February 1917, 4.

42. Key's motives for blocking the proposed cuts to the black seventh grade were not entirely altruistic. Despite disfranchisement, several hundred African Americans remained on the voting rolls in the city of Atlanta. Running in a tight four-way race for mayor, Key may have been angling for the votes that he thought the NAACP could deliver. White to Nash, 5 March 1917; Toppin, "Walter White," 15; *Atlanta Constitution,* 9 June 1918, A1.

43. *Savannah Tribune,* 10 March 1917, 4.

44. Walter White to James Weldon Johnson, 3 March 1917, NAACP Papers—Microfilm Edition, Part 12, Series A, Reel 9, frame 633.

45. *Atlanta Independent,* 24 March 1917, 8.

46. Toppin, "Walter White," 11.

47. Walter White to Royal Nash, 19 March 1917, NAACP Papers—Microfilm Edition, Part 12, Series A, Reel 9, frames 630–31.

48. Appeal signed "Atlanta Branch of the National Association for the Advancement of Colored People," 1917, NAACP Papers—Microfilm Edition, Part 12, Series A, Reel 9, frames 665–66.

49. *Atlanta Constitution,* 20 August 1917, 5.

50. *Atlanta Constitution,* 8 September 1917, 6.

51. *Atlanta Constitution,* 11 September 1917, 1, 4; 12 September 1917, 8; 14 September 1917, 5; and 15 September 1917, 5.

52. *Atlanta Constitution,* 18 September 1918, 1.

53. *Atlanta Constitution,* 21 September 1918, 6.

54. *Atlanta Constitution,* 18 September 1917, 6.

55. Walter White to James Weldon Johnson, 27 September 1917, NAACP Papers—Microfilm Edition, Part 12, Series A, Reel 9, frames 667–68.

56. *Atlanta Constitution*, 15 September 1917, 5; White to Johnson, 27 September 1917.

57. White, *Man Called White*, 32.

58. White to Johnson, 27 September 1917.

59. *Atlanta Independent*, 25 August 1917, 4.

60. *Atlanta Constitution*, 18 September 1917, 6; *Atlanta Independent*, 25 August 1917, 4.

61. *Atlanta Independent*, 29 September 1917, 4.

62. Ibid.

63. *Atlanta Independent*, 29 September 1906, 4.

64. *Atlanta Independent*, 29 September 1917, 4.

65. *Atlanta Constitution*, 28 September 1917, 8.

66. Ibid.

67. Toppin, "Walter White," 14; *Atlanta Constitution*, 28 September 1917, 8.

68. *Atlanta Constitution*, 24 January 1918, 8; and 14 June 1918, 1, 13, 16.

69. *Atlanta Independent*, 6 October 1917, 1.

70. *Atlanta Independent*, 10 November 1917, 4.

71. *Atlanta Constitution*, 28 September 1917, 8.

72. Walter White to James Weldon Johnson, 1 October 1917, NAACP Papers—Microfilm Edition, Part 12, Series A, Reel 9, frames 648–50.

73. James Weldon Johnson to Harry Pace, 10 December 1917; Harry Pace to James Weldon Johnson, 12 December 1917; Harry Pace to James Weldon Johnson, 4 January 1918, all in NAACP Papers—Microfilm Edition, Part 12, Series A, Reel 9, frames 655–56, 670.

74. James Weldon Johnson to Harry Pace, 18 January 1918, NAACP Papers—Microfilm Edition, Part 12, Series A, Reel 9, frame 671.

75. *Atlanta Independent*, 20 October 1917, 7.

76. White to Johnson, 1 October 1917. Walter White wrote James Weldon Johnson in October that he considered Davis to be one of the "strongest and most consistent workers in forwarding the work of the Atlanta branch."

77. Walter White to James Weldon Johnson, 5 December 1917, NAACP Papers—Microfilm Edition, Part 12, Series A, Reel 9, frames 659–60.

78. Harry Pace to James Weldon Johnson, 15 July 1918, NAACP Papers—Microfilm Edition, Part 12, Series A, Reel 9, frames 698–99.

79. Walter White to James Weldon Johnson, 5 December 1917, NAACP Papers—Microfilm Edition, Part 12, Series A, Reel 9, frames 659–60.

80. Ibid.

81. Janken, *White*, 27–28.

82. Kuhn, *Living Atlanta*, 20, 26.

83. Pomerantz, *Where Peachtree Meets Sweet Auburn*, 84–85; Kuhn, *Living Atlanta*, 26.

84. *Atlanta Constitution*, 25 May 1917, 13.

85. *Atlanta Independent,* 26 May 1917, 8; and 2 June 1917, 4.

86. Kuhn, *Living Atlanta,* 27.

87. Keegan, *First World War.*

88. *Atlanta Journal,* 2 April 1917, 1.

89. *Atlanta Journal,* 5 June 1917, 1, 3; and 6 June 1917, 1; *Atlanta Constitution,* 6 June 1917, 1–2.

90. *Atlanta Constitution,* 6 June 1917, 1–2.

91. *Atlanta Journal,* 5 June 1917, 1, 3, 6. Despite its praise, the *Journal* claimed that two-thirds of the black registrants had shown up on the first day of registration only to file exemptions to the draft.

92. *Atlanta Constitution,* 5 October 1917, 7.

93. *Crisis* 16, no. 3 (July 1918): 111; Lewis, *W. E. B. Du Bois: Biography of a Race,* 552–60.

94. *Atlanta Constitution,* 2 April 1917, 2. For the full text of Roosevelt's speech in which he declared that "there is no room in this country for hyphenated Americans," see *New York Times,* 13 October 1915, 1, 5.

95. *Atlanta Constitution,* 6 April 1917, 6.

96. *Atlanta Constitution,* 2 April 1917, 2.

97. *Atlanta Independent,* 14 April 1917, 1.

98. *Atlanta Independent,* 7 April 1917, 3; *Atlanta Constitution,* 11 April 1917, 4.

99. *Atlanta Constitution,* 7 April 1917, 11; 13 April 1917, 3; and 21 April 1917, 11.

100. *Atlanta Independent,* 7 April 1917, 5; *Atlanta Constitution,* 8 April 1917, 10.

101. *Atlanta Independent,* 5 May 1917, 3; Walter White to Royal Nash, 9 May 1917, NAACP Papers—Microfilm Edition, Part 12, Series A, Reel 9, frames 644–45.

102. *Atlanta Independent,* 12 May 1917, 1.

103. According to the *Constitution,* "there were no fewer than 5000 negroes" present for the dedication of the Colored Building at the Expo. For "Negro Day" at the Expo, the *Constitution* predicted that no fewer than 30,000 African Americans would be in attendance. See *Atlanta Constitution,* 26 December 1895, 5; and 22 October 1895, 4. Twelve thousand attended the 1902 Negro Young People's Christian Congress. See *Atlanta Constitution,* 11 August 1902, 5.

104. *Atlanta Independent,* 19 May 1917, 1; *Atlanta Independent,* 24 March 1917, 8.

105. White, *Man Called White,* 36.

106. *Atlanta Constitution,* 13 April 1918, 4; 18 April 1918, 1; and 19 April 1918, 1, 8.

107. On concerns over black disloyalty during World War I, see Kornweibel, *Seeing Red,* 1–18.

108. *New York Age,* 29 March 1917, 4.

109. See *Atlanta Constitution,* 5 April 1917, 3; 6 April 1917, 5; 8 April 1917, 3; and 18 May 1917, 9.

110. *Atlanta Journal,* 6 April 1917, 12.

111. *Atlanta Constitution,* 5 April 1917, 3.

112. *Atlanta Constitution,* 10 April 1917, 1.

113. *Atlanta Constitution,* 15 April 1917, A5.

114. Raymond F. Crist, ed., *Student's Textbook: A Standard Course of Instruction*

for Use in the Public Schools of the United States for the Preparation of the Candidate for the Responsibilities of Citizenship (Washington, D.C.: Government Printing Office, 1918), 100–102.

115. Jordan, *Black Newspapers*, 61.

116. *Atlanta Independent*, 31 March 1917, 4.

117. *Atlanta Independent*, 24 March 1917, 4.

118. Though Ben Davis's "train of grievances" may have been notable for its length, these sentiments were by no means unique. Similar assertions of qualified black loyalty can also be found in the *Crisis* 14, no. 1 (June 1917): 8. See also the *Baltimore Afro-American, Savannah Tribune, Cleveland Gazette,* and *New York Age.* See Jordan, *Black Newspapers,* 70–71, 92, 118.

119. *Atlanta Independent*, 7 April 1917, 4.

120. *Atlanta Independent*, 7 July 1917, 1. See also *Atlanta Independent*, 20 October 1917, 4; 23 March 1918, 4; and 30 March 1918, 4.

121. *New York Age*, 3 November 1917, 12.

122. Capozzola, *Uncle Sam Wants You*, 14.

123. *Atlanta Independent*, 31 March 1917, 4.

124. Scott, *Official History*, 32–33.

125. Jordan, *Black Newspapers*, 40–41.

126. *Chicago Defender*, 12 February 1916, 8.

127. Jordan, *Black Newspapers*, 42.

128. *Atlanta Journal*, 8 October 1915, 10.

129. *Savannah Tribune*, 16 October 1915, 4.

130. *Atlanta Constitution*, 2 April 1917, 10.

131. *Crisis* 13, no. 2 (December 1916): 89. Many of these migrants were doubtless passing through Atlanta on their way north.

132. Chambers, *To Raise an Army*, 347, n.82.

133. Walter White, notes, n.d., NAACP Papers, Series I, Group C, Box 417.

134. Walter White, "Work or Fight 1917/1918" research notes, NAACP Papers, Series I, Group C, Box 417.

135. Chambers, *To Raise an Army*, 226; Williams, *Torchbearers of Democracy,* 55.

136. *Crisis* 15, no. 4 (February 1918): 192.

137. Shenk, *Work or Fight*, 27.

138. Dittmer, *Black Georgia*, 197–98; Shenk, *Work or Fight*, 27–29.

139. "Results of Observations in Alabama and Part of Georgia," n.d., NAACP Papers, Series I, Group C, Box 417.

140. Shenk, *Work or Fight*, 11–47.

141. Walter White, "Work or Fight 1917/1918" research notes; *Atlanta Constitution,* 14 June 1918, 1; and 20 July 1918, 7.

142. *Atlanta Constitution*, 16 July 1918, 6; and 3 September 1918, 6.

143. *New York Age*, 28 September 1918, 4.

144. *Atlanta Constitution*, 25 August 1918, A6; Shenk, *Work or Fight*, 41–42; Capozzola, *Uncle Sam Wants You*, 36.

145. *Atlanta Constitution*, 9 May 1918, 2; 13 July 1918, 12; and 20 July 1918, 7.

146. Dittmer, *Black Georgia,* 198.

147. Walter White, "Work or Fight in the South," *New Republic* 18 (March 1, 1919). Typescript copy in NAACP Papers, Series I, Group C, Box 417.

148. Chambers, *To Raise an Army,* 347, n.82; Shenk, *Work or Fight,* 45; Hunter, *To 'Joy My Freedom,* 52–53.

149. Dittmer, *Black Georgia,* 191; Hunter, *To 'Joy My Freedom,* 227.

150. "Report of Conditions Found in Investigation of 'Work or Fight' Laws in Southern States—Georgia," n.d., NAACP Papers, Series I, Group C, Box 417.

151. Hunter, *To 'Joy My Freedom,* 242.

152. *Atlanta Constitution,* 8 September 1918, C10. See also *Atlanta Constitution,* 23 January 1919, 10; 13 February 1919, 2; and 11 July 1919, 11.

153. "Report of Conditions Found in Investigation of 'Work or Fight' Laws."

154. *Atlanta Constitution,* 3 August 1918, 5.

155. Shenk, *Work or Fight,* 42.

156. James Jordan to the NAACP, 14 August 1918; Walter White to A. D. Williams, 21 August 1918; Walter White to James Jordan, 21 August 1918; Walter White to F. R. Belcher, 22 August 1918; W. H. Harris to Walter White, 23 October 1918; Walter White to G. H. Hutto, 17 October 1918, all in NAACP Papers, Series I, Group C, Box 417.

157. Walter F. White to John R. Shillady, 26 October 1918, NAACP Papers, Series I, Group C, Box 417.

158. White, "Work or Fight in the South."

159. Walter F. White to John R. Shillady, 14 November 1918, NAACP Papers, Series I, Group C, Box 417.

160. "Report of Conditions Found in Investigation of 'Work or Fight' Laws."

161. G. R. Hutto to Walter F. White, 21 October 1918, NAACP Papers, Series I, Group C, Box 417; "The 'Work or Fight' Edict," *Crisis* 18, no. 2 (June 1919): 97; White, "Work or Fight in the South."

162. Hunter, *To 'Joy My Freedom,* 229–30.

163. White to Shillady, 26 October 1918.

164. "Report of Branches—Atlanta, GA, A. D. Williams," 28 June 1919, NAACP Papers, Series I, Group B, Box 2; Hunter, *To 'Joy My Freedom,* 230; Dittmer, *Black Georgia,* 199.

165. "Report of Conditions Found in Investigation of 'Work or Fight' Laws."

166. *Atlanta Constitution,* 3 August 1918, 5; *Atlanta Independent,* 31 August 1918, 4; James Jordan to the NAACP, 14 August 1918, NAACP Papers, Series I, Group C, Box 417; "The Negro in Labor and Industry," Remarks by Rev. P. J. Bryant, 24 June 1919, NAACP Papers, Series I, Group B, Box 2; White, "Work or Fight in the South."

167. *Atlanta Constitution,* 10 September 1918, 1; 2 October 1918, 9; 29 October 1918, 7; and 5 November 1918, 6.

168. *Atlanta Constitution,* 9 November 1918, 5.

169. "Negro in Labor and Industry"; Dittmer, *Black Georgia,* 198.

170. *Atlanta Independent,* 24 February 1917, 1.

171. "Negro in Labor and Industry."

172. Capozzola, *Uncle Sam Wants You,* 33.

173. Edgar H. Webster, *Chums and Brothers* (Boston: Gorham Press, 1920), 148, 152; Williams, *Torchbearers of Democracy,* 50. Williams erroneously attributes this quote to Edgar Webster, the principal of Atlanta University's Normal Department. However, it comes from a letter sent to him, included in Webster's autobiography.

174. Williams, *Torchbearers of Democracy,* 50.

175. Lentz-Smith, *Freedom Struggles,* 81; Williams, *Torchbearers of Democracy,* 69. On black men in labor battalions, see Lentz-Smith, *Freedom Struggles,* 109–29.

176. Williams, *Torchbearers of Democracy,* 70.

177. Gatewood, *Black Americans and the White Man's Burden,* 93–95. During World War I, the Eighth Illinois was folded into the 370th Infantry. See Williams, *Torchbearers of Democracy,* 71.

178. Gatewood, *Black Americans and the White Man's Burden,* 118–28; Williams, *Torchbearers of Democracy,* 70.

179. Williams, *Torchbearers of Democracy,* 70–71.

180. Franklin, "Birth of a Nation"; Williamson, *Rage for Order,* 98–115, 244–45.

181. Goodson, *Highbrows, Hillbillies, & Hellfire,* 102–6.

182. Holmes, *White Chief,* 326–27.

183. *Crisis* 18, no. 1 (May 1919): 16–17.

184. Barbeau and Henri, *Unknown Soldiers,* 38–39; *Crisis* 18, no. 1 (May 1919): 19.

185. *Atlanta Independent,* 24 March 1917, 4.

186. *Savannah Tribune,* 10 March 1917, 4.

187. Scott, *Official History,* 9.

188. *Crisis* 14, no. 2 (June 1917): 59, 61.

189. *Baltimore Afro-American,* 17 March 1917, 4.

190. *Atlanta Constitution,* 6 April 1917, 6.

191. *Atlanta Independent,* 7 April 1917, 1.

192. *Atlanta Constitution,* 7 April 1917, 9.

193. Higginbotham, *Righteous Discontent,* 225.

194. Capozzola, *Uncle Sam Wants You,* 132.

195. Rouse, *Lugenia Burns Hope,* 93–96; Barbeau and Henri, *Unknown Soldiers,* 41–42; Williams, *Torchbearers of Democracy,* 102.

196. Williams, *Torchbearers of Democracy,* 103.

197. Shivery, "History of Organized Social Work," 142–62.

198. Ibid., 149–51.

199. Dykeman and Stokely, *Seeds of Southern Change,* 50–51.

200. Quoted in Williams, *Torchbearers of Democracy,* 225–26.

201. Myrdal, *American Dilemma,* 2:567.

202. Ibid. See also Rudwick, *Race Riot at East St. Louis;* and Tuttle, *Race Riot.*

203. Dittmer, *Black Georgia,* 204–5.

204. Brundage, *Lynching in the New South,* 227–28.

205. *Crisis* 17, no. 2 (December 1918): 63.

206. Williams, *Torchbearers of Democracy,* 230.

207. Ibid., 239.

208. Ibid., 233.

209. Dittmer, *Black Georgia*, 204–5.

210. Williams, *Torchbearers of Democracy*, 237.

211. Shivery, "History of Organized Social Work," 163–64.

212. *Washington Bee*, 18 January 1919, 1, 4.

213. *Georgia Equal Rights Convention*, 12.

214. *Washington Bee*, 18 January 1919, 1, 4.

215. *New York Age*, 7 June 1919, 4.

5. "A Satisfied Part of Our Composite Citizenship"

1. Newman, "Atlanta Public School Teachers' Association," 44.

2. On the 1915 bond issue, see the *Atlanta Constitution*, 16 May 1915, 2; 21 May 1915, 1; 23 July 1915, 1; 1 August 1915, 1; 28 August 1915, 9; 3 September 1915, 6; 8 September 1915, 6; and 23 September 1915, 8. Louie Shivery suggests that black voters defeated the 1915 bond issue. However, there is nothing in the *Atlanta Independent,* the white press, or the NAACP papers to suggest that this was the case. See Shivery, "History of Organized Social Work," 106.

3. Georgia State Constitution of 1877, Section VII, Paragraph I.

4. *Atlanta Constitution*, 15 March 1918, 8. In 1915, the city attorney attempted to circumvent these rules, but was stymied by the state supreme court. See *Atlanta Constitution,* 11 June 1915, 2; 23 September 1915, 8; and 19 November 1916, D12.

5. *Atlanta Constitution*, 11 June 1915, 2; and 2 January 1918, 4. See also *Atlanta Constitution* 14 March 1918, 11; and 4 July 1918, 6.

6. White, *Man Called White*, 33.

7. *Atlanta Constitution*, 21 April 1917, 1. See also *Atlanta Constitution*, 23 April 1917, 5; 1 May 1917, 1; 8 May 1917, 4; 9 May 1917, 8; 15 May 1917, 1; 27 May 1917, C6; 31 May 1917, 16; 1 June 1917, 16; and 12 June 1917, 6.

8. *Atlanta Constitution*, 23 April 1917, 5.

9. *Atlanta Constitution*, 1 June 1917, 16; and 12 June 1917, 6.

10. *Atlanta Constitution*, 15 May 1917, 1.

11. *Atlanta Constitution*, 21 December 1917, 1; and 20 January 1918, 5.

12. *Atlanta Constitution*, 21 December 1917, 1; 20 January 1918, 1; and 31 January 1918, 4; *Atlanta Independent*, 23 February 1918, 4.

13. Philippians 4:7 (King James Version): "And the peace of God, which surpasses all comprehension, will guard your hearts and your minds in Christ Jesus."

14. *Atlanta Independent*, 23 February 1918, 4.

15. *Atlanta Constitution*, 9 October 1917, 1–2; 11 October 1917, 3; 13 October 1917, 1; and 15 February 1918, 1.

16. *Atlanta Constitution*, 19 February 1918, 1; and 11 July 1918, 1, 5. These four bonds were for the modernization of the city waterworks, the modernization of the fire department, a fireproof building to house the cyclorama, and an electric generating plant for the city crematorium.

17. *Atlanta Constitution,* 27 October 1917, 6; 30 October 1917, 8; and 8 January 1918, 1–2.

18. *Atlanta Constitution,* 3 January 1918, 6; and 16 February 1918, 6.

19. *Atlanta Constitution,* 9 March 1918, 1; 14 March 1918, 1; 19 March 1918, 1, 9; 6 April 1918, 2; and 7 May 1918, 1, 6.

20. Turner-Jones, "Political Analysis of Black Educational History," 153; *Atlanta Journal,* 7 April 1918, 3.

21. *Atlanta Constitution,* 16 June 1918, 1, 5; 6 July 1918, 5; 7 July 1918, 6; 8 July 1918, 1; and 9 July 1918, 1, 4.

22. *Atlanta Constitution,* 26 June 1918, 4; and 27 June 1918, 9.

23. *Atlanta Constitution,* 28 June 1918, 5.

24. *Atlanta Constitution,* 30 June 1918, A15; 3 July 1918, 1; and 4 July 1918, 1.

25. *Atlanta Constitution,* 4 July 1918, 1; and 7 July 1918, 6.

26. *Atlanta Constitution,* 4 July 1918, 6; and 9 July 1918, 1.

27. *Atlanta Journal,* 5 July 1918, 1.

28. Ibid. See also *Atlanta Journal,* 9 July 1918, 1.

29. *Atlanta Journal,* 9 July 1918, page number unknown; 10 July 1918, 1; and 10 July 1918, 4.

30. *Atlanta Journal,* 10 July 1918, 1.

31. Toppin, "Walter White," 15–16.

32. *Atlanta Journal,* 7 July 1918, 1; 9 July 1918, 1; *Atlanta Constitution,* 10 July 1918, 1–2; and 11 July 1918, 1, 5.

33. *Atlanta Constitution,* 11 July 1918, 1, 5. Total black registration is given in *Atlanta Constitution,* 8 July 1918, 1.

34. *Atlanta Journal,* 7 July 1918, 1; *Atlanta Constitution,* 8 July 1918, 1.

35. *Atlanta Journal,* 7 July 1918, page number unknown.

36. *Atlanta Constitution,* 8 July 1918, 1.

37. *Atlanta Constitution,* 11 July 1918, 1, 5; and 8 July 1918, 1.

38. *Atlanta Journal,* 4 July 1918, page number unknown; 7 July 1918, 1; and 11 July 1918, 1, 8; *Atlanta Constitution,* 4 July 1918, 1; 11 July 1918, 1, 5; 12 July 1918, 1–2; and 12 July 1918, 1–2.

39. *Atlanta Constitution,* 12 July 1918, 1–2.

40. Turner-Jones, "Political Analysis of Black Educational History," 154.

41. James Weldon Johnson to Harry Pace, 29 June 1918, NAACP Papers—Microfilm Edition, Part 12, Series A, Reel 9, frame 694.

42. *Atlanta Journal,* 7 July 1918, 1; and 9 July 1918, page number unknown; *Atlanta Constitution,* 8 July 1918, 1. For the denominational identification of Revs. Carter and Bryant, see *Atlanta Constitution,* 3 March 1913, 3.

43. *Atlanta Journal,* 11 July 1918, 1, 8.

44. Walter White to John Shillady, 9 July 1918, NAACP Papers—Microfilm Edition, Part 12, Series A, Reel 9, frames 695–96.

45. Ibid.

46. Circular letter authored by Harry Pace, 7 July 1918, NAACP Papers—Microfilm Edition, Part 12, Series A, Reel 9, frame 700.

47. Ibid.

48. Harry Pace to James Weldon Johnson, 12 July 1918, NAACP Papers—Microfilm Edition, Part 12, Series A, Reel 9, frames 698–99.

49. Circular letter authored by Harry Pace, 7 July 1918.

50. Walter White to John Shillady, 11 July 1918, NAACP Papers—Microfilm Edition, Part 12, Series A, Reel 9, frame 697.

51. Pace to Johnson, 12 July 1918.

52. Branch, *Parting the Waters,* 30–38. Rev. A. D. Williams was also Rev. Martin Luther King Jr.'s maternal grandfather.

53. "Report of Branches."

54. For a list of the major Baptist churches in Atlanta in 1919, see *Atlanta Constitution,* 15 March 1919, 10.

55. Pace to Johnson, 12 July 1918.

56. L. C. Crogman to John Shillady, 4 December 1918, NAACP Papers—Microfilm Edition, Part 12, Series A, Reel 9, frame 719. See also *Atlanta Constitution,* 3 September 1911, C7; and 12 June 1918, 9. The addition of Mrs. Bryant to the leadership of the branch was especially significant, since her husband had earlier opposed the NAACP's strategy of opposing all municipal bonds.

57. *Atlanta Constitution,* 18 April 1912, 10; 21 June 1914, A7; 29 September 1915, 12; and 19 November 1919, 3.

58. Rev. Williams's absence is commented upon in satirical cartoons in the *Atlanta Independent,* 3 May 1919, 1; 24 May 1919, 1; and 31 May 1919, 2. See also Mary White Ovington to Rev. A. D. Williams, 2 June 1919, NAACP Papers—Microfilm Edition, Part 12, Series A, Reel 9, frames 772–73.

59. On Truman K. Gibson, see *Atlanta Constitution,* 6 February 1912, 1; 8 February 1912, 13; and 8 April 1916, 12. See also Gibson's obituary in the *New York Times,* 2 January 2006, page number unknown.

60. Truman K. Gibson to James W. Johnson, 7 March 1919, NAACP Papers, Series I, Group G, Box 43.

61. Pace to Johnson, 12 July 1918; Circular letter authored by Harry Pace, 7 July 1918.

62. O. A. Toomer to John Shillady, 17 September 1918, NAACP Papers—Microfilm Edition, Part 12, Series A, Reel 9, frame 715.

63. Truman K. Gibson to James Weldon Johnson, 7 March 1919, NAACP Papers, Series I, Group G, Box 43; *Atlanta Constitution,* 19 December 1918, 12; *Crisis* 18, no. 2 (June 1919): 90–91.

64. *Atlanta Constitution,* 8 August 1918, 8.

65. *Atlanta Constitution,* 7 January 1919, 1, 7.

66. *Atlanta Independent,* 15 February 1919, 1; *Crisis,* 18, no. 2 (June 1919): 90–91.

67. Toppin, "Walter White," 15.

68. Williams, *Torchbearers of Democracy,* 60.

69. White, *Man Called White,* 33.

70. Freeman, "On the Origins of Social Movements."

71. Godshalk, *Veiled Visions,* 234.

72. Shivery, "History of Organized Social Work," 166.

73. Lerner, "Early Community Work of Black Club Women," 166.

74. Shivery, "History of Organized Social Work," 48.

75. White, *Man Called White*, 33.

76. Ibid.

77. Gibson to Johnson, 7 March 1919; *Atlanta Georgian*, 27 February 1919, NAACP Papers, Series I, Group G, Box 43.

78. *Atlanta Independent*, 9 March 1918, 4.

79. *Atlanta Independent*, 18 January 1919, 4.

80. *Atlanta Independent*, 15 February 1919, 1.

81. *Atlanta Independent*, 18 January 1919, 4.

82. *Atlanta Independent*, 15 February 1919, 1.

83. *Atlanta Independent*, 9 March 1918, 4.

84. *Atlanta Independent*, 18 January 1919, 4; and 9 March 1918, 4.

85. *Atlanta Independent*, 22 February 1919, 4. Candler was the founder of the Coca Cola Company and mayor from 1906 to 1919. Inman, one of Atlanta's wealthiest men, made his fortune in real estate, railroads, and cotton.

86. *Atlanta Independent*, 22 March 1919, 4–5.

87. *Atlanta Independent*, 18 January 1919, 4.

88. Since the poll tax was part of residential property taxes, anyone who paid the full tax on his home also wound up paying his poll tax. This, of course, undermined the efficacy of the poll tax as a disfranchising mechanism, and it is possible that Atlanta's repeated budget shortfalls prompted its inclusion into city property taxes. Pomerantz, *Where Peachtree Meets Sweet Auburn*, 148.

89. White, *Man Called White*, 33.

90. Gibson to Johnson, 7 March 1919.

91. *Atlanta Independent*, 8 February 1919, 2; *Atlanta Constitution*, 16 January 1919, 7.

92. *Atlanta Independent*, 15 February 1919, 1.

93. *Atlanta Independent*, 1 February 1919, 4.

94. *Atlanta Independent*, 15 February 1919, 1.

95. *Atlanta Constitution*, 23 January 1919, 1, 9.

96. *Atlanta Constitution*, 24 January 1919, 1–2; and 23 January 1919, 1, 9; *Atlanta Journal*, 24 January 1919, 11.

97. *Atlanta Constitution*, 26 January 1919, 1, 5; *Atlanta Journal*, 10 January 1919, 10.

98. Newman, "History of the Atlanta Public School Teachers' Association," 54. The APSTA represented 750 white teachers.

99. *Atlanta Constitution*, 24 January 1919, 1–2.

100. *Atlanta Constitution*, 27 January 1919, 1; *Atlanta Journal*, 19 January 1919, 1, 3.

101. *Atlanta Journal*, 23 January 1919, 1; and 26 January 1919, 1; *Atlanta Constitution*, 28 January 1919, 1, 3.

102. *Atlanta Constitution*, 28 January 1919, 1, 3; and 1 February 1919, 1, 7.

103. *Atlanta Constitution*, 24 January 1919, 1–2; 26 January 1919, 1, 5; 11 February 1919, 5; and 18 February 1919, 1–2; *Atlanta Journal*, 7 July 1918, page number unknown; 27 January 1919, 1, 14; 28 January 1919, 4; and 4 February 1919, 3.

104. *Atlanta Journal*, 2 February 1919, 6.

105. *Atlanta Journal*, 13 February 1919, 3; 17 February 1919, 10; 20 February 1919, 10; 25 February 1919, 10; and 27 February 1919, 1; *Atlanta Constitution*, 9 February 1919, 2; and 23 February 1919, 10.

106. *Atlanta Journal*, 23 February 1919, 7; and 23 February 1919, 1, 12.

107. *Atlanta Journal*, 26 February 1919, 4; 27 February 1919, 1; 2 March 1919, 6; 2 March 1919, 10; and 4 March 1919, 10.

108. *Atlanta Journal*, 19 February 1919, 8; 2 March 1919, 1; and 3 March 1919, 1, 16; *Atlanta Constitution*, 4 March 1919, 1–2.

109. *Atlanta Constitution*, 28 February 1919, 9.

110. *Atlanta Journal*, 4 March 1919, 4.

111. Ibid., 1, 11; *Atlanta Constitution*, 4 March 1919, 1–2.

112. *Atlanta Journal*, 2 March 1919, 1–2.

113. One of the few exceptions was a resolution by the Atlanta School Improvement Committee recommending that any future bond issues passed for the construction of new schools also "make a provision for the education of negro children." However, the committee was unwilling to fight the city on this point. *Atlanta Journal*, 22 January 1919, 1; *Atlanta Constitution*, 28 January 1919, 1, 3.

114. *Atlanta Journal*, 27 February 1919, 7.

115. On Proctor, see Godshalk, *Veiled Visions*, 187–90, 211–12, 220–21, 254–56.

116. *Atlanta Journal*, 2 March 1919, 1–2.

117. *Crisis* 18, no. 2 (June 1919): 90–91.

118. "Address Delivered by Miss Cora Finley," 25 June 1919, NAACP Papers, Annual Conference Files, Series I, Group B, Box 2.

119. T. K. Gibson, "Dear Friend and Fellow-Citizen," 26 February 1919, NAACP Papers, Atlanta Branch Files, Series I, Group G, Box 43.

120. *Crisis* 18, no. 2 (June 1919): 90–91.

121. Walter White's recollection of this fight, written almost three decades later, gets the date wrong. He places it prior to World War I. White, *Man Called White*, 38.

122. The heavy black vote before noon indicates a high degree of organization. These were voters committed enough to turn out to vote without extra prodding. *Atlanta Journal*, 5 March 1919, 1–2; and 6 March 1919, 1.

123. *Atlanta Journal*, 4 March 1919, 1; and 5 March 1919, 1, 3.

124. *Atlanta Constitution*, 6 March 1919, 1.

125. The heaviest opposition to the tax increase had come from the city's two predominantly black wards, where 79 and 65 percent of the voters had rejected it. Since those percentages mirrored almost exactly the black population in these two wards and the tax increase had lost by such a narrow margin, it is safe to conclude that the black vote had defeated the taxes. See Newman, "History of the Atlanta Public School Teachers' Association," 44.

126. *Atlanta Constitution*, 6 March 1919, 1; and 11 March 1919, 1. The vote totals for the bonds were: waterworks: 4,017 for and 1,042 against; crematory: 3,859 for and 1,169 against; fire department: 4,036 for and 1,012 against; cyclorama: 3,898 for and 1,167 against.

127. *Atlanta Constitution,* 11 March 1919, 1; *Atlanta Journal,* 11 March 1919, 1, 3.

128. *Atlanta Journal,* 9 March 1919, 1; *Atlanta Constitution,* 11 March 1919, 1.

129. *Atlanta Journal,* 5 March 1919, 1, 3.

130. *Atlanta Journal,* 6 March 1919, 1; and 7 March 1919, 1; *Atlanta Independent,* 8 March 1919, 1; 15 March 1919, 4; and 29 March 1919, 4.

131. *Atlanta Journal,* 11 March 1919, 1, 3; 18 March 1919, 2; and 21 March 1919, 13.

132. *Atlanta Constitution,* 7 March 1919, 1.

133. Written appeal from the Atlanta Branch of the NAACP to "Dear Friend and Fellow-Citizen," 26 February 1919, NAACP Papers—Microfilm Edition, Part 12, Series A, Reel 9, frame 736.

134. *Atlanta Independent,* 8 March 1919, 1.

135. Ibid., 4.

136. Ibid.

137. *Atlanta Independent,* 5 April 1919, 4.

138. *Atlanta Journal,* 6 April 1919, B1; *Atlanta Constitution,* 7 April 1919, 2; *Crisis* 18, no. 2 (June 1919): 90–91.

139. *Crisis* 18, no. 2 (June 1919): 90–91.

140. White to Johnson, 27 September 1917; *Atlanta Constitution,* 15 September 1917, 5.

141. *Atlanta Constitution,* 9 April 1919, 6.

142. *Atlanta Journal,* 8 April 1919, 6.

143. *Crisis* 18, no. 2 (June 1919): 90–91.

144. Godshalk, *Veiled Visions,* 249.

145. L. C. Crogman to J. R. Shillady, 18 April 1919, NAACP Papers, Series I, Group G, Box 43.

146. *Atlanta Independent,* 22 March 1919, 4.

147. "Report of Branches."

148. Godshalk, *Veiled Visions,* 249–50.

149. Kelley, "We Are Not What We Seem" (quotation on 77–78).

150. *Crisis* 18, no. 2 (June 1919): 90–91.

151. Ibid. (emphasis added).

152. For example, see Fortune, *Black and White,* 127; and *New York Age,* 13 December 1906, 4. For other examples of calls for black political independence, see Logan, *Betrayal of the Negro,* 55–57; and Wynne, "Brownsville," 153–60.

153. *Crisis* 18, no. 2 (June 1919): 90–91.

154. *Atlanta Journal,* 12 March 1919, 2.

155. *Atlanta Journal,* 1 April 1919, 1.

156. *Atlanta Journal,* 28 March 1919, 14; 29 March 1919, 9; 30 March 1919, A5; 31 March 1919, 2; 3 April 1919, 3; 4 April 1919, 11, 26; 7 April 1919, 16; 10 April 1919, 2; 11 April 1919, 4; 17 April, 1919, 13; 18 April 1919, 8; and 19 April 1919, 2.

157. *Atlanta Journal,* 18 April 1919, 12; 19 April 1919, 1; and 20 April 1919, A8.

158. *Atlanta Journal,* 4 April 1919, 16; 13 April 1919, A6; 20 April 1919, A1–2; cartoon on 22 April 1919, 1; and 22 April 1919, 16.

159. *Atlanta Journal,* 20 April 1919, A1–2.

160. *Atlanta Journal*, cartoon on 13 April 1919, B1.

161. *Atlanta Journal*, 11 April 1919, 1; 23 April 1919, 1, 3; *Atlanta Constitution*, 24 April 1919, 1–2; *Atlanta Independent*, 26 April 1919, 4.

162. Bayor, *Race and the Shaping of Twentieth Century Atlanta*, 204; *Atlanta Journal*, 14 April 1919, 2.

163. *Atlanta Journal*, 23 April 1919, 1, 3.

164. *Atlanta Constitution*, 24 April 1919, 1–2; *Atlanta Journal*, 24 April 1919, 1, 11. The vote tallies were: tax increase: 4,184 for and 5,064 against; waterworks: 6,161 for and 2,955 against; crematory: 4,972 for and 4,181 against; cyclorama: 5,716 for and 3,232 against; fire department: 5,854 for and 3,228 against.

165. *Atlanta Constitution*, 6 March 1919, 1.

166. On the number of black voters participating in the election, see Henry Rucker's testimony before the board of education in *Atlanta Constitution*, 20 May 1919, 4. A good portion of the city's conservative white establishment also opposed the referenda as well and mounted an extensive and well-funded campaign against the referenda. The heaviest opposition against the tax rate and the bonds arose from the predominantly black First and Fourth Wards as well as the city's upscale, white Eighth Ward. *Atlanta Constitution*, 24 April 1919, 1–2. See also the fourteen advertisements paid for by the Taxpayers' League and the Georgia Railway & Power Co. in *Atlanta Journal*, 9 April 1919, 2, 10; 17 April 1919, 22; 18 April 1919, 14; 19 April 1919, 2, 8; 20 April 1919, B5–6, D8; 21 April 1919, 2, 11; 22 April 1919, 7, 11; and 23 April 1919, 23.

167. *Atlanta Journal*, 5 May 1919, 6.

168. *Atlanta Journal*, 24 April 1919, 1, 11.

169. *Atlanta Journal*, 7 May 1919, 20; 20 May 1919, 13; and 29 May 1919, 1.

170. *Atlanta Journal*, 5 May 1919, 2.

171. *Atlanta Journal*, 6 May 1919, 4; and 20 May 1919, 2.

172. *Atlanta Journal*, 28 April 1919, 1–2.

173. *Atlanta Journal*, 20 May 1919, 4; *Atlanta Constitution*, 20 May 1919, 4.

174. *Atlanta Journal*, 20 May 1919, 4.

175. *Atlanta Journal*, 13 May 1919, 2; James, "Policies of Organized Labor," 36.

176. Newman, "History of the Atlanta Public School Teachers' Association," 53; *Atlanta Constitution*, 7 October 1919, 1, 11.

177. Newman, "History of the Atlanta Public School Teachers' Association," 55.

178. James, "Policies of Organized Labor," 36.

179. *Atlanta Journal*, 7 March 1919, 3.

180. Quoted in Bayor, *Race and the Shaping of Twentieth Century Atlanta*, 204.

181. Newman, "History of the Atlanta Public School Teachers' Association," 56.

182. *Atlanta Constitution*, 21 January 1920, 6.

183. Newman, "History of the Atlanta Public School Teachers' Association," 57–58.

184. *Atlanta Constitution*, 1 February 1920, 1; and 15 February 1920, A1; Newman, "History of the Atlanta Public School Teachers' Association," 59.

185. Newman, "History of the Atlanta Public School Teachers' Association," 62.

For white rank-and-file dissension, see ibid., 59–61, 65–66; and James, "Policies of Organized Labor," 63–64.

186. Harry H. Pace to A. D. Williams, 25 June 1919; and Harry Pace to Mary White Ovington, 7 November 1919, both in NAACP Papers, Annual Conference Files, Series I, Group B, Box 2.

187. James L. Key to A. D. Williams, 25 June 1919, NAACP Papers, Series I, Group B, Box 2.

188. Atlanta Chamber of Commerce to A. D. Williams, 25 June 1919; and Hugh Dorsey to Moorfield Storey, 25 June 1919, both in NAACP Papers, Annual Conference Files, Series I, Group B, Box 2.

189. Hall, *Revolt against Chivalry*, 62–65.

190. Dykeman and Stokely, *Seeds of Southern Change*, 75.

191. John J. Eagan to James L. Key, 20 October 1919; James L. Key to the Atlanta City Council, 20 October 1919; and James L. Key to John J. Eagan, 25 October 1919, all in NAACP Papers, Annual Conference Files, Series I, Group B, Box 2.

192. Bayor, *Race and the Shaping of Twentieth Century Atlanta*, 148–50; Hickey, *Hope and Danger*, 179–80.

193. James L. Key to John J. Eagan, 25 October 1919, NAACP Papers, Series I, Group B, Box 2; Dykeman and Stokely, *Seeds of Southern Change*, 62–63, 78.

194. Harry Pace to Mary White Ovington, 7 November 1919, NAACP Papers, Annual Conference Files, Series I, Group B, Box 2.

195. *Atlanta Constitution*, 6 January 1920, 9.

196. Shivery, "History of Organized Social Work," 218–19.

197. Mary White Ovington to Harry Pace, 13 December 1919; C. E. Robertson to Mary White Ovington, 15 December 1919; Harry Pace to Mary White Ovington, 20 December 1919; Hugh Dorsey to Mary White Ovington, 20 December 1919, all in NAACP Papers, Annual Conference Files, Series I, Group B, Box 2; Minutes of the Atlanta Conference Committee, 18 March 1920; Press Release, "For New Epoch in Race Relations: Governor of Georgia and Mayor of Atlanta to Address National Association for Advancement of Colored People," 22 March 1920; Program—Atlanta Conference, 26 April 1920, all in NAACP Papers, Annual Conference Files, Series I, Group B, Box 3; Dykeman and Stokely, *Seeds of Southern Change*, 58, 63, 67.

198. *Atlanta Constitution*, 9 January 1920, 1, 6; and 6 February 1921, 1; Newman, "History of the Atlanta Public School Teachers' Association," 63–64.

199. *Atlanta Journal*, 22 May 1919, 7; *Atlanta Constitution*, 23 May 1919, 4; 4 January 1920, A1, 16; 14 January 1920, 1; and 23 February 1920, 2.

200. Newman, "History of the Atlanta Public School Teachers' Association," 63–64.

201. *Atlanta Constitution*, 9 March 1921, 1, 16.

202. Godshalk, *Veiled Visions*, 250.

203. NAACP Press Release, "Negro Vote against Atlanta Bond Issue Wins 5 New Schools Costing $1,200,000," 11 January 1924, NAACP Papers—Microfilm Edition, Part 12, Series A, Reel 9, frame 874.

Epilogue

1. Newman, "History of the Atlanta Public School Teachers' Association," 64; *Atlanta Constitution,* 10 August 1923, 1, 10; 16 September 1923, 1–2; 20 October 1923, 1, 9; and 3 November 1923, 1, 5.

2. Dittmer, *Black Georgia,* 208.

3. *Atlanta Constitution,* 2 September 1923, 6.

4. Kuhn, *Living Atlanta,* 140–141.

5. Walter White to John Hope, 21 January 1924. NAACP Papers, Atlanta Branch Files, Series I, Group G, Box 43; Godshalk, *Veiled Visions,* 253.

6. Godshalk, *Veiled Visions,* 251–53.

7. R. W. Bagnall to A. T. Walden, 3 September 1924, NAACP Papers, Atlanta Branch Files, Series I, Group G, Box 43.

8. Jackson, *Ku Klux Klan,* 31, 37–39.

9. *Atlanta Independent,* 19 April 1919, 4.

10. *Atlanta Independent,* 26 April 1919, 4.

11. Ibid.

12. "Address Delivered by Dr. W. E. B. Du Bois," 25 June 1919, NAACP Papers, Annual Conference Files, Series I, Group B, Box 2.

13. *Atlanta Constitution,* 10 November 1899, 7.

14. Goings, *NAACP Comes of Age,* 24.

15. Ferguson, *Black Politics,* 138–41, 152–60.

16. Brown-Nagin, *Courage to Dissent,* 45–46.

17. Ibid., 53–56.

18. *Atlanta Independent,* 26 April 1919, 4.

19. Quoted in Singh, *Black Is a Country,* 123.

20. *Crisis* 18, no. 2 (June 1919): 90–91.

Bibliography

Allen, Ernest, Jr. "Du Boisian Double Consciousness: The Unsustainable Argument." *Massachusetts Review* 43 (Summer 2002): 217–53.

Anderson, James D. *The Education of Blacks in the South, 1860–1935.* Chapel Hill: University of North Carolina Press, 1988.

Astor, Gerald. *The Right to Fight: A History of African Americans in the Military.* New York: Da Capo Press, 1998.

Ayers, Edward L. *The Promise of the New South: Life after Reconstruction.* New York: Oxford University Press, 1992.

Bacote, Clarence A. "The Negro in Georgia Politics, 1880–1908." Ph.D. diss., University of Chicago, 1955.

———. "Some Aspects of Negro Life in Georgia, 1880–1908." *Journal of Negro History* 43, no. 3 (July 1958): 186–213.

Baker, Ray Stannard. *Following the Color Line: American Negro Citizenship in the Progressive Era.* 1908. Reprint, New York: Harper and Row, 1964.

Baldwin, Davarian. *Chicago's New Negroes: Modernity, the Great Migration and Black Urban Life.* Chapel Hill: University of North Carolina Press, 2007.

Bauerlein, Mark. *Negrophobia: A Race Riot in Atlanta, 1906.* San Francisco: Encounter Books, 2001.

Barbeau, Arthur, and Florette Henri. *The Unknown Soldiers: African-American Troops in World War I.* Philadelphia: Temple University Press, 1974.

Bartley, Numan V. *The Creation of Modern Georgia.* 2nd ed. Athens: University of Georgia Press, 1990.

Bayor, Ronald H. *Race and the Shaping of Twentieth Century Atlanta.* Chapel Hill: University of North Carolina Press, 1996.

Bederman, Gail. *Manliness and Civilization: A Cultural History of Gender and Race, 1880–1917.* Chicago: University of Chicago Press, 1995.

Berg, Manfred. *"The Ticket to Freedom": The NAACP and the Struggle for Black Political Integration.* Gainesville: University Press of Florida, 2005.

Blackmon, Douglas A. *Slavery by Another Name: The Re-Enslavement of Black Americans from the Civil War to World War II.* New York: Anchor Books, 2008.

Branch, Taylor. *Parting The Waters: America in the King Years, 1954–1963.* New York: Simon and Schuster, 1988.

Breen, William J. "Black Women and the Great War: Mobilization and Reform in the South." *Journal of Southern History* 44, no. 3 (August 1978): 421–40.

Brown, Elsa Barkley. "Negotiating and Transforming the Public Sphere: African American Political Life in the Transition from Slavery to Freedom." In *Jumpin' Jim Crow: Southern Politics from Civil War to Civil Rights,* ed. Jane Dailey et al., 28–66. Princeton, N.J.: Princeton University Press, 2000.

Brown, Nikki. *Private Politics and Public Voices: Black Women's Activism from World War I to the New Deal.* Bloomington: Indiana University Press, 2006.

Brown-Nagin, Tomiko. *Courage to Dissent: Atlanta and the Long History of the Civil Rights Movement.* New York: Oxford University Press, 2012.

Brundage, W. Fitzhugh. *Lynching in the New South: Georgia and Virginia.* Urbana: University of Illinois Press, 1993.

Bullock, Penelope L. "Profile of a Periodical: 'The Voice of the Negro.'" *Atlanta Historical Bulletin* 21, no. 1 (Spring 1977): 95–114.

Capeci, Dominic J., Jr., and Jack C. Knight. "Reckoning with Violence: W. E. B. Du Bois and the 1906 Atlanta Race Riot." *Journal of Southern History* 62, no. 4 (November 1996): 727–66.

———. "W. E. B. Du Bois's Southern Front: Georgia 'Race Men' and the Niagara Movement, 1905–1907." *Georgia Historical Quarterly* 83, no. 3 (Fall 1999): 479–507.

Capozzola, Christopher. *Uncle Sam Wants You: World War I and the Making of the Modern American Citizen.* New York: Oxford University Press, 2008.

Cecelski, David S. *Along Freedom Road: Hyde County, North Carolina, and the Fate of Black Schools in the South.* Chapel Hill: University of North Carolina Press, 1994.

Chambers, John Whiteclay. *To Raise an Army: The Draft Comes to Modern America.* New York: Free Press, 1987.

Coon, Charles L. *Public Taxation and Negro Schools: A Paper read before the Twelfth Annual Conference for Education in the South.* Cheyney, Pa.: Committee of Twelve for the Advancement of the Interests of the Negro Race, 1909.

Cooper, Anna Julia. *A Voice from the South by a Black Woman of the South.* Xenia, Ohio: Aldine Printing House, 1892.

Cooper, Walter G. *Official History of Fulton County.* Atlanta: Walter W. Brown, 1934.

Crowe, Charles. "Racial Violence and Social Reform: Origins of the Atlanta Riot of 1906." *Journal of Negro History* 53, no. 3 (July 1968): 234–56.

———. "Tom Watson, Populists and Blacks Reconsidered." *Journal of Negro History* 55, no. 2 (April 1970): 99–116.

Curtin, Mary Ellen. *Black Prisoners and Their World: Alabama, 1895–1900.* Charlottesville: University of Virginia Press, 2000.

Davis, Allen. *Spearheads for Reform.* New York: Oxford University Press, 1967.

Davis, Benjamin J., Jr. *Communist Councilman from Harlem: Autobiographical Notes Written in a Federal Penitentiary.* New York: International, 1969.

Dittmer, John. *Black Georgia in the Progressive Era, 1900–1920.* Urbana: University of Illinois Press, 1977.

Donaldson, Bobby J. "New Negroes in a New South: Race, Power, and Ideology in Georgia, 1890–1925." Ph.D. diss., Emory University, 2002.

Dorsey, Allison. *To Build Our Lives Together: Community Formation in Black Atlanta, 1875–1906.* Athens: University of Georgia Press, 2004.

Doyle, Don H. *New Cities, New Men, New South: Atlanta, Nashville, Charleston, Mobile, 1860–1910.* Chapel Hill: University of North Carolina Press, 1990.

Du Bois, W. E. B. *The Autobiography of W. E. B. Du Bois: A Soliloquy on Viewing My Life from the Last Decade of Its First Century.* New York: International Publishers, 1968.

———. *The Souls of Black Folk.* 1903. Reprint, Boston: Bedford/St. Martin's Press, 1997.

Dykeman, Wilma, and James Stokely. *Seeds of Southern Change: The Life of Will Alexander.* Chicago: University of Chicago Press, 1962.

Elshtain, Jean Bethke. *Jane Addams and the Dream of American Democracy.* New York: Basic Books, 2002.

Englehardt, E. L. *Report of the Survey of the Public School System of Atlanta, Georgia.* Vol. 1. New York: Institute of Educational Research, Teachers College, Columbia University, 1922.

Englehardt, E. L., and E. S. Evenden. *Report of the Survey of the Public School System of Atlanta, Georgia.* Vol. 2. New York: Institute of Educational Research, Teachers College, Columbia University, 1922.

Feimster, Crystal N. *Southern Horrors: Women and the Politics of Rape and Lynching.* Cambridge, Mass.: Harvard University Press, 2011.

Ferguson, Karen. *Black Politics in New Deal Atlanta.* Chapel Hill: University of North Carolina Press, 2002.

Fortune, Timothy Thomas. *Black and White: Land and Labor and Politics in the South.* New York: Fords, Howard & Hulbert, 1884.

Franklin, John Hope. "*The Birth of a Nation:* Propaganda as History." In *Race and History: Selected Essays, 1938–1988,* 10–23. Baton Rouge: Louisiana State University Press, 1989.

Fredrickson, George M. *The Black Image in the White Mind: The Debate on Afro-American Character and Destiny, 1817–1914.* Hanover, N.H.: Wesleyan University Press, 1971.

Freeman, Jo. "On the Origins of Social Movements." In *Waves of Protest: Social Movements since the Sixties,* ed. Jo Freeman and Victoria Johnson, 7–24. New York: Rowman and Littlefield, 1999.

Frymer, Paul. *Uneasy Alliances: Race and Party Competition in America.* Princeton, N.J.: Princeton University Press, 1999.

Gaines, Kevin K. *Uplifting the Race: Black Leadership, Politics, and Culture in the Twentieth Century.* Chapel Hill: University of North Carolina Press, 1996.

Garrett, Franklin M., and Harold H. Martin. *Atlanta and Environs: A Chronicle of Its People and Events.* Vol. 2. New York: Lewis Historical Publishing, 1954.

Gatewood, Willard B., Jr. *Black Americans and the White Man's Burden, 1898–1903.* Urbana: University of Illinois Press, 1975.

Giddings, Paula J. *Ida: A Sword among Lions.* New York: Amistad, 2008.

Gilmore, Glenda Elizabeth. *Gender and Jim Crow: Women and the Politics of White Supremacy in North Carolina, 1896–1920.* Chapel Hill: University of North Carolina Press, 1996.

Godshalk, David Fort. *Veiled Visions: The 1906 Atlanta Race Riot and the Reshaping of American Race Relations.* Chapel Hill: University of North Carolina Press, 2005.

Goings, Kenneth W. *"The NAACP Comes of Age": The Defeat of Judge John J. Parker.* Bloomington: Indiana University Press, 1990.

Goodson, Steve. *Highbrows, Hillbillies, & Hellfire: Public Entertainment in Atlanta, 1880–1930.* Athens: University of Georgia Press, 2007.

Goodwyn, Lawrence. *The Populist Moment: A Short History of the Agrarian Revolt in America.* New York: Oxford University Press, 1978.

Gordon, Linda. "Black and White Visions of Welfare: Women's Welfare Activism, 1890–1945." *Journal of American History* 78, no. 2 (September 1991): 559–90.

———. *Pitied, But Not Entitled: Single Mothers and the History of Welfare.* Cambridge, Mass.: Harvard University Press, 1994.

Grant, Colin. *Negro with a Hat: The Rise and Fall of Marcus Garvey.* New York: Oxford University Press, 2008.

Grantham, Dewey W., Jr. "Hoke Smith: Progressive Governor of Georgia, 1907–1909." *Journal of Southern History* 15, no. 4 (November 1949): 423–40.

———. *Hoke Smith and the Politics of the New South.* Baton Rouge: Louisiana State University Press, 1958.

Griggs, A. C. "Notes: Lucy Craft Laney." *Journal of Negro History* 19, no. 1 (January 1934): 97–102.

Grossman, James R. *Land of Hope: Chicago, Black Southerners and the Great Migration.* Chicago: University of Chicago Press, 1989.

Guy-Sheftall, Beverly. *Daughters of Sorrow: Attitudes towards Black Women, 1880–1920.* Brooklyn, N.Y.: Carlson, 1990.

Hahn, Stephen. *A Nation Under Our Feet: Black Political Struggles in the Rural South from Slavery to the Great Migration.* Cambridge, Mass.: Harvard University Press, 2003.

Hale, Grace Elizabeth. *Making Whiteness: The Culture of Segregation in the South, 1890–1940.* New York: Pantheon Books, 1998.

Hall, Jacquelyn Dowd. *Revolt Against Chivalry: Jessie Daniel Ames and the Women's Campaign Against Lynching.* New York: Columbia University Press, 1993.

Harlan, Louis R. *Booker T. Washington: The Making of a Black Leader, 1856–1901.* New York: Oxford University Press, 1975.

———. *Booker T. Washington: The Wizard of Tuskegee, 1901–1915.* New York: Oxford University Press, 1983.

———. "Booker T. Washington and the Voice of the Negro, 1904–1907." *Journal of Southern History* 45, no. 1 (February 1979): 45–62.

Harrison, Joanne K., and Grant Harrison. *The Life and Times of Irving Garland Penn.* Philadelphia: Xlibris, 2000.

Henderson, Alexa Benson. "Heman E. Perry and Black Enterprise in Atlanta, 1908–1925." *Business History Review* 61, no. 2 (Summer 1987): 216–42.

Hickey, Georgina. *Hope and Danger in the New South City: Working-Class Women and Urban Development in Atlanta, 1890–1940.* Athens: University of Georgia Press, 2003.

Higginbotham, Evelyn Brooks. *Righteous Discontent: The Women's Movement in the Black Baptist Church, 1880–1920.* Cambridge, Mass.: Harvard University Press, 1993.

Hine, Darlene Clark. "Rape and the Inner Lives of Black Women in the Middle West." *Signs* 14, no. 4 (Summer 1989): 912–20.

Holmes, William F. *The White Chief: James Kimble Vardaman.* Baton Rouge: Louisiana State University Press, 1970.

Horne, Gerald. *Black Liberation/Red Scare: Ben Davis and the Communist Party.* Newark: University of Delaware Press, 1994.

Hunter, Tera. *To 'Joy My Freedom: Southern Black Women's Lives and Labor after the Civil War.* Cambridge, Mass.: Harvard University Press, 1997.

Jackson, Kenneth T. *The Ku Klux Klan in the City, 1915–1930.* Chicago: Ivan R. Dee, 1967.

James, Leonard Hammock. "The Policies of Organized Labor in Relation to Negro Workers in Atlanta, 1869–1937." M.A. thesis, Atlanta University, 1937.

Janken, Kenneth. *White: The Biography of Walter White, Mr. NAACP.* New York: New Press, 2003.

Jones, Jacqueline. *Labor of Love, Labor of Sorrow: Black Women, Work and the Family from Slavery to the Present.* New York: Vintage Books, 1985.

Jones, Martha S. *All Bound Up Together: The Woman Question in African American Public Culture, 1830–1900.* Chapel Hill: University of North Carolina Press, 2007.

Jordan, William G. *Black Newspapers and America's War for Democracy, 1914–1920.* Chapel Hill: University of North Carolina Press, 2001.

Kantrowitz, Stephen. *Ben Tillman and the Reconstruction of White Supremacy.* Chapel Hill: University of North Carolina Press, 2000.

Keegan, John. *The First World War.* New York: Vintage Books, 1998.

Kelley, Blair L. M. *Right to Ride: Streetcar Boycotts and African American Citizenship in the Era of Plessy v. Ferguson.* Chapel Hill: University of North Carolina Press, 2010.

Kelley, Robin D. G. "'We Are Not What We Seem:' Rethinking Black Working-Class Opposition in the Jim Crow South." *Journal of American History* 80, no. 1 (June 1993): 75–112.

Kennedy, David M. *Over Here: The First World War and American Society.* New York: Oxford University Press, 1980.

Kerber, Linda K. *Toward an Intellectual History of Women: Essays by Linda K. Kerber.* Chapel Hill: University of North Carolina Press, 1997.

Knight, Louise W. *Citizen: Jane Addams and the Struggle for Democracy.* Chicago: University of Chicago Press, 2005.

———. *Jane Addams: Spirit in Action.* New York: W. W. Norton, 2010.

Kornweibel, Theodore, Jr. *"Seeing Red": Federal Campaigns against Black Militancy, 1919–1925.* Bloomington: Indiana University Press, 1998.

Kousser, J. Morgan. *The Shaping of Southern Politics: Suffrage Restriction and the Making of the One-Party South, 1880–1910.* New Haven, Conn.: Yale University Press, 1974.

Kuhn, Clifford, et al., eds. *Living Atlanta: An Oral History of the City, 1914–1948.* Athens: University of Georgia Press, 1990.

Lane, Ann J. *The Brownsville Affair: National Crisis and Black Reaction.* Port Washington, N.Y.: Kennikat Press, 1971.

Lasch-Quinn, Elisabeth. *Black Neighbors: Race and the Limits of Reform in the American Settlement House Movement, 1890–1945.* Chapel Hill: University of North Carolina Press, 1993.

Lentz-Smith, Adrienne. *Freedom Struggles: African Americans and World War I.* Cambridge, Mass.: Harvard University Press, 2009.

Lerner, Gerda, "Early Community Work of Black Club Women." *Journal of Negro History* 59, no. 2 (April 1974): 158–67.

Lewinson, Paul. *Race, Class and Party: A History of Negro Suffrage and White Politics in the South.* New York: Grosset and Dunlap, 1965.

Lewis, David Levering. *W. E. B. Du Bois: Biography of a Race, 1868–1919.* New York: Henry Holt, 1993.

———. *W. E. B. Du Bois: The Fight for Equality and the American Century, 1919–1963.* New York: Henry Holt, 2000.

Lichtenstein, Alex. *Twice the Work of Free Labor: The Political Economy of Convict Labor in the New South.* New York: Verso, 1996.

Litwack, Leon. *Trouble in Mind: Black Southerners in the Age of Jim Crow.* New York: Vintage Books, 1998.

Logan, Rayford W. *The Betrayal of the Negro: From Rutherford B. Hayes to Woodrow Wilson.* New York: Collier Books, 1965.

Maclachlan, Gretchen Ehrmann. "Women's Work: Atlanta's Industrialization and Urbanization, 1879–1929." Ph.D. diss., Atlanta University, 1992.

Mancini, Matthew J. *One Dies, Get Another: Convict Leasing in the American South.* Columbia: University of South Carolina Press, 1996.

McCurry, Stephanie. *Masters of Small Worlds: Yeoman Households, Gender Relations, and the Political Culture of the Antebellum South Carolina Low Country.* New York: Oxford University Press, 1995.

McGuire, Danielle. *At the Dark End of the Street: Black Women, Rape, and Resistance— A New History of the Civil Rights Movement from Rosa Parks to the Rise of Black Power.* New York: Vintage Books, 2011.

McMillen, Neil R. *Dark Journey: Black Mississippians in the Age of Jim Crow.* Urbana: University of Illinois Press, 1990.

Meier, August, and Elliott Rudwick. "The Boycott Movement against Jim Crow Streetcars in the South, 1900–1906." *Journal of American History* 55, no. 4 (March 1969): 756–75.

Merritt, Carole. *The Herndons: An Atlanta Family.* Athens: University of Georgia Press, 2002.

Morgan, Francesca. *Women and Patriotism in Jim Crow America.* Chapel Hill: University of North Carolina Press, 2005.

Muncy, Robyn. *Creating a Female Dominion in American Reform, 1890–1935.* New York: Oxford University Press, 1991.

Myrdal, Gunnar. *An American Dilemma: The Negro Problem and Modern Democracy.* Vol. 2. New York: Harper and Row, 1944.

Nalty, Bernard C. *Strength for the Fight: A History of Black Americans in the Military.* New York: Free Press, 1986.

Neverdon-Morton, Cynthia. *Afro-American Women of the South and the Advancement of the Race, 1895–1925.* Knoxville: University of Tennessee Press, 1989.

Newman, Joseph Whitworth. "A History of the Atlanta Public School Teachers' Association, Local 89 of the American Federation of Teachers, 1919–1956." Ph.D. diss., Georgia State University, 1978.

Ortiz, Paul. *Emancipation Betrayed: The Hidden History of Black Organizing and White Violence in Florida from Reconstruction to the Bloody Election of 1920.* Berkeley: University of California Press, 2005.

Ovington, Mary White. *The Walls Came Tumbling Down.* New York: Schocken Books, 1970.

Peiss, Kathy. *Cheap Amusements: Working Women and Leisure in Turn-of-the-Century New York.* Philadelphia: Temple University Press, 1986.

Perman, Michael. *Struggle for Mastery: Disfranchisement in the South, 1888–1908.* Chapel Hill: University of North Carolina Press, 2001.

Pomerantz, Gary M. *Where Peachtree Meets Sweet Auburn: A Saga of Race and Family.* New York: Penguin Books, 1996.

Prather, H. Leon, Sr. "We Have Taken a City: A Centennial Essay." In *Democracy Betrayed: The Wilmington Race Riot of 1898 and Its Legacy,* ed. David S. Cecelski and Timothy B. Tyson, 15–42. Chapel Hill: University of North Carolina Press, 1998.

Rabinowitz, Howard N. *Race, Ethnicity and Urbanization: Selected Essays by Howard N. Rabinowitz.* Columbia: University of Missouri Press, 1994.

———. *Race Relations in the Urban South, 1865–1890.* New York: Oxford University Press, 1978.

Rachleff, Peter. *Black Labor in Richmond, 1865–1890.* Urbana: University of Illinois Press, 1989.

Ransom, Roger L., and Richard Sutch. *One Kind of Freedom: The Economic Consequences of Emancipation.* New York: Cambridge University Press, 1977.

Redkey, Edwin S. *Black Exodus: Black Nationalist and Back-to-Africa Movements, 1890–1910.* New Haven, Conn.: Yale University Press, 1969.

——, ed. *Respect Black: The Writings and Speeches of Henry McNeal Turner.* New York: Arno Press, 1971.

Reed, Adolph L. *W. E. B. Du Bois and American Political Thought: Fabianism and the Color Line.* New York: Oxford University Press, 1997.

Rose, Elizabeth. *A Mother's Job: The History of Day Care, 1890–1960.* New York: Oxford University Press, 1999.

Rosen, Hannah. *Terror in the Heart of Freedom: Citizenship, Sexual Violence and the Meaning of Race in the Postemancipation South.* Chapel Hill: University of North Carolina Press, 2009.

Rotundo, E. Anthony. *American Manhood: Transformations in Masculinity from the Revolution to the Modern Era.* New York: Basic Books, 1993.

Rouse, Jacqueline. "The Legacy of Community Organizing: Lugenia Burns Hope and the Neighborhood Union." *Journal of Negro History* 69, nos. 3/4 (Summer–Autumn 1984): 114–33.

——. *Lugenia Burns Hope: Black Southern Reformer.* Athens: University of Georgia Press, 1989.

Rudwick, Elliott M. "An Accommodationist in Wartime." In *W. E. B. Du Bois: A Profile,* ed. Rayford W. Logan, 158–82. New York: Hill and Wang, 1971.

——. *Race Riot at East St. Louis: July 2, 1917.* New York: Atheneum, 1972.

Ryan, Mary P. "Gender and Public Access: Women's Politics in Nineteenth-Century America." In *Habermas and the Public Sphere,* ed. Craig Calhoun, 259–88. Cambridge, Mass.: MIT Press, 1992.

Salem, Dorothy. *To Better Our World: Black Women in Organized Reform, 1890–1920.* Brooklyn N.Y.: Carlson, 1990.

Sanders, Elizabeth. *Roots of Reform: Farmers, Workers and the American State, 1877–1917.* Chicago: University of Chicago Press, 1999.

Scott, Anne Firor. "Most Invisible of All: Black Women's Voluntary Associations." *Journal of Southern History* 56, no. 1 (February 1990): 3–22.

Scott, Emmett J. *Scott's Official History of the American Negro in the World War.* New York: Underwood & Underwood, 1919.

Shapiro, Karin. *A New South Rebellion: The Battle against Convict Labor in the Tennessee Coalfields, 1871–1896.* Chapel Hill: University of North Carolina Press, 1998.

Shenk, Gerald E. *"Work or Fight!" Race, Gender and the Draft in World War One.* New York: Palgrave MacMillan, 2005.

Sherman, Richard B. *The Republican Party and Black America from McKinley to Hoover, 1896–1933.* Charlottesville: University of Virginia Press, 1973.

Shivery, Louie Delphia Davis. "The History of Organized Social Work among Atlanta Negroes, 1890–1935." M.A. thesis, Atlanta University, 1936.

——, and Hugh H. Smythe. "The Neighborhood Union: A Survey of the Beginnings of Social Welfare Movements among Negroes in Atlanta." *Phylon* 3, no. 2 (2nd Qtr., 1942): 149–62.

Singh, Nikhil Pal. *Black Is a Country: Race and the Unfinished Struggle for Democracy.* Cambridge, Mass.: Harvard University Press, 2004.

Sklar, Kathryn Kish. *Florence Kelley and the Nation's Work: The Rise of Women's Political Culture, 1830–1900.* New Haven, Conn.: Yale University Press, 1995.

Slotkin, Richard. *Lost Battalions: The Great War and the Crisis of American Nationality.* New York: Henry Holt, 2005.

Sullivan, Patricia. *Lift Every Voice: The NAACP and the Making of the Civil Rights Movement.* New York: New Press, 2009.

Summers, Martin. *Manliness and Its Discontents: The Black Middle Class and the Transformation of Masculinity, 1900–1930.* Chapel Hill: University of North Carolina Press, 2003.

Thornbrough, Emma Lou. "The Brownsville Episode and the Negro Vote." *Mississippi Valley Historical Review* 44, no. 3 (December 1957): 469–93.

Toppin, Edgar A. "Walter White and the Atlanta NAACP's Fight for Equal Schools, 1916–1917." *History of Education Quarterly* 7, no. 1 (Spring 1967): 3–21.

Turner-Jones, Marcia Elaine. "A Political Analysis of Black Educational History: Atlanta, 1865–1943." Ph.D. diss., University of Chicago, 1982.

Tuttle, William M., Jr. *Race Riot: Chicago in the Red Summer of 1919.* New York: Atheneum, 1977.

Washington, Booker T. *The Story of My Life and Work: An Autobiography.* Toronto: J. L. Nichols, 1901.

———. *Up From Slavery: An Autobiography.* New York: Carol Publishing Group, 1989.

Weiss, Nancy J. *Farewell to the Party of Lincoln: Black Politics in the Age of FDR.* Princeton, N.J.: Princeton University Press, 1983.

White, Deborah Gray. *Ar'n't I a Woman? Female Slaves in the Plantation South.* New York: W. W. Norton, 1985.

———. *Too Heavy Load: Black Women in Defense of Themselves, 1894–1994.* New York: W. W. Norton, 1999.

White, Shane, and Graham White. *Stylin': African American Expressive Culture from Its Beginnings to the Zoot Suit.* Ithaca, N.Y.: Cornell University Press, 1998.

White, Walter F. *A Man Called White: The Autobiography of Walter White.* New York: Viking Press, 1948.

Williams, Chad L. *Torchbearers of Democracy: African American Soldiers in the World War I Era.* Chapel Hill: University of North Carolina Press, 2010.

Williamson, Joel. *Crucible of Race: Black-White Relations in the American South since Emancipation.* New York: Oxford University Press, 1984.

———. *A Rage for Order: Black-White Relations in the American South since Emancipation.* New York: Oxford University Press, 1986.

Wolcott, Victoria. *Remaking Respectability: African American Women in Interwar Detroit.* Chapel Hill: University of North Carolina Press, 2001.

Woodward, C. Vann. *Origins of the New South, 1877–1913.* Baton Rouge: Louisiana State University Press, 1951.

———. *Tom Watson: Agrarian Rebel.* New York: Oxford University Press, 1963.

Wynne, Lewis N. "Brownsville: The Reaction of the Negro Press." *Phylon (1960–)* 33, no. 2 (2nd Qtr., 1972): 153–60.

Index

Italicized page numbers refer to illustrations.

Adams, Mattie, 86

Addams, Jane, 122; Hull House, 17, 107, 109, 122, 129; on "social control," 110. *See also* Hull House (Chicago)

African Methodist Episcopal (AME) Church, 42, 43, 170, 216

Akins, Coleman, 171–72

Alexander, Will, 191. *See also* Young Men's Christian Association

Allen Temple AME Church, 170

Allen, Peyton A., *155*

American Federation of Labor (AFL), 238

American Federation of Teachers, Local 89, 229–30. *See also* Atlanta Public School Teachers' Association

American Missionary Association, 140

Ansley Park (white neighborhood), 75

Ashley, Claude, 203

Atlanta Anti-Tuberculosis Association, 125, 155, 208

Atlanta Baptist College, 127. *See also* Morehouse College

Atlanta Baptist Ministers' Union, 81, 206. *See also* Williams, Adam Daniel

Atlanta Board of Education, 140, 148, 182, 232, 234; 1913 schools survey, 142, 143–44; bond referendum, July 1918, 207, 214; —, March 1919, 215; —, April 1919, 221, 222, 234; NAACP campaign to abolish double sessions in black schools, 160, 162, 165, 166; NAACP

fight to save seventh grade (1916–17), 155, 157–58, 236; teacher salaries, 207, 214, 228, 230; "Wake Up, Daddy" movement, 197–98. *See also* Guinn, R. J; Wardlaw, J. C.

Atlanta Chamber of Commerce: 1906 Atlanta Race Riot, 91, 92, 98; 1920 NAACP Annual Meeting, 231, 232; bond referendum, July 1918, 200; —, March 1919, 215. *See also* Hopkins, Charles T.

Atlanta City Council, 40, 49, 74, 76, 140, 126; 1913 schools survey, 142, 143–44, 146; bond referendum, July 1917, 198–99, 214; —, March 1919, 214; —, April 1919, 218, 226; —, March 1921, 234; ends double sessions for white students, 162, 198–99; Klan membership in, 236; reluctance to fund public education, 143–44, 148, 198; teacher salaries, 230; "Wake Up, Daddy" movement, 198–99; "work or fight" ordinance, 181. *See also* Orme, A. J.

Atlanta Civic and Political League, 239

Atlanta Civic League, 105, 132; politics of respectability, 92–93, 94, 105, 106; post-riot negotiations, 90, 91–93, 94, 107, 255n137. *See also* Atlanta Race Riot

Atlanta Colored Women's War Council, 190

Atlanta Community Chest, 117

"Atlanta Compromise," 10–11, 29, 57, 62, 90, 135. *See also* Atlanta Cotton States and International Exposition (1895); Washington, Booker T.

Atlanta Constitution, 185; 1906 election, 39; 1913 schools survey, 143, 146; black loyalty in WWI, 171, 188; bond referendum, July 1918, 199; double sessions in white schools, 161, 163; "work or fight" laws, 178, 179. *See also* Howell, Clark

Atlanta Cotton States and International Exposition (1895), 10, 29, 171. *See also* "Atlanta Compromise"

Atlanta Evening News, 84, 94. *See also* Graves, John Temple

Atlanta Federation of Trades, 199, 229, 230

Atlanta Georgian, 61, 224, 253–54n82. *See also* Graves, John Temple

Atlanta Independent, 64; 1906 Atlanta Race Riot, 83, 85; black loyalty in WWI, 172; bond referendum, July 1918, 209–10; Gate City Kindergarten Association, 262n90; NAACP fight to save seventh grade (1916–17), 148. *See also* Davis, Ben, Sr.

Atlanta Journal, 39; 1906 election, 40; bond referendum, July 1918, 199, 201; —, March 1919, 214–15; questions black wartime loyalty, 171; "rape scare," 78; World War I, 168–69, 176. *See also* Gray, James; Smith, Hoke

Atlanta Life Insurance Company, 117, 169. *See also* Herndon, Alonzo

Atlanta Negro Voters League, 240

Atlanta Parent-Teacher Association, 215

Atlanta Public School Teachers' Association (APSTA), 214, 229–30, 275n98

Atlanta public schools: 1913 schools survey, 141–47; access as a civic right, 4, 107–8, 144–46, 149–50; attempted elimination of the seventh grade in black schools, 147–48, 155–57, 236; Bailor Street School, 265n1; Booker T. Washington High School, 2, 6, 12, 22–23, 233, 234–35, 243n8; Carrie Steele School, 265n1; desegregation, 6, 243n9; Dimmock School, 265n1; double sessions in black schools, 141–42, 156–57, 159–65, 198, 229; double sessions in

white schools, 161–62, 165–66, 197–98, 234; elimination of eighth grade in black schools, 144–45; English Avenue School, 161; enrollment, 140, 143, 148, 232; first established, 139–40; funding, 3, 38–39, 42, 143–44, 148, 196, 197, 214, 227–28, 229, 234; funding inequities between black and white schools, 33–34, 45, 47, 140–42, 144, 160, 264n137; Girls' High School, 161; Gray Street School, 265n1; Houston School, 265n1; Mitchell Street School, 265n1; Pittsburg School, 265n1; Roach School, 265n1; "second-taxing," 34, 247n28; South Atlanta School, 265n1; Storrs School, 139–40, 265n1; Summer Hill School, 139–40, 265n1; Tenth Street School, 161; as vehicle for race uplift, 12–13, 33–34; Wesley Avenue School, 265n1; Yonge Street School, 206, 265n1. *See also* Atlanta Public School Teachers Association (APSTA); bond referenda

Atlanta Race Riot (1906), 3, 9–10, 17, 19, 22, 84–93; aftermath, 91; Atlanta Civic League, 90, 91–93, 94, 105, 106, 107, 132, 255n137; Jesse Mar Barber, 91, 93–105; Ben Davis Sr., 81–84, 91, 92–93, 99–101, 102, 103; W. E. B. Du Bois, 78, 90, 105; Lugenia Burns Hope, 90, 255n127; politics of respectability, 62, 78, 87, 90–91, 92, 96, 97, 98; rape scare, 78–82, 84–85; victims, 86–87, 89; Booker T. Washington, 62, 99, 101–2, 105; Walter Francis White, 88, 255n120. *See also* Commission on Interracial Cooperation

Atlanta University, 71, 183, 251n33, 259n31, 271n173; Ben Davis Sr., 64; W. E. B. Du Bois, 27, 43, 90, 122; Gate City Kindergarten Association, 117; John Hope, 17, 45; Neighborhood Union, 125, 127; private school for black students, 141; Walter Francis White, 153, 154. *See also* Atlanta University Conferences

Atlanta University Conferences, 9; black women's sexual purity, 77–78; cross-class solidarity, 120, 130; Gate City Kindergarten Association, 117; welfare of black children, 109, 110–16

Atlanta University Studies. *See* Atlanta University Conferences

Bacon, Edward, 73
Bacon, Susie, 73
Bacote, Clarence, 34
Bainbridge, GA, 180
Baker, Newton Diehl, Jr., 192
Baker, Ray Stannard, 68, 87, 91, 93
Ballou, Charles, 183
Baltimore Afro-American, 176, 187
Barber, Jesse Max, 45, 64–65, 67, 224, 251n16; on 1906 Atlanta Race Riot, 91, 93–99, 256n159, 256n162; attacked by Ben Davis Sr., 99–101; attacked by Booker T. Washington, 101–5, 257–58n183; criticizes Hoke Smith's hypocrisy, 65–66; exile from Atlanta, 19, 96–97, 106, 191, 256n160, 257n173, 258n186; Georgia Equal Rights Convention, 55, 57–58, 63; politics of respectability, 65–66, 9–99, 104–5, 250n125, 251n15. See also *Voice of the Negro*
Barnes, J. Lee, 179. *See also* Hotel Men's Association
Barnett, Hattie, 130, 132. *See also* Neighborhood Union
Bartow County, 61
Bayor, Ron, 16,
Benevolent and Protective Order of Elks, 62
Berkeley, GA, 192
Birth of a Nation (1915), 184–85
Blakely, GA, 193
Blount, Samuel, 151
Bond, James, 169. *See also* Rush Memorial Congregational Church
bond referenda, 2, 6, 13, 196; 1919 voter registration drive, 2, 207–12; NAACP "manifesto" (April 1919), 221–22, 224–25; NAACP's rejection of politics of respectability, 21, 22, 222, 236–37; referendum, 1872, 140; —, 1903, 141; —, 1910, 141; —, 1915, 196; —, July 1918, 198–204, 206, 209–10, 272n16; —, March 1919, 214–20, 276n113, 276n126; —, April, 6, 218, 220–23, 225–28, 230, 231, 235, 237, 239, 240, 278n166; —,

March 1921, 229, 232–34, 235; —, 1935, 239; —, 1938, 239; state laws regarding, 42, 196–97, 207. *See also* Atlanta Board of Education; Atlanta City Council; city budget, Atlanta
Booker T. Washington High School, 6, 12, 23, 239, 243n8; construction of, 233; overcrowding, 234–35
Bowen, John Wesley Edward, 81–82, 89. *See also* Gammon Theological Seminary
Bradford, Perry, 76
Brawner, Mary, 130. *See also* Neighborhood Union
Brown v. Board of Education (1954), 6
Brown, Charlie, 240
Brown, Elsa Barkley, 53
Brown, J. Epps, 226. *See also* Southern Bell Telephone and Telegraph Company
Brown, Joseph E., 48
Brownsville (black neighborhood), 88–89, 91, 256n153
Brownsville Affray, 22, 154
Bruce, John E., 65
Bruce, Philip, 15–16
Bryan, William Jennings, 39, 154
Bryant, Mrs. Peter James, 206, 274n56
Bryant, Peter James, 181, 182–83, 206. *See also* Wheat Street Baptist Church
Buchanan v. Warley (1917), 75
Bugg, Laura, 130
Burke, John, 74
Burroughs, Nannie Helen, 112
Butler, H. R., 188, 233
Butler, Selena Sloan, 112

Camp Funston, KS, 189
Camp Gordon, GA, 169, 171, 190, 193, 200
Camp Upton, NY, 21, 151, 189
Candler, Allen D., 27
Candler, Asa, 169, 211, 275n85; bond referendum, July 1918, 198, 207; overcrowding in black schools, 157; "work or fight" law, 182. *See also* Coca-Cola Company
Capeci, Domenic J., 105
Carter, E. R., 203, 206. *See also* Friendship Baptist Church
Charleston, SC, 64

Chatham County, 28, 65
Chattahoochee Brick Company, 48–49, 50
Chattooga County, 61,
Chicago Conservator, 102
Chicago Defender, 152, 176
Chicago, IL, 122, 255n127; exile of Jesse Max Barber, 19, 97, 256n160, 258n188; Great Migration, 176; Lugenia Burns Hope, 17, 109; Red Summer, 152, 191
city budget, Atlanta, 203, 275n88; 1913 fiscal crisis, 135; bond referendum, 1915, 196–97; —, July 1918, 214; —, April 1919, 227–28; —, March 1921, 234; education, 148, 161, 214, 227–28, 230, 232; income from convict-leasing and criminal fines, 49, 249n93
City Federation of Women's Clubs (Atlanta), 143
Civil Rights Act of 1875, 21
Civil Rights Cases (1883), 21, 22
Clark University, 71, 89, 90, 144, 153
Clemmons, Estelle, 235
Cleveland, Grover, 39
Cleveland, OH, 182, 231
Coca-Cola Company, 157, 275n85
College Park, GA, 234
Colored American Magazine, 63
Colored Co-operative League, 132
Colored Press Association, 21
Columbia County, 179
Columbus Ledger, 177
Commission on Interracial Cooperation (CIC), 231, 232, 234. *See also* Durham, Plato; Eagan, John; Jones, Ashby
Communist Party, 64
Covington, GA, 64
Cranford, Alfred, 26, 246n4
Crawford, Ella N., 130
Crisis, 186
Crogman, L. C., 222
Crogman, William H., 90. *See also* Clark University
Crowe, Charles, 36

Darktown (black neighborhood), 88, 90, 152
Darwin, Charles, 113
Davis, Ben, Jr., 64, 253n74

Davis, Ben, Sr., 70, 71, 102, 103, 117, 138; 1906 Atlanta Race Riot, 98, 99–101; 1906 election, 63; 1906 rape scare, 81, 82, 253–54nn81–82; abandons politics of respectability, 153, 163–64, 198, 213, 237–38; Atlanta Civic League, 91; bond referendum, July 1918, 198, 201, 202; —, March 1919, 212, 213, 219–21; —, April 1919, 222, 237–38, 240–41; —, March 1921, 233; on black patriotism, 173–74, 175, 186, 188; on black working-class, 92–93, 135; Brownsville affray, 22; career, 64; criticizes Barber's flight from Atlanta, 101; on disfranchisement, 66; double sessions in black schools, 162–64; Gate City Kindergarten Association, 262n90; Georgia Equal Rights Convention, 44, 58–60; on morals of the black family, 83–84, 107; leadership in Atlanta NAACP, 154, 155, 155, 166, 167, 203, 206, 265n26, 267n76; NAACP fight to save seventh grade (1916–17), 149–50, 158; Republican Party, 106, 206, 235, 265n26; World War I, 169, 170. *See also Atlanta Independent;* Grand United Order of Odd Fellows; Odd Fellows' Lodge
Davison, J. W., 188. *See also Atlanta Independent*
Dawson, GA, 64
Decatur, GA, 234
Decatur Street (Atlanta), 76–77, 83, 85, 93, 94
Democratic Party, 37–39, 41, 79, 257n183
Deveaux, John H., 28
Dittmer, John, 76
Dobbs, John Wesley, 239–40
Dorsey, Allison, 12, 132
Dorsey, Hugh, 181, 231, 232
Douglass, Frederick, 137
Doyle, H. S., 36
Druid Hills (white neighborhood), 75
Du Bois, W. E. B., 9, 65, 75, 78, 109, 122; 1906 Atlanta Race Riot, 90, 105; bond referendum, April 1919, 238; Brownsville affray, 154; "Close Ranks" editorial, 20, 150, 169; conflict with Booker T. Washington, 7, 65, 105; and Ben Davis Sr., 43–44, 248n69; Georgia Equal

Rights Convention, 43–44, 45, 47, 53, 55, 209; Hardwick memorial (1899), 31; leaves Atlanta, 106; on lynching of Sam Hose, 27; on segregation, 4, 5; politics of respectability, 245n24; "talented tenth," 130; Walter Francis White, 154. *See also* Atlanta University Conferences

Durham, Plato, 232. *See also* Commission on Interracial Cooperation

Eagan, John, 232. *See also* Commission on Interracial Cooperation

East Point, GA, 234

East St. Louis Riot (1917), 191,

Ebenezer Baptist Church, 167, 205–6. *See also* Williams, Adam Daniel

Eighth Illinois Infantry, 184, 271n177

Eighth Ward House (Philadelphia), 110

Emory University, 232

English, James W., 99, 102; 1906 Atlanta Race Riot, 85, 256n164; Chattahoochee Brick Company, 48–49, 50; convict-leasing, 48–49, 50; Fourth National Bank, 48, 85; threatens Jesse Max Barber, 96–97

Estill, J. H., 41

Farmers' Alliance, 35

Feimster, Crystal N., 99

Finley, Cora B., 206, 216

First Congregational Church (Atlanta), 45; as elite institution, 76, 133; contrast with Neighborhood Union, 128; social services supported by white philanthropy, 128, 215–16; supports Gate City Kindergarten, 117; World War I, 169. *See also* Proctor, Henry Hugh

Five Points (neighborhood), 61, 171

Fort Des Moines, IA, 183

Fortune, Timothy Thomas, 28, 65; on black independence from the GOP, 22; on racial voting blocs, 21, 225; supports Jesse Max Barber, 258n186. See also *New York Age*

Fourth National Bank, 48, 85

Friendship Baptist Church, 201, 203. *See also* Carter, E. R.

Fulton County, 177

Gammon Theological Seminary, 71, 81–82, 89. *See also* Bowen, John Wesley Edward

Gate City Kindergarten Association, 17, 18, 109–18, 129; "civic rights," 136; engenders black solidarity, 115–16, 121, 137, 259–60n32; precursor to Neighborhood Union, 118, 119, 125, 129; race uplift, 110–16, 117–18, 259–60n32; roots in 1897 Atlanta University Conference, 109–16; sustained by black community, 116–17, 127, 262n90; transforms politics of respectability, 115–16, 117–18, 136. *See also* Hope, Lugenia Burns; Neighborhood Union

Georgia Baptist, 43

Georgia Equal Rights Convention (GERC), 42–60, 92, 93–94, 100, 106, 107, 119, 138–39, 143, 204; Jesse Max Barber, 45, 55, 57–58; black education, 43, 47–48, 49, 55; black working-class, 53–57, 60, 117–18, 136; "colored yeomanry," 45–46; convict leasing, 45, 47, 48–49, 50, 55; criticized by Ben Davis Sr., 44, 58–60; defense of black women, 50–53, 73, 77, 80, 107, 111; W. E. B. Du Bois, 43–45, 55; Du Bois–Washington conflict, 43–44, 57–58, 105; politics of respectability, 44, 45, 49–50, 56–57, 59–60, 156, 194; poll taxes, 56–57, 59, 136; Henry McNeal Turner, 42–43, 44, 45, 46, 55; William Jefferson White, 42–45, 46, 47, 49, 54–55, 56–57, 59–60

Georgia State Library Commission, 222

Georgia State Parent Teacher Association, 143

Gibson, Truman K., 206, 212, 216,

Godshalk, David Fort, 92, 123

Gordon, Asa H., 183

Grady Hospital, 196

Grady, Henry, 86

Grand United Order of Odd Fellows, 62; Atlanta lodge and auditorium, 76, 159, 167, 201; Ben Davis Sr., 64, 203; World War I, 169

Grant, Jim, 193

Graves, John Temple, 99, 102; 1906 Atlanta Race Riot, 94–96, 98, 101, 253–54n82; support for First Congregational

Graves, John Temple (*continued*)
Church, 128. See also *Atlanta Evening News; Atlanta Georgian*
Gray, James, 78–79. See also *Atlanta Journal*
Great Atlanta Fire (1917), 168, 198
Great Migration, 176–77, 244n13
Greer, Allen J., 185–86
Griffith, David Wark, 184, 186. See also *Birth of a Nation*
Guinn, R. J., 157, 158, 161, 165. *See also* Atlanta Board of Education

Haines Normal and Industrial School (Augusta, GA), 114, 259n31. *See also* Laney, Lucy Craft
Harding, Warren G., 235
Hardwick Bill of 1899, 24, 25, 26, 27; campaign against, 28–34, 63, 152; Booker T. Washington, 28–31, 80. *See also* Hardwick memorial (1899); Hardwick, Thomas
Hardwick Memorial (1899), 31–34, 135, 152; black education, 32–34, 48, 156; politics of respectability, 31–33, 35, 50, 56, 145–46. *See also* Hardwick Bill of 1899
Hardwick, Thomas: 1906 election, 39, 40; disfranchisement bills, 24, 34; Hoke Smith, 38–39; Tom Watson, 37–38; World War I, 192. *See also* Hardwick Bill of 1899; Hardwick memorial (1899)
Harlan, Louis T., 102
Hartsfield, William B., 240
Herndon, Adrienne, 117, 259n31
Herndon, Alonzo, 86, 117, 169, 259n31. *See also* Atlanta Life Insurance Company
Herne, Ben, 193
Hickey, Georgina, 15
Higginbotham, Evelyn Brooks, 8, 11
Hillyer, George, 220–21
Hope, John, 17, 31, 45, 109, 154, 155
Hope, Lugenia Burns, 152, 154, 259n31; 1906 Atlanta Race Riot, 90, 255n127; bond referendum, April 1919, 222–23; career, 17; cross-class solidarity, 136–37; Gate City Kindergarten Association, 109, 116–18, 129; Neighborhood Union, 107, 123, 124, 125, 129, 130, 131, 222–23,

239; politics of respectability, 20, 90, 117–18, 134–35, 136–37; World War I, 20–21, 189, 208. *See also* Gate City Kindergarten Association; Neighborhood Union
Hopkins, Charles T., 91, 92. *See also* Atlanta Chamber of Commerce
Hose, Sam, 26–27, 246n4
Hotel Men's Association, 179. *See also* Barnes, J. Lee
Houston Riot (1917), 191
Houston, Charles Hamilton, 183
Howard, David T., 117, 255n127
Howell, Clark, 80; 1906 election, 39, 41, 42, 61, 62, 65; black wartime loyalty, 187–88; NAACP fight to save seventh grade (1916–17), 166; support for First Congregational Church, 128. *See also* *Atlanta Constitution*
Hull House (Chicago), 17, 107, 109, 110; as a model for the Neighborhood Union, 122. *See also* Addams, Jane
Hunter, Tera, 74

Inman Park (white neighborhood), 75
International Cotton Exposition (1881), 74

James, C. L. R., 240–41
Jenningstown (black neighborhood), 71
Johnson, Charles H., 155
Johnson, Greenleaf, 193–94
Johnson, Henry L., 31
Johnson, James Weldon: Atlanta NAACP, 154, 159–60, 167, 203, 205, 206, 265–66n26, 266n30; bond referendum, March 1919, 212; —, March 1921, 233; NAACP campaign to abolish double sessions in black schools, 162, 166; NAACP fight to save seventh grade (1916–17), 157; Red Summer, 151–52; World War I, 151–52, 171, 175–76, 194–95. *See also* National Association for the Advancement of Colored People (NAACP)
Jones, Ashby, 232. *See also* Commission on Interracial Cooperation
Jones, Jacqueline, 69

Jones, Jerome, 229
Journal of Labor, 229

Kantrowitz, Stephen, 79
Keith, Hardy, 103–4
Kelley, Charles, 193
Kelley, Florence, 122
Kelley, Robin D. G., 223
Key, James L.: 1913 schools survey, 143;
   1920 NAACP Annual Meeting, 231–32;
   bond referendum, March 1919, 207,
   214–16, 218; —, April 1919, 221, 226;
   NAACP campaign to abolish double
   sessions in black schools, 165; NAACP
   fight to save seventh grade (1916–17),
   157, 158, 266n42; politics of respectabil-
   ity, 215–16; teacher salaries, 214
King, L. H., *155*
King, Martin Luther, Jr., 167
Knight, Jack C., 105
Ku Klux Klan, 184, 235–36. *See also* Sims,
   Walter

Lamarck, Jean-Baptiste, 113, 118
Laney, Lucy Craft. *See also* Haines Normal
   and Industrial School
Lasch-Quinn, Elisabeth, 114, 259n31
Little, Wilbur, 193
Logan, Adella Hunt, 113, 114

Mack, Daniel, 192–93
Macon, GA, 170; Georgia Equal Rights
   Convention, 43, 46, 47, 48, 56; "work or
   fight" laws, 178, 180
Maddox, Leola, 86
Maddox, Robert F., 94
Manly, Alexander, 19
Marietta, GA, 234–35
Mayson, James L., 203, 217
McClelland, John S., 217, 218
McCoy, Frank, 179
McCrary, Rufus, 178–79
McDonough, J. J., 28
McHenry, Jackson, 1–2, 4, 6, 13–14, 211
McKellar, Kenneth, 185
McTeir, G. G., 11
Mechanicsville (black neighborhood), 71
Milledgeville, GA, 192
Millen, GA, 191–92

Miller, Kelly, 65
Mitchell, John, 22
Morehouse College, 17, 109, 118, 141. *See
   also* Atlanta Baptist College
Morris Brown College, 141

Nash, Royal, 160
National Association for the Advancement
   of Colored People (NAACP), 4, 6, 20,
   88, 102, 106, 233, 240, 255n120; 1920
   NAACP Annual Meeting, 231–32; black
   progressivism, 5–6; defeats nomination
   of Judge John Parker, 238–39, 240;
   lynching, 9, 151–52; school segregation,
   6, 243–44n9; "work or fight" laws,
   178, 180–82. *See also* Johnson, James
   Weldon; White, Walter Francis
—, Atlanta Branch, 23, 153–60, 195, 229,
   234; 1919 membership drive, 207; 1919
   voter registration drive, 207–13; 1920
   NAACP Annual Meeting, 231–32;
   black progressivism, 158, 163, 225; bond
   referendum, July 1918, 197, 201–4; —,
   March 1919, 207–8, 215–19; —, April
   1919, 2, 3, 6, 207, 226–27; —, March
   1921, 232–33; —, 1935, 239; —, 1938, 239;
   campaign to abolish double sessions
   in black schools, 156, 159–65; demobilization, 235; executive committee, *155;*
   factionalism, 165–68, 203–6; fight to
   save seventh grade, 154–59, 236, 266n42;
   Great Atlanta Fire (1917), 168; NAACP
   "manifesto" (April 1919), 221–22, 223–25;
   partisan divisions, 154, 206, 265–66n26;
   politics of respectability, 23, 163–64, 205,
   209, 225, 236; relationship with Atlanta
   Public School Teachers Association,
   229–30; relationship with Commission
   on Interracial Cooperation, 231–32;
   relationship with Neighborhood Union,
   155, 160, 164, 182–83, 196, 208, 213, 221,
   222–23, 235, 239; reorganization (1918),
   203–6, 274n56; reorganization (1924),
   235; school segregation, 243–44n9;
   teacher salaries, 229–30; World War
   I, 158, 169–71, 174, 177, 209–11. *See also*
   Davis, Ben, Sr.; Pace, Harry; Walden,
   Austin T.; White, Walter Francis; Williams, Adam Daniel

National Association of Colored Women, 116, 189
National Baptist Convention, 206
National Guard, 170
National Negro Business League, 104
National Urban League, 235
Negro Knights of Pythias, 62
Negro Young People's Christian Congress (1902), 171
Neighborhood Union, 17–18, 20–21, 23, 118–31, 240; 1913 schools survey, 141–47; 1919 voter registration drive, 208, 211, 222–23; black progressivism, 5–6, 121–22, 158; bond referendum, March 1919, 211; —, April 1919, 2, 216, 222–23; —, March 1921, 233; —, 1935, 239; campaign to abolish double sessions in black schools, 161, 164, 229; civic rights, 108, 125–27, 136; community centers, 127–28, 128; defense of black women, 118–20, 122–23; demobilization, 235; domestic workers, 123–24, 130; enforcers of black morality, 131–35, 263n119; finances, 127–29; Gate City Kindergarten Association, 17–18, 110, 118; Great Atlanta Fire (1917), 168; Investigating Committee, 131–35; "mediator/enforcers," 134–35, 263n112; neighborhood surveys, 108–9, 123–25, 133, 155; organizing, 123–24, 130–31, 136–38, 182–83, 196, 208, 213; politics of respectability, 17–18, 20, 107–9, 118, 127, 136, 138–39, 142–43, 146–47, 150–51, 189–91; relationship with Atlanta NAACP, 148, 149, 153, 154–55, 160, 167, 170, 196, 204, 206, 213, 221, 233; relationship with police, 132–34, 263n111; settlement house movement, 127–29, 261n58; Washington Park, 232; World War I, 150–51, 170, 174, 182–83, 189–91, 193, 208. See also Hope, Lugenia Burns
New York Age, 22, 178, 258n186. See also Fortune, Timothy Thomas
Newnan, GA, 26–27
Norfolk Journal and Guide, 176
Nutting, J. R., 228,

Odd Fellows' Lodge, 76, 159, 167, 201. See also Davis, Ben, Sr.; Grand United Order of Odd Fellows

Orme, A. J., 203, 218
Ovington, Mary White, 90

Pace, Harry: 1920 NAACP Annual Meeting, 231; bond referendum, March 1921, 232; president of Atlanta NAACP, 154, 155, 166, 170; reorganization of Atlanta NAACP, 203–6; teacher salaries 230. See also National Association for the Advancement of Colored People: Atlanta Branch
Parker, John J., 238, 240
Pelham, GA, 178–79
Penn, Irving Garland, 256n153
Penn, William F., 93, 155, 157, 255n137
People's Party. See Populist Party
Perry, Heman, 117, 169. See also Standard Life Insurance Company
Pickens, William, 102–3
Pippen, Horace, 183–84
Pittsburg (black neighborhood), 71
Pledger, William, 31
Polk County, 61
Pope City, GA, 193
Populist Party, 34, 35–37, 38, 40, 84. See also Watson, Tom
Porter, James, 140
Price, Minnie Wright, 120,
Proctor, Adeline Davis, 77–78
Proctor, Henry Hugh, 45, 133; Atlanta Civic League, 91, 92; black working-class morals, 76–78; bond referendum, March 1919, 215–16; Gate City Kindergarten Association, 117; relationship with white philanthropists, 128, 215–16; World War I, 169. See also First Congregational Church (Atlanta)

Red Cross, 20, 125
Red Summer (1919), 3, 152, 191, 238
Republican Party, 25, 31, 61, 203, 218, 228, 240; black independence from, 22, 36, 213, 238–39; Brownsville affray, 21–22, 154; Civil Rights Cases (1883), 21; contrast with Neighborhood Union, 139; defeat of Judge John Parker, 238–39; factionalism, 43–44, 64, 106; Georgia Equal Rights Convention, 43–44, 46, 57–58, 139; patronage, 25, 106, 120, 235;

politics of respectability, 59–60; relationship with Atlanta NAACP, 154, 203, 206, 265–66n26. *See also* Davis, Ben, Sr.; Harding, Warren G.; Roosevelt, Theodore; Rucker, Henry A.
Roosevelt, Franklin Delano, 239, 257–58n183
Roosevelt, Theodore, 21, 44, 66, 169, 172, Rucker, Henry A., 31, 43–44, 218–19, 228, 248n69
rural free delivery, 69
Rush Memorial Congregational Church, 169. *See also* Bond, James
Ryan, Mary P., 15

Sammons, J. W., 192
Savannah, GA, 11, 28, 178
Savannah Tribune, 81, 158–59, 175, 176, 186
Scott, Anne Firor, 121
Scott, Emmett J., 186
Scott, James C., 223
Selective Service Act (1917), 181, 189, 210
Sherman, William Tecumseh, 70
Shermantown (black neighborhood), 71
Shillady, John, 180–81
Shivery, Louie, 122, 124, 131, 141, 146
Simmons, Roscoe Conkling, 174
Sims, David H., 155
Sims, Walter, 236. *See also* Ku Klux Klan
Slaton, William, 143
Smith, Hoke, 39–40; 1906 Atlanta Race Riot, 78, 80, 94; 1906 election, 38–42, 61, 62–63, 78, 82–83, 96–97, 99; 1906 rape scare, 81, 82–83, 96–97; disfranchisement, 40–42, 65–66; Thomas Hardwick, 38; progressivism, 39–40; politics of respectability, 62, 63, 65–66, 96–97, 251n15; support for First Congregational Church, 128; Tom Watson, 38
Smith, Frank, 86
Southern Bell Telephone and Telegraph Company, 215, 226. *See also* Brown, J. Epps
Spanish-American War, 171, 184
Spelman College, 126, 127, 141
Standard Life Insurance Company. *See also* Perry, Heman
Stone Mountain, GA, 184

Storrs School, 139–40. *See also under* Atlanta public schools
Summer Hill (black neighborhood), 71
Summer Hill School, 139–40, 265n1

Talbot, Marion, 17
Terrell County, 64
Terrell, Joseph, 88, 97
Terrell, Mary Church, 65
Terrell, W. H., 162, 222, 226–27, 228
Thomasville, GA, 180
Thompson, Richard W., 22
Towns, George A., 155, 166–67
Turner, Henry McNeal, 24–25, 106, 137, 175; Georgia Equal Rights Convention, 42–43, 44, 45, 46, 55, 135
Tuskegee Institute, 103, 113. *See also* Washington, Booker T.

United States Department of the Interior, 39
United States Bureau of Naturalization, 172
United States Department of War, 127, 190–91, 193

Valdosta, GA, 180
Vardaman, James K., 185–86
Villa, Pancho, 184
Villard, Oswald Garrison, 101
Virginia Union University, 64
Voice of Missions, 43. *See also* Turner, Henry McNeal
Voice of the Negro, 55, 64–65, 95, 102, 256n160, 258n186; 1906 Atlanta Race Riot, 19, 94, 97, 257n173. *See also* Barber, Jesse Max

Walden, Austin T., 239–40
Walker, C. T., 44
Wardlaw, J. C., 161, 162–63
Ware Colored High School (Augusta, GA), 43
Washerwomen's Strike (1881), 74
Washing Society, 74
Washington, Booker T., 64, 99, 258n186; 1906 Atlanta race riot, 90, 257n177; 1906 election, 62, 80; "Atlanta Compromise," 10–11, 29, 57, 90; attacks Jesse

Washington, Booker T. (*continued*)
Max Barber, 65, 101–2, 257–58n183;
conflict with Du Bois, 7, 43, 105,
114, 248n69; Georgia Equal Rights
Convention, 43–44, 57–58; Hardwick
Bill of 1899, 28–32, 80, 238; politics of
respectability, 7, 30–31, 103–5; support
for Henry Hugh Proctor, 128. *See also*
Tuskegee Institute
Washington, D.C., 116, 173, 215; Red
Summer, 152, 191, 215
Washington Park, 231–32
Watson, John, 263n111
Watson, Tom, 35–38, 40, 63, 83
Webster, Edgar, 271n173
Wells, Ida B., 19
Wheat Street Baptist Church, 182, 203. *See
also* Bryant, Peter James
White, Walter Francis, 153–54; 1906
Atlanta Race Riot, 88, 255n120; 1919
voter registration drive, 208, 212;
Atlanta NAACP, 153–55, 155, 166–67,
266n30, 267n76; bond referendum,
July 1918, 197; —, March 1919, 276n121;
defeat of Judge John Parker, 238; joins
NAACP national staff, 203; NAACP
campaign to abolish double sessions
in black schools, 159–60, 162, 164–67;
NAACP fight to save seventh grade,
157–58; on Great Migration, 177;
reorganization of Atlanta NAACP,
204–6; "work or fight" laws, 180–81;
World War I, 170. *See also* National
Association for the Advancement of
Colored People (NAACP)
White, William Jefferson: on black
working class, 54–55, 59–60, 135, 209;
on convict leasing, 49; Georgia Equal
Rights Convention, 42–45, 46, 47,
106; on poll taxes, 56–57; politics of
respectability, 59–60, 106
Willard, Frances, 129–30
Williams, Adam Daniel, 167, 205–6, 223,
235. *See also* Ebenezer Baptist Church

Williams, Maggie F., 130
Wilmington Race Riot (1898), 19, 38
Wilson, Woodrow, 154, 168; war aims, 20,
169, 177, 181, 237; wartime citizenship,
172–73, 174–75, 210
Winn, W. Tom, 201
Woodward, James, 85
Worth County, 192
Wright, Howard, 172
Wright, Louis T., 155
Wright, Richard, 28
Wrightsville, GA, 180
"work or fight" laws, 178–82
World War I, 1, 3, 196, 222, 225, 236, 238,
239, 271n177; anti-black violence,
151–52, 191–93; assertions of black
loyalty, 169–74, 186, 187–89; Atlanta
NAACP, 169–71; black ambivalence
towards, 175–76; black response to
the draft, 20, 168–69, 175, 177–78, 183;
black soldiers, 183–86; bond referenda,
226–27; changes meaning of poll tax,
210–11; Commission on Interracial Cooperation, 231; Du Bois's "Close Ranks"
editorial, 150, 158–59, 169; Great Migration, 176–77, 244n13; hostess houses,
189–90; Neighborhood Union, 190–91,
208; new terms of black solidarity, 151,
158–59, 163, 168, 174–75, 183–84, 209;
politics of respectability, 13, 20–21, 127,
149–52, 158–59, 174–75, 187–91, 193–95,
209, 244n13; racist characterizations of
black soldiers, 184–86; "re-masculin-
ization" of black politics, 150, 152–53,
182–83; rumors of black disloyalty,
171–72; "servant crisis," 179–80; "Work
or Fight" laws, 177–82
World War II, 6, 90, 239

Young Men's Christian Association, 191,
204, 231
Young Women's Christian Association,
20–21, 189

Recent Books in the Carter G. Woodson Institute Series

Midori Takagi, *"Rearing Wolves to Our Own Destruction":*
Slavery in Richmond, Virginia, 1782–1865

Alessandra Lorini, *Rituals of Race: American Public Culture*
and the Search for Racial Democracy

Mary Ellen Curtin, *Black Prisoners and Their World, Alabama, 1865–1900*

Philip J. Schwarz, *Migrants against Slavery: Virginians and the Nation*

Armstead L. Robinson, *Bitter Fruits of Bondage: The Demise of Slavery*
and the Collapse of the Confederacy, 1861–1865

Francille Rusan Wilson, *The Segregated Scholars: Black Social Scientists*
and the Creation of Black Labor Studies, 1890–1950

Gregory Michael Dorr, *Segregation's Science:*
Eugenics and Society in Virginia

Glenn McNair, *Criminal Injustice: Slaves and Free Blacks in Georgia's*
Criminal Justice System

William Dusinberre, *Strategies for Survival:*
Recollections of Bondage in Antebellum Virginia

Valerie C. Cooper, *Word, Like Fire: Maria Stewart, the Bible,*
and the Rights of African Americans

Michael L. Nicholls, *Whispers of Rebellion: Narrating Gabriel's Conspiracy*

Henry Goings, *Rambles of a Runaway from Southern Slavery,* edited by
Calvin Schermerhorn, Michael Plunkett, and Edward Gaynor

Philip J. Schwarz, ed., *Gabriel's Conspiracy: A Documentary History*

Kirt von Daacke, *Freedom Has a Face: Race, Identity,*
and Community in Jefferson's Virginia

Deborah E. McDowell, Claudrena N. Harold, and Juan Battle, eds.,
The Punitive Turn: New Approaches to Race and Incarceration

Jay Winston Driskell Jr., *Schooling Jim Crow: The Fight for Atlanta's*
Booker T. Washington High School and the Roots of Black Protest Politics

CPSIA information can be obtained
at www.ICGtesting.com
Printed in the USA
LVHW041935011222
734343LV00004B/557